Learning on the Shop Floor

International Studies in Social History
General Editor: Marcel van der Linden, International Institute of Social History, Amsterdam

Volume 1
Trade Unions, Immigration and Immigrants in Europe 1960–1993
Edited by Rinus Penninx and Judith Roosblad

Volume 2
Class and Other Identities
Edited by Lex Heerma van Voss and Marcel van der Linden

Volume 3
Rebellious Families
Edited by Jan Kok

Volume 4
Experiencing Wages
Edited by Peter Scholliers and Leonard Schwarz

Volume 5
The Imaginary Revolution
Michael Seidman

Volume 6
Revolution and Counterrevolution
Kevin Murphy

Volume 7
Miners and the State in the Ottoman Empire
Donald Quataert

Volume 8
Anarchism, Revolution and Reaction
Angel Smith

Volume 9
Sugarlandia Revisited
Edited by Ulbe Bosma, Juan Giusti-Cordero and G. Roger Knight

Volume 10
Alternative Exchanges
Edited by Laurence Fontaine

Volume 11
A Social History of Spanish Labour
Edited by José A. Piqueras and Vicent Sanz Rozalén

Volume 12
Learning on the Shop Floor
Edited by Bert De Munck, Steven L. Kaplan and Hugo Soly

Volume 13
Unruly Suburbs
Wolfgang Maderthaner and Lutz Musner

Learning on the Shop Floor

Historical Perspectives on Apprenticeship

Edited by
Bert De Munck, Steven L. Kaplan
and Hugo Soly

Berghahn Books
NEW YORK • OXFORD

First published in 2007 by

Berghahn Books

www.berghahnbooks.com

Library of Congress Cataloging-in-Publication Data

Learning on the shop floor : historical perspectives on apprenticeship / edited by Bert De Munck, Steven L. Kaplan and Hugo Soly.
p. cm.
Includes bibliographical references and index.
ISBN 978-1-84545-341-1 (hardback : alk. paper)
1. Apprenticeship programs--History. 2. Apprenticeship programs--Case studies. I. Munck, Bert De, 1967- II. Kaplan, Steven L. III. Soly, Hugo.

HD4881.L43 2007
331.25'922--dc22

2007044678

British Library Cataloguing in Publication Data

A catalogue record for this book is available from the British Library

Printed in the United States on acid-free paper

ISBN 978-1-84545-341-1 (hardback)

Contents

List of Figures and Tables

Figures

Tables

Preface

The initial versions of the contributions to this volume were presented at a colloquium organized by the Centre for the Study of Pre-Industrial Production Processes and Labour Relations (PIPA; director: Hugo Soly) of the *Vrije Universiteit Brussel*, Free University of Brussels, and the Flemish Centre for the Study of Popular Culture (VCV; director: Marc Jacobs), Brussels, in December 2000. Dr Jacobs thought of convening the participants in the Landcommanderij Alden Biesen at Bilzen, Belgium. This proved a flash of inspiration, as these surroundings were truly magnificent, both in historical and artistic respects and because of their scenic beauty, and were the ideal setting for an intensive exchange of ideas; the gathering was particularly successful because Hilde Schoefs, a senior researcher at the VCV, attended to absolutely every one of the many practical details that arise at such events. On behalf of all other participants, we wish to convey our deepest gratitude to these two mainstays of the VCV.

We are also indebted to our colleagues Catharina Lis from the Free University of Brussels, Jan Lucassen from the International Institute of Social History in Amsterdam, Maarten Prak from Utrecht University and Frank Simon from the University of Ghent, who willingly served as commentators. Their valuable and constructive remarks enlightened the debates enormously and revealed new perspectives. Last but not least, we would like to honor S.R. (Larry) Epstein from the London School of Economics and Politcial Science, who did not only attend the conference in Alden Biesen, but has stimulated the debate on apprenticeship. Unfortunately, this brilliant and amicable colleague died unexpectedly on 3rd February 2007. We dedicate this book to him.

Despite the enthusiasm during and after the colloquium, this book has taken far longer to produce than anticipated. The reason is both simple and complex at the same time: as director of the VCV, Dr Jacobs became so overwhelmed by his new responsibilities that he had to resign as co-editor, and others involved in this exercise suffered extended medical problems or encountered all kinds of unexpected events.

We are very grateful to all the authors, both for their exceptional patience and above all for their willingness – in some cases under difficult circumstances – to submit revised versions of their conference paper. Special thanks are due to Clare Crowston in this respect: she completed her contribution shortly after giving birth to twins. We are pleased to dedicate this volume also to her children Kian, Lili and Reza Banihashem.

Introduction

Chapter 1

'Learning on the Shop Floor' in Historical Perspective

Bert De Munck and Hugo Soly

In memory of Stephen R. (Larry) Epstein

Apprenticeship, which might be described very concisely as 'learning on the shop floor' or simply as 'learning by doing', is not a practice of bygone days. On the contrary, many new economic sectors have a growing need for highly skilled and specialized professionals with the flexibility to accommodate the rapidly changing needs of the labour market. This trend has affected educational systems as well. Not only is lifelong learning increasingly perceived as an absolute necessity, but in several countries two tracks are emerging: specialized modules and curricula at traditional schools on the one hand and shop-floor learning on the other. The process brings education and corporate industry closer together. While schools are under increasing pressure to meet the demands of trade and industry, companies arrange employee training internally. The authorities try to stipulate curricula and issue certificates upon course completion to ensure that training meets labour market demand. Moreover, the seals of quality issued matter to entrepreneurs and potential and current employees alike and thus function as cultural capital.

The changes explain not only the revived interest in the German *duale System*[1] – where shop-floor learning occurs parallel to learning at school – but have also revitalized vocational training overall. Applied sciences and generalized training contents became important in occupational training programmes from the nineteenth century onward, but recently this approach has progressively fallen out of favour. Occupational skills are increasingly learned in settings that at least resemble those of their ultimate application. While this arrangement may be beneficial, it can also lead to the neglect of more general schooling for young workers. In some West European countries, the trend to focus almost entirely on occupational training in the context of shop-floor learning has reduced the value of the diploma to an admission ticket to the labour market. Conceptions of general culture are tacitly relegated to the realm of the useless and the superfluous.[2]

At any rate, educational sciences reflect greater emphasis on 'situated learning'. Imparting decontextualized and generalized knowledge is making way for producing knowledge and skill in context.[3] Assuming that occupational skills inevitably depend on the context in which they are acquired, the shop floor would be the best place to learn them. Such skills are to be interpreted very broadly as including social and communication skills as well. The same holds true for a concept such as 'cognitive apprenticeship', as it can be argued that acquiring cognitive skills depends largely on the material and social context of learning.[4] More generally, a 'constructivist approach' automatically presumes that knowledge is constructed in the course of learning: youngsters produce knowledge rather than passively adopting it, whether they are on the shop floor or at an educational institution. Students are therefore expected to incorporate new knowledge and new skills in the cognitive structure acquired in their youth. Educators use the terms 'assimilation' and 'accommodation': processes previously described by Jean Piaget.[5]

Current changes in the prevalence and the practice of apprenticeship, and in the ways that educators identify 'learning on the shop floor', may inspire historical research. This idea was the basis for an international congress on apprenticeship in pre-industrial Europe organized in Alden Biezen (Belgium) in 2000.[6] The theme seemed particularly appealing, as historians have paid relatively little attention to shop-floor learning, especially during the late Middle Ages and the early modern period. In some measure, this is understandable. After all, few institutions for occupational training existed until the mid-nineteenth century, and source collections focused on apprenticeship are therefore rare. Moreover, the early modern craft guilds, which in many cities were authorized to regulate all local matters related to apprenticeship in their own trade, seemed oriented more toward the past than the future. Yet, the revived interest in urban corporatism since the 1980s, which has led to fundamental revisions,[7] has coincided with rising interest in the historical aspects of shop-floor learning, as is apparent from the recent studies by scholars such as Kurt Wesoly, Reinhold Reith and Andreas Griessinger in Germany;[8] Ilja Krausman Ben-Amos, Joan Lane and Jane Humphries in England;[9] Michael Sonenscher and Steven Kaplan in France;[10] Sven Steffens and Bert De Munck in Belgium;[11] Annemarie Steidl in Austria;[12] and Estelle Fallet in Switzerland.[13]

The history of apprenticeship relates to a great many research fields, ranging from the history of education and childhood, the history of guilds and corporatism, labour history, migration history and family history, to economic history and legal history. Apprenticeship is essentially an economic contract and may need to be enforced by economic on other institutions. Such is the interpretation of economic historians interested in the role of learning methods in increasing the supply and improving the quality of *human capital*. The training also comprises an important socio-cultural component: apprentices are inculcated into the way of life associated with the trade and are introduced to the norms and values of the social group, class or trade to which their master belongs. Accordingly, research on apprenticeship and 'on-the-job training' addresses the interface between social and cultural history.

In organizing a congress and compiling this volume, we have obviously had to make some difficult choices. All the same, a broad focus has been the idea from the outset. Mary Louise Nagata's contribution on apprenticeship in early modern Japan reveals similarities and differences that might easily be overlooked from a European perspective. The most important similarities were the dominance of on-the-jobtraining and a life-cycle trend. Young adolescents were sent to live under their master's roof from about the age of thirteen, passing through stages similar to the European journeyman and master. Both informal and formal training figured in the process. Although the informal component was somewhat similar to the learning processes experienced by unfree journeymen in Europe, the difference in the training was much more striking. One of the most important of these differences was the far more comprehensive training required of 'apprentices' in Japan. Japanese 'apprentices' received general education, including reading, writing and arithmetic – which in Europe was very often relegated to religious instruction at Sunday schools. In addition, the Japanese counterparts often acquired managerial skills as well, in contrast (as far as research shows) to most apprentices in Europe.[14] With the possible exception of England, apprenticeship in Europe was focused far less on general education and far more on specialized vocational training, which was just a stage in and part of the training and education. This emerges clearly from the case study by Clare Crowston (see below), who opens this volume together with the article by Nagata.

Authors throughout the collection emphasize the need for an integral approach. An indenture was not merely a contract between economic actors but was also an agreement between families, fellow professionals and/or guild brothers. Both parties might have material as well as nonutilitarian concerns. Institutional and socio-cultural contexts were similarly essential factors with respect to the economic added value of the contracts.

Understanding both the economic and the social impact of pre-industrial apprenticeship systems requires examining to what extent and in what manner such systems materialized, and what they added to the 'free market' of contracts. The authors of several contributions therefore focus on the institutional context of the apprenticeship contracts. Was institutionalization driven by economic motives? And, if it was, what were the effects that ensued, and what was their impact on the craft guilds, on the one hand, and on the regulating activities of municipal authorities or central governments, on the other hand? Three contributions address these questions. Karel Davids and Bert De Munck examine in what measure an official apprenticeship system was conducive to imparting and producing knowledge and skills during the early modern period. Jonathan Reinarz presents a case study that occurs in a very different institutional context but raises the same questions. He demonstrates that even in the late nineteenth century in a technologically highly complex sector, the absence of an institutionalized educational system was not necessarily perceived as a shortcoming.

Three other contributions highlight the socio-cultural dimensions of apprenticeship. Annemarie Steidl, in addition to relating her questions about social and geographic mobility to the regulating mechanisms of craft guilds, considers the issue from a gender perspective, in which she examines the ages of apprentices and the length of their training. Peter Stabel admittedly regards apprenticeship in late-medieval Flanders as a 'cornerstone' of the social and economic organization of the pre-industrial city but also emphasizes the importance of cultural elements, such as paternalism and guild solidarity. Reinhold Reith contemplates the function of boarding apprentices and questions the *ganze Haus* model, which reflects an almost exclusively disciplinary perspective on apprenticeships and consistently labels economic aspects as secondary in importance.

In this introduction, the contributions are identified in a broader historiographic context, by consecutively addressing occupational training institutions in pre-industrial Europe, the economic importance of self-enforcing contracts, the complex relationship between corporatism and apprenticeship, on-the-job training and skill acquisition, forms of mobility and family strategies, boarding with a master and socialization, and gender perspectives.

Occupational Training Institutions in Pre-industrial Europe

Except for the professions taught exclusively at universities and (from the eighteenth century) academies, few alternatives to shop-floor learning were available in Europe until the mid-nineteenth century.

During the early modern period para-university educational networks emerged in several countries. The most important ones were undeniably in surgery. As early as 1578, the Amsterdam municipal authorities established the position of *praelector anatomiae*, which was soon entrusted to the professor of medicine at the *illustre school* (illustrious school). Rembrandt has immortalized this position in his painting *The Anatomy Lecture of Dr. Nicolaes Tulp*.[15] In the course of the seventeenth century the authorities in many large cities formed *collegia medica* (boards of health), which often trained surgeons.[16] In most cases, university-educated physicians aimed to seize control from the barber-surgeons and often from the pharmacists as well, who were practitioners without university degrees. The barber-surgeons and pharmacists, however, were either already organized in guilds or requested permission to form a corporation soon after the establishment of the board of health. From the outset, the two types of institutions were therefore at odds on issues such as training and education. In 1641 in Antwerp, even master surgeons with ten years of experience or more were required to attend a two-year course at the local *collegium medicum*. Sitting for a theoretical examination became an additional requirement for attaining master status.[17]

To meet the growing need for civil and military engineers, specialized schools were established. In the United Provinces the first such institution opened in Leiden in 1600; the renowned mathematician Simon Stevin designed the curriculum. Similar institutions soon opened in other cities in the Dutch Republic, offering programmes in pilotage and cartography in addition to technical training for engineers. While many such institutions were affiliated with universities in the seventeenth century, they started to be replaced by occupational schools founded at the initiative of the local authorities toward the end of the Ancien Régime.[18] The course of events was similar elsewhere in Europe.[19]

Schools for drawing started to open in northern Italy in the second half of the sixteenth century and in other parts of Europe after 1600. In the eighteenth century, drawing academies and painting and sculpture academies became commonplace. Instruction was free of charge at most of these institutions. Lessons were provided both during the day and in the early evening, since in addition to offering artists lessons in figure sketching or drawing life models, these institutions were intended as places for craftsmen to master architectural drafting. Many offered courses on perspective and architecture.[20] The socio-cultural significance of these schools was considerable. The drawing academy in Bruges, for example, averaged 192 students a year between 1775 and 1802, including many cabinetmakers, carpenters and masons, who regarded the lessons as an opportunity for social advancement.[21]

What made drawing schools so popular? Did guild-based apprenticeship systems somehow fail to provide complete training? Were the tasks learned at most workshops exclusively or primarily executive, leaving aside the basics of design and creativeness? The evidence available reveals nothing on that subject. We have little or no information about learning by apprentices at the workshops of gold- and silversmiths, cabinetmakers, or other artisans whose prestige and profits depended largely on their ability to design new models. Yet, the increasing specialization in many industries raises questions. Shop-floor learning meant that learning covered only the operations on the shop floor, which could be highly limited in view of the whole range of products manufactured in the trade. In some cities in the late sixteenth and early seventeenth centuries paintings were produced through extensive division of labour, both at and between the workshops.[22] In the course of the eighteenth century, this procedure was adopted in increasing measure by 'mass production' industries. In her contribution to this volume, Crowston shows that the free drawing schools established in Ancien Régime France were all part of a 'pre-apprenticeship' system. In addition to completing guild-based on-the-job training by bridging the gap years before an apprenticeship began, they supplemented training on the shop floor with basic skills. Moreover, relationships between the apprenticeships and drawing schools were mutually reinforcing.[23]

Other forms of institutionalized occupational education existed as well. Boys and girls at some orphanages were taught technical skills in addition to reading and the basics of writing. Some boys' orphanages even had several specialized workshops, each run by a skilled craftsman.[24] Since orphanage trustees usually preferred arranging apprenticeships at the workshops of master artisans, however, most orphans were boarded out. The parochial schools, which opened in some Catholic countries during the second half of the seventeenth century, were far more important in quantitative terms. In France they offered free schooling for poor children, providing the girls with occupational training appropriate for their 'class', which was basically needlework. This also held true for the *écoles de charité*. Run by lay women, these schools admitted girls only in nearly all cases and were dedicated to preparing them for the labour market.[25] Spinning schools became widespread during the eighteenth century, especially in regions with substantial proto-industrial growth, at least on the Continent. They emerged in small towns and rural communities and were nearly all private operations, motivated by both philanthropic intentions and demand for cheap labour among textile entrepreneurs. While some of these schools were for boys, the data available suggest that most students were girls.[26] Schools where pupils were trained in lace making admitted only young girls. They arose in various parts of Western Europe throughout the eighteenth century and especially toward the end of the Ancien Régime. They were particularly numerous in the towns of the Duchy of Brabant, where the lace industry grew spectacularly. More than 10,000 women and children worked in this industry in both Antwerp and Brussels, 4,500 in Mechelen, and between 2,000 and 3,000 in the small town of Lier.[27] Since the products from all these cities and towns were of good or superior quality, training young girls in this craft received special emphasis. By 1780 Antwerp had no fewer than 149 private schools run by lay people and a dozen religious institutions where children learned to make lace from the age of six or seven. In lieu of paying tuition, their parents or guardians agreed to have their daughters work for the mistress for a number of years without pay.[28]

Overall, except for craft guilds, institutions that organized occupational training in pre-industrial Europe remained the exceptions. In some countries institutions were established for relatively large groups of girls. They provided vocational training in addition to religious instruction and the basics of reading and writing, in virtually all cases with a view toward helping them join the labour market. The proliferation of such schools at a time when production of garments and accessories was increasing substantially as prices dropped was far from coincidental. The overwhelming majority of all male occupations were learned informally, however, in the home of a merchant or master artisan or at the site where the activity was performed, such as with skippers, foremen or workers specialized in loading and unloading cargo.

The Economic Importance of Self-enforcing Contracts

More efficient general training is certain to have been crucial for increasing labour productivity, and this may be assumed to have been particularly true for craft production.[29] Economic historians have recently observed that apprenticeship was pivotal in improving the availability and quality of human capital in early modern Europe and have noted that this system of technical training was conducive to the first Industrial Revolution in various respects.

Jan Luiten van Zanden has calculated that the skill premium, i.e. the wage discrepancy between skilled and unskilled workers, decreased considerably in Western Europe during the century following the Black Death and hovered around 60 percent until circa 1914, whereas in Japan and India the skill premium was 150 to 250 percent throughout this period. In other words: from the late Middle Ages onward, human capital in Western Europe was far cheaper than in large parts of Asia. The author attributes this remarkable difference to a combination of two factors: the more efficient capital market in Western Europe, which was accessible to broad segments of the population, and the greater efficiency of a training system controlled largely by craft guilds.[30] Larry Epstein has even argued that craft guilds in many parts of late medieval and early modern Europe existed essentially because their organization of occupational training solved what is known as the free rider problem, where some employers might benefit from the investments of their colleagues in training apprentices. Organizing apprenticeship within the guilds restricted qualified workers to a limited number of employers and therefore gave individual masters a greater incentive to invest in their training. As a consequence, the apprenticeship system promoted innovation through the production and transfer of technical skills, which in turn made craft guilds fundamental operators in the transition to the industrial society.[31]

In her innovative study on the causes of the English Industrial Revolution, Jane Humphries explores the relationship between apprenticeship and structural economic change. Humphries argues that the English national system of apprenticeship, established in 1563, promoted general industrial training. In conjunction with the Elizabethan Poor Law of 1602, the system moreover contributed to 'the premature exodus of labour out of agriculture that is the hallmark of English exceptionalism'. In other words, the author considers the apprenticeship system's facilitation of rural to urban migration to be one of the factors behind the relatively widespread urbanization and large share of nonagrarian labour in England as early as 1700.[32]

While the efficiency – and consequently the economic significance – of a training system may depend on various factors, the enforcement issue is by far the most important in the case of apprenticeship. The master-apprentice contract is by definition an 'incomplete contract' in economic terms.[33] There are two fundamental problems: 'first the exchanges are not synchronized in time; either the master trains first and the apprentice works subsequently as skilled labour, or the unskilled apprentice works first to be trained subsequently... Second, the commodities to be exchanged, training and maintenance on the one hand and service on the other, are difficult to define and specify'.[34] Both problems could clearly be cause for differences of opinion and conflicts between the parties to the contract.

Quantitative data indicate that a great many apprentices failed to complete their contract. Between 1540 and 1590 nearly 45 percent of the apprentices in the London cabinetmakers' guild were in fact listed as 'gone' or 'run away'.[35] At the end of the Ancien Régime, drop-out rates for apprentices in the French guilds on which information is available averaged 30 percent,[36] while rates in Vienna in the eighteenth and nineteenth centuries ranged from 20 percent (bookbinders) to 57 percent (locksmiths).[37] In most cases, apprentices left because of ill treatment, which might consist of physical abuse, or because their master was unwilling to assign them anything other than demeaning tasks (which meant that they were taught nothing). In other cases, masters terminated the arrangement, because apprentices had a physical ailment, were chronically ill or proved unsuitable for other reasons.[38]

The available figures also reveal, however, that the overwhelming majority of the apprentices *did* serve out their contract. How is this possible? This question is difficult to answer. After all, in addition to the vast geographic and chronological differences in both apprenticeship systems and enforcement mechanisms, socio-economic, legal and cultural contexts often varied widely as well. The current studies nonetheless enable a few general conclusions. England had two efficiency-inducing measures that were not observed anywhere else in Europe. From 1563, England had national legislation regarding apprenticeship: the renowned Statute of Artificers – effective until 1814 – entitled a young man who had served out his contract to practice his trade everywhere, which was not the case on the Continent. From 1662 onward, working people in England could also use legal apprenticeships to establish settlement rights, entitling them to poor relief in times of need.[39]

Do both arrangements indeed suggest that breaches of contract were less likely in England than on the Continent? Not necessarily. A complex transaction, such as an apprenticeship contract, had to be based largely on trust, which demanded far more than legal measures. It was essential that both masters and apprentices be able to take legal action in the event of breach of contract. Still, legal coercion appears to have been a measure of last resort. Social coercion tactics tended to be far more efficient. That was why apprenticeship contracts in Germany, France, Austria and the southern Netherlands were no less self-enforcing than in England during the early modern period. On the one hand, the parties concerned cared deeply about maintaining or establishing a good reputation in the family, peer group and local community, as notions of honour and dishonour were major factors determining both their material and their emotional chances of survival. On the other hand, in many urban occupations apprenticeship contracts were embedded in institutions that supervised compliance with contractual obligations by both parties and arbitrated in the event of disputes: the guilds.[40]

Corporatism and Apprenticeship: A Complex Relationship

In both late medieval and early modern Europe (and elsewhere in the world), craft guilds were formed primarily in cities and towns. Any corporative organizations established in rural areas were usually restricted to export industries,[41] and the data available suggest that they were unusual even in proto-industrial areas. Although no exact figures can be provided, the overwhelming majority of manufacturers in the countryside were noncorporative. This does not mean that apprenticeship was unregulated. In England, the Statute of Artificers applied to both the countryside and the cities. Under the Statute the apprenticeship period in all sectors was seven years, and no master was allowed more than three apprentices.[42] Since no such national apprenticeship regulations existed on the Continent, local craft guilds determined the number of apprentices in each workshop and the duration of their training.

It is not clear where the artisans who ran workshops in villages without corporative organizations had received their training. Fragmentary data indicate that some urban craft guilds took on a great many apprentices from the countryside. Perhaps most of them later returned to the village of their birth to practise their trade, although this is far from certain.[43] It is quite possible that even occupations requiring special skills could be learned informally in the countryside. At any rate, in most towns and cities in Western and central Europe a great many trades were organized in guilds until the end of the Ancien Régime, or even until the second half of the nineteenth century (especially in Germany and Austria). Both contemporaries and later generations of historians have consistently acknowledged the close ties between urban corporatism and apprenticeship. Discussions about the significance of shop-floor learning in the pre-industrial period are therefore inextricably linked with those on the significance of craft guilds.

Traditional views tended to associate urban apprenticeship in the pre-industrial period with what has been called an immutable society of orders in which master artisans formed an important stratum. Their organizations were said to have impeded the rise of the free market, blocked technological change and curtailed social mobility. Apprenticeship figured prominently in each of these three perspectives – in each case negatively. It was associated with maintaining the status quo and reproducing the established social order. Karl Stratmann, who establishes a rigid distinction between the Old Regime and 'modernity', situates shop-floor learning in precisely this context.[44] He presumes a nearly static social order, with the guilds as major defenders. Apprentices were expected to observe and emulate the honourable conduct of their masters and to follow in their footsteps later on. In Stratmann's opinion, this explains why apprentices lived with their masters in addition to working for them, and why apprenticeship was integrated within the guild system. Masters seemed to have a corporative mandate, and the objective of the education was to mould a new member of the community rather than create a sovereign individual. According to this perspective, craft guilds were regarded as a *Gemeinschaft* (community) and were consequently a counterweight to the *Gesellschaft* (society) of the industrial era.[45]

Most scholars no longer consider craft guilds to be incompatible with the rise and development of capitalism.[46] Nonetheless, opinions continue to vary widely with respect to both the socio-economic[47] and the socio-cultural dimensions of urban corporatism – and therefore with respect to apprenticeship as well. In his contribution to this volume Davids argues that the needs of masters and apprentices in the Dutch Republic could be reconciled through oral or written agreements. These contracts were negotiated in a free market without any interference from corporative organizations. If necessary, the town council intervened by enacting regulations. Any supervision by the local authorities of apprenticeship contracts through compulsory registration tended to figure within a social policy that related care for orphans or children of paupers to labour-market needs. This left craft guilds in the Republic with little or no say in the duration, content or cost of apprenticeships during the seventeenth and eighteenth centuries. Their sole opportunity for exercising control was ex post facto in some cases: they could test the competence of a prospective master through a master's test, but that practice was not ubiquitous. Such tests were often arranged through institutions supervised by the municipal authorities, known as *neringen*, or civil servants.[48] The free rider problem could also be solved through private contracts; this is apparent from clauses where the apprentice agreed to continue working for his master for a period after the training had been completed so that the master could recover his investment. A similar, frequently recurring, mechanism was the practice of charging high fees for brief apprenticeship contracts and lower ones for more extended commitments. Payments were usually due in advance to discourage apprentices from running off once they had mastered the skills they needed.[49]

While guilds were indeed very numerous in the Dutch Republic, they did not have the same extensive authority there as they did in many other countries. In the Spanish/Austrian Netherlands[50] and German-speaking regions,[51] for example, apprenticeship regulations were enshrined in most guild statutes, and these organizations were entitled to exercise control. In such cases the role of guilds *did* become important and even decisive with respect to apprenticeship, in both economic and cultural respects. Understanding how this worked requires considering the economic and socio-cultural context in greater detail.

The late Middle Ages and early modern period were a time of product innovation rather than process innovation. This was particularly true for textile manufacturing, which was the most important industrial sector in terms of capital investment, employment and profits: the available techniques could be used to produce infinite varieties of new fabrics.[52] Moreover, the more affluent employers sometimes used their trained apprentices as cheap labour and therefore had little incentive to pursue technological change.[53] Precisely because product innovation was so important in the pre-industrial period, urban corporatism and apprenticeship were often closely linked: corporative control over 'shop-floor learning' helped guarantee and legitimize product quality.

Some historians assert that compulsory apprenticeship also regulated access to a prestigious status and reproduced the harmonious image of the independent, competent craftsman. Reality could be very different, however. The descriptions of some of the master-pieces required in guild-based trades suggest that apprentices in certain occupations learned very few specializations. In seventeenth-century Paris, the test for becoming a master in the goldsmith industry was even determined *ad hoc*, based on the candidate's area of specialization during his apprenticeship.[54] Division of labour may have prevented apprentices from becoming familiar with more than a small part of the production process and made their status similar to that of young, unskilled workers. Alternatively, specialization may have improved their chances on the labour market by creating distinction.[55]

In this volume the changing features of the apprenticeship system are examined from the perspective of both changing labour relations and shifts on the product market. In the Antwerp cabinetmakers' guild, the formal apprenticeship system loosened up precisely when master artisans and merchant-entrepreneurs began focusing on luxury markets, offering complex, quality products instead of standardized fabrics. Up to the late sixteenth century, the apprenticeship term and the master-piece were consonant with the skills required to produce a well-defined range of manufacture of goods, but the close correspondence between product and training disappeared once trust in the more 'baroque' products was no longer guaranteed by standardization. From then on, other 'conventions' were required to establish agreement on product quality and price. The new aim of the formal apprenticeship system may have been to link the collective trademark to the superior 'quality' of the producers through a representative level.[56]

Some authors are inclined to subordinate economic logic entirely to rhetorical and discursive logic.[57] In our view, this is as questionable as reducing corporatism to an institution to capitalize training costs. Strategies focused on controlling competition and regulating prices cannot be completely reduced to a discourse. We advocate combining the two perspectives rather than favouring one. In his recent study on the decline of craft guilds in France, Steven Kaplan regards the guild system as a relatively autonomous intermediary body, in which socio-economic and moral registers were inextricably linked, with the understanding, however, that corporative discourse was essentially a post-facto construction that neutralized the underlying contradiction between masters and journeymen, and legitimized the established order.[58] Kaplan's view is somewhat compatible with the argument presented by Michael Sonenscher, who emphasizes that in France at the end of the Ancien Régime the economic need for labour was related to maintaining ethical or moral stability. Master artisans had little effective control over workers, whose willingness to work was subject to fundamental conditions, such as acknowledgement of their 'property in skill' and decent treatment. Sonenscher attributes the compromise between the two groups to their support for a sort of fictional intimacy. Masters and journeymen offset labour market insecurities by devising customs and codes, which underlay a measure of collective identity and ensured the necessary trust and stability.[59] While Sonenscher appears to base himself on Durkheim's harmony model, Kaplan advances a conflict model and the corresponding false class consciousness. Both authors, however, regard the apprenticeship period as initiation to a cultural context (i.e. socialization and acculturation), whether within a guild or in a different setting. In accordance with recent sociological views on learning and socialization processes, they tend to interpret learning on the shop floor as encompassing far more than skill acquisition alone.

'On-the-Job Training' and Skill Acquisition

Skill acquisition was the objective of those who were apprenticed to a master, but to what extent did the apprenticeship system meet this expectation? In some industries parents or guardians of apprentices entered an oral or written contract with a master stipulating how long the training would last and how much it would cost, as well as all kinds of mutual rights and obligations.[60] This procedure was expected to reconcile supply with demand and was up to a certain degree unrelated to the term of apprenticeship institutionalized by the craft guilds. In medieval Flanders the negotiated terms did not necessarily match what was officially prescribed.[61] As noted above, the duration of the training usually varied according to the fees paid. Children from humble or poor homes tended to be apprenticed for longer periods than those whose parents or guardians were more comfortable financially. In German towns during the eighteenth century apprenticeships were nearly always shorter for more costly apprenticeship contracts, as extensive quantitative data have demonstrated.[62] In this volume, Steidl reveals that poor apprentices in seventeenth-century Vienna had to spend an extra year with a master silk weaver or a master purse maker.[63] Munich even had official regulations on the subject around 1800: children of paupers were entitled to be apprenticed to master artisans free of charge, provided they signed on for an extra year.[64] Several arrangements from earlier periods covered the opposite situation. In sixteenth-century London, for example, well-to-do families often bought off years of apprenticeship.[65] Employers, in turn, might engage their apprentices in production immediately (possibly by assigning them preparatory or repetitive tasks) or recruit apprentices who would eventually repay them with extra work. While both the nature of the production process and the economic and social position of the individual employer may be assumed to have figured in the decision between the different strategies, insufficient information is available to identify these elements at this time.

Studies of apprenticeship contracts enable examination of actual transactions between masters and apprentices (or their parents or guardians) and provide insight into the socio-economic positions of different groups and the leeway available to them. In his contribution Stabel shows that guilds in medieval Flanders did not ordinarily intervene in apprenticeship conditions, preferring to leave most issues to custom and negotiations between the master and the apprentice's family. Until the sixteenth century a minimum term and a maximum number of apprentices per master were the only guild regulations concerning apprenticeship. Even the social mobility of apprentices did not depend on the juridical and financial thresholds the guilds established. An apprentice's prior status (as a master's son, for example) or his financial assets seem to have been far more important in determining if and when he became a master. Guilds are likely to have been preoccupied especially with their monopoly on the product market and the corresponding standardization of (the quality of) their products.[66]

But the question remains: what did apprentices learn on the shop floor? The answer seems obvious: the technical aspects of a certain occupation. In fact, the situation could be more complex. Based on autobiographical writings of Belgian and German master artisans from the late eighteenth and nineteenth centuries, Sven Steffens has hypothesized that neither masters nor journeymen were inclined to make an effort to train apprentices, preferring to use them as general helpers. Apprentices with a strong desire to learn (i.e. to master skills) had to 'steal with their eyes'.[67] However, should these 'testimonies' not be regarded as very free translations of alternative trajectories?[68] After all, the authors in most of these cases did not practise the trade for which they had been apprenticed. Instead, in the eyes of most of their contemporaries – and certainly in their own eyes – they had worked their way up to being entrepreneurs, politicians, syndicalists, journalists or professional writers. This experience probably made them particularly inclined to distinguish practical experience from intellectual education, on the one hand, and to highlight their career as self-taught men, on the other.

The view that apprentices had to steal with their eyes corresponds with the longstanding interest in the 'mysteries' or 'secrets' of the trade, which were believed to be jealously guarded within the guild framework. It may, however, be argued that journeymen's travels from town to town – a common practice in England and France and characteristic of the social constitution of trades in Central Europe[69] – was in fact conducive to learning and disseminating new techniques. Note that trade or craft 'secrets' largely concerned process-innovation methods, whereas product innovation was the main focus during the pre-industrial period. It has been demonstrated, for example, that journeymen tailors who had worked in many towns mastered the broadest range of styling and cutting.[70] In some guild-based occupations, efforts were made at any rate to integrate innovations systematically. Upon arriving in a town, for example, a travelling surgeon might be required to perform in public with a local guild official in attendance to ensure the distribution of knowledge.[71]

Technical knowledge was probably regarded as an economic commodity on which the owner could capitalize, for example, through an apprenticeship contract. In seventeenth-century London, some agreements prohibited apprentices from immediately passing on the knowledge they acquired to protect their masters from losses in the event of breach of contract.[72] In apprenticeship contracts in Antwerp during the same period, master artisans were often obliged to teach their apprentices everything they knew about their occupation, without concealing anything.[73] Basically, technical knowledge was the property of the master, and a contract was an agreement to transfer that property in exchange for money and/or labour. Anyone unable to establish himself as a master could at least claim 'property in skill' as a journeyman.[74] The higher premiums paid to brewers, goldsmiths and barber surgeons than to tailors or shoemakers, and the far higher amounts given to some master artisans than to others, reflected the 'potential profitability' of an occupation or firm,[75] as well as the degree of specialization, the time required for learning the occupation, the individual expertise, the scale of business involved and, last but not least, the social prestige of the owner.[76]

Detailed information about the actual learning process is very difficult to obtain. All available data, however, indicate that the lamentations from the eighteenth century onward about the regressive and obnoxious nature of corporative organizations have misrepresented the early modern apprentice system. According to the critics, most apprentices simply copied what they saw and heard from their masters with respect to both work and lifestyle. As a result, the guild-based apprenticeship system has been considered responsible for purely 'reproducing' and consequently impeding all forms of creativity and even autonomous operation. The absence of systematic clarification and explanatory information was believed to have needlessly delayed the training programme. Only in a modern context was imparting knowledge dissociated from the concrete, immediate and empirical, and did learning supposedly become more than copying and imitating.[77] This sharp contrast between Ancien Régime and modernity is invalid, on the one hand, because in many industrial sectors large numbers of apprentices neither expected nor even hoped to attain master status (see below), and on the other hand, because of the pre-industrial state of technology and economic development. Product innovation was achieved not by specialists in applied sciences but by craftsmen who imitated established patterns and shapes and 'invented' new combinations.[78]

The focus in most occupations was on acquiring experience and learning in stages and through trial and error. This arose not from a lack of modern educational insights and instructional methods but from the specific technological and economic operating conditions. In nearly all branches of industry apprentices needed to learn how the raw materials would react to the mechanical and chemical production processes, in a context of variable surrounding conditions, such as temperature, level of humidity, quality of the materials used, and other elements that were often impossible to measure accurately. The only way to understand these processes and to learn how to anticipate all possible reactions was to do the work and to keep evaluating the reactions. Didactic skills were of secondary importance: masters were merely expected to point out what had gone wrong and what might be improved, while apprentices, in turn, had only to acquire sufficient practical experience.[79]

These circumstances applied not only in the pre-industrial period. After 1800 shop-floor learning remained the best option in some trades. In his contribution to this volume Reinarz demonstrates that on-the-spot learning continued in the brewing industry in England through the late nineteenth and early twentieth centuries, despite the vast technological and economic changes. This case is remarkable not only because of the abundance of vocational schools and increasingly systematic instruction in reading and writing at the time, but also because the rapid advances in technology received only secondary consideration in industrial training. The entrepreneurs – and probably the apprentices as well – were not interested in fostering an understanding of zymotechnology (the science of fermentation). By rotating between the different departments of the brewery, apprentices gained comprehensive insight into the production process without understanding the science. All their energies were devoted to gaining experience, which meant understanding the relationship between the production process and the outcome.[80] Practical, empirical and specific knowledge were thus valued over theories, abstractions and generalizations – know-how took precedence over knowledge.

Forms of Mobility and Family Strategies

Decisions to enter one apprenticeship or another should also be considered from a broader perspective, including geographical mobility, urbanization and de-urbanization, family economy, life-cycle trends, guild traditions and the like.

Stabel calls attention to geographical mobility, not only of untrained youngsters looking for a job or a training opportunity, but also of journeymen wanting to settle as a master in a renowned city (i.e. Bruges).[81] While journeymen were undoubtedly highly mobile in many parts of Europe during the late Middle Ages and the early modern period, was this true for apprentices as well? In England this was indeed the case: in all major towns for which data are available, migrants from smaller centres or rural areas were the largest single group among the apprentices. In mid-sixteenth century London, migrants accounted for 90 percent of the apprentice population, compared with 85 percent by the mid-seventeenth century. Around 1550, approximately 1,400 youths started as apprentices every year, compared with twice this figure around 1650. While there were fewer migrants among the apprentices in the provincial towns, their share never dropped below one-third, and ranged from 75 to 80 percent in Bristol.[82] The only data available for the Continent concern the eighteenth century. In Vienna most apprentices came from the city or the surrounding countryside (the province of Lower Austria), but considerable differences existed among occupations: while only 22 percent of the bookbinders were migrants, 52 percent of the cabinetmakers and 65 percent of the chimney sweeps came from other places; over half the chimney sweeps came from southern Switzerland (Grisons, Ticino) or Italy, and had thus travelled hundreds of kilometres to be trained in a metropolis such as Vienna.[83] The research cannot yet explain these differences. Unfortunately, the same holds true for various aspects of occupational and social mobility.

Children from poor families obviously had few or no choices about their occupational future. While no exact figures are available, all the information suggests that many young adults never even started apprenticeships but performed wage labour when they were very young to supplement the family income. This was the case in England and on the Continent, both in the cities and in the countryside.[84] In cases where orphanage trustees allowed their wards to learn an occupation, the selection was invariably very limited and comprised exclusively low-prestige trades.[85] In England, children whose parents were unable to support them were apprenticed at the expense of the parish and thus entered the poorer trades in the seventeenth century and the impoverished trades in the eighteenth century; in the late eighteenth and early nineteenth centuries batches of children were increasingly apprenticed at centralized workshops, often at a considerable distance from their parish.[86]

Among the middle classes, the party choosing the occupation is often impossible to determine: was it the prospective apprentice him/herself or the parents or guardians of the youth, or was the decision reached mutually? Age at the start of apprenticeship was undoubtedly a factor and varied widely, depending on the trade. In many cases, the vast differences between the periods and regions have yet to be identified. In early fourteenth-century London young people generally started apprenticeships at around the age of fourteen. A century later the average age of new apprentices was fifteen or sixteen years, and by 1550 it had risen to nineteen-and-a-half years, although this last average includes a broad range from twelve to twenty-five years of age.[87] By the late sixteenth century the average age of new London apprentices appears to have declined again, while elsewhere in England it varied between fourteen and sixteen years during the early modern period.[88] Only indigent apprentices tended to be younger, although even they rarely started before they were twelve or thirteen years old.[89] On the Continent wide fluctuations occurred as well, although the available data suggest that in the eighteenth century apprentices started earlier there than in England. In both Paris and Vienna the majority started at twelve, thirteen or fourteen years of age,[90] while in Berlin the age of new apprentices ranged from fourteen to sixteen years.[91] In the seventeenth and eighteenth centuries in Antwerp the average age of new apprentices was between fifteen and sixteen, but the range was broad: from twelve to twenty-five years.[92]

Presumably, the duration of apprenticeships was related to the age at which young people entered them. While these terms could be seven years or longer everywhere, such durations were exceptional on the Continent. In Vienna they ranged from three to five years in most occupations, in Berlin from three to six years. They were usually four years in towns in southern Germany and lasted about two years in the United Provinces, the Habsburg Netherlands and north-German coastal cities, except in highly technical occupations (e.g. surgeons and goldsmiths), where the apprenticeship periods were longer.[93] Since they were older upon starting *and* served longer apprenticeships, English apprentices might have been older when they started as free journeymen. The effective term of apprenticeship, however, was not always the same as the one prescribed. Perhaps apprentices in England completed their terms in less time than the period prescribed, while those on the Continent might often generally have taken longer than the official term allotted.

The contributions to this volume from Reith and Steidl reveal that microstudies are needed to explain why in some cities and periods the official terms of apprenticeship were longer or shorter than in others, and why exceptions were made if necessary. Steidl demonstrates that among the Viennese silk weavers during the late eighteenth and nineteenth centuries, the actual duration of the apprenticeship was in some cases longer but more often shorter than the prescribed terms. Longer periods of apprenticeship usually arose from social factors.[94] Reith attributes the lengthening terms of apprenticeship in German towns from the sixteenth century onward to a combination of population growth and the more sophisticated qualifications that were required as a consequence of product innovation.

The primary concern of a great many master artisans was whether the son would be following in his father's footsteps and, if this was the case, whether he would be trained at home. Simply passing on the torch offered several advantages: in nearly all cases entrance fees for sons of masters were lower than for other candidates, and sons trained by their fathers were not required to pay a premium. Moreover, in this case fathers were entitled to take on one apprentice more than the maximum number allowed for that trade. But matters were rarely that simple, as studies about occupations practised by fathers and sons demonstrate. Based on a few Parisian family trees, for example, David Garrioch has observed a gradual shift in occupational continuity during the eighteenth century. Up to the 1740s, sons customarily succeeded their fathers in the same occupation, and daughters married men with the same occupation from the same neighbourhood. After 1750, however, sons and daughters started to marry outsiders in increasing numbers. Because their fathers were sufficiently successful in their own occupation, more young people were able to take up other trades and activities.[95]

Understanding what motivated sons to enter or avoid their father's occupation will require a host of microstudies. The fields examined should include family composition, social status of the head of the household, systems of inheritance and economic prospects, not to mention more obscure elements, such as relations between family members and relatives, the physical condition of the son and the way his virtues (or flaws) were perceived. Each of these elements could deeply influence an individual career from the outset. Some occupations were effectively closed to nonrelatives. This was the case in many corporations of butchers, who often stipulated the succession from father to son in their by-laws,[96] as well as in guilds of locksmiths, pewterers and goldsmiths.[97] Most trades were open to varying degrees, however, although the sons (and sometimes also the sons-in-law) of masters nearly always had privileged access. Yet the purpose of these supposed 'privileges' is not always properly understood. Gervaise Rosser, for example, has suggested that the lower entrance fee for the sons of masters may have served not to save the few vacancies for the sons of masters but rather to deter these sons from pursuing alternative careers.[98] Additional personal characteristics might also surface in different fields and in different directions. If an apprentice was less physically fit, for example, it might affect both the amount of the premium owed to a master artisan and the term of apprenticeship.[99]

The guilds obviously played a role as well. In Lyon and Nantes, growing difficulties among the small masters led some corporations to increase their efforts to prevent nonfamily members from joining despite economic expansion in these trades. In Dijon the socio-economic stability made for greater openness among the craft guilds and led to a substantial and ongoing inflow of men who were not the sons of masters, as well as journeymen from other places. After all, in this city the career prospects of masters' sons extended beyond the guilds.[100] Efforts to make guilds less accessible – through professional endogamy, marriages between families of equal status, and/or complicating accession for those who were not the sons of masters – were abandoned when the decline proved irreversible: why should a master artisan have his son learn and practise the same occupation if its future prospects were gloomy?[101]

In addition to the corporative strategies themselves, three factors were particularly important: the economic situation, the labour market and the familial context. As far as demand was concerned, the economic means of individual masters may have determined whether they could take on apprentices. The decline in the number of new apprentices during an economic slump may simply have been attributable to lack of work, but masters may also have been more inclined to employ their own sons. The final decision as to who would stay at home to work and who would register as an apprentice was reached within individual households rather than by the guilds (also with respect to the sons of nonmasters). In addition to financial help from parents, assistance from elder brothers or sisters or other relatives could be vital to start an apprenticeship both during and after training. Family context and all its ramifications for relations and networks were thus crucial.[102] This may be inferred first of all from the origins of the new masters registered in a given trade: sons of masters in that trade were not necessarily in the majority, but most new masters were sons of masters from *other* corporations.[103]

Fragmentary data suggest that such decisions were the outcome of family or group strategies. Genealogical analysis of producers of quality goods and of merchants who traded in them during the seventeenth and eighteenth centuries reveals that many male members – whether related by blood or by marriage – were involved in industries with close economic ties.[104] The huge impact of changed economic prospects on occupational choices in the families of master artisans is aptly illustrated by the variations in economic strategies concerning succession in early modern Antwerp. During this city's 'Golden Age', not only did master artisans often have one of their sons learn their occupation, but in many cases they arranged for two or more of their sons – whether from the same marriage or a different one – to be apprenticed in the same trade as well. This was due to economic expansion, which enabled several sons to succeed in the same industry. After 1585, this became far more difficult, and families opted in increasing measure to have only one son – generally the eldest – follow in his father's craft.[105]

Other factors include technological changes and whether or not a guild existed, as Steidl demonstrates in her contribution to this volume. Whereas the Viennese purse makers appear to have attracted apprentices through technological innovations, the number of registrations with the silk weavers plummeted once this guild was abolished. Apparently, a period of apprenticeship was no longer necessary to become an independent silk weaver.[106] All in all, additional research will need to cover a broad range of strategies and options, from the need for wages to contribute to the family income and the need for labour in the family business, to the practice among masters in more prestigious occupations of sending their first-born sons to university.

Boarding With a Master and Socialization

While many apprentices were the offspring of guild members, those from lower social groups often acted out of rather basic survival strategies. The rising number of apprentices in England and the high drop-out rates were the outcome of socio-economic changes in the countryside, which drove ever more young people from poor households to the cities, where they had difficulty adapting to new working and living conditions. The adjustment was especially difficult, as they were by definition the most vulnerable parties in their master's household. Obviously, however, not all apprentices were the same. The chief distinctions were 'living-in' versus 'external' apprenticeship, small versus large workshops, and the prospect of master status versus the virtual certainty of remaining a journeyman throughout one's life.

Living in a different household was a very common practice during the Ancien Régime. According to some authors, boarding with a master was even regarded as a kind of cultural ideal, where the master acted *in loco parentis* and raised his apprentice as he would his own son.[107] This seems very plausible indeed as far as England is concerned, where the exceptional geographic mobility would have forced many apprentices to seek accommodation far from home. On the Continent, most apprentices (including masters' sons) are believed to have lived with their masters as well, although no systematic research has been performed on the subject. The question as to whether apprentices moved in with their masters even if they were from the same town (and, if so, why), for example, has yet to be answered. Was it the custom for children to leave the home of their parents at an early age, as has been suggested for Vienna in the eighteenth and nineteenth centuries?[108] Or were some families unable to support all their members, so that a tradition of social responsibility arose in communities of the Ancien Régime?[109] At any rate, more businesslike procedures in the eighteenth century are believed to have affected the practice of apprentices boarding with their masters.[110] This would appear to result from changing labour relations, which meant that some masters no longer had journeymen or apprentices, while others might have a dozen – too many to board in their home.[111] Recent research suggests, however, that small, autonomous workshops with a few resident helpers had ceased to be commonplace well before the eighteenth century, and that, conversely, small-scale businesses remained important until well after 1800.[112] Understandably, therefore, most apprentices in Paris still boarded with their master in 1845,[113] and compulsory boarding was abolished in Germany only in 1875. Although many journeymen also lived with their masters until well into the nineteenth century, they were the first ones to depart from the *ganze Haus* ('whole house'). In the end, apprentices from outside the area were the ones most likely to board for extended periods, such as with bakers, shoemakers, tailors and cabinetmakers. The traditionally large representation of apprentices from the countryside in these occupations is believed to have perpetuated the practice of boarding with the master.[114]

Relations in a master's household were not always harmonious. In addition to becoming direct competitors of the journeymen, apprentices were a threat to the power of journeymen in the long run. By swelling the ranks of the journeymen, they reduced wages and employment. Even when their employers observed legal or corporative regulations, apprentices at large workshops interacted with several skilled workers and were primarily dependent upon them for their training and other experiences. Two factors influenced relations between journeymen and apprentices in such cases: the question as to whether or not the members of both groups would remain wage labourers indefinitely, and the question as to whether or not the journeymen had organizations of their own. At this time, however, insufficient information is available to shed light on the relations between the two groups.

Masters and apprentices might also clash. Both parties had complaints that were not always attributable to individual personality conflicts. The nature of the conflicts sometimes depended, at least in part, on the trade and labour relationships that prevailed. Industries characterized by concentration of production differed from trades that were small-scale operations well into the nineteenth and even the twentieth centuries, where apprentices were integrated in the master's household. In the first case, masters treated their apprentices as employers would treat poorly paid workers, while apprentices in the second case were subject to rigid patriarchal authority and might be ordered to do household chores as well.[115] If apprentices boarded with their master, they expected decent accommodation along with associated symbolic conditions in addition to good training. In the garment industry, in the Southern Netherlands, the debate extended beyond physical abuse and neglect of instructional responsibilities by the masters to include the quality of the food provided.[116] Even sleeping arrangements could be cause for conflict.[117]

Apprentices complained not only of physical abuse and neglect,[118] but also about the training provided.[119] Their reasons were twofold. First, the more affluent entrepreneurs were inclined to take on as many apprentices as possible to use them as cheap labour.[120] Some apprentices were involved only in preparatory procedures or learned only part of the production process. At small workshops, in addition to being subject to the direct and generally strict authority of their master, apprentices became involved in conflicts over performing household chores, degrading them to mere servants who did not learn at all.[121] Second, while many apprenticeship contracts stipulated that the master was supposed to teach everything that happened at the workshop or that he knew,[122] division of labour and specialization were hardly conducive to this objective. While masters often complained that their apprentices failed to serve out their term, apprentices were inclined to move on, once they felt they had learned all they could and could expect nothing more than a stint as free workers. All contracts that combined labour with learning thus comprised an ongoing dynamic, which often resulted in mutual suspicion between the master and the apprentice.[123]

Different value systems often figured in the background. Young boys and girls from poor rural households were not the only ones who had difficulty adjusting. In early modern England, for example, the growing numbers of apprentices from the lower landed gentry led to clashes in the homes of master artisans between urban bourgeois values and the more libertine values common to the gentry.[124] This demonstrates once again the need to consider the broader social and cultural context, including moral and educational concerns. The perception of apprenticeship agreements as both economic and moral understandings is cause for examining the factors that determined the placement of apprentices. In his contribution to this book, Reith questions the '*ganze Haus*' model, which depicts trades as a framework for harmonious coexistence under the master's roof in the late Middle Ages. Given such models, it is not surprising that the practice of paying wages to apprentices was associated with decadence or the rise of industrial society, which was not necessarily the case. Based on apprenticeship contracts, the apprenticeship period may also be regarded as an economic transaction comparable to an employment arrangement, and the workshop as a type of enterprise involving labour by family and nonfamily.[125] From this perspective, the assertion that wages increased as parents grew more inclined to send their sons to work at factories – especially with older apprentices who, moreover, had often already worked in the same craft as unskilled labourers – certainly merits additional research. Paying higher wages may have been necessary to maintain apprentice recruitment. Various data indicate that in some trades on the Continent, employment opportunities in noncorporate branches – where in some cases unskilled youths could earn wages relatively early on – labour recruitment became a problem by the eighteenth century.[126] Information about the southern Netherlands suggests that apprentices entered occupations considered to be undesirable (e.g. shoemakers and tailors) primarily when other guilds were doing badly, which suggests the same mechanism.[127]

Gender Perspectives

Because of the focus on the corporative and urban contexts, women are not covered in sufficient measure in this volume. Both during the pre-industrial period and in the nineteenth century nearly all guild-based apprentices in Europe were male. Although little is known about the opportunities for girls to learn skills, and the data available reflect substantial local and even regional variations, social expectations regarding the roles and skills of young women must have consistently differed from those of young men everywhere. One clear sign of this discrepancy is that the apprenticeship system offered far fewer opportunities to young women than to young men, both in the Middle Ages and during the early modern period, in England and on the Continent alike. Indications are, moreover, that women faced better prospects for learning and training in the late Middle Ages than they did in the early modern period.

Although the pace and exact nature of the changes depended on the place and often on the trade, the trend was unmistakable: during the sixteenth and seventeenth centuries nearly everywhere in Europe where craft guilds were in control, entering occupations organized in guilds became more difficult or even impossible for women. In many cases female apprentices were no longer taken on, and the only women allowed to run workshops were the widows of masters. In some guilds even these widows faced myriad restrictions; for example, they were allowed to carry on their late husband's business only if they entrusted supervision to a journeyman, or they might be prohibited from training apprentices. By the eighteenth century women were allowed to join only a very small number of guilds directly and had their own corporations in very few towns; their official role in the corporate system had been restricted largely to trades in the urban economy associated with some form of domestic production, such as the garment trades or food processing, certain branches of the textile industry, or retail.[128] While the reasons for these changes are unclear, fluctuations in the demand for labour were undoubtedly a factor. In the first half of the seventeenth century, the London population soared, and the city absorbed thousands of male apprentices from all over the country, which left very few women eligible for apprenticeships. The arrival of male apprentices later decreased, and more women were registered again.[129] During the second half of the eighteenth century in Nantes, labour participation reflected economic changes as well: employment opportunities for women increased, both legally, supervised by the craft guilds, and illegally, as textile manufacturing, the garment trades and the food processing industries expanded significantly and became more specialized in the process.[130]

Of course, formal criteria for admission to or exclusion from craft guilds were not always of overriding importance. First, the significance of occupational training in corporative organizations that accepted both male and female apprentices was very different for each of the two groups, as the example of eighteenth- and nineteenth-century Vienna indicates: both female and male apprentices were accepted for the production of silk fabrics, but the apprentice period for young women was generally three years, after which they would take poorly paid jobs, whereas men spent five or six years as apprentices and learned to design patterns in addition to weaving.[131] Second, the *rate* of female labour participation did not necessarily diminish in guild-based trades during the early modern period. In addition to the reversal of this trend in some cities toward the end of the Ancien Régime, as the case of Nantes illustrates, wives of master craftsmen were generally entitled to work for their husband, at his workshop and under his privilege, as were his daughters. Daughters of guildsmen thus received informal occupational training at home. After all, where else would the young women who ran workshops in Brussels during the eighteenth century – where a brother or other family member acted as the official master – have learnt the skills required?[132]

Finally, some labour-intensive trades were not organized in guilds. Women involved in these trades could set up economically independent operations, provided they had the necessary financial means. Still, occupational choices were far more limited for girls than for boys. Research on England has demonstrated that during the sixteenth and seventeenth centuries young girls were a tiny minority among apprentices. Most ended up as housewives or in domestic service, which in many cases included training in some type of needlework. The social composition of female apprentices changed as well. The increasing share of girls apprenticed at the expense of the municipal or parochial authorities suggests a decline in prestige.[133] Whether a similar trend occurred on the Continent is impossible to determine from existing data. The rising demand for needlework in the eighteenth century certainly did not coincide with greater appreciation for female apprentices.[134] On the contrary, the rising numbers of women trained as lace makers (who generally attended private schools for many years) were paid abysmally low wages in nearly all cases,[135] despite being highly skilled; seamstresses and spinsters rarely fared any better. Neither the eighteenth-century practice among trustees of girls' orphanages of opening workshops where their wards learned to sew[136] nor the spinning schools opened for poor girls raised the standing of female apprentices. Young girls who were apprenticed in the fashion industry were often depicted as prospective prostitutes by their contemporaries, while those trained in certain textile industries were held in very low esteem because of their miserable career prospects.[137]

Notes

1. K. Stratmann and M. Schlösser, *Das Duale System der Berufsbildung. Eine historische Analyse seiner Reformdebatten* (Frankfurt am Main, 1992); G. Kutscha, 'Das Duale System der Berufsausbildung in der Bundesrepublik Deutschland – Ein Auslaufendes Model'?, *Die Berufsbildende Schule* (1992): 145–56; D. Soskice, 'Reconciling Markets and Institutions: The German Apprenticeship System', in L.M. Lynch (ed.), *Training and the Private Sector: International Comparisons* (Chicago, 1994), 25–60; K.U. Mayer and D. Konietzka, 'Formation professionnelle et débuts de carrière: crise ou stabilité du modèle allemand'?, *Revue Française de Sociologie*, 39 (1998): 269–304; and A. Lattard, 'Permanence et mutations du système dual. Où va le modèle allemand?', *Revue Française de Pédagogie,* 131 (Spring 2000): 75–85.
2. See Gilles Moreau, 'L'enseignement professionnel ou la défaite d'un projet émancipateur', *Le Monde Diplomatique*, 51, 601 (April 2004): 22–23.
3. Cf. J. Lave and B. Rogoff, *Everyday Cognition: Its Development in Social Context* (Cambridge, 1984); J. Brown, A. Collins and P. Duguid, 'Situated Cognition and the Culture of Learning', *Educational Researcher*, 18 (1989): 32–42; and R. Driver, H. Asoko, J. Leach, E. Mortimer and P. Scott, 'Constructing Scientific Knowledge in the Classroom', *Educational Researcher*, 23 (1994): 5–12.
4. J. Brown, A. Collins and S.E. Newman, 'Cognitive Apprenticeship: Teaching the Crafts of Reading, Writing, and Mathematics', in L.B. Resnick (ed.), *Knowing, Learning, and Instruction: Essays in Honor of Robert Glaser* (Hillsdale, 1989): 453–94; S. Henessy, 'Situated Cognition and Cognitive Apprenticeship: Implications for Classroom Learning', *Studies in Science Education* 22 (1993): 1–42.
5. Cf. R. Siegler, *Childrens' Thinking* (Englewood Cliffs, 1991); and R. Vasta, M.M. Haith and S.A. Miller, *Child Psychology: The Modern Science* (New York, 1995).
6. The twentieth century is not covered, because occupational training in Western Europe became highly institutionalized and was provided through schools during the decades before and after 1900 and thus instigated an entirely different dynamic. Between the Franco-Prussian War and World War I, the dual system emerged in Germany, while in France the wellknown Astier Act introduced German-style compulsory occupational training (*cours professionnels*).
7. See especially R. Mackenney, *Tradesmen and Traders. The World of the Guilds in Venice and Europe, c.1250–c.1650* (London and Sydney, 1987); C. Lis and H. Soly, 'Corporatisme, onderaanneming en loonarbeid. Flexibilisering en deregulering van de arbeidsmarkt in Westeuropese steden (veertiende-achttiende eeuw)', *Tijdschrift voor Sociale Geschiedenis*, 20 (1994): 365–90; and C. Lis and H. Soly, 'Different Paths of Development: Capitalism in the Northern and Southern Netherlands during the Late Middle Ages and the Early Modern Period', *Review*, 20 (1997): 228–38; G. Crossick (ed.), *The Artisan and the European Town, 1500–1900* (Aldershot, 1997); R.S. DuPlessis, *Transitions to Capitalism in*

Early Modern Europe (Cambridge, 1997): 127–34; J. Farr, 'On the Shop Floor: Guilds, Artisans, and the European Market Economy, 1350–1750', *Journal of Early Modern History*, 1 (1997): 24–54; and J. Farr, *Artisans in Europe, 1300–1914* (Cambridge, 2000); J. Ehmer, 'Traditionelles Denken und neue Fragestellungen zur Geschichte von Handwerk und Zunft', in F. Lenger (ed.), *Handwerk, Hausindustrie und die historische Schule der Nationalökonomie. Wissenschafts- und gewerbegeschichtliche Perspektiven* (Bielefeld, 1998) 19–77; W. Reininghaus, 'Stadt und Handwerk. Eine Einführung in Forschungsprobleme und Forschungsfragen', in K.H. Kaufhold and W. Reininghaus (eds), *Stadt und Handwerk in Mittelalter und früher Neuzeit* (Cologne, 2000), 1–19; and H.-G. Haupt (ed.), *Das Ende der Zünfte. Ein europäischer Vergleich* (Göttingen, 2002).

8. K. Wesoly, *Lehrlinge und Handwerksgesellen am Mittelrhein. Ihre soziale Lage und ihre Organisation vom 14. bis ins 17. Jahrhundert* (Frankfurt, 1985); A. Griessinger and R. Reith, 'Lehrlinge im deutschen Handwerk des ausgehenden 18. Jahrhunderts. Arbeitsorganisation, Sozialbeziehungen und alltägliche Konflikte', *Zeitschrift für Historische Forschung*, 13 (1986): 149–99; R. Reith, 'Zur beruflichen Sozialisation im Handwerk vom 18. bis ins frühe 20. Jahrhundert. Umrisse einer Sozialgeschichte der deutschen Lehrlinge', *Vierteljahrschrift für Sozial- und Wirtschaftsgeschichte*, 76 (1989): 1–27.
9. I. Krausman Ben-Amos, *Adolescence and Youth in Early Modern England* (New Haven and London, 1994), chs 3–5, and the following articles by the same author: 'Service and the Coming of Age in Seventeenth-Century England', *Continuity and Change*, 3 (1988): 41–64, and 'Failure to Become Freemen: Urban Apprentices in Early Modern England', *Social History*, 16 (1991): 155–72; J. Lane, *Apprenticeship in England, 1600–1914* (London, 1996); and J. Humphries, 'English Apprenticeship. A Neglected Factor in the First Industrial Revolution', in P.A. David and M. Thomas (eds), *The Economic Future in Historical Perspective* (Oxford, 2003): 73–102.
10. M. Sonenscher, *Work and Wages: Natural Law, Politics and the Eighteenth-century French Trades* (Cambridge, 1989); S. Kaplan, 'L'apprentissage à Paris au XVIIIe siècle: le cas de Paris', *Revue d'Histoire Moderne et Contemporaine*, 40 (1993): 436–79, and the book by the same author *La fin des corporations* (Paris, 2001). See also the contributions of Alain Cabantous, Anne-Marie Cocula, Jean-Marc Moriceau and Nicole Pellegrin in the special issue on 'Apprentissages (XVIe–XXe siècles)' of the *Revue d'Histoire Moderne et Contemporaine*, 40 (1993).
11. S. Steffens, *Untersuchungen zur Mentalität belgischer und deutscher Handwerker anhand von Selbstzeugnissen (spätes 18. bis frühes 20. Jahrhundert)* (Unpublished Ph.D. Thesis, Université Libre de Bruxelles, Brussels, 2000) and the article by the same author 'Le métier volé. Transmission des savoir-faire et socialisation dans les métiers qualifiés au XIXe siècle (Belgique-Allemagne)', *Revue du Nord*, 15 (2001) (Volume hors série: *Les ouvriers qualifiés de l'industrie, XVIe-XXe siècle. Formation, emploi, migrations*, ed. by B. Gayot and P. Minard): 121–35; B. De Munck, *Leerpraktijken. Economische en sociaal-culturele aspecten van beroepsopleidingen in Antwerpse ambachtsgilden, 16de–18de eeuw* (Unpublished Ph.D. Thesis, Vrije Universiteit Brussel, Brussels, 2002), the chapters by the same author in B. De Munck and D. Dendooven, *'Al doende leert men'. Leertijd en ambacht in het Ancien Régime, 1500–1800* (Bruges, 2003), 9–52, and B. De Munck's 'La reproduction d'une crise. L'apprentissage des menuisiers et des charpentiers à Anvers (XVIe-XVIIIe siècle)', *Revue du Nord*, 17 (2003) (*Volume hors série: Formation professionnelle et apprentissage, XVIIIe-XXe siècle*, ed. G. Bodé and P. Minard), 31–51.
12. A. Steidl, *Auf nach Wien! Die mobilität des mitteleuropäischen Handwerks im 18. und 19. Jahrhundert am Beispiel der Haupt- und Residenzstadt* (Vienna and Munich, 2003).
13. See E. Fallet, *Apprendre l'horlogerie dans les Montagnes neuchâteloises, 1740–1810* (La Chaux-de-Fonds, 2001) and the article by the same author 'Des modalités de l'apprentissage de l'horlogerie à Neuchâtel, 1740–1810', *Revue du Nord*, 17 (2003) (Volume hors série: *Formation professionnelle et apprentissage, XVIIIe-XXe siècle*, ed. G. Bodé and P. Minard), 79–97.
14. M.L. Nagata, 'Apprentices, Servants and Other Workers: Apprenticeship in Japan', in this volume.

15. W. Frijhoff, *La societé néerlandaise et ses gradués, 1575–1814* (Amsterdam, 1981), 26–27.
16. C.D. O'Mally (ed.), *The History of Medical Education* (Berkeley, Los Angeles and London, 1970). See also M. Lindeman, *Medicine and Society in Early Modern Europe* (Cambridge, 1999), 111–112.
17. B. De Munck, 'Medische praktijken. Conflicten rond competentie in de Antwerpse medische sector in de zeventiende en achttiende eeuw', *Tijdschrift voor Sociale Geschiedenis*, 27 (2001): 459–484.
18. Frijhoff, *La société néerlandaise*, 27–28, 31–32.
19. G. Bodé, 'L'enseignement technique en France et en Allemagne: écoles de perfectionnement et cours professionnels, 1820–1940', *Revue du Nord*, 15, (2001 [Hors série]): 147–148; E. Charlot and M. Figeat, *Histoire de la formation des ouvriers, 1789-1984* (Minerva, 1985); and P. Pelpel and V. Troger, *Histoire de l'enseignement technique* (Paris, 1993).
20. N. Pevsner, *Academies of Art: Past and Present* (Cambridge, 1940), 42–47, 55-63, 83–107; D. Roche, *Le Siècle des Lumières en province. Académies et académiciens provinciaux, 1680–1789* (Paris, 1978): I, 126–128; and B. De Munck, 'Le produit du talent ou la production de talent? La formation des artistes à l'Académie royale des Beaux-Arts à Anvers aux XVIIe et XVIIIe siècles', *Paedagogica Historica*, 37 (2001): 569–607.
21. See the excellent (but as yet unpublished) M.A. thesis of D. Dendooven, *De Brugse academie in de achttiende eeuw*, 2 vols. (Vrije Universiteit Brussel, Brussels, 1994); See also De Munck, *Leerpraktijken*, 356–62.
22. See, for example, E.A. Honig, *Painting and the Market in Early Modern Antwerp* (New Haven and London, 1998).
23. See C. Crowston, 'From School to Workshop: Pre-training and Apprenticeship in Old Regime France', in this volume.
24. See, for example, E. Geudens, *Het Antwerpsche knechtjeshuis sedert zijn voorhistorisch tijdperk tot op onze dagen* (Antwerp, 1895).
25. Crowston, 'From School to Workshop'. See also the article by the same author 'L'apprentissage hors des corporations. Les formations professionnelles à Paris sous l'Ancien Régime', *Annales. Histoire, Sciences sociales*, 60 (2005): 409–41.
26. M. D'Hoker, 'Arm onderwijs voor arme kinderen. Bijdragen tot de studie van het lager beroepsonderwijs in de Zuidelijke Nederlanden tijdens de achttiende eeuw', *Werkgroep Achttiende Eeuw, Onderwijs en opvoeding in de achttiende eeuw*, 1983: 103–12; and H. Deceulaer, 'Connaissances et concurrence transfrontalières. Aptitudes techniques et éducation professionnelle dans la filature entre le Nord de la France et les Pays-Bas autrichiens au XVIIIe siècle', *Revue du Nord*, 17 (2003) (*Volume hors série: Formation professionnelle et apprentissage, XVIIIe-XXe siècle*, ed. G. Bodé and P. Minard), 15–30.
27. H. Soly, 'Social Aspects of Structural Changes in the Urban Industries of Eighteenth-century Brabant and Flanders', in H. van der Wee (ed.), *The Rise and Decline of Urban Industries in Italy and in the Low Countries (Late Middle Ages – Early Modern Times)* (Louvain, 1988), 239–51, p. 243.
28. C. Lis, *Social Change and the Labouring Poor: Antwerp, 1770–1860* (New Haven and London, 1986), 12. See also M. Coppens, 'Lois et usages réglant les rapports des différents acteurs de l'industrie dentellière dans les Pays-Bas autrichiens au XVIIIe siècle', *Revue Belge d'Archéologie et d'Histoire de l'Art*, 65 (1996): 157–70; and M. Coppens, 'Règlementation de l'apprentissage du métier de dentellière sous l'Ancien Régime: quelques exemples', *Revue Belge d'Archéologie et d'Histoire de l'Art*, 67 (1998): 93–112.
29. Humphries, 'English Apprenticeship', 81.
30. J.L. van Zanden, 'De timmerman, de boekdrukker en het ontstaan van de Europese kenniseconomie. Over de prijs en het aanbod van kennis voor de Industriële Revolutie', *Tijdschrift voor Economische en Sociale Geschiedenis*, 2 (2005): 105–20. For data and calculations, see the paper by the same author 'The Skill Premium and the Great Divergence', on the Internet: http://www.iisg.nl/hpw/papers/vanzanden.pdf.
31. S.R. Epstein, 'Craft Guilds, Apprenticeship, and Technological Change in Preindustrial Europe', *Journal of Economic History*, 58 (1998): 684–713.

32. Humphries, 'English Apprenticeship', 99. See also D. Mitch, 'Education and Skill of the British Labour Force', in R. Floud and P. Johnson (eds), *The Cambridge Economic History of Modern Britain*, Vol. I: *Industrialisation, 1700–1860* (Cambridge, 2004), 338–39.
33. See especially F. Grubb, 'Does Bonded Labour Have to Be Coerced Labour?', *Itinerario: European Journal of Overseas History*, XXI (1999): 28–51; and F. Grubb 'The Statutory Regulation of Colonial Servitude. An Incomplete-Contract Approach', *Explorations in Economic History*, 37 (2000), pp. 42–75. For theoretical discussions, see A. Schwartz, 'Incomplete Contracts', in P. Newman (ed.), *The New Palgrave Dictionary of Economics and the Law*, Vol. II (London, 2002), 277–82 and H. Lorne Carmichael, 'Self-Enforcing Contracts, Shirking, and Life Cycle Incentives', *Journal of Economic Perspectives*, 3, 4 (1989): 65–84.
34. Humphries, 'English Apprenticeship', 75; and Schwartz, 'Incomplete Contracts'.
35. S. Rappaport, *Worlds Within Worlds: Structures of Life in Sixteenth-century London* (Cambridge, 1989), 77 and 311–12, and S.R. Smith, 'The London Apprentices as Seventeenth-Century Adolescents', *Past and Present*, 61 (1973): 149–61.
36. Sonenscher, *Work and Wages*, 109–11.
37. Steidl, *Auf nach Wien*, 253.
38. P. Rushton, 'The Matter in Variance: Adolescents and Domestic Conflict in Northeast England, 1600–1800', *Journal of Social History*, 25 (1991): 94–97; Kaplan, 'L' apprentissage', 443–46; Krausman Ben-Amos, *Adolescence*, 100–107; Lane, *Apprenticeship*, chs 9 and 10; and Steidl, *Auf nach Wien*, 254–60.
39. K.D.M. Snell, *Annals of the Labouring Poor: Social Change and Agrarian England, 1660-1900* (Cambridge, 1985), ch. 5.
40. B. Elbaum, 'Why Apprenticeship Persisted in Britain But Not in the United States', *Journal of Economic History*, 49 (1989): 337–49; G. Hamilton, 'Enforcement In Apprenticeship Contracts: Were Runaways a Serious Problem? Evidence From Montreal', *Journal of Economic History*, 55 (1995): 551–74; Epstein, 'Craft Guilds'; and Humphries, 'English Apprenticeship'.
41. See, for example, S. Ogilvie, *State Corporation and Proto-Industry: The Württemberg Black Forest, 1580–1797* (Cambridge, 1995).
42. M.G. Davies, *The Enforcement of English Apprenticeship: A Study in Applied Mercantilism, 1563–1642* (London, 1956). For the Tudor context of the Statute, see D. Woodward, 'The Background to the Statute of Artificers: The Genesis of Labour Policy, 1558-63', *Economic History Review*, 2nd ser., 33 (1980): 32–44.
43. Krausman Ben-Amos, 'Failure to Become Freemen'.
44. K. Stratmann, *Die gewerbliche Lehrlingserziehung in Deutschland. Modernisierungsgeschichte der betrieblichen Berufsbildung*, Vol. I: *Berufserziehung in der ständischen Gesellschaft (1648–1806)* (Frankfurt am Main, 1993), 227–38.
45. On this subject, see A. Black, *Guilds and Civil Society in European Political Thought* (London, 1984).
46. See note 7, above.
47. See especially S. Ogilvie, 'Guilds, Efficiency, and Social capital: Evidence from German Proto-Industry', *Economic History Review*, 57 (2004): 286–333, who criticizes the 'rehabilitation' views.
48. K. Davids, 'Apprenticeship and Guild Control in the Netherlands, c. 1450–1800', in this volume.
49. Griessinger and Reith, 'Lehrlinge', 153; Reith, 'Zur beruflichen Sozialisation', 5–6; H. Schulz, *Das Ehrbare Handwerk. Zunftleben in alten Berlin zur Zeit des Absolutismus* (Weimar, 1993), 62; B. De Munck, 'Kiezen of delen? Sociale mobiliteit in ambachtsgilden (17de–18de eeuw)', in De Munck and Dendooven, *Al doende leert men*, 26–30.
50. C. Lis and H. Soly, 'Craft Guilds in Comparative Perspective: The Northern and Southern Netherlands. A Survey', in M. Prak, C. Lis, J. Lucassen and H. Soly (eds), *Craft Guilds in the Early Modern Low Countries: Work, Power, and Representation* (Aldershot, 2006), 9–39.
51. See the surveys of R. Reith, W. Reininghaus and J. Ehmer in Haupt (ed.), *Ende der Zünfte*, 39–126.

52. In this connection, see M. Berg, 'From Imitation to Invention: Creating Commodities in Eighteenth-Century Britain', *Economic History Review*, 55 (2002): 1–30; and C. Lis and H. Soly, 'Subcontracting in Guild-based Export Trades, Thirteenth-Eighteenth Centuries', in S.R. Epstein and M. Prak (eds), *Guilds and the Economy* (forthcoming).
53. For some examples, see J. Munro, *Textiles, Towns and Trade: Essays in the Economic History of Late Medieval England and the Low Countries* (Aldershot, 1994); and N. Harte (ed.), *The New Draperies in the Low Countries and England* (Oxford, 1997).
54. M. Bimbenet-Privat, 'Goldsmiths' Apprenticeship During the First Half of the Seventeenth Century: The Situation in Paris', in D. Mitchell (ed.), *Goldsmiths, Silversmiths and Bankers: Innovation and the Transfer of Skill, 1500–1800* (Stroud, 1995; Centre for Metropolitan History, Working Paper Series, no. 2), 23–32, p. 29.
55. On this subject, see the interesting remarks of M. Garden, 'The Urban Trades: Social Analysis and Representation', in S. Kaplan and C. Koepp (eds), *Work in France. Representations, Meaning, Organization, and Practice* (London, 1986), 287–296, p. 288.
56. B. De Munck, 'Construction and Reproduction: The Training and Skills of Antwerp Cabinetmakers in the Sixteenth and Seventeenth Centuries', in this volume.
57. See, for example, Farr, *Artisans*, 20–21.
58. Kaplan, *La fin des corporations*. See also the following articles by the same author: 'Social Classification and Representation in the Corporate World of Eighteenth-century France: Turgot´s "Carnival"', in Kaplan and Koepp (eds), *Work in France*, 176–228; and 'Conflit, idéologie et pratiques politiques dans les corporations parisiennes au XVIIIe siècle', *Revue d'Histoire Moderne et Contemporaine*, 49 (2002): 5–55.
59. See Sonenscher, *Work and Wages*, and the same author's article 'Journeymen's Migrations and Workshop Organization in Eighteenth-century France', in Kaplan and Koepp (eds), *Work in France*, 74–96. See also G. Hanne, 'Le travail et son monde: transition historique (1750–1850) et représentations historiennes (1850–1990)', *Revue d'Histoire Moderne et Contemporaine*, 44 (1977): 703–705.
60. See the special issue of the *Revue d'Histoire Moderne et Contemporaine,* 40, 3 (1993): 'Apprentissages, XVIe–XXe siècles'.
61. P. Stabel, 'Social Mobility and Apprenticeship in Late Medieval Flanders', in this volume.
62. See note 8, above.
63. A. Steidl, 'Silk Weaver and Purse Maker Apprentices in Eighteenth- and Nineteenth-Century Vienna', in this volume.
64. U. Puschner, *Handwerk zwischen Tradition und Wandel. Das Münchner Handwerk an der Wende vom 18. zum 19. Jahrhundert* (Göttingen, 1988; *Göttinger Beiträge zur Wirtschafts- und Sozialgeschichte*, vol. XIII), 242–43.
65. Rappaport, *Worlds Within Worlds*, 321.
66. Stabel, 'Social Mobility'.
67. Steffens, *Untersuchungen*, and the article by the same author: 'Le métier volé'.
68. On this subject, see the relevant remarks of Sonenscher, *Work and Wages*, 10–41; and N. Pellegrin, 'L'apprentissage ou l'écriture de l'oralité. Quelques remarques introductives', *Revue d'Histoire Moderne et Contemporaine*, 40, 3 (1993): 366-67.
69. See the literature cited in C. Lis and H. Soly, 'An Irresistible Phalanx: Journeymen Associations in Western Europe, 1300–1800', in C. Lis, J. Lucassen and H. Soly (eds), *Before the Unions: Wage Earners and Collective Action in Europe, 1300-1850* (Cambridge, 1994; *International Review of Social History,* Supplement 2), 11–52, p. 18, notes 22 and 23.
70. J. Schwarzmüller, *Vom Lehrling zum Meister im alten Schneiderhandwerk Oberösterreichs (vom Mittelalter bis zur Gewerbeordnung 1859)* (Linz, 1984), 50. See also R. Reith, 'Arbeitsmigration und Technologietransfer in der Habsburgmonarchie in der zweiten Hälfte des 18. Jahrhunderts – Die Gesellenwanderung aus der Sicht der Kommerzienkonzesse', *Blätter für Technikgeschichte*, 56 (1994): 9–33; and R.S. Elkar, 'Lernen durch Wandern? Einige kritische Anmerkungen zum Thema "Wissenstransfer durch Migration"', in K. Schulz (ed.), *Handwerk in Europa vom Spätmittelalter bis zur Frühen Neuzeit* (Munich, 1999): 213–33.

71. See, for example, A. Meulemans, 'Leuvense ambachten. De barbiers en de chirurgijns', *Eigen Schoon en de Brabander*, 39 (1956): 52–63, p. 56.
72. Smith, 'The London Apprentices', 150.
73. De Munck, *Leerpraktijken*, 352.
74. See the important article of J. Rule, 'The Property of Skill in the Period of Manufacture', in P. Joyce (ed.), *The Historical Meanings of Work* (Cambridge, 1987), 50–53. Although the meaning of 'skill' in the Early Modern period is a subject of debate, journeymen's sense of possessing property in skill undoubtedly distinguished them from common workers. See Lis and Soly, 'An Irresistible Phalanx', 17.
75. C. Brooks, 'Apprenticeship, Social Mobility and the Middling Sort, 1550–1800', in J. Barry and C. Brooks (eds), *The Middling Sort of People: Culture, Society and Politics in England, 1550–1800* (London, 1994), 52-83, p. 60.
76. For some examples, see Krausman Ben-Amos, *Adolescence*, 90–91; and De Munck, 'Kiezen of delen?', 27.
77. See note 44, above.
78. J. Styles, 'Manufacturing, Consumption and Design in 18th-century England', in J. Brewer and R. Porter (eds), *Consumption and the World of Goods* (London, 1993); J. Styles, 'Product Innovation in Eearly Modern London', *Past and Present*, 168 (2000): 124–170; and Berg, 'From Imitation to Invention'.
79. B. De Munck, 'Leren en werken in de praktijk. Beroepsopleidingen in het kader van ambachtsgilden: maatschappelijke en institutionele aspecten (13de–18de eeuw)', in De Munck and Dendooven, *Al doende leert men*, 9–24.
80. J. Reinarz, 'Learning by Brewing: Apprenticeship and the English Brewing Industry in the Late Victorian and Early Edwardian Period', in this volume.
81. Stabel, 'Social Mobility'.
82. Krausman Ben-Amos, *Adolescence*, 86.
83. J. Ehmer, 'Worlds of Mobility: Migration Patterns of Viennese Artisans in the Eighteenth Century', in Crossick (ed.), *The Artisan and the European Town*, 185; Steidl, *Auf nach Wien*, 156–67.
84. For England, see Brooks, 'Apprenticeship', 73.
85. In 1725, the master hosiers in Antwerp invoked the fact that many of their apprentices came from the boys' orphanage as evidence of the poor economic prospects in their sector: H. Deceulaer, *Pluriforme patronen en een verschillende snit. Sociaal-economische, institutionele en culturele transformaties in de kledingsector in Antwerpen, Brussel en Gent, 1585–1800* (Amsterdam, 2001), 280.
86. M.B. Rose, 'Social Policy and Business: Parish Apprenticeship and the Early Factory System, 1750–1834', *Business History*, 31 (1989): 5–29.
87. B.A. Hanawalt, *Growing Up in Medieval London. The Experience of Childhood in History* (New York, 1993), 82 and 113; Rappaport, *Worlds Within Worlds*, 296–97.
88. A. Yarborough, 'Apprentices as Adolescents in Sixteenth-Century Bristol', *Journal of Social History*, 13 (1979): 67–82; Snell, *Annals of the Labouring Poor*, 324–25.
89. In Colyton, Devon, poor children started their indentures at about the age of ten-and-a-half, but they were generally younger than those mentioned in comparative studies. P. Sharpe, 'Poor Children as Apprentices in Colyton, 1598–1830', *Continuity and Change*, 6 (1991): 254–57.
90. Kaplan, 'L' apprentissage', 453; and Ehmer, 'Worlds of Mobility', 186.
91. Schulz, *Das Ehrbare Handwerk*, 61.
92. De Munck, *Leerpraktijken*, 92–93.
93. C. Wiskerke, *De afschaffing der gilden in Nederland* (Amsterdam, 1938), 80–81; Griessinger and Reith, 'Lehrlinge', 152; Ehmer, 'Worlds of Mobility', 186; Schulz, *Das Ehrbare Handwerk*, 63; and De Munck, 'Kiezen of delen', 25.
94. See R. Reith, 'Apprentices in the German and Austrian Crafts in Early Modern Times: Apprentices as Wage Earners?'; in this volume and Steidl, 'Silk Weaver and Purse Maker Apprentices'.
95. D. Garrioch, *The Formation of the Parisian Bourgeoisie, 1690–1830* (London, 1996), 105–22.

96. On the butchers of Paris, see R. de Lespinasse, *Les métiers et corporations de la ville de Paris*, Vol. I (Paris, 1886-1897), 260 and 270. As for the Southern Netherlands, in Antwerp the butchers made their occupation hereditary by law from 1354, in Mechelen from around 1441, and in Brussels from 1446. See M. Jacobs, 'De ambachten in Brabant en Mechelen (12de eeuw-1795)', in R. Van Uytven, C. Bruneel, H. Coppens and B. Augustyn (eds), *De gewestelijke en lokale overheidsinstellingen in Brabant en Mechelen tot 1795* (Brussels, 2000), 558–624, p. 576.
97. See Farr, *Artisans*, 248.
98. G. Rosser, 'Crafts, Guilds and the Negotiation of Work in the Medieval Town', *Past and Present*, 154 (1997): 17.
99. Reith, 'Zur beruflichen Sozialisation', 6; and Steidl, 'Silk Weaver and Purse Maker Apprentices'.
100. E.J. Shephard, 'Social and Geographic Mobility of the Eighteenth Century Guild Artisan: An Analysis of Guild Receptions in Dijon, 1700–1790', in Kaplan and Koepp (eds), *Work in France*, 97–131.
101. Garden, 'The Urban Trades', 287–97.
102. Krausman Ben-Amos, *Adolescence*, 158-70; and Kaplan, 'L' apprentissage', 455–56.
103. Farr, *Artisans*, p. 250; De Munck, *Leerpraktijken*, 282–86.
104. See especially S. Cerutti, 'Group Strategies and Trade Strategies: The Turin Tailors' Guild in the Late Seventeenth and Early Eighteenth Centuries', in S. Woolf (ed.), *Domestic Strategies: Work and Family in France and Italy, 1600–1800*, (Cambridge, 1991), 103–47.
105. De Munck, *Leerpraktijken*, pp. 217–36.
106. Steidl, 'Silk Weaver and Purse Maker Apprentices'.
107. Smith, 'The London Apprentices'; and S.R. Smith, 'The Ideal and the Reality: Apprentice-Master Relationships in Seventeenth-century London', *History of Education Quarterly*, 21 (1981): 449–60.
108. J. Ehmer, 'The Artisan Family in Nineteenth-century Austria: Embourgeoisement of the Petite Bourgeoisie', in G. Crossick and H.-G. Haupt (eds), *Shopkeepers and Master Artisans in Nineteenth-century Europe* (London and New York, 1984), 195–218, p. 197.
109. D. Thomson, 'Welfare and the Historians', in L. Bonfield, R.M. Smith and K. Wrightson (eds.), *The World We Have Gained: Histories of Population and Social Structure. Essays Presented to Peter Laslett on His Seventieth Birthday* (Oxford, 1986), 355–78; and D. Van Damme, *Armenzorg en de staat. Comparatief-historische studie van de origines van de moderne verzorgingsstaat in West-Europa* (Ghent, 1990), 43–45.
110. H. Deceulaer, 'Arbeidsregulering en loonvorming in de Antwerpse haven, 1585–1796', *Tijdschrift voor Sociale Geschiedenis*, 18 (1992): 41–42; Hanne, 'Le travail et son monde', 686.
111. Ehmer, 'The Artisan Family', 204–205.
112. See R. Samuel, 'Workshop of the World: Steam Power and Hand Technology in Mid-Victorian Britain', *History Workshop*, 3 (1977): 6–72; G. Stedman Jones, 'The Mid-century Crisis and the 1848 Revolutions: A Critical Comment', *Theory and Society*, 12, 4 (1983): 505–20; and C. Sabel and J. Zeitlin, 'Historical Alternatives to Mass Production', *Past and Present*, 108 (1985): 133–76.
113. M. Perrot, 'La jeunesse ouvrière: de l'atelier à l'usine', in G. Lévi and J.-C. Schmitt (eds), *Histoire des jeunes en Occident*, Vol. II, *L'époque contemporaine* (Paris, 1996), p. 107.
114. Reith, 'Zur beruflichen Sozialisation', 10–12.
115. Griessinger and Reith, 'Lehrlinge', 150–99.
116. Deceulaer, *Pluriforme patronen*, 273.
117. De Munck, 'Leren en werken', 19.
118. P. Griffiths, *Youth and Authority: Formative Experiences in England, 1560–1640* (Oxford, 1996), 321.
119. Rushton, 'The Matter in Variance', 96.
120. See especially J. Rule, *The Experience of Labour in Eighteenth-century Industry* (London, 1981), 104–19; Also Lis and Soly, 'An Irresistible Phalanx', 22, 28–30.
121. Reith, 'Zur beruflichen Sozialisation', 15–16; Steffens, *Untersuchungen*, Vol. I, 179–217; De Munck, 'Leren en werken', 19.

122. De Munck, 'Leren en werken', 14.
123. De Munck, 'Leren en werken', 18–22; also Deceulaer, *Pluriforme patronen*, 275.
124. Brooks, 'Apprenticeship', 75 ff.
125. Reith, 'Apprentices in the German and Austrian Crafts'.
126. Regarding England, youths proved less inclined to become apprentices when demand for (unskilled) labour was high: Brooks, 'Apprenticeship', 73.
127. De Munck, 'Kiezen of delen', 33–34.
128. For recent surveys of the literature, see M.E. Wiesner, *Women and Gender in Early Modern Europe* (Cambridge, 1993), 102–106; O. Hufton, *The Prospect Before Her: A History of Women in Western Europe*, Vol. I: *1500–1800* (London, 1995), 91–93, 161–166, 238–45; G. Crossick, 'Past Masters: In Search of the Artisan in European History', in Crossick (ed.), *The Artisan and the European Town*, 13–15; and Farr, *Artisans*, 39–41.
129. Krausman Ben-Amos, *Adolescence*, 136.
130. E. Musgrave, 'Women and the Craft Guilds in Eighteenth-century Nantes', in Crossick (ed.), *The Artisan and The European Town*, 162–63, 167–68.
131. Steidl, *Auf nach Wien*, 251.
132. S. Vastesaeger, *Vrouwen in ambachten in Brussel in de achttiende eeuw.* (Unpublished M.A. thesis (Vrije Universiteit Brussel, Brussels, 1998).
133. Krausman Ben-Amos, *Adolescence*, 136–43.
134. Hufton, *The Prospect*, 93–4; J.G. Coffin, *The Politics of Women's Work: The Paris Garment Trades, 1750-1915* (Princeton, 1996); C.H. Crowston, *Fabricating Women: The Seamstresses of Old Regime France, 1675–1791* (Durham, 2001); and Deceulaer, *Pluriforme patronen*.
135. Lis, *Social Change*, 14–15 and 176.
136. B. Panhuysen, *Maatwerk. Kleermakers, naaisters, oudkleerkopers en de gilden, 1500–1800* (Amsterdam, 2000), 190–93; and Deceulaer, *Pluriforme patronen*, 212–14.
137. Lane, *Apprenticeship*, 39–40.

Part I

Between School and Household

CHAPTER 2

APPRENTICES, SERVANTS AND OTHER WORKERS

APPRENTICESHIP IN JAPAN

Mary Louise Nagata

The word 'apprenticeship' induces images of teenage boys living and working under a master artisan, later to become journeymen and travel from place to place plying their skilled trade until they become master artisans themselves. This is primarily a pre-modern image associated with the small artisan workshop. In Japan, however, apprenticeship was not limited to artisan skills, the small artisan workshop, or teenage boys, even in the early modern context. The apprentice did not later become a journeyman and travel around the countryside plying his trade. Apprenticeship was a way of training managers in larger firms as well as skilled workers and artisans. Moreover, this system has continued to influence the way modern Japanese firms work as well as skilled artisans in craft industries. This study uses data from several early modern firms to show the role of apprenticeship in the early modern context. Secondary research and contemporary data are then used to show the continuing role of apprenticeship in modern Japan.

Apprenticeship has two common aspects. One is on-the-job training which necessarily tends to focus on the practical aspects of education. The second is the combination of living, working and learning under one roof, if not necessarily the same space. When Harry Braverman talks of his apprenticeship as a coppersmith he notes that he worked in a naval shipyard for seven years thereafter which he describes as 'probably the most complete product of two centuries of industrial revolution.' Moreover, he continues to note that the apprentices of all the mechanics crafts gathered for sessions in a trade school.[1] His brief description suggests that on-the-job training was possibly an essential aspect of apprenticeship rather than living, learning and working in the same space at the same time. Since he uses the term 'apprenticeship' even though he is speaking of his personal experience in twentieth century America, I think we can agree that apprenticeship continues to play a role in modern society even though it is no longer the main form of education today. Moreover, the introduction of other formal education such as the trade school coexists with apprenticeship. The term 'informal apprenticeship' will be used in this chapter to refer to situations where on-the-job training is the normal and expected system for gaining skills and training skilled workers, but there may be no mention of apprenticeship in the situation.

The more formal or traditional form of apprenticeship often entails the apprentices living with the master, often in his home. In Europe this system has been connected with a traditional system of fostering in which the apprentice gives service in return for room, board and training.[2] Local authorities in England also used the apprenticeship system as a way to find caretakers for impoverished children and orphans. During the period of early industrialization when labour was scarce, these youths were frequently apprenticed in factories and manufactories. This is an historical example of apprenticeship describing on-the-job training on the factory floor. As a result 'apprenticeship' gained an association with the poor as well as with serious hardship and poor working conditions.[3]

Japan did not have a tradition of fostering as a way for the children of the elite to gain training in other households outside of the apprenticeship system. This type of apprenticeship/fostering was, however, sometimes practised among the merchant houses of the early modern period. The system was almost never associated with the poor except in unusual circumstances as I will explain below. Japanese entrepreneurs filled the labour shortage of early industrialization with casual labour rather than with the labour of impoverished children. On the contrary, the youths who entered into formal apprenticeships were often destined to become the elite members and managers of their employers' businesses, with a chance to be adopted as heir to the business.[4]

This chapter outlines the labour hierarchy of the early modern Japanese firm. Then the roles formal and informal apprenticeship played in this labour hierarchy and in the labour market will be discussed. The final section will discuss cases of apprenticeship in modern Japan and the role the system has continued to play over the years. Early modern data, labour contracts and miscellaneous documents collected from twenty-six early modern firms between 1672 and 1873 are used. These firms range in size from small, single-shop businesses in Kyoto to major manufacturers with multiple retail shops spread in various parts of Japan. Many of these firms remain in business today. For the modern data, a sample case study supported by secondary research is usual. The case is the apprenticeship and career of a young man, M, in a traditional Japanese confectionery shop (*wagashiya*) called Tsuruya.

Apprenticeship in Early Modern Japan

Apprentices were near the bottom of the labour hierarchy in most early modern firms, particularly small, single-shop businesses and those that relied upon skilled production labour. The standard career in an early modern firm was to begin as an apprentice at around age thirteen. For commercial enterprises the term was *detchi* and artisan apprentices were *deshi*. In the smaller artisan workshops the apprentice graduated to become an artisan in the craft at around age seventeen; however, this was not the end of his apprenticeship. Apprentices in commercial enterprises and those in management tracks of larger businesses became *tedai* which included clerks and other low-ranking managers or assistants.[5]

A 1672 register of domicile residents away for temporary labour migration from Tondabayashi village in southern Osaka lists fifty-two migrants identified as serving either serving contracts or apprenticeships. Eight of the sixteen apprentices listed fall in the 10–14 age group with four apprentices under 10 and four apprentices ages 15–19.[6] The apprentices in the latter group were probably finishing their apprenticeships; there were none listed over age 20. Two sets of draft population registers for family businesses in Kyoto provide more information regarding apprentices. The first set is for the Tanaka family business, Ōmiya, a carpenter workshop, for the years 1780–1781 and 1784–1788 or roughly nine years with two years missing. These registers do not record ages, but cross-referencing with contracts from the same business contributes to understanding the overall pattern. The registers list, on average, three male servants and one female servant each year with a total of seven male servants during the data period, and I could match these 'servants' with labour contracts for six of these male workers, revealing that they were actually carpenters. The contracts, moreover, are dated several years after their appearance as servants on the registers, suggesting that they received contracts upon completion of their apprenticeships. Moreover, two workers changed their names upon receiving contracts after appearing in the registers for four years.

The Endō family business, Hiranoya, was textiles and tailoring. Hiranoya served as one of the major retail outlets for Nishijin silks. The Endō registers cover two households of the Endō business that happened to be in the same neighborhood; 1840–1843 and 1853–1866 for one household/shop, 1857–1867 for the other household/shop. These registers record ages from 1843. Each of the sixty-three male employees appearing on these registers is identified by place of birth, temple of registration including address, and status as servant (*genin*) or tedai as well as by name and age. The position could represent either servant or apprentice, but examination of the records reveals that nearly all of the genin became tedai at around age seventeen if they remained with the employer. The eldest genin in the record is eighteen and those who did not become tedai left the household before the age of twenty. I assume, therefore, that the genin were all apprentices. This record also reveals that all the apprentices changed their names when they became tedai. Murai Masuo has also noted this practice among the employees of a money-changing shop in Osaka during the same period and I have noted the same among the carpenters of the Tanaka family employees above.[7] The name change represented a change in family membership and status and probably marked not only the transition from apprentice to full employee, but from outsider to insider in the employer's household and business.[8] Although the registers reveal twenty-nine employees listed as tedai during this short period and I have fifteen contracts from the Endō collection during the same data period, I could only cross-reference two of the contracts. The remaining contracts were probably for tedai sent to other branches of the business as will be explained below. Nevertheless, these contracts also match the dates for the transition from apprentice to tedai as do the contracts for the Tanaka family business.

In short, young men (and some women, as the data for some other businesses reveal) entered into apprenticeships around the age of thirteen and graduated to become tedai or artisans at around age seventeen. Of course, there were probably variations regarding the transition age according to the craft, but the data thus far has been remarkably consistent with age seventeen, whether we look at textile retailers, carpenters or clerks in a money-changing shop. Furthermore, this timing is also consistent over time, using data from various circumstances and sources from the seventeenth, eighteenth and nineteenth centuries. The younger tedai, however, were probably not yet considered full artisans in the first few years. But they were eligible for contract and wage. The apprenticeship probably continued during the first years as a tedai. The next major transition was usually to a commuting tedai, or at least one who lived separately from his employer. Whether this transition marked the change from apprenticeship to journeyman, or if the transition to full artisan was made earlier, is unclear and there may have been differences between crafts.

Apprentices did not actually work for their employers' businesses during the detchi period of their apprenticeship. They were under the authority of the wife of the employer who tutored them in reading, writing and calculating while they did minor errands and worked as servants in the employer's household.[9] They learned business skills – craft or trade – from older apprentices and tedai as well as by helping out in the shop. Nevertheless, by the time they became tedai they had at least the basic skills of the craft to the extent that they were eligible to earn wages and could be sent out. In larger businesses, the new tedai might then be sent to work in one of the branch shops of the business. The Endō business mentioned above, Hiranoya, probably followed this pattern. This was the case for the tedai of the Konishi sake breweries in Itami. The apprentices were all hired and trained by the main house in Itami, now a suburb of Osaka, and then sent to one of the Edo shops or to the Osaka shop upon receiving a contract as a tedai.[10] Even when the Konishi breweries took an apprentice from Edo, he was brought to the main house in Itami for his apprenticeship. In a letter from the director of the Edo branch the director requested that the directors of the main brewery would 'mold him into something useful by using him like the other children for various tasks.' This request is rather vague since the apprentices had no specific duties. Nevertheless, it reveals something of the situation.[11]

After several years as a tedai working for the employer in either the main business or one of the branches, the tedai might be allowed to establish his own branch business as an expansion of the employer's business. This was the way the two Edo branches of the Konishi breweries were established. The tedai might also move out, but continue to work for the employer as a commuting manager and establish his own business. This was the case with Magoshichi at the Hakutsuru breweries. He worked as a manager of one of their breweries for five years while establishing his own business before he caused a major scandal.[12] In this case, Magoshichi apparently also learned brewing skills during his apprenticeship as well as management skills as the scandal he caused was to secretly brew sake from leftover materials and market it under the Hakutsuru brand name while pocketing the profits. Up until then, Magoshichi had also been in charge of the various contracts with suppliers as well as retailers, managing two of the Hakutsuru breweries and establishing his own shop. This gives some idea of the scope of duties tedai handled as well as the management skills included in the training of apprentices in the larger businesses.

In all these examples the lucky apprentice who became tedai had the potential to become a manager in his employer's business and even one of the directors and elders with the responsibility for his own branch. Managers, after all, were also skilled workers and apprenticeship was the main method for training them in the early modern system. However, some firms did not use this system to train managers. The Mitamura family that manufactured paper in Okamoto village, Echizen province relied upon their hereditary servants for the top levels of their management labour. Indeed, this employer did not appear to use the apprentice system at all except in the informal fashion of on-the-job training. Many of the labour contracts for this firm also explicitly mention economic hardship and most of the labour force came from local communities without written contracts.[13] Thus, apprentices and skilled workers did not comprise the entire labour hierarchy, nor the only way to gain craft skills.

Much of the brewery labour and labour in larger manufacturing, where the process could be accomplished by many unskilled or semiskilled workers under the direction of a skilled few, was casual labour. In Japan, casual labour was largely taken from the agricultural labour force during their free time and agricultural off-periods. The casual labourers usually worked by the day or the month and were paid a daily rate. However, they could also learn the skills and gain the contracts of skilled workers through an informal type of apprenticeship. Casual labourers in the brewing trade, for example, could acquire the necessary skills of an assistant brewer in three years. In this case, their skills were more valuable if they had been gained at a wide variety of breweries as they would have the experience of many tastes and varieties of sake or soy sauce and could presumably know the differences and what created them.[14]

Such casual labour became an informal apprenticeship when the labourer successfully gained the skills that invited an employer to offer him a management contract. This was not the usual method to gain such a contract;

formal apprenticeship was more common. Nevertheless, two documents in the data set attest to the possibility. The first document is a letter from drifter Shohachi to the directors of the Endō family business, Hiranoya. In this letter dated the tenth month of 1823, Shohachi writes, 'I recently drifted here and everyone has kindly arranged for me to work for you.'[15] The second document is a reply to Matsuya, a safflower processing and dyeing company, agreeing to a future contract for a skilled worker who had come to work as casual labour in the Matsuya manufactory.[16]

In summary, apprenticeship was the way for early modern firms to train and recruit skilled labour. The labour hierarchy in these firms and the use of unskilled casual labour in early modern manufacturing resulted in apprentices becoming the managers of early modern firms. In most cases these skilled workers gained their skills through formal apprenticeships with their employers and their training continued through various phases and positions within the employer's business with the successful apprentices becoming directors of branch shops or manufactories. In rare cases, however, these skills were gained through informal apprenticeships such as on-the-job training through casual labour. In either case, skilled labour was short and therefore a precious asset to the employer, who would not worry too much about how the employee gained his skills.

Apprenticeship in Modern Japan

The Meiji Restoration in 1868 resulted in major political and institutional changes for Japan as it opened to Western trade and competition. New industries were established, often with foreign technicians brought in to teach the new techniques. One major institutional change was the establishment of public education, at least for a few years at the elementary level. Nevertheless, the traditional sector with traditional industries organized in traditional ways continued to be of major importance. By 1884 even government bureaucrats recognized the importance of the traditional economic sector to the economy as a whole and it remained vital to Japan's economic development until WW I. The traditional sector slackened off after 1920, but remained important even if in decline.[17] This sector has not entirely disappeared today, although it is no longer of major economic importance. Nevertheless, Japan has one of the highest proportions of self-employed among the employable population of the seven industrialized nations, second only to Italy, at twenty-five percent.[18] The traditional sector includes many of those who are self-employed as well as medium sized and small businesses. The traditional crafts in this sector have benefited from mechanization and other aspects of a modern economy, yet continue to pass on skills by formal apprenticeship and much of the work is by hand.

My first case study, M, underwent his apprenticeship in Japanese confectionery at a shop and small factory in Kyoto called Mibu Tsuruya, in 1988–1998. 'Mibu' refers to the district of Kyoto the main shop and factory are located in. Tsuruya is primarily a family-owned corporation like many such confectionery shops *(wagashiya)* in Kyoto, but has several branch shops and retail outlets in Kyoto and Osaka. M is from Mito, north of Tokyo, and his family also owned a confectionery business for several generations, but the shop closed when his father died early, when M was a child. M determined to reopen the family business and began looking around for a way to learn the necessary skills when he was in high school. He was introduced to Tsuruya by the friend of a friend of his cousin and began his apprenticeship immediately after graduation from high school.[19] The apprenticeship period was set at ten years.

Like the apprentices of the early modern period, M lived in the household of his employer, waking at five every morning to sweep the garden and make tea for the family before beginning work. For the first three years, he worked entirely at retail outlets in various places and only began learning the various techniques and recipes for making the confectionery from the end of his third year. By the end of his apprenticeship, M was in charge of virtually every aspect of the business, including contracts with suppliers, overseeing the preparation of confections in the factories, managing the various retail shops and their personnel, and all other aspects of the business. He even reported participating with the owner in the creation of new confections to the point that he worried that his employer would not willingly let him go at the end of the apprenticeship. When the ten years were finished, however, M and his guarantor persuaded his employer to let him do an additional year of training at a shop in the Tokyo region. M's reasoning was that the supplier routes and contacts for Mito, north of Tokyo, would be different from those of Kyoto in the west. Now M has successfully reopened his family business in Mito.

In this modern example of apprenticeship, the first detchi period was skipped as it had been fulfilled by public education. Nevertheless, M underwent a training course that not only taught him the craft of creating traditional confections, but also trained him in all aspects of managing and running a confectionery business. This course was similar to that of the early modern firms with the exception that M graduated from secondary education before beginning his apprenticeship rather than receiving his basic education from his employer's wife.

The introduction of Western technology to Japan in the mid-nineteenth century relied much upon the apprenticeship system as found in the metal crafts. Apprenticeship in these crafts was not the same as in a larger business as described above. Instead, it bore a certain resemblance to the informal apprenticeships of casual labour. Young men were apprenticed to a master artisan at around the age of twelve or thirteen and lived in his household. Originally the apprenticeship lasted for ten years, but the need for skilled labour reduced the term to around seven years. Once the apprentice reached the standing of journeyman, he travelled from workshop to workshop or factory to factory building his skills with varied experience, much like the casual labourer, in hopes of either starting his own business or gaining a management contract from a major employer. The masters in these trades were called *oyakata* and often acted also as employment agents for factory work, gathering wandering journeymen as well as their own apprentices to supply whatever jobs were around.[20]

In the new industries, foreign technicians were brought in to train workers in the new technology, but they frequently lamented that workers, finally trained with great difficulty, soon left for jobs elsewhere, leaving behind only inexperienced workers.[21] This sort of problem, found when the foreign technology was first introduced in the 1850s, continued to be a problem for Japanese firms in the modern sector until about 1920. The skilled and experienced workers wanted independence and most either established their own, small factories or changed professions. Japanese firms used a number of strategies to tie the skilled labour to the firm that trained them and these strategies are reminiscent of the strategies used by early modern firms to maintain their skilled labour force. For one, oyakata were offered jobs as foremen and firms also offered long-term contracts to a few select, skilled men. School education did not easily replace the apprenticeship system for training such skilled workers. The technical supervisors trained in school were ineffective relative to those trained in traditional apprenticeship. On the other hand, relying on oyakata meant that factory work continued on a casual labour basis with a wide variety of skill levels and it was difficult for a firm to gain control of its skilled labour force.[22]

In the end, firms sent new workers on training programmes within the firm and created company schools. At the same time, companies would hire a small number of workers directly from public education – elementary or secondary – and train them to become workshop leaders and career employees.[23] This is essentially the same course as followed by Magoshichi and other apprentices of larger early modern firms with one exception. The basic education that Magoshichi and other apprentices gained in the employer's household under the direction of the employer's wife was supplanted by public school education. The remainder of the training, however, was a combination of on-the-job training and technical courses also provided by the employer.

Thus far this chapter has focused upon the technical worker with the artisan or factory worker directly involved with production or managing the production labour. However, similar strategies can be found in management and white-collar work as well. Certainly firms tend to hire university graduates for white-collar or management work. The large corporations have typically hired the graduates of a handful of top universities. However, these universities do not provide practical business training and the graduates have usually not received any special training as managers when they are hired. Instead, the universities serve as a recruitment screening device while the employing firm provides all management training after employment. Therefore, non-graduates also can sometimes reach a management position with good results.[24] Moreover, most top management including nearly 80 percent of directors, come up through the ranks of the employer's company. Most of those remaining are sent from parent companies or related companies in the corporate group called keiretsu, where they come up through the ranks.[25] In other words, although large firms hire university graduates for their white collar and management workers, their training continues to be largely on-the-job training reminiscent of the management employees in early modern or traditional firms whose managers gained their training through apprenticeship.

Firms train their future managers in the necessary expertise in a variety of ways. There are company-sponsored training classes for white-collar workers as well as in technical skills. These classes include English, typing and a number of other courses. Employees are transferred from department to department, spending an average of three to four years in each department, until they have experience in nearly all aspects of the business. For example, one airline executive began his career taking tickets and assisting passengers at Osaka airport. After three years in this position he was transferred to the ticketing counter, then the financing department, an overseas post in Rome, Italy, back to the home office department of international relations, sales, marketing, an overseas post handling ticketing and personnel, a Japan regional post for inbound sales and public relations, and a variety of other posts including cargo, information and research, aero-politics and corporate planning. In this career, he reached management level during his second foreign transfer and the top of the employed management hierarchy in the corporate planning department. This career provided the airline executive with experience and expertise in nearly every aspect of airline management through on-the-job training. Many firms also send more promising young managers to universities, sometimes foreign universities, for higher education as deemed necessary. Many of the Japanese students at business schools in the USA and other places have been sent by their employers.

Discussion and Conclusions

This chapter outlines the role of apprenticeship in early modern and modern Japanese business. Apprenticeship is usually associated with training in specialized artisan skills. Early modern Japanese businesses, however, also used apprenticeship to develop management skills. In such a career the transition from apprentice to journeyman became less important than the acquisition of greater responsibility in the employer's business and gaining the financing to establish either a branch or one's own business. Apprenticeship in the large, integrated, early modern firms, therefore, had a dual purpose: training and maintaining a skilled labour force and training management employees.

At the same time, some trades maintained a more Western form of apprenticeship. Journeymen travelled from workshop to workshop and factory to factory, polishing their skills with a broad range of work experience. These journeymen hoped eventually to be offered long-term contracts by major employers or collect the money to establish their own workshops or factories, much like the apprentices in larger businesses described above. Unskilled casual labour also had similar opportunities. Sometimes a persistent worker could learn the skills of a trade while roaming as a casual labourer. If successful, these labourers also could gain such long-term contracts, making casual labour an opportunity for an informal apprenticeship through on-the-job training.

Modern Japanese business inherited this complicated system for gaining the skills necessary for industries using new technologies. The work and skills may have been different, but the strategies taken by workers to acquire, polish and market their skills and the strategies taken by businesses to train workers and maintain a skilled labour force have been influenced by the early modern system. The more traditional apprenticeship system was incorporated into modern business and transformed into something that had remarkable similarities with the skilled labour and management apprentice system of larger early modern businesses.

School education did not supersede apprenticeship. Instead, school education was also incorporated into the new system in several ways. Basic public education grew from three years to nine years and took the place of the first few years of apprenticeship that were devoted to basic skills such as reading, writing and arithmatic. School education, although recognized as important, proved inferior to apprenticeship in teaching technical skills. Therefore, the technical training gained in trade schools was incorporated in the apprenticeship system and provided by firms after employment as a supplement to on-the-job training and apprenticeship rather than instead of it. This policy also extended into less technical, white-collar and management training as well. Although firms have tended to hire university graduates for white-collar positions, these graduates are given the necessary training for their various jobs after employment contracts are signed. This training is largely on-the-job training, but is also supplemented with courses in a variety of subjects provided by the employer and the opportunity to pursue higher education, again subsidized by the employer.

Thus, apprenticeship has had an important influence upon modern Japan and modern Japanese employment practices. At the same time, the traditional form of apprenticeship as adopted by early modern firms for training skilled and management workers continues to survive in the more traditional sectors of the economy. The history of apprenticeship in Japan, therefore, continues from the past to the present.

Notes

1. H. Braverman, *Labor and Monopoly Capital: The Degradation of Work in the Twentieth Century* (New York: Monthly Review Press, 1974), 9.
2. J. Lane, *Apprenticeship in England, 1600–1914* (London: UCL Press, 1996), 9.
3. Lane, *Apprenticeship in England*, 15, 238–39.
4. M.L. Nagata, *Labour Contracts and Labour Relations in Early Modern Central Japan* (London and New York: CurzonRoutledge Press, 2005), 61; Nakano Takashi, *Shōka dōzokudan no kenkyū*, vol. 1 (Tokyo: Miraisha, 1978), 6; Yasuoka Shigeaki, 'Kinsei Kyōto shōnin no kagyō to sōzoku', in *Kyōto shakai shi kenkyū* (Kyōto: Hōritsu Bunkasha, 1971), 295–326, and 'Mitsui bekke no sōzoku kō shiryō', *Shakai Kagaku*, 26 (1979): 125–41.
5. Nagata, *Labour Contracts and Labour Relations*, 55–62.
6. 'Taryō e kakari mōsu hōkōnin no chō', 1672, Sugiyama collection, Kyōto Daigaku Hakubutsukan.
7. Murai Masuo, 'Toshi seikatsu no han'ei', Kimura Isono (ed), *Seikatsu shi* (Tokyo: Yamakawa Shuppansha, 1981) 228–59.

8. Mary Louise Nagata, 'Balancing Family Strategies and Individual Choice: Name Changing in Early Modern Japan', *Japan Review*, 11 (1999): 145–66.
9. Ogura Eiichirō, *Omi shōnin no keiei* (Kyōto: Sanburaito Shuppan, 1988), 106; Murai, 'Toshi seikatsu no han'ei', 248–53.
10. Nagata, *Labour Contracts and Labour Relations*, 65–66.
11. Ichibei and Teikichi [to Honke shihainin toshiyori], 'Issatsu no koto', Letter accompanying new apprentice, 4/1834, Konishi collection No. 6–2–22, Itami Shiritsu Hakubutsukan, Itami; Nagata, *Labour Contracts and Labour Relations*, 65–66.
12. Nagata, *Labour Contracts and Labour Relations*, 211–27.
13. Kichitayu et al.[to Sei'uemon], 'Hōkōnin ukejō no koto', Labour contract, 12/12/1776, Mitamura collection No. 1–283, Imadatechō Rekishi Minzoku Shiryōkan, Imadatechō; Bun'uemon et al. [to Sei'uemon] 'Hōkōnin ukejō no koto', Labour contract, 12/1808, Mitamura collection No. 1–285, Imadatechō Rekishi Minzoku Shiryōkan, Imadatechō; Tasaburōsuke et al. [to Seiuemon], 'Hōkōnin ukejō no koto', Labour contract, 11/1813, Mitamura collection No. 1–289, Imadatechō Rekishi Minzoku Shiryōkan, Imadatechō; Nagata, *Labour Contracts and Labour Relations*, 88–93.
14. Aburai Hiroko, 'Chōshi shōyu jōzōgyō ni okeru koyō rōdō: Higeta Tanaka ke monjo wo chōshin to shite', *Ronshū Kinsei*, 4 (Tokyo: Tōkyō Daigaku Kinsei Shi Kenkyūkai, 1980), 24–40; Mark W. Fruin, *Kikkoman: Company, Clan and Community* (Cambridge, MA: Harvard University Press, 1983), 36–47.
15. Shōhachi et al.[to Hiranoya Chōbei and Zenbei], 'Issatsu no Koto', Labour agreement, 10/1823, Endō collection No. 693, Kyoto City Library of Historical Documents, Kyoto.
16. Haiya Rinzaemon, 'Issatsu', Agreement for a future contract, 6/1859, Matsuya collection No. 164, Kyōto Furitsu Shiryōkan, Kyoto.
17. E. Sydney Crawcour, 'Industrialization and Technological Change, 1885–1920', in Peter Duus, *The Cambridge History of Japan: The Twentieth Century*, 6 vols (Cambridge: Cambridge University Press, 1988), VI, 403–406, 414–21.
18. Toshiaki Tachibanaki and Atsuhiro Taki, *Capital and Labour in Japan: The Functions of Ttwo Factor Markets* (London and New York: Routledge, 2000), 30–31.
19. My husband and I were part of this link (the friend of M's cousin) and the situation I explain here comes from personal communications, 1988–1998.
20. Andrew Gordon, *The Evolution of Labor Relations in Japan: Heavy Industry, 1853–1955*, (Cambridge, MA: Harvard University Press, Council on East Asian Studies, 1988), 22–29.
21. Ibid. 19.
22. Ibid. 36–40.
23. Ibid. 126.
24. Hiroshi Okumura, *Corporate Capitalism in Japan*, (London: Macmillan Press, 2000),110; Yutaka Kosai, 'The Post-war Japanese Economy, 1945–1973', in Duus (ed.), *The Cambridge History of Japan*. VI, 504–505.
25. Tachibanaki and Taki, *Capital and Labour in Japan*, 124; Kosai, 'The Post-ar Japanese Economy', 527–28.

Chapter 3

From School to Workshop
Pre-training and Apprenticeship in Old Regime France

Clare Crowston

To the extent that we understand apprenticeship in Old Regime France, we understand it through the prism of the guild system. Guilds established regulations regarding apprenticeship and maintained a supervisory role in the training offered by their masters. A 1691 royal edict required apprentices to obtain notarized contracts for their training, signed by guild officers. Apprentices' families paid fees to the guild and its officials as well as any charges demanded by the child's master. In return, the apprentice acquired a recognized qualification vis-à-vis the corporation. Upon completion of the training period, the youth had acquired not only useful skills and professional contacts, but the capacity to become a master in turn one day. Apprenticeship was not a guarantee of entry; the finished apprentice still had to overcome major obstacles, including an entry fee, masterpiece, various ancillary fees and charges, and, often, quotas on the number of finished apprentices accepted each year. Still, he or she possessed an official qualification denied to those who had not undertaken a formal apprenticeship or who had done so in a different city. This privilege was even greater for Parisian apprentices, whose training was valid for guilds across the kingdom. Journeymen who lacked formal apprenticeship – or the superior qualification of being a master's son – could only hope to become masters by buying an expensive letter of mastership or marrying a master 's widow.[1]

Even before the question of independent establishment arose, finished apprentices held a privileged position in the labour market. In addition to the prestige of their official training with a guild master, they were legally the sole workers eligible for employment in corporate workshops. Most guild regulations stipulated that masters could hire only finished apprentices and no male or female '*faux-ouvriers*'. Without being an official guild member, therefore, the apprentice belonged to the corporate orbit and benefited from a series of privileges denied to outsiders.

Given the strong links between guilds and apprenticeship, studies of vocational skill and its acquisition in Old Regime France have, as a rule, fallen within histories of the guilds. Historians have thus echoed corporate prejudices by assuming formal apprenticeship to be the sole path to becoming a skilled artisan. Viewing the world of work through the eyes of the guilds, they have regarded other forms of training as inherently lesser and numerically insignificant, as forms of charity rather than real training. This perspective in turn derives from the assumptions of an earlier historiography that guild regulations awarding control over the trades actually created a functioning monopoly over production and distribution.

Twenty years of revisionist histories of work and the guilds have revealed the extent to which these assumptions were mistaken. Not only were false-workers legion, along with illicit work practices by legitimate masters, but many varieties and shades of 'regulation' existed. These included the privileged areas that existed in Paris until the late seventeenth century, the ongoing privileges of the faubourg Saint-Antoine, royal manufactures, privileged individuals etc. Through the work of Steven L. Kaplan, Michael Sonenscher, Philippe Minard and Simona Cerutti, among others, we now possess a much more complex and multifaceted image of the world of work.[2] This chapter contributes to this reconceptualization of work by broadening our perspectives on apprenticeship. In particular, it will focus on the relationship between education and apprenticeship in Paris from the late seventeenth to the eighteenth centuries. By stepping back from the rigid perspective of the guilds, we find that the acquisition of skills relevant for the labour market took place in a much longer and more variegated process than the term 'apprenticeship' implies. As we will see, schools – in different forms and with different curricula – played a significant role in this process.

My notion of 'pre-apprenticeship' thus questions the distinction most historians take for granted between 'education' and 'work,' between intellectual learning and vocational training. This distinction draws on a venerable history in the eighteenth century itself. Harvey Chisick has emphasized the hesitancy of important Enlightenment figures regarding the extent to which the poor should be educated.[3] Although committed to banishing ignorance and extending enlightenment, most philosophes stopped short of advocating massive education campaigns for peasants or urban labourers. Indeed, some of the most liberal spokesmen of the Enlightenment explicitly opposed teaching reading and writing to the lower classes. They feared that education would make humble people dissatisfied with their lot in life, leading to the abandonment of farms and workshops in favour of the seminary. Opening the life of the mind – particularly by spreading reading and writing – threatened productive work.[4]

The separation between work and education in the historical imagination is reinforced by the ongoing division that exists between the fields of education history and labour history. As discussed above, labour historians focus on apprenticeship as the normative process and dismiss everything else

– including skills imparted in schools – as unrelated to vocational training. For their part, perhaps naturally, historians of education seem to have an implicit bias towards the notion of education as a form of intellectual awakening and as a path to self-improvement and social mobility. They presume that it was inherently better to send poor children to school than have them apprenticed in a workshop. As a result, they treat apprenticeship as the perpetuation of existing inequalities, or worse, in the case of pauper apprenticeships, as a form of social control and exploitation.

Of course, historians of education are not naive about processes of social control at work in education itself. In particular, they have demonstrated the primacy of religious impulses in charity schools established from the late seventeenth century in Paris and other urban areas. Religious education in schools was viewed by the Church and the state as a means to disseminate knowledge of the 'true faith' to children – and their families – and also as a form of social control which taught children to fear and obey God as a model for fearing and obeying their parents and secular authorities. Historians have emphasized the great limits of what was actually learned in charity schools, stemming from the limited ambitions of educators for their humble pupils. Reading was the key skill, given its utility for religious indoctrination; writing and, to a lesser extent, arithmetic took a secondary place in the curriculum.[5]

What is missing from the literature – in educational history and labour history – is a consideration of the relationship between intellectual and vocational learning. Questions about the parallels or discrepancies between the strategies, practices, results and theories at work in these two forms of learning have not been raised. Nor have historians looked for institutional links between forms of popular education and forms of vocational training, or between the guilds and the charity schools. This chapter begins to address these issues by investigating the preparatory training children received for apprenticeship in school, that is, the way forms of popular education were conceived of and delivered as a form of preparation for apprenticeship. Over the course of the eighteenth century, individuals and institutions from a number of different perspectives became increasingly involved in such projects across France. Without separating apprenticeship from the guilds, these interventions sought to supplement and correct perceived shortcomings of the guild-based training system. They also demonstrated a new awareness of and attention to the different stages of childhood and adolescence and a concern with the appropriate way to mold young minds and bodies through these distinct stages.

This essay will focus on two types of schools in particular. First will be free schools, created for poor children by the Parisian parishes, starting in the late seventeenth century and continuing through to the late eighteenth century. The second type of school will be the free drawing schools created in Paris and the provinces from the 1740s to the 1760s. Very different motivations lay behind the creation of these two types of schools and, as a result, they held quite different relations to work and vocational training. Priests and religious communities inspired by the Catholic reform movement were responsible for creating parish schools, while the drawing schools were the work of painters under the patronage of municipal and royal government. The two projects, nonetheless, shared a common concern with the 'gap years' in a child's education. Parish administrators worried about the problems of poor children before they entered apprenticeship. They believed that children would, as a rule, enter apprenticeship around age fifteen. Their question was: how would the children spend their time prior to age fifteen? If no formal training was offered to them before apprenticeship, how could they spend their time profitably, avoid debauchery and acquire necessary skills for apprenticeship? Their answer was to create schools intended to provide two years of education for children from age ten. Apart from practical skills in reading and writing, they were concerned with imparting knowledge of faith, moral principles and the capacity for social integration that they believed were necessary to complete apprenticeship successfully and become disciplined and productive adults.

Founders of the drawing schools worried, initially, about the phase between the completion of school and the beginning of apprenticeship. If children finished two or three years of school around age twelve, what would they do with themselves before entering apprenticeship? Drawing schools were intended to fill the gap years from twelve to fifteen by providing training in drawing and drafting that would be useful for a wide array of trades. Over time, this goal evolved into a questioning of the efficacy of apprenticeship itself. Some observers wondered if young men were learning enough in apprenticeship. Were there essential skills that apprentices did not acquire? Were the limitations of apprenticeship hindering French economic progress? Rather than morality and self-discipline, the drawing schools reflected concerns with the French national economy and with the quality and reputation of French production. These were secular institutions, although social integration and social control remained implicit matters of concern.

Both these forms of charitable education held important, albeit ambivalent, relationships with the guild system. The parish charity schools often envisioned guild-based apprenticeship as the normative next phase of life for boys after two or three years of parish education. Indeed, some parish schools did their best to ensure that their pupils could achieve this goal, by sponsoring apprenticeships for their best students. They were aware that apprenticeship was difficult to obtain and sought to open doors for the worthiest students. The drawing schools offered a more radical critique of the guilds. Their founders stated explicitly that apprenticeship was failing apprentices. They conceived of drafting and other skills as a remedy for the deficiencies of apprenticeship. Nevertheless, drawing schools also retained tight links with the guilds. The royal government encouraged guilds to create fellowships at the drawing school for members of their trade and diverted funds from guild receptions to the school. Annual prizes for the best students, moreover, came in the form of sponsored apprenticeships or masterships. Despite their criticisms, administrators still saw entry to the guild as the highest reward for an aspiring artisan.

Before continuing, it is important to note the limitations of my evidence. My sources on the charity schools and the drawing schools do not allow me to evaluate the effectiveness or utility of the instruction offered in them. I have little to offer in terms of understanding how the schools actually operated. What my sources do permit is an examination of the intentions of the schools' founders, the nature of the educational projects they devised, as well as the organization and enrolment of the institutions they founded. This essay is therefore focused more on perceptions about children, vocational and intellectual training, work and economic production, than on the concrete skills children acquired and how they acquired them. Another important point is that this essay focuses exclusively on the education and training of boys. This choice does not imply that girls did not attend charity schools. There were, indeed, numerous charity schools for girls, where they acquired even more directly useful skills – in needlework primarily – than the boys. I have treated the question of girls' charitable education and vocational skill elsewhere.[6] Girls were not admitted to the free drawing schools, although plans did exist for a girls' drawing school in Paris at the time of the Revolution.

Pre-apprenticeship in Parish Charity Schools

Most Parisian parishes established one or more free charity schools in the second half of the seventeenth century. The impulse behind this effort lay to a great extent with the religious revival sparked by the Catholic Reform and accompanying fears of Protestant conversion. They were the work of charity companies within the parishes created between the 1650s and 1680s as parallel organizations, under the authority of the *curé* but outside the official parish administration.[7] The motivations behind the schools were summed up by the 1665 regulations of the charity schools of Saint Paul parish, which stated that because most poor children 'live ordinarily without the Fear of God and without knowing the first elements of Christianity; because they do not have the opportunity to learn to read; they [the administrators] thought that the most infallible means to help these little children to go to Our Lord… was to institute Charity Schools.' Charity schools were intended to prevent poor children from falling into the ignorance that caused not only vice and impiety but brought the wrath of God in the form of cholera and other scourges. The parish officers' intention was to teach children the 'Catholic, Apostolic, and Roman Faith, to pray to God, to read and write; and by this instruction give them all the knowledge necessary for their salvation; and also by their example show their fathers and mothers to serve God.'[8] In 1665, they founded a total of five schools: two for boys and one for girls within Paris and one each for boys and girls in the outlying Faubourg Saint Antoine. Each school would have 72 children, making a total enrolment of 360.

Students entered the charity schools between ages eight and ten for approximately two years of education. As might be expected, the most important element of the schools' curriculum was religious instruction. Morning and afternoon prayers, as well as attendance at Mass in the parish church were integral parts of the daily routine. The schools were segregated by sex, with a female mistress for the girls and a male master for the boys. Girls' and boys' schools were also distinguished by their curricula. Boys generally studied religion, reading, writing and some arithmetic. Girls learned religion and reading, but little or no writing, and arithmetic was replaced with needlework. As I have argued elsewhere, girls' training in needlework was intended not only to enforce cultural norms of female behaviour, but to offer preliminary preparations for a future on the labour market. In 1698, Saint Sulpice parish ran eight schools for girls and four schools for boys. A report on charity in the parish outlined the curriculum of these schools in hierarchical order: catechism, reading, writing, arithmetic, 'trades appropriate to their sex and condition' [such as knitting, embroidery etc.], drawing, and the principles of architecture and sculpture. Following this programme, 'we instruct in Religion, and we raise for different trades almost two thousand poor children, who without this help would err in the streets and be exposed to all sorts of dangers and disorders.'[9]

The fact that boys did not learn concrete vocational skills seems at first to rule out the role of their education as pre-apprenticeship, but a closer look indicates the utility of such skills as literacy, drawing or arithmetic. Learning to write and read were important skills for future artisans, who would need to read clients' orders and do bookkeeping. Besides simple calculations for account-books, lessons in geometry could help future craftsmen draft plans for and successfully execute their clients' orders. Apart from these useful intellectual skills, the discipline involved in attending school regularly, sitting through lessons and submitting to the authority of the teacher, were all seen as a crucial step in acquiring the bodily and mental self-control necessary to become a good worker. The most intellectually skilled among the boys might be selected to continue learning and become priests or school teachers, while girls might become teachers or enter domestic service. For the vast majority of boys and many girls, however, the future would involve an artisanal trade of some kind.

At the time of the Revolution, the practical utility of popular education was being expressed in terms of patriotic nationalism. The Frères des Ecoles Chrétiennes, founded in 1680 by Jean-Baptiste de La Salle, was dedicated to offering free instruction to poor boys. By 1789, it was a national organization, with 116 houses across France and some 1,000 brothers. According to a statement written at the time of the Revolution, 'They teach prayers, the catechism of the diocese, reading, writing, arithmetic and spelling; they take their pupils to the parish services.' The brothers explicitly defended their educational programme as a useful form of pre-training for future artisans. Writing to justify their existence to the National Assembly, they stated:

> It is not for the Frères des Ecoles Chrétiennes to decide if it is important to the Nation that the children of the people have religion, morals and some openness of spirit; that they are accustomed in good time to subordination, rules of conduct and continual occupation appropriate to their age and sphere, that, drawing them away from the dangers of idleness and opportunities to learn vice, gives them more aptitude for the different professions they should embrace.

Even if they were not judged useful to the nation, they argued, their education gave students important advantages in the labour market: 'It is clearly useful to artisans and craftsmen to know their religion, read, write and calculate. Also, is there anyone, in need of choosing a worker or a servant who would not prefer one who knows his duty and has some intelligence over someone who lacks those two things?'[10]

What was the relationship of popular education to apprenticeship and the guilds? The first item to note is that parish administrators did not intend charity education to serve the poorest children. Instead, they looked to enrol the children of the settled and respectable poor. As regulations for the Saint Paul parish charity schools stated, school wardens were to record pupils' name, age and address, 'without forgetting the condition and the trade of their mothers and fathers.' This requirement carried with it the assumption of a fixed residence and profession on the parents' part. Beneath this level, children would not be accepted at school. Education and apprenticeship were thus not so much a step up for these children as a way to ensure they could maintain their families' precarious hold on a stable position among the working poor. This prejudice extended to all charitable aid provided by the parish. The 1689 Saint Paul charity company regulations state that for adult men to be eligible for any charitable aid: 'They must know a trade, or have a vocation (*vacation)*, such that they could subsist following the assistance that we give them'.[11] The company refused to pay debts, rent or wages, but would purchase raw materials or tools, to enable men to pursue their trades. Company regulations also warned of the need for prudence and charity in dealing with the respectable poor who were loathe to admit their poverty, in particular artisans who feared 'that one would no longer want to confide anything to them, if they were known to be poor, which would ruin them totally'.[12] Other parish charities echoed these concerns, often requiring at least one year's residence in the parish and refusing to help those living in lodging rented on a weekly basis.

The parish of Saint Eustache went furthest in linking charitable giving to the world of the trades. The regulations of its charity company declared that: 'The poor, needing different help, because of the diversity of their trades, commerce and affairs (*négoce*), which are not known by all, the Company will be composed not only of Ecclesiastics, Officers and Merchants, but also of tradesmen of honorable condition (*condition honneste*)'.[13] Unlike other parishes, where merchants and office-holders dominated charitable companies, Saint Eustache made room for the ordinary masters who comprised such an important element of this commercial district. The regulations also imposed a preference for guild masters as candidates for charitable assistance: 'Among the eligible, worthy poor, merchants and artisans, masters of their trades, married or widowed, will always be the first and the truest objects of the company' Ordinary workers – daily labourers, seamstresses, fruit-sellers etc. – were also eligible, but would receive less than masters.

For administrators, apprenticeship in a trade was the ideal outcome of popular education. Education could help students succeed in apprenticeship by making them literate and teaching them to sit still and obey their betters, but it was no substitute for training in specific techniques. Their intention was thus to support not replace apprenticeship. They also acknowledged, however, that their pupils might have difficulty gaining access to apprenticeship. Since most apprentices paid for their apprenticeship and access to a willing guild master might not be available to all, apprenticeship was the hoped-for outcome of education rather than the assumed outcome. Having invested time and money in schooling children, administrators often attempted to ensure that the boys would be able to enter apprenticeship. The 1665 regulations of the charity schools of Saint Paul parish explicitly required administrators to help place out-going students in apprenticeship. As they stated: 'When poor children are ready to leave school, the officers will bring their names to the two Charity Companies of Men and of Women, so as to establish funds to put the boys in apprenticeship and the girls, who cannot be placed in service'. The administrators were to keep records on the students, including the day they left the school and where they went.[14]

Some parishes maintained fellowships guaranteeing free apprenticeship to the best students in the charity schools. For administering apprenticeship subventions, the rules of the charity company of Saint Gervais parish stated: 'children of the parish will be preferred over all others and chosen from the number of those who were most assiduous in the charity schools'. In 1779, sieur Maréchal, a wealthy parishioner of Saint-Jean-en-Grève, established annuities to fund six apprenticeships each year at a cost of 250 livres each. In exchange, he appropriated the right to choose the recipients. After his death, two choices remained in the hands of his widow and the others fell to parish secular and religious officials.[15] A poster publicizing the awards detailed the selection process. As it stated, the awards were restricted to students at the parish's charity schools, who had a 'perfect knowledge' of their religion, had attended catechism classes and school for several years, and completed their First Communion. The prizes were to be awarded based on pure merit to boys or girls 'who will have made the most progress in study and knowledge of Religion'. To assist in determining the winners, the school teachers were required to keep records noting their students' attendance, behaviour in class and progress in study. Each year, the teachers would bring eight girls and boys to be reviewed by a panel composed of the curé, several priests and some lay notables. Based on an examination of school records and an oral quiz on religion, the panel picked eight children to present to the parish foundation administrators, who chose six award-winners from among them. Maréchal's encouragement of religious education was intended to have an effect not only on the children involved, but on their families as well.[16]

To add a further incentive to this programme of good behaviour and religious devotion, M. Maréchal created a second award. This time, he set aside a fund of 600 livres to be awarded each year as a dowry to the most worthy among beneficiaries of his apprenticeship prizes. In order to be eligible for this award, the youths would have to attend confession every month during their apprenticeship and obtain a letter from their master or mistress every three months testifying to their hard work and good behaviour. Once the period of apprenticeship was finished, they would continue to attend confession at least once a month and supply their employer' s name and address, so they too could be solicited for testimony of conduct. The apprentice's choice of husband or wife was also to be declared to the administrators, so that an investigation of his or her lifestyle and background could be conducted.

Despite their assumption that apprenticeship was the ideal culmination of a child's formal education, parish administrators at times expressed doubts about the accessibility of apprenticeship for poor children. The parish company of Saint Eustache parish – which was the most outspoken in linking charitable assistance to the guilds – was extremely pessimistic about the outcome of apprenticeship. Given what it perceived to be the closed nature of the guild system, the charity company forbade using funds to place children in apprenticeship or help journeymen become masters. As the regulations stated:

> Journeymen craftsmen being obliged to work at their Masters' and their goods being subject to seizure that would cause the loss of what was given to them, and the fees for mastership and apprenticeship being too high, and the utility of this help being too uncertain to be undertaken by the company, no [charity] tickets will be given to journeymen nor any assistance to have them received as Masters, nor to put anyone in apprenticeship.

This was a particularly harsh stipulation, given that charity in the parish was directed primarily toward guild masters. Those who already belonged to the corporate sphere would be assisted to remain in it; outsiders could not hope for charitable aid in order to enter the privileged world of the guilds.

Institutional Training for Younger Children

From the 1670s, parish schools in Paris offered rudimentary education that was concerned primarily with the religious instruction of poor children but also with their capacity to profit from apprenticeship and become productive and useful adults. By the 1770s, some charity administrators had begun to conclude that school alone was an insufficient preparation for apprenticeship. In 1777, the administrators of Saint Sulpice parish undertook a reform of their charity programme. This reform included new works projects for women and children, the distribution of bread and cribs, as well as fellowships for apprenticeship. In examining the education of children in the parish, the administrators decided that by the time children entered school, at age ten or eleven, they had already acquired ingrained habits of indolence and sloth. For children who had been neglected until school age, education became a source of danger rather than redemption. Learning to read and write served only to heighten potential sources of corruption rather than to preserve them from it. Outside school hours, they ran in the streets and depraved each other. Those who were not instructed in a trade perished miserably after a life of misfortune and crime. The lucky ones who entered apprenticeship after school were unable to profit from it: 'The majority of apprentices, already weakened by idleness and the disorders that follow it, become bad workers'. Based on these fears, they decided that children must be taught to work by age seven or eight, if they were to be preserved from a life of debauchery. This early work experience would prepare them for the education they received in school:

> If we succeed, the development of their intellectual faculties in school, far from being harmful, will be to the profit of Religion, morals and virtue. Reading, writing, arithmetic, drawing, will be a variety of occupations, that will make them make better use of their time and they will acquire a greater facility in the arts and crafts.[17]

The parish administrators thus resolved to establish two institutions in the parish where young children would be put to work. One institution would serve two hundred boys aged eight, who would 'be employed in spinning silk' to be used to make velvet and other types of fabric. The income earned from selling the boys' work would be used to feed and clothe them. Charity administrators estimated that they would be able to cover these costs – and the costs of raw materials – and still give each boy 20 sols a week in wages. Such payment, they believed, was essential to encourage the boys to work hard and improve their skills. This institution was also to serve as a school where the boys would learn to read, do their catechism and perform 'pious exercises'. At age thirteen or fourteen, they would be put in apprenticeship 'following their taste and the custom in the Parish.' In the second institution, girls would spin cotton before learning how to spin silk. The purpose of these two institutions was both vocational and educational. The spinning work was not intended to give the children a trade, but to give them a taste for work. Acquiring good work habits and discipline, along with a veneer of education, were seen as necessary prerequisites to undertaking a successful apprenticeship.

Charity administrators also reported that an anonymous benefactor (who was in fact Chevalier Pawlet) had recently established a house for the orphaned children of soldiers. Based on his agreement to grant preference to children of the parish, the administrators accorded him a house large enough to house three hundred children. Pawlet's plan was 'to accustom them in good time to work and to study their dispositions to have them take the estate or trade for which they have the most aptitude and attraction.' He would lodge artisans on the premises to give work to young children. Another group of artisans would take the children into their homes once they had reached the appropriate age to test their aptitude for different trades. It was only after these initial stages that the children would be placed in apprenticeship. As in the parish-based institution, the children would be paid for their work: 'The most effective means to induce young people to work being to pay them exactly, each will receive the price of his work'. However, the cost of the children's care would be deducted from their wages.[18]

These plans were put into effect. In 1780, the parish administrators reported that 160 boys were employed in 'the manufacture of cotton cloth' (rather than silk). Another 60 boys had been placed in apprenticeship following education in the school. Seventy girls were employed in spinning cotton. The institution founded by Pawlet for orphaned soldiers' children housed seventy-two children and an additional seventeen had been placed in apprenticeship. By 1783, the chevalier reported that 150 children were housed in the orphanage.[19]

Once more, these initiatives were conceived as a support for apprenticeship rather than an attack on it. Charity administrators assumed that apprenticeship was a necessary prerequisite for becoming an artisan. They also agreed, however, that apprenticeship alone was not enough. A period of elementary schooling should precede apprenticeship, where children would acquire rudimentary proficiency in reading, writing and arithmetic. Moreover, even this period in school might be insufficient. To ensure good work habits and discipline, poor children might have to enter institutional training by age seven or eight. Interestingly, the early training needed by young children was not in intellectual skills – the extra time would not be spent in reading or writing – but in habits and methods of work. Conceived as a support for apprenticeship, these plans contained an implicit criticism of the apprenticeship system. Thus, we find, particularly in Pawlet's plan, the notion that the system of apprenticeship offered children insufficient information or guidance for picking the appropriate trade. If they were to succeed, more attention should be paid to choosing trades that matched each child's individual talents and dispositions. The emphasis on paying youngsters for their work also constituted an implicit break with guild traditions of apprenticeship. Treated by law and custom as a substitute father to the child, masters offered no wages to their apprentices and usually charged fees to the parents for the child's training, room and board. By replacing the master's paternal care and attention with a monetary motivation, these plans reveal their distance from traditional conceptions of apprenticeship.

The *Ecole royale gratuite de dessin*

The notion of pre-training received the most explicit attention in the series of free drawing schools established across France from the 1740s onward. Plans for such a school began in 1746, when the painter Ferrand de Monthelon published his 'Project for the Establishment of Free Drawing Schools'. His project was motivated by concerns about the idleness of children, not before they entered school but after leaving school and before beginning apprenticeship. Ferrand de Monthelon thus identified three distinct periods of children's lives: from ages five to ten they learned to read and write at school; from ages fifteen to twenty they learned their trades in apprenticeship; from ages ten to fifteen, however, he worried that children wasted their time in idleness, which made them lazy and vulnerable to corruption. To address this problem, he proposed the creation of free drawing schools for adolescents, where they would spend their time in the period after leaving school and before entering apprenticeship.

Ferrand de Monthelon explicitly conceived of the drawing schools as a form of pre-training that would form a sound basis for further training in many different trades:

> to what does drawing not lead? A worker, in whatever profession it may be, derives an infinite aid from drawing. Drawing forms taste for all works; it produces fertility of the imagination and conveys facility in execution; it raises the worker above his estate; nothing stops him; nothing seems difficult to him; he conceives; he gives birth to new projects and leads them to a happy conclusion.

According to Ferrand de Monthelon drawing was useful for a dizzying list of trades, from the mason to the carpenter, the goldsmith, clock maker, tapestry maker and cloth maker. Even the simple soldier, he declared, armed with the principles of drawing and a little geometry, could become an engineer who rendered invaluable services to the king. De Monthelon's suggestion was echoed by other enlightened thinkers, notably in the *Mercure de France*, where his own essay was reprinted. This ambitious project was realized by a painter named Descamps in Rouen in 1747. Free drawing schools opened subsequently in Marseille in 1753, Lille in 1755, Lyon in 1756 and Amiens in 1758.

In Paris, the painter Jean-Jacques Bachelier, former artistic director of the royal porcelain manufacture at Sevres, opened the first free drawing school in 1766.[20] The following year he received royal letters patent giving the school the title of *Ecole royale gratuite de dessin*. In explaining his reasons for opening the school, Bachelier was openly critical of the guild-based apprenticeship system. He complained of the lack of skill and taste of French workers and their laziness and inadequacy in comparison to foreign workers. According to Bachelier, French workers were slaves to routine: 'let us not hide from ourselves the ineptitude of a multitude of workers, men without taste, without precision, dedicated to a routine of operations that degrade the best conceived projects'. French workers were incapable of conceiving good designs and unable to execute them. Bachelier also underlined the difficulties involved in sponsoring children for apprenticeship, given its high price and the uncertainty of its outcome:

> How many people would wish to procure the advancement of children who are of interest to them and to enable them to earn a living, who are prevented from doing so by a lack of opportunities or by being unable to profit from those that present themselves!
>
> One makes an effort to have a child taught a trade; one exhausts one's family, has recourse to acquaintances, makes use of protectors to furnish the fees of an apprenticeship for which he often has no aptitude; but if the child responds to the care one takes of his instruction and if after finishing his time, he is in a position to become a master, it arrives only too often that the good will of his benefactor cedes to the impotence of the benefactor's ability to execute it.[21]

Bachelier argued that his school was a much better investment for charitable donors than apprenticeship, which he estimated to cost up to one thousand livres.[22] For a donation of only 30 livres, a student would receive free materials and drawings to take home and copy. (The school itself charged no tuition and relied on funds from donors to meet operating costs.) According to Bachelier, this was a much cheaper option than funding an apprenticeship and it was also a more trustworthy means to produce a worker who would always be able to find employment. Bachelier stopped short of declaring apprenticeship unnecessary, but he argued that, after six years of training at the school, his students would have an advantage over all other workers. He also argued that the school had the benefit of allowing children to discover their natural aptitudes and thus make better choices about future career paths and apprenticeship. Without free drawing schools, parents sent their children to apprenticeship

> to be their whole lives only journeymen who work without knowing why; such are almost all our workers, obliged to recommence several times the same thing to arrive at a point of apparent perfection; they raise manpower to excessive prices and their lack of principles conceals the talents that culture could have germinated and made to bear fruit.[23]

The school was apparently an immediate success. Enrolment was set at a total of 1,500 students, all male. Despite this large size, Bachelier claimed that demand always exceeded the available number of places.[24] The curriculum consisted of three distinct courses of study: architecture and geometry; the human figure and animals; and flowers and ornamentation. Students were divided equally among these subjects based on the utility of the subject matter to their chosen trade. These groups occupied the school by rotation, with each having the school to itself for two days a week. Within each group, five classes of 125 students each spent two hours in class on each of their school days, so each student spent four hours in class a week. Children were admitted from the age of eight and there was no upper age limit or any other formal requirement for entry. Each student was admitted for six years of study, the time period Bachelier deemed necessary to acquire adequate skill in drawing.

The school's patrons, listed in its annual brochure, ranged from the king and the royal family, through various nobles, royal and municipal officers, and many of the Parisian guilds. There was heavy pressure on the guilds to contribute funds to the school and many of them did despite initial reluctance.[25] By 1774, ten guilds, including the six merchant guilds of the Six Corps, had established foundations in favour of the school. By establishing such foundations, they gained the right to name children admitted to the school (at thirty livres per child).[26] With the royal government's consent, a total of forty-eight guilds (including the ten who constituted foundations) agreed to award the school a share of their fees from the admission of masters, apprenticeship contracts and the election of guild officers.[27] This money went to pay operating expenses and help fund the prizes. The school's ties to the royal government and the guild system were emphasized in the annual awards ceremony held in the Tuileries. Each year on the day after Christmas, the *lieutenant general de police* – the nominal head of school – distributed awards to students before an audience consisting of the school's noble and guild patrons.

The prizes represented another link between the guild system and the drawing school. In addition to smaller prizes, school administrators awarded six grand prizes to winners of an annual drawing contest. Contestants were drawn from the winners of 96 quarterly prizes awarded during the year. The grand prizes consisted of 36 livres-worth of books or engravings and a promise from the school to pay for the student's mastership in a guild or, if the student had not already entered apprenticeship, to pay for apprenticeship. In order to qualify for the mastership prize, students had to be eligible for mastership in the eyes of the guild and had to perform a master-piece before guild officials, in the usual manner.[28] The funds for these awards came from charitable donations, including guilds' share of their fees. The royal government also agreed to abandon its share of guild mastership fees for prize winners. In 1790, when the school's existence was threatened, the guilds spoke in its favour to the National Assembly, declaring: "Who better than artists could know how much this suppression could influence their zeal to train apprentices?"[29] Bachelier not only succeeded in saving the school at that date; he remained as director until 1806 and the school survives to this day as the *Ecole nationale supérieure des arts décoratifs*.

It appears that Ferrand de Monthelon's original intention of preparing children for apprenticeship was not realized in the Parisian school. Bachelier's written accounts of the school often assumed that the pupils were not only apprentices, whose masters had chosen to send them to the school, but also journeymen in search of additional training or, even, masters who sought to perfect their skills. Rather than pre-training, therefore, the school appears to have functioned as a supplement to apprenticeship and as a form of continuing education. The prizes distributed by the school bear out this impression. Many more prize-winners chose the mastership option than apprenticeship, suggesting that they had already begun or completed apprenticeship when they won the prize. From 1768 to 1772, the school distributed a total of thirty-seven grand prizes (an average of more than seven a year). Sixteen prize-winners received payment for mastership and only three for apprenticeship. The remaining eighteen prize-winners chose neither mastership nor apprenticeship. No indication is given regarding their career status. We may assume that they would have been journeymen and apprentices who were not yet eligible for mastership, finished masters, and some individuals who established themselves in provinces.[30]

Conclusion

Despite the separation historians have posited between education and labour, we find that eighteenth-century educators were keenly interested in vocational training and the labour market, and framed their educational projects within the context of apprenticeship and the guilds. They viewed apprenticeship as the desired goal for poor youths – of a certain social status

– and they sought to prepare children for it. Parish leaders believed children would need social, intellectual and physical preparation for apprenticeship that could only be imparted in schools. They were also aware, however, of limitations of accessibility and used charity schools as a means to funnel charitable support to the most deserving young people. Conceived as a support and preparation for apprenticeship, these projects also addressed the perceived weaknesses of apprenticeship. Apprenticeship was too expensive, too difficult to obtain and led to an uncertain future. Plunged into vocational training with no prior experience, children had little opportunity to test their skills and interests before being wedded to a craft for life. It is striking to note the extent to which these criticisms were shared by educators, from parish charity officers concerned with salvation and social control to enlightened artists anxious to improve French industrial competitiveness.

Another shared concern was a growing awareness of the child as a much more complex creature than the docile apprentice depicted in guild statutes. Children's lives were broken into distinct stages, to which different activities and forms of learning should correspond. Their success in life relied on a combination of religious, social, intellectual and vocational training. In this broad perspective, it is clear that guilds played an important role in preparing youths for the labour market, but they shared this terrain with a much more diverse array of institutions and authorities than has been acknowledged. In this focus on the stages of childhood and the ideal employment for each of them, we may see a parallel to the intensification and rationalization of the rhythms of labour for adult workers underway in the same period.

We know little about the guilds' responses to these criticisms. They must have been aware of them, for they maintained close relations with parish charity officers and with the administrators of the drawing schools, as they did, moreover, with charity workshops in the *Hôpital général* and other institutions that provided vocational training to poor children. These relations were indeed ambiguous for the guilds, for educators both acknowledged corporate privilege in the world of work and sought to rectify perceived failings of the guild system. These examples demonstrate, once again, the porosity of the guild system and the multiplicity of the world of work, where guild privileges interacted with a host of parallel, competing and contradictory set of privileges. For children and their families, faced with limited resources and an uncertain future, the path to vocational training was longer, more variegated and more open-ended than the current notion of apprenticeship suggests.

Notes

1. In some guilds, marriage to a master's daughter also offered eased conditions for access to the guild. On apprenticeship in eighteenth-century France, see Steven L. Kaplan, 'L'apprentissage au XVIIIe siècle: le cas de Paris', *Revue d'histoire moderne et contemporaine* 40 (juillet-septembre 1993): 436–79.
2. On work and guilds in eighteenth-century Paris, see Steven L. Kaplan, 'Réflexions sur la police du monde du travail, 1700–1815', Revue historique 261 (janvier–mars 1979):

17–77; 'Les Corporations, les faux-ouvriers et le fauxbourg Saint-Antoine', *Annales: Economies, Sociétés, Civilisations* (mars–avril 1988): 253–88; 'La lutte pour le contrôle du marché du travail', *Revue d'histoire moderne et contemporaine* 36 (juillet–septembre 1989): 436–79; and *The Bakers of Paris* (Durham, N.C.: Duke University Press, 1999). See also Michael Sonenscher, *Work and Wages: Natural Law, Politics and the Eighteenth-Century French Trades* (Cambridge, U.K.: Cambridge University Press, 1989); Simona Cerutti, *La Ville et les métiers. Naissance d'un langage corporatif (Turin, 17e–18e siècles)* (Paris: Editions de l'Ecole des Hautes Etudes en Sciences Sociales, 1990); Gail Bossenga, *The Politics of Privilege: Old Regime and Revolution in Lille* (Cambridge: Cambridge University Press, 1991); and Philippe Minard, *La Fortune du colbertisme. Etat et industrie dans la France des Lumières* (Paris: Fayard, 1998).

3. Harvey Chisick, *The Limits of Reform in the Enlightenment: Attitudes Toward the Education of the Lower Classes in 18th-Century France* (Princeton: Princeton University Press, 1981).
4. In private correspondence, Voltaire wrote 'Je vous remercie de proscrire l'étude chez les laboureurs. Moi, qui cultive la terre, je vous présente requête pour avoir des manoeuvres, et non des clercs tonsurés. Envoyez moi sur-tout des fréres ignorantins pour conduire mes charrues, ou pour les atteler'. Cited in Chisick, *The Limits of Reform in the Enlightenment*, 94. The letter was written to de La Chalotais Louis René de Caradeuc, author of *Essai d'education nationale*, (Rennes, 1985) which had similarly criticized popular education.
5. On education in Old Regime France, see Roger Chartier, Dominique Julia and Marie-Madeleine Compère, *L'Education en France du XVIe au XVIIIe siècle* (Paris: Société d'edition d'enseignement supérieur, 1976); Bernard Grosperrin, *Les petites écoles sous l'Ancien Régime* (Rennes: Ouest-France, 1984); and Chisick, *The Limits of Reform in the Enlightenment.* On female education see Jean Perrel, 'Les écoles de filles dans la France d'Ancien Régime', in *The Making of Frenchmen: Current Directions in the History of Education in France, 1679–1979*, eds Donald N. Baker and Patrick J. Harrigan (Waterloo, Ont.: Historical Reflections Press, 1980) and Martine Sonnet, *L'éducation des filles au temps des Lumières* (Paris, 1987).
6. Clare Haru Crowston, 'An Industrious Revolution in Late Seventeenth- and Eighteenth-Century Paris: New Vocational Training for Adolescent Girls and the Creation of Female Labor Markets', in *Secret Gardens, Satanic Mills: Placing Girls in European History, 1750–1960,* eds Mary Jo Maynes et al. (Bloomington, 2004).
7. On these companies, see Marcel Fosseyeux, *Les Ecoles de charité;* Harvey Chisick, 'French Charity Schools in the Seventeenth and Eighteenth Centuries with Special Reference to the Case of Amiens', *Histoire sociale – Social History*, vol. 16, 32 (November 1983): 241–77; and Léon Cahen, "Les Idées charitables à Paris au XVIIe et au XVIIIe siècles d'après les règlements des compagnies paroissiales," *Revue d'histoire moderne et contemporaine*, t. II (1900–1901): 5–22.
8. *Archives nationales,* Series L (AN L) 716 ; *Règlemens pour les Escholes de charité de la paroisse de Saint Paul* (Paris, 1665).
9. AN L 716; *Etat présent des bonnes oeuvres et Ecoles charitables de la Paroisse de Saint Sulpice du 1. Decembre 1698.*
10. AN S 7046; *Idée générale de l'Institut des Frères des Ecoles Chrétiennes.*
11. (Article IV p. 20).
12. See also AN L 716; *Règlemens de la Compagnie de la Charité de Saint-Severin* (Paris, 1673), which contain a similar emphasis on helping the respectable poor by giving them vocational training and raw materials, and helping them negotiate with creditors.
13. AN L 716; *Règlemens de la compagnie employée au secours et rétablissement des pauvres familles honteuses de la paroisse de Saint-Eustache* (Paris, 1684).
14. AN L 716, *Règlemens pour les Escholes des charité de la paroisse de Saint-Paul.* Another indication of the importance placed on apprenticeship was the routine stipulation in charity company regulations that no request for aid would be accepted from individuals who placed their children in apprenticeship with a Protestant master.
15. During his lifetime, he maintained the right to choose four of the recipients each year, regardless of their parish of origin or their attendance at the charity school. When he died,

his widow retained the choice of two children. After her death, the choice of all six children reverted to the parish, under the conditions described in this paragraph.

16. AN L 665B; *Instruction pour les enfans des écoles de charité de la Paroisse de Saint Jean en Grève qui concourent aux Apprentissages de Métier, fondés en 1779.* As elaborate as it was, this process accounted for only six of the parish's twelve charity apprentices. The acting director of the parish foundation named another six children and the masters or mistresses for whom they were destined. The choice of age, sex and trade was thus left entirely in his hands.
17. *Ordre d'administration pour le soulagement des pauvres de la paroisse de Saint-Sulpice* (Paris: chez Crapart, 1777).
18. *Ordre d'administration pour le soulagement des pauvres de la paroisse de Saint-Sulpice,* 27–33.
19. *Ordre d'Administration établi, en 1777, pour le soulagement des Pauvres de la Paroisse de Saint-Sulpice, Compte des dépenses depuis le premier Octobre 1779, jusqu'au premier Oct. 1780.*
20. See Arthur Birembaut, 'Les Ecoles gratuites de dessin', in *Enseignement et diffusion des sciences en France au XVIIIe siècle*, ed. René Taton (Paris: Hermann, 1964).
21. *Mémoire concernant l'Ecole royale gratuite de dessin* (Paris: Imprimerie royale, 1774), 13.
22. *Mémoire concernant l'Ecole royale gratuite de dessin*, 15.
23. *Mémoire concernant l'Ecole royale gratuite de dessin*, 15.
24. *Mémoire concernant l'Ecole royale gratuite de dessin*, 5.
25. Arthur Birembaut reports that the Six Corps at first refused to sponsor the school, because they viewed it as another form of disguised taxation. The school's royal letters patent, and the royal patronage they represented, helped to convince the guilds. Birembaut, 'Les Ecoles gratuites de dessin', 445.
26. According to Birembaut, the mercers sponsored two places in the school, the wine merchants and clock makers five each, the tailors and painter-sculptors four each, and the grocers, cabinetmakers, *limonadiers, gaziers* and saddle-makers each sponsored one place in the school annually. (Les Ecoles gratuites de dessin, 449). Students who entered without the benefit of a fellowship received free instruction but did not receive drawings to take home and had to make do with materials available during school hours. (*Mémoire concernant l'Ecole royale gratuite de dessin*, 13).
27. The ten guilds who had established foundations in favour of the school were the merciers, epiciers, orfevres, horlogers, marchands de vins, menuisiers, limonadiers, tailleurs, gaziers and serruriers (*Mémoire concernant l'Ecole royale gratuite de dessin*, 24–25).
28. *Mémoire concernant l'Ecole royale gratuite de dessin*, 10.
29. *Attestation et supplication des Corps et Communautés* (1790)
30. In 1768, 5 prizes were given: 3 for mastership and 2 unspecified; in 1769, 7 prizes, 2 for mastership, 1 for apprenticeship and 4 unspecified; in 1770, 8 prizes, 4 for mastership and 4 unspecified; in 1771, 9 prizes, 4 for mastership, 1 for apprenticeship and 4 unspecified; in 1772, 8 prizes, 3 for mastership, 1 for apprenticeship and 4 unspecified.

Part II

Between Contract and Practice

Chapter 4

Apprenticeship and Guild Control in the Netherlands, c.1450–1800

Karel Davids

Apprenticeship at present seems to enjoy a higher reputation than ever before. In his recent survey of artisans in Europe from the late Middle Ages into the era of industrialization, James Farr has stated that apprenticeship was not only an initiation to a trade but an instrument of 'moral and political socialization' as well. Apprenticeship was one of the principal means to discipline labour and maintain a distinction between ranks in society and thus to uphold order and hierarchy. Guild regulations served to institutionalize this central role of apprenticeship for the preservation of the established social order.[1] Steven Kaplan, in a pioneering case-study on apprenticeship in Paris in the eighteenth century, which formed the *pièce de resistance* of a special issue on this subject of the *Revue d'histoire moderne et contemporaine*, has claimed that apprenticeship was 'une des pierres angulaires du système de reproduction du monde des arts et métiers', which primarily served for the transmission of knowledge and skills but also contributed to the survival of the corporate system by acting as a vehicle of socialization. Apprenticeship, according to Kaplan, was based on a notion of reciprocity between master and apprentice which found concrete expression in a contract drawn up before a notary. But each contract had a corporate and public dimension as well: guilds were not only normally cosignatories of the contract, but also acted as its supervisors and guarantor.[2] For German cities in the eighteenth century, Andreas Griessinger and Reinhold Reith have stressed the corporate and public dimensions of contracts between master and apprentice and the supervisory role of guilds as well.[3] In England, the enactment of the Statute of Artificers in 1563, according to Joan Lane and James Farr, led to the replacement of the old system of total control by the guilds by a new regime of apprenticeship regulated by state laws and a relative openness of admission to mastership, although guilds still maintained some powers of inspection and control of apprentices' conditions until the beginning of the eighteenth century.[4]

How did the Netherlands fit into this pattern? Thanks to the work by Jan Lucassen, Piet Lourens, Maarten Prak and others, the rough outline of the history of guilds in the Netherlands is now much better known than about ten or twenty years ago. In the northern part of the Low Countries, which after the Revolt against the Habsburg regime would constitute the Republic of the United Provinces, the spread of guilds in many cities did not start until the fourteenth or fifteenth century. The number and membership of guilds reached their highest rate of expansion during the period between c. 1580 and 1670, when urbanization and economic growth were at their peak. By the end of the seventeenth century, according to a recent estimate made by Lucassen and Prak, even in the 'undisputed centre of Dutch capitalism', Amsterdam, 70–85 percent of the adult male workers were included within the guild system. Although the period after 1670 could be seen as 'one of consolidation' rather than continued expansion, guilds remained 'strong and full of vitality' until the very end of the Old Regime. In common with corporations in other countries of Europe, Dutch guilds normally possessed a local economic monopoly and tended to protect the interests of established masters (and their sons). In contrast to their counterparts in many other countries, however, they were relatively inclusive as far as migrants were concerned, showed neutrality in the matter of religion (except towards Jews) and, as a rule, did not play a major role in political affairs.[5] As far as apprenticeship is concerned, it is still an open question whether the Netherlands conformed to the 'standard' pattern exhibited in France and Germany, followed the somewhat different route of England or, perhaps struck out an entirely different path.

Apprenticeship can only have fulfilled its supposed role as a key instrument for the transmission of knowledge and skills and as a means for socialization into the corporate order, if it really served as the predominant institution in the field of training and education and if it was indeed to a large extent supervised by guilds. But there are no compelling reasons why either of these suppositions should always have been true. It is, after all, not self-evident why training and education could only, or mainly, have been provided by a system of apprenticeship. The structure of training and education may, among other things, also have depended on the nature of the knowledge and skills involved. As for supervision: the fundamental problem in the case of apprenticeship, in terms of historical institutional analysis, was the question of how to ensure that each of the parties involved would really honour its side of the bargain. It is hard to see why this problem could only have been solved by having guilds act as supervisors and guarantor. Other solutions may have been practised as well.

The historical reality of these alternative scenarios becomes evident in the case of the Netherlands. In this chapter I will argue, first, that apprenticeship in the Netherlands from an early date was, in fact, only to a limited degree controlled by guilds, and second, that the role of apprenticeship in training and education compared with other routes of vocational training and education was decreasing long before the end of the eighteenth century. This happened in a different way and for different reasons than in England, however. The chapter will conclude by suggesting a number of factors or circumstances that may be relevant for an explanation of this particular development.

Guild Control of Apprenticeship

As far as guild regulations in Dutch cities in the late Middle Ages and early modern period touched upon the subject of apprenticeship, they usually referred to no more than four aspects: registration of apprentices, apprenticeship fees, duration of apprenticeship and the number of apprentices per master. By-laws laid down the date and procedure of registration with the guild, fixed the amount in money or in kind that had to be paid to the guild by an apprentice or a master at the start of an apprenticeship term, stipulated the minimum number of years an apprenticeship should last and determined the number of apprentices that might be taken on per master per year or the maximum number allowed per master at any given time. It was rare to find any regulations on the qualifications of masters who were permitted to take on apprentices, such as the regulations of the fullers' and weavers' guilds in Bois-le-Duc of 1377 and 1421, respectively, which said that masters were not allowed to take on apprentices until one year after they had acquired the mastership[6], or any by-laws similar to those issued for the stocking-knitters' guild in Leiden in 1595, which required that 'in order to prevent all future quarrels' all apprenticeship agreements had to be noted down in detail by officers of the guild.[7]

The extent of guild control of apprenticeship, however, was in reality even more limited than this brief outline might suggest. Guild regulations, to begin with, seldom defined the actual *contents* of the training of apprentices: by-laws of guilds normally did not prescribe what apprentices had to learn during the period they were supposed to serve their apprenticeship or how and when they should be taught. The exception to the rule were surgeons' guilds.[8] From the late sixteenth century onwards, many cities in the Netherlands saw the creation of new, institutional facilities in the field of medical education in the form of the building of anatomical theatres, laying-out of botanic gardens and appointment of lecturers or professors, who were charged with the task of giving public lectures or demonstrations on anatomy, surgery or botany. These public lecturers usually received their income from the town government, but in a few cases (as in Amsterdam) figured on the payroll of the surgeons' guild. Their lectures or demonstrations were open to doctors, master surgeons, journeymen, members of the government and other interested citizens as well as to surgeons' apprentices. Attendance sometimes even formed a compulsory part of the apprentice's training programme. In Amsterdam, for example, all surgeons' apprentices were, from 1606 onwards, obliged to attend the public lectures on anatomy. A similar obligation was introduced by the magistrate of Rotterdam in 1705.[9] Guild officers tried to ensure that apprentices complied with this regulation and in the eighteenth century sometimes even pressed for further improvement of these facilities for the sake of enhancing the quality of apprentices.[10] No other guild has matched the surgeons in their concern for regulating the contents of professional education.

The competence of an apprentice, as S.R. Epstein has remarked, generally could only be assessed *ex post*, namely by the requirement of producing a masterpiece as a precondition for admittance to mastership.[11] But this retroactive instrument of guild control on apprenticeship was by no means universal. It did not possess a comprehensive range. For one thing, in many crafts or trades the making of a masterpiece did not become a necessary condition for admittance to mastership until the late sixteenth or seventeenth century, even in occupations which were organized in guilds long before that date. The shipcarpenters' guild of Dordrecht, for instance, which received its first by-laws in 1437, did not introduce a formal proof requirement until 1587. The shoemakers' guild of Arnhem, which was founded in the fifteenth century, did not require the making of a masterpiece until 1674. Some guilds, like that of the shoemakers in Gouda, first established the proof requirement at the end of the eighteenth century.[12] Moreover, many corporations never introduced this test as a precondition for admittance to the mastership at all. The incidence of proof requirements was not necessarily related to particular crafts or trades. Whereas bakers' guilds in Amsterdam, Utrecht or Nijmegen succeeded in introducing proof requirements, those in Arnhem and Gouda did not. In the shipbuilding industry, the only guilds ever to introduce proof requirements remained those of Dordrecht, Amsterdam and Arnemuiden. In the printing trade, on the other hand, the only printers', bookbinders' and booksellers' guilds *not* to establish the making of a masterpiece as a precondition for admission to mastership were those in Leiden and Amsterdam.[13]

Besides, the existence of guild regulations on particular aspects of apprenticeship did not mean that guild control in practice was very tight or extensive. Guilds, after all, did not always uphold their own laws. Apprenticeship registers kept by the officers of the carpenters' and painters' guilds in The Hague in the seventeenth century reveal that masters often engaged a higher number of apprentices per year than the guild laws permitted.[14] But the officers apparently saw no reason to take action. Guild regulations on apprenticeship terms allowed individual masters and apprentices (or their parents and guardians) a considerable measure of leeway, as these normally only prescribed a minimum duration of the apprenticeship period. Apprenticeship terms were in fact often much longer than the two (or sometimes three, four or five) years enshrined in guild statutes. Among 68 contracts and certificates of apprenticeship drawn up in Amsterdam between 1595 and 1670, no less than 47 refer to an apprenticeship period that was longer than the term stated in the relevant guild laws; in three cases, the term was shorter than the official one, while in eighteen cases the actual and formal terms were exactly equal.[15] Only one certificate of apprenticeship (concerning a hatmaker in 1624) explicitly declared that the term of apprenticeship served was precisely as long as prescribed in the by-laws of the guild.[16] And most apprenticeship cases were never recorded in the form of a written contract before a notary. They were defined in an oral agreement between a master and the parents or guardians of an apprentice, or simply arranged between father and son. The only elements of apprenticeship that really have been susceptible to some measure of effective guild control appear to have been the registration of apprentices at the start of their term, the payment of apprenticeship fees to the treasury of the guild and, in a number of cases, the *ex post* test of competence that was required before admission to mastership.

Up to now, I have argued on the assumption that guilds at least made an attempt to exert control on apprenticeship and that apprenticeship was closely intertwined with the existence of guilds. Reality was different, however. Many guilds in Dutch cities, especially in the sector of distribution, never knew any regulations concerning the admission, registration, training or examination of apprentices at all. Guilds of merchants, brokers, pedlars, boatmen, bargemen, fishmongers, carters or beer, peat and market porters did not distinguish a separate category of apprentices.[17] These guilds belonged to the largest corporate organizations of the day. In Amsterdam in 1688, they comprised more than 40 percent of the (estimated) total membership of corporations.[18] Even inside the guild system, apprenticeship was a far from universal institution.

Moreover, apprenticeship was, in fact, not dependent on the existence of guilds. The rural district of the Zaanstreek, which in the seventeenth century led the way in the development of industrial windmills, has hardly known any guilds at all.[19] Yet, this very region saw the emergence and expansion of a distinct group of craftsmen specialized in the making and repairing of mills, who developed their own system of apprenticeship as well. A millwright, Pieter Johannes de Vries from Zaandam, for example, who in 1769 applied for a job as master millwright in the service of the Dutch East-India Company, sought to establish his credentials by the presentation of a kind of curriculum vitae stating that 'from childhood he had been taught by his uncle Jan Douwes de Vries the art of drawing and the making of all sorts of mills and gear of mills' and that in the mean time 'he had made such progress that for a few years past he had built with success a number of mills in the Netherlands as a master millwright himself (lastly in Flushing in 1768)'.[20] Around 1800, the Zaanstreek numbered ten workshops of millwrights, each of which probably employed twenty to thirty adult craftsmen and five boys.[21] The persistence of the apprenticeship system in this region was probably more based on the confidence of each of the parties involved that the other naturally would honour its obligations because they were all bound by family and kin relations, than on any formal contracts guaranteed by public institutions.

In cities, where guilds were much thicker on the ground, training of apprentices was not always embedded in a corporate structure either. Apprenticeship did not only exist in crafts or trades that were organized in the form of guilds. Of the 159 apprenticeship contracts concluded between individual persons in Amsterdam dating from the period 1595–1670 that have been collected by J.G. van Dillen, no more than 62 (39 percent) relate to occupations which at the time of the drafting of the contract were subject to guild regulations. The vast majority (61 percent) concern trades or crafts which at the time of drafting were not yet organized in a guild or which were never organized in a guild at all (such as watchmaking, diamond cutting, gold- and silver-wire drawing and most branches of the wholesale trade).[22] The few apprenticeship contracts relating to the textile industry in Leiden, which were published by N.W. Posthumus, mostly refer to occupations which remained outside the orbit of guild regulation, such as camlet, cloth or serge drapery.[23] In contrast to eighteenth-century Paris or cities in Germany, it was evidently possible in Amsterdam and Leiden to conclude formal arrangements concerning vocational instruction between an individual craftsman or tradesman and the parents or guardians of a prospective pupil even if there were no guild which could test and certify its outcome. Corporations were not necessary agencies for the enforcement of apprenticeship contracts.[24]

These apprenticeship contracts from Amsterdam moreover reveal that the relationship between master and apprentice was not always so close that the master could wield an almost comprehensive disciplinary power over the apprentice's life. While about 75 percent of the contracts stipulated that the master would be obliged to furnish the apprentice with board and lodging and thus allowed the former to exercise a nearly round-the-clock surveillance on the latter, the rest of the contracts charged the master – in addition to his commitment with regard to instruction – only with obligations of a monetary nature. Instead of providing support in kind, the master would pay the apprentice a certain wage, which would become higher as the latter's abilities increased. The master's supervision in these cases thus did not extend beyond working hours at all. Besides, many apprenticeship contracts were not concluded between individual persons, but between an individual master and the board of an institution that represented the interest of the apprentice and his (or her) family, such as an orphanage. Apprentices placed by an orphanage were often not taken in by the master, but continued to receive their board and lodging from the institute.[25]

Alternatives to Guild Control

The fact that guild control on apprenticeship in Dutch cities was not as firm and extensive as current views on the corporate system in Continental Europe would lead us to expect, does not imply that supervision on vocational training and education on the whole was weakly developed. In many professions outside the guild system in the seventeenth and eighteenth centuries, entrants were only admitted after having undergone a test similar to the making of a 'masterpiece', namely a formal examination under the auspices of local magistrates, provincial governments, church authorities, institutions of the central government, or semi-public bodies. Schoolmasters, in cities at least, were often obliged to pass a formal exam by a board appointed by local authorities before they could take up their job.[26] Surveyors were subjected to a test of competence by officials appointed by a provincial government.[27] Ministers of the Dutch Reformed Church were examined by a classis.[28] Army engineers and artillery officers for a time had to undergo an examination before the Council of State.[29] Officers, mates and surgeons in the Navy had to pass an exam before officials appointed by an Admiralty. Masters, mates and surgeons of East-Indiamen and West-Indiamen were subjected to a test by examiners in the service of Chambers of the VOC (*Verenigde Oostindische Compagnie*) and WIC (*West Indische Compagnie*).[30]

In export industries, notably textile manufacture, apprenticeship could be supervised by *neringen* instead of guilds. Neringen were organizations established by a town government, which were charged with regulating and controlling a particular branch of export industry. In contrast with guilds, they knew no formal membership but included *all* persons working in a specific sector of production. They were administered by a board consisting both of entrepreneurs and of representatives from the urban government.[31] Regulations with regard to neringen usually covered the subject of apprenticeship as well. The order on the *nering* of gold- and silver-wire drawing issued by the government of Amsterdam in 1696 stipulated that all apprentices had to be registered and that apprentices were obliged to complete the agreed term of service.[32] By-laws of neringen in Leiden from the late sixteenth century normally contained clauses on the number of apprentices per master, the length of apprenticeship and the procedure of registration at the beginning and end of the apprenticeship period.[33] A number of neringen-regulations went much further than that. Nering-regulations about the manufacture of *changeants* (fabric of varying lustre) in 1602 and the weaving of camlets and mock velvets in 1759, for instance, contained prescriptions on the making of masterpieces.[34] The by-laws of the nering of serges and camlets manufacture issued in 1585 stipulated that apprentices should only be trained indoors and that any master who engaged an apprentice had to give evidence before the board of supervisors of the nering that he was indeed able to teach the apprentice himself. In 1663, a regulation was issued to the effect that apprenticeships in camlet manufacture would only be valid if they were properly registered by the directors of the inspection hall (*greinhal*) of this particular branch of industry.[35] the board of supervisors of the nering of fine cloth making was authorized by the city government in 1641 to visit the houses of drapers or spinners in order to check whether apprentices were well treated and looked after. Another by-law of 1646 laid down rules on working hours of apprentices in summer and winter. The contents of apprenticeship contracts were carefully noted in a register kept by the supervisors of the nering.[36]

The finding that many apprenticeship contracts were not related to occupations that were subject to guild regulations is, on closer inspection, hardly surprising at all. The spread of registration of apprenticeship contracts in Dutch cities since the end of the sixteenth century was not due to the guild system. Guild regulations on registration of apprentices, after all, seldom extended beyond prescriptions about enrolment in a register kept by guild officers, the payment of a fee, the duration of apprenticeship and the number of apprentices per master. They rarely required a formal contract. It was not the guilds, but the provincial government of which Holland, at the request of the city of Amsterdam, actually made an effort to bring apprenticeship contracts into more general use. On 2 September 1597, the States of Holland issued a decree to the effect that all masters who engaged a poor boy as apprentice were henceforth obliged to have a formal contract drawn up before the local magistrates or public commissioners in charge of poor relief in order to guarantee that the boy would be properly looked after. In contrast with England, the States of Holland did not proceed to establish a record of apprenticeship contracts at a supralocal level. The principal purpose of this measure was to reduce beggary by apprentice boys. The reason why the States of Holland interfered with this matter was the argument, put forward by the burgomasters of Amsterdam that local measures aimed at ensuring a decent sustenance for apprentice boys could only be effective if all cities in the province would fall into line.[37] In the city of Delft, the urban magistrate shortly thereafter indeed established a public committee on poor relief, the *Kamer van Charitate*. One of its principal tasks was the regulation and supervision of apprenticeship contracts.[38]

In addition to urban and provincial governments, the most important promoters of the registration of apprenticeship contracts were the urban institutions that served as large suppliers of apprentices: orphanages. Orphanages in Dutch cities were interested in a formal arrangement of apprenticeship relations for a number of reasons. By entering into a contract of apprenticeship with a master craftsman on behalf of the children put under their care, regents of those institutions could ensure not only that the children during at least part of their stay would contribute to the income of the institute, but also that the orphans would be able to earn their own living once they had left and that the whole operation could be properly accounted for both to the orphan's family and/or the municipal authorities.[39] In Amsterdam, the position of the municipal board in charge of orphan care vis-à-vis the guild masters was strenghtened by the formal prescription issued by the urban authorities in 1634 that 'in order to prevent orphaned children from wandering from one master to another, without learning their craft well or without handing over any earnings to the regents of the orphanage', orphans could only be employed by guild masters if they were properly apprenticed by the 'regents' of the orphan board.[40]

This does not imply that the interest of regents in concluding apprenticeship contracts was immutable across time and unvarying by category of orphans. The aim of making orphans generate income for the institute could also be achieved by having them placed in unskilled jobs in the textile industry, as happened, for example, in the seventeenth century with many orphaned children under fourteen in Leiden (see Table 4.1), Delft, Amsterdam, Alkmaar, Kampen, Zwolle and a number of cities in Friesland,[41] and the aim of making orphans earn their own living could also be realized by having older boys enlisted into the service of the East-India Company, the West-India Company or the Navy. The latter practice began as early as about 1615 and continued until the beginning of the nineteenth century. Although the numbers leaving the orphanage for the East-Indies in the later eighteenth century were much lower than in the second or fourth quarter of the seventeenth century, the *Burgerweeshuis* in Amsterdam, for example, between

Table 4.1 *Employment of Orphaned Boys in Leiden, 1607–1611*

Type of Employment	Economic Sector *Textile Trades*	 *Other Trades*
Apprenticeship	47 (of whom 39 were 14 years or older)	17 (of whom 14 were 14 years or older)
Unskilled Job	51 (of whom 11 were 14 years or older)	0
Total:	98 = 85 %	17 = 15 %

Source: GA Leiden, Archief Heilige Geest en Arme Wees- en Kinderhuis nr.3845

1765 and 1794 still placed on average five boys each year in the service of the VOC. The Burgerweeshuis in Haarlem between 1766 and 1805 sent fifty-six boys to sea, fifteen of whom were placed on a naval vessel and forty-one placed aboard an East-Indiaman.[42]

As Anne McCants has shown in her study on the Burgerweeshuis in Amsterdam, however, regents of this institution, which housed orphaned children of burghers, strove to place boys under their care primarily in occupations that gave them access to the 'guild-organized craft sector', which was characterized by 'relatively high wages, stable employment, and the queuing of applicants', rather than in jobs that formed part of the 'casual, or proletarian sectors, of the labor market' and hardly offered any reliable prospects at all. Of the 2700 apprenticeship contracts from the period 1669–1767 kept in the archives of the Burgerweeshuis, all but a few related to placements in trades organized in guilds, especially in the sectors of building, shipbuilding and woodworking. The ultimate goal of this policy of the regent board, which was heavily dominated by the urban elite, was to secure the long-term allegiance of the middle strata of the population to the existing social and political order by making a manifest effort to prevent the downward mobility of their orphaned offspring.[43] A similar mechanism can be observed in the policy of the regents of the Walloon orphanage in the seventeenth and eighteenth centuries: according to Isabella van Eeghen, orphans from this institution were preferably apprenticed in the crafts or trades that had been practised by their fathers.[44] In the other municipally managed orphanage in Amsterdam, the Aalmoezeniersweeshuis, which in contrast with the Burgerweeshuis primarily cared for the children of the poor, orphans were 'left to the mercy of the casual labor market', however.[45] There is no evidence of any effort to secure for them placements in the guild-based craft sector.

In other cities in Holland, differences between orphanages were not as clear-cut as in Amsterdam. Evidence from municipally managed orphanages in Dordrecht and Leiden suggests that, in the later decades of the eighteenth century at least, orphaned boys were mostly apprenticed in the guild-organized craft sector, although the specific distribution of apprenticed orphans over various occupations differed of course by city, depending on its economic structure (Table 4.2).[46] In the principal orphanage in Leiden, the Heilige Geesthuis, employment of orphaned children in the textile industry, which had largely remained outside the guild system, drastically declined in comparison with the early seventeenth century (see table 4.1) and the share of placements in guild-organized trades correspondingly increased.[47]

Orphanages influenced apprenticeship relations in other ways than by concluding apprenticeship contracts. Thanks to the support of urban governments, orphans obtained a kind of special position among apprentices by receiving exemptions from particular obligations to guilds. In 1523, the very year that saw the foundation of the Burgerweeshuis, orphans in Amsterdam were declared exempt from paying apprenticeship dues and other contributions to the guilds.[48] Orphans from the Heilige Geesthuis in Leiden enjoyed a similar exemption from paying dues to the guild. This privileged position was, at the request of the regents of the institute, expressly confirmed by the urban magistrate in 1766. In 1790, it was granted to orphans from the Walloon orphanage, too. The only guilds in Leiden that have *not* been obliged to honour this privilege are the shearers and the gold- and silversmiths.[49]

Table 4.2 *Occupations of Apprenticed Orphan Boys from Municipally Managed Orphanages in Dutch Cities, c.1720–1805*

Trades	**Amsterdam**	**Dordrecht**	**Leiden**			
	1720–1767	*1732–1760*	*1745*	*1765*	*1785*	*1805*
Building	32.0 %	24.7 %	14.3 %		5.2 %	5.4 %
Woodworking	19.5	9.9	11.4	50 %	12.3	7.3
Shipbuilding	16.8	25.8	2.8			1.8
Pictorial Arts and Glaziery	11.3	0.3	2.8		10.5	5.4
Metalworking	6.2	1.4	5.7	4.2	8.8	9.0
Leatherworking	5.1	12.7	8.6	8.4	10.5	7.3
Precious-metal Working	2.5		2.8		3.5	6.4
Bookbinding/ Printing/Selling	1.7	7.0	5.7		8.8	4.5
Tailoring	0.4	9.2		4.2	1.7	4.5
Basket-Brush-Broommaking	0.4	0.6		4.2	7.0	13.6
Textile Making		4.6	37.1	25.0	19.3	11.0
Other	4.1	4.8	8.6	4.2	12.3	22.7
Total Number of Apprentices	1098	283	35	24	57	110

Sources: McCants, *Civic Charity*, 71-72; Esseboom, *Onderwijsinghe*, 197; GA Leiden, Archief Heilige Geest of Arme Wees- en Kinderhuis nr. 3862.

The degree of control over apprenticeship relations exerted by orphanages reached its height in the case of institutions that were fully financed from private funds. The pre-eminent examples of this type of charity were the Fundaties van Renswoude in Delft, The Hague and Utrecht, which were founded in 1756 as a result of the testamentary dispositions by a widow of a member of the Utrecht aristocracy, Maria Duyst van Voorhout. The establishments funded from the legacy of Maria Duyst were charged with the task of selecting a small number of gifted children from a local orphanage, lodging them in a separate institute and giving them a training in 'mathematics, drawing or painting, sculpting or carving, construction of dykes to protect the country against inundation, or similar liberal arts'. The theoretical part of the training was entrusted to teachers in the service of the Fundaties themselves. The practical, vocational part was provided by a master craftsman or an organization in accordance with a contract concluded between the regents of the Fundatie and these external instructors. In contrast with ordinary apprenticeship contracts, these agreements contained detailed stipulations about the actual contents of the training programme. The emphasis was squarely on the instruction side of the apprenticeship relationship, not on an eventual contribution by the orphan to the income of the institute. The Fundaties made an effort to monitor the progress of their pupils during their period of training as closely as possible and to assist them in getting an appointment or setting up shop once their training had been completed.[50]

Alternatives to Apprenticeship

For all their exceptional features, the Fundaties were still indicative of a general trend. The importance of apprenticeship compared with other ways of vocational training and education relatively declined during the very period that has been marked as an era of 'consolidation' of the guild system, viz. between c.1670 and 1800. Willem Frijhoff has characterized this transformation as a shift from an individual learning process in the context of a hierarchical craft relationship towards an autonomous, more codified 'package' of schooling, which no longer was directly related to the workplace and did not require the same degree of individual commitment as in the past.[51]

In many trades and professions outside the guild system in Dutch cities, alternative facilities for training and education first emerged in the late sixteenth and early seventeenth centuries. Next to apprenticeship contracts, which made provisions for instruction during a specific period of *time*, contracts were concluded which arranged instruction on a particular *piece* of knowledge. On 28 November 1642, for example, Hendrick Wildens in Amsterdam bound himself by contract to teach Jacob de Coninck the art of borax refining in the same manner as he had taught Johannes van Ceulen for the sum total of 150 guilders.[52] In 1674, an agreement was concluded between dyers Jacob Loys and Marcelis Bunnens, from Rotterdam and Eindhoven, respectively, which stipulated that Loys would teach Bunnens the art of dying with madder, in return for a payment of 600 guilders.[53] These were not atypical examples. These contracts for instruction 'by the piece' normally related to operations that (still) remained outside the orbit of guild regulation, such as soap boiling, lacquer making or the manufacturing of saltpetre.[54] Moreover, knowledge and skills needed for jobs like surveying, constructing dykes, locks, houses, fortifications or public buildings; or navigating a ship across the ocean could be learned not only through personal instruction from a 'practised hand' but also by attending classes taught by private schoolmasters or lecturers paid from the public purse, who established themselves in the urban centres in the western and northern parts of the United Provinces. In Amsterdam, for instance, it became very easy to find private instructors who were willing and able, at good pay, to teach a variety of courses on mathematical topics, ranging from gauging and bookkeeping to surveying and the art of navigation. Although a number of cities knew separate guilds of schoolmasters,[55] most of these entrepreneurs in the education business were never included in the corporate system.[56] Surgeons in many cities received part of their education from lecturers and professors in the service of town governments. Around the middle of the eighteenth century, schools for professional training of officers, pilots and gunners in the Navy and navigating personnel of the East-India Company and the merchant marine were jointly created by the governments of Amsterdam and Rotterdam and the Admiralties of Amsterdam and De Maze.

In addition, several universities or other institutions of higher learning in the Netherlands in the early seventeenth century began to provide courses, taught in Dutch, on practical mathematics for a nonacademic public. At the 'Duytsche mathematicque', founded as a branch of Leiden University in 1600 at the instance of Prince Maurits, instruction was given on surveying, gauging and fortification. At the University of Franeker, Dutch courses on surveying, fortification and the art of navigation were offered from 1600. At the Athenaeum Illustre in Amsterdam, teaching in Dutch on the art of navigation was, with a few interruptions, provided from 1635 until 1838.[57]

From the late seventeenth century onwards, the range of facilities for training and education outside the apprenticeship system widened in several respects. First, additional facilities for training emerged from the rise of technological literature and collections of models as means for the diffusion of technical knowledge. While the supply of technological literature in Dutch up to the end of the seventeenth century was largely restricted to spheres of knowledge and skills that remained outside the scope of guild regulation (like surveying, gauging, bookkeeping, fortification and the art of navigation), the period between c. 1680 and 1740 saw the appearance of book-length descriptions concerning domains of technical practice, which – in the cities, at least – could be claimed to lie within the realm of competence of craft guilds. The outstanding example were the so-called 'mill books'. The first millbook was published by the Amsterdam publisher Justus Danckerts in 1686. It had been composed by a Swedish millwright, Pieter Linpergh, who had come to the Netherlands with the express purpose of studying Dutch windmills. The *Architectura Mechanica Moole boek* contained both images and verbal explanations of the exterior, gear and annexes of various types of windmills. Linpergh's book, which was reprinted in 1727, was in the 1730s supplanted by two new millbooks composed by millwrights from Holland itself, which surpassed the work of their predecessor in both the quality and quantity of descriptions: the *Theatrum machinarum universale, of groot algemeen moolen-boek* by Johannis van Zyl (with engravings by Jan Schenk) and the *Groot volkomen moolen-boek* by Leendert van Natrus and Jacob Polly (with engravings by Cornelis van Vuuren). In these works, every type of windmill was carefully described and depicted, including specific measurements. The engravings, printed on folio-sized pages, showed almost every relevant detail. Van Zyl's book was later extended to include an equally detailed manual on the construction of other feats of the carpenter's craft, such as the making of staircases.[58]

A similar development took place in the use of models. 'Models', in the sense of three-dimensional representations of real (or potentially real) constructions on a reduced scale, were not unknown in the Netherlands in the sixteenth and early seventeenth centuries. It was not until the end of the seventeenth century, however, that models became increasingly used as instruments for the diffusion of knowledge by the formation and display of large numbers of new or representative specimens of technical capability. The Amsterdam bookseller, theologian and architectural writer Willem Goeree at around 1680 boasted of a large collection of 'architectural models and instruments of force and practice, most accurately drawn in their measures and use', which he opened for public view. In addition to copies of all sorts of buildings and building components, this collection included models of locks, sluices, bridges, cranes, drop hammers, windlasses, pumping devices, minting presses and mechanisms of mills.[59] In the eighteenth century, such 'cabinets' of technical models and instruments were also established at public or private institutions such as naval boards, universities and scientific societies.[60]

Secondly, from the late seventeenth century onwards technical education by way of curricular teaching in groups was extended to include parts of the manufacturing sector as well. The *Amsterdamsche Courant* from the 1680s onwards more than once featured advertisements from private instructors, who offered to teach courses on chemistry or on preparing dyes for calico printing.[61] In the course of the eighteenth century this type of vocational training spread to the building trades, too. Those who aspired to become a master-mason or carpenter, increasingly – in addition to learning craft skills in a workshop by day – took to attending evening classes on drawing and mathematics in order to improve their knowledge of the artistic and theoretical aspects of the building process. These additional facilities for training and education were not only offered by *konstscholen* or *tekencollegies* directed by private instructors, but also after c.1750 by drawing masters in the service of orphanages and drawing schools founded by scientific, drawing or improvement societies, such as *Mathesis Scientiarum Genitrix* in Leiden, *Kunstoefening* in Arnhem or the nationwide *Maatschappij tot Nut van 't Algemeen*, who considered it their duty to promote 'enlightened education'.[62] In contrast with the arrangement in the surgeons' guilds, however, attendance at these courses by apprentices was never made compulsory.

Conclusion

As guilds in the Netherlands had only a limited hold on apprenticeship and the importance of apprenticeship compared with other ways of vocational training, and education was decreasing before the end of the eighteenth century, the abolition of the guilds in the early nineteenth century must have mattered less to the practice of apprenticeship or to the system of training and professional education as a whole than often has been assumed.[63] In the public debate about the pros and cons of guilds, which flared up between 1795 and 1798 and again in 1806–1807, the uses of apprenticeship figured only as a minor argument on the defenders' side. Partisans of the guild system pointed to the vital importance of guilds and guildmembers for the maintenance of quality of goods, the income of the public treasury, the arbitration of disputes within the urban community, the support of the ill, infirm and aged through mutual insurance schemes and the protection of the citizen's livelihood against the intrusion of foreigners and other types of 'outsiders'. Linking up with the new revolutionary discourse, they also argued that liberty could only flourish if bound by a set of social rules and that guildmembers, as 'men and citizens', were entitled to the protection of their rights as well, namely the property right vested in their mastership of a particular craft or trade. As far as the maintenance of quality of goods was concerned, the thrust of the argument was that consumers should be assured that producers of goods were wellqualified in their craft and therefore that entrance to crafts should be restricted to those who had shown proof of their abilities by the making of a masterpiece. In some cases, this call for admission requirements was extended with the demand that new entrants also should have served a certain term of apprenticeship.[64]

In contrast with claims made by a number of Dutch historians, the demise of the guild system did *not* spell the end of vocational training. Craftsmen continued to take on apprentices. Orphanages continued to apprentice their pupils to local craftsmen.[65] Complaints on vocational training which emerged between c.1820 and 1860 did not concern the absence of vocational training as such, but rather aimed at a putative lack of theoretical education, more specifically among native craftsmen in the building trades.[66] This observation suggests that the bottleneck (if there was any) in the training of craftsmen primarily resided in the inability of institutions which in the late eighteenth century had arisen outside the guild system (such as the drawing schools managed by private organizations) to keep up with changing demands of design and production in the building industry. It was not until after about 1860, that criticism of the competence of craftsmen widened to include their practical skills as well and to embrace the entire industrial sector of the Dutch economy.[67]

Why was guild control on apprenticeship in cities in the early modern Netherlands only of relatively limited importance? The explanation cannot merely reside in the generally restricted role of Dutch guilds in political affairs. There is no indication that guild control on appenticeship was more firm and extensive in the few cities in the Netherlands where guilds for a time *did* maintain a certain degree of political power, such as Bois-le-Duc before

1629 or Dordrecht from the Middle Ages to the end of the Old Regime. The stark fact is, that guilds in the Netherlands, with few exceptions, have not even attempted to get a stronger grip on the system of apprenticeship, in order to improve the quality of training and/or to promote the `moral and political socialization' of their future members. Guild regulations on apprenticeship in general rather served as a means to generate corporate revenue by the levying of fees, as a tool to realize a modicum of control on the inflow of new entrants by issuing rules on registration and the duration of apprenticeship and as an instrument to achieve a modest degree of equality among their members by fixing a maximum number of apprentices per master. In this respect, there was no difference between the various *Zunftlandschaften* which Lourens and Lucassen have discerned within the territory of the Dutch Republic.[68] The only exceptions to the rule were the surgeons' guilds, who aspired to a status on a par with a reference group (doctors of medicine) which did not receive its professional training within the guild system at all.

But guilds were not charged to expand their control on apprenticeship either. They were not pressed to extend their supervision of the apprenticeship system. At a deeper level of analysis, the explanation of the relatively limited extent of guild control on apprenticeship in Dutch cities, in my view, should be sought in the ideology and politics of urban elites and the complex of institutions in the urban community they helped to create or preserve. The centre of political power in the Netherlands after c.1580, as is wellknown, was in the provinces and the cities rather in the central agencies of the state. In the context of the Dutch Republic, it would have been extremely unlikely that the matter of apprenticeship, as in England, would have been settled by a state law like the Statute of Artificers. Even the power of provincial governments was in large parts of the Republic heavily circumscribed by the interests of cities. It is significant that the only direct intervention by the States of Holland in apprenticeship affairs (the decree of 1597) was made at the request of the leading city of the province and aimed to combat a perceived social nuisance in the region as a whole rather than to improve training and education of urban apprentices. From the point of view of the most relevant actors, the elites in Dutch cities, guilds were (perhaps to a greater extent than for urban elites in England) very valuable institutions for the regulation of economic life, the preservation of social order and the promotion of the general welfare of the urban community, but by no means the only medium by which these political and ideological goals could be achieved. In this long-term strategy of urban elites, the creation and maintenance of neringen, of charity institutes such as orphanages; of educational facilities such as city schools; or of public institutions for the cultivation of scholarship, such as universities or illustrious schools, anatomical theatres, botanic gardens or municipal chairs in anatomy or botany, assumed no less importance than the protection of the guild system. There was no compelling reason why, in particular, the task of moral socialization and the disciplining of young entrants to the labour force should have been delegated to guilds rather than to other institutions. In 1614, the magistrate of Amsterdam ordered master craftsmen to report every four months on the behaviour of their apprentices and apprentices to report on their treatment by their masters, not to the officers of the guilds, but to the regents of the municipal board of orphans.[69] Finally, urban elites in the highly market-oriented economy of the Netherlands were probably, in contrast to France or Germany, more inclined, if no orphaned children of citizens were involved, to leave the arrangement of apprenticeship relations by and large to the relevant parties themselves rather than ensure that all contractual agreements would be supervised and guaranteed by corporate organizations. Thus, alternative scenarios for the role of guilds in the field of apprenticeship became a historical reality in the case of the Netherlands.

Notes

1. J.R. Farr, *Artisans in Europe, 1300–1914* (Cambridge, 2000), 33–34.
2. S.L. Kaplan, 'l'Apprentissage au XVIIIe siècle : le cas de Paris', *Revue d'histoire moderne et contemporaine*, 40 (1993): 436–79, esp. 436–37, 455–57.
3. A. Griessinger and R. Reith, 'Lehrlinge im deutschen Handwerk des ausgehenden 18. Jahrhunderts', *Zeitschrift für Historische Forschung*, 13 (1986): 149–99, p. 152.
4. J. Lane, *Apprenticeship in England, 1600–1914* (London, 1996), 3–4; Farr, *Artisans.*, 35–36, p. 83.
5. J. Lucassen and M. Prak, 'Guilds and Society in the Dutch Republic (16th–18th Centuries)', in S.R. Epstein et al. (eds), *Guilds, Economy and Society* (Madrid, 1998), 63–77, p. 68–69.
6. N.H.L. van den Heuvel, *De ambachtsgilden van 's-Hertogenbosch vóór 1629* (Utrecht, 1946), 62.
7. N.W. Posthumus (ed.), *Bronnen tot de geschiedenis van de Leidsche textielnijverheid*, vol. VI (The Hague, 1922) no. 450, p. 743, article 14.
8. For detailed information on guild regulations on apprenticeship in one particular craft (tailoring): B. Panhuysen, *Maatwerk. Kleermakers, naaisters, oudkleerkopers en de gilden (1500–1800)* (Amsterdam, 2000): 137–42. For the exception of the surgeons: H. van Eeghen, *De gilden. Theorie en praktijk* (Bussum, 1924), 24.
9. C.A. Davids, 'Amsterdam as a Centre of Learning in the Dutch Golden Age, c. 1580–1700', in P. O'Brien, D. Keene and M.C. 't Hart (eds), *Urban Achievement in Early Modern Europe* (Cambridge, 2001); Van Eeghen, *De gilden*, 83–86; S. Bos, *'Uyt liefde tot malcander'. Onderlinge hulpverlening binnen de Noord-Nederlandse gilden in internationaal perspectief (1570–1820)* (Amsterdam, 1998) 59–60; M.A. van Andel, *Chirurgijns, vrije meesters, beunhazen en kwakzalvers. De chirurgijnsgilden en de praktijk der heelkunde (1400–1800)* (The Hague, 1981) 46–49; M.J. van Lieburg, *Het medisch onderwijs te Rotterdam (1467–1967)* (Amsterdam, 1978), 27–31.
10. GA (Gemeentearchief) Amsterdam 27, Archief Collegium Medicum nr. 3 minutes, 14 January 1734, f. 273–74; A.E. Leuftink, *Harde heelmeesters. Zeelieden en hun dokters in de 18de eeuw* (Zutphen, 1991), 30–36; Van Lieburg, *Het Medisch onderwijs*, 28–32.
11. S.R. Epstein, 'Craft Guilds, Apprenticeship and Technological Change in Preindustrial Europe', *The Journal of Economic History*, 58 (1998): 684–713, p. 694 note 43.
12. R.W. Unger, *Dutch Shipbuilding Before 1800* (Assen, 1978), 76; A. de Groot, 'De Arnhemsche ambachtsgilden in de 17de en 18de eeuw', *Bijdragen en Mededeelingen Gelre* XLII (1930), 79–119, p.102; M. Hulshof, 'De gilden', in: K. Goudriaan et al. (eds), *De gilden in Gouda* (Zwolle, 1997), 115.
13. Hulshof, 'De gilden', 91; De Groot, 'Arnhemsche ambachtsgilden', 103; Unger, *Dutch Shipbuilding*, 76; Van Eeghen, *De gilden*, 109.

14. C. Plomp, 'Het leerlingwezen in Den Haag van de 15de tot de 18de eeuw', *Die Haghe Jaarboek* 1936, 3–35, pp. 17–18.
15. J.G. van Dillen (ed.), *Bronnen tot de geschiedenis van het bedrijfsleven en het gildewezen van Amsterdam*, 3 vols. I–III, (The Hague 1929–1974); see also Plomp, 'Het leerlingwezen', 24, and R. de Jager, 'Meester, leerjongen, leertijd. Een analyse van zeventiende-eeuwse Noord-Nederlandse leerlingcontracten van kunstschilders, goud- en zilversmeden', *Oud Holland*, 104 (1990): 69–111, pp. 70, 80.
16. Van Dillen (ed.), *Bronnen*, II, 523 nr. 920.
17. See, for example, Van Eeghen, *De gilden*, and H. Noordkerk (ed.), *Handvesten, ofte privilegien ende octroyen ... der stad Amsterdam* (Amsterdam, 1748–1778) (Amsterdam), De Groot, 'Arnhemsche ambachtsgilden' (Arnhem), Van den Heuvel, *De ambachtsgilden van 's-Hertogenbosch;* M. Prak, *Republikeinse veelheid, democratisch enkelvoud. Sociale verandering in het Revolutietijdvak 's- Hertogenbosch 1770–1820* (Nijmegen 1999) 88–92, 98–101 (Bois-le-Duc); Hulshof, 'De gilden' (Gouda); Plomp, 'Het leerlingwezen in Den Haag van de 15de tot de 18de eeuw', *Die Haghe Jaarboek* 1936, 3-35 (The Hague); and P.H.M.G. Offermans, *Arbeid en levenstandaard in Nijmegen (1550–1600)* (Zutphen, 1972), 77–99, and F.C. Berkenvelder, 'De gilden te Zwolle tot 1600', *Overijsselse Historische Bijdragen,* 104 (1989): 7–32 (Zwolle).
18. P. Lourens and J. Lucassen, 'Ambachtsgilden binnen een handelskapitalistische stad: aanzetten voor een analyse van Amsterdam circa 1700', *NEHA-Jaarboek voor de economische, bedrijfs- en techniekgeschiedenis*, 61 (1998): 121–62, pp.160–62.
19. According to the survey of guilds in the Netherlands by P. Lourens and J. Lucassen, 'Ambachtsgilden in Nederland: een eerste inventarisatie', *NEHA-Jaarboek voor de economische, bedrijfs- en techniekgeschiedenis*, 57 (1994): 34–62, esp. 61, the number of guilds in the Zaanstreek amounted to no more than three; Unger, *Dutch Shipbuilding*, 5, 84–85.
20. Algemeen Rijksarchief Archief (ARA) Verenigde Oostindische Compagnie (VOC) 277, 27 April 1769.
21. A.M. van der Woude (ed.), 'De Goldberg-enquête in het Departement van Texel, 1801', *AAG Bijdragen* 18 (1973): 95–251, esp. 132, 136, 151, 159, 170, 179, 202, 218. The informed guess on the number of workers per shop is based on the figures from the shop of Pieter Schram & Co in Zaandijk.
22. See Van Dillen (ed.), vols I–III. Information on guild-regulated crafts was derived from Van Eeghen, *De gilden*, and Lourens and Lucassen, 'Ambachtsgilden', esp. 157–59.
23. See Posthumus (ed.), *Bronnen*, III–VI.
24. In notarial deeds concerning conflicts about the implementation of apprenticeship contracts no reference is made to intervention by a guild. See, for example, Van Dillen (ed.), *Bronnen*, III, 63–64 nr. 134, 91 nr. 187, 109–110 nr. 224.
25. A.E.C. McCants, *Civic Charity in a Golden Age: Orphan Care in Early Modern Amsterdam* (Urbana/Chicago, 1997), 70; S. Groenveld, J.J.H. Dekker, Th.R.M. Willemse, *Wezen en boefjes. Zes eeuwen zorg in wees- en kinderhuizen* (Hilversum, 1997), 210.
26. J. Spaans, *Armenzorg in Friesland 1500–1800. Publieke zorg en particuliere liefdadigheid in zes Friese steden* (Hilversum, 1997), 152; C. Esseboom, *Onderwysinghe der jeught. Onderwijs en onderwijstoezicht in de 18e eeuw op het Eiland van Dordrecht* (Ridderkerk, 1995), 39.
27. E. Muller and K. Zandvliet, *Admissies als landmeter in Nederland vóór 1811* (Alphen a/d Rijn, 1987), 17–19, 61, 75–77, 95–98, 109, 124, 151–54, 194; in some provinces a certificate of competence could be issued by a provincial university.
28. F.A. van Lieburg, *Profeten en hun vaderland. De geografische herkomst van de gereformeerde predikanten in Nederland van 1572 tot 1816* (Amsterdam, 1996), 77–78.
29. J.A.M.M. Janssen, *Op weg naar Breda. De opleiding van officieren voor het Nederlandse leger tot aan de oprichting van de Koninklijke Militaire Academie in 1828* (The Hague, 1989), 82–89.
30. C.A. Davids, *Zeewezen en wetenschap. De wetenschap en de ontwikkeling van de navigatietechniek in Nederland tussen 1585 en 1815* (Amsterdam/Dieren, 1986), 294–300;

Leuftink, *Harde heelmeesters*, 29–36, 183; surgeons of whalers and merchants were examined by officers of the surgeons' guilds in the main port cities of the Dutch Republic.

31. C.A. Davids, 'Neringen, hallen en gilden. Kapitalisten, kleine ondernemers en stedelijke overheid in de tijd van de Republiek', in C.A. Davids, W. Fritschy and L.A. van der Valk (eds), *Kapitaal, ondernemerschap en beleid. Studies over economie en politiek in Nederland, Europa en Azië van 1500 tot heden* (Amsterdam, 1996), 95–121, pp. 95–97.
32. Noordkerk (ed.), *Handvesten*, I, Ordonnantie op de neeringe van het goud- en zilverdraadtrekken en voor het werkvolk, 11 July 1696, 1096, art. 11 and 12.
33. Posthumus (ed.), *Bronnen*, vols III–VI, passim.
34. Posthumus (ed.), *Bronnen*, III, no. 271, p. 489–90, VI, no. 128, pp. 205–206.
35. Posthumus (ed.), *Bronnen*, III, no. 100, pp. 115–16, V, no. 236 pp. 301–302; see also VI, no. 128 p. 205–206 (1759).
36. Posthumus (ed.), *Bronnen*, IV, no. 302, pp. 363–64, V, no. 366, pp. 475–77, VI, no. 463, p.773.
37. C. Cau (ed.), *Groot placaet-boeck vervattende de placaeten en ordonnanciën en de edicten van de Staten-Generaal etc*, I, (The Hague, 1658); Placaet waer nae alle ambachts-jongens ende haerluyden meesters hen sullen reguleren binnen den landen van Hollandt ende West-Vrieslandt, 2 September 1597, 514–16; res. States of Holland, 1 January 1596, ff.1–7, 2 September 1597 f. 421–22. Cf. Lane, *Apprenticeship*, 4.
38. I. van der Vlis, *Leven in armoede. Delftse bedeelden in de zeventiende eeuw* (Amsterdam, 2001), 38–39, 45.
39. McCants, *Civic Charity*, 63–64, 70–82; W. Frijhoff, *Wegen van Evert Willemsz. Een Hollands weeskind op zoek naar zichzelf 1607–1647* (Nijmegen, 1995), 262; Groenveld et al., *Wezen en boefjes*, 209–11, H. Van Wijngaarden, *Zorg voor de kost. Armenzorg, arbeid en onderlinge hulp in Zwolle 1650–1700* (Amsterdam, 2000), 187.
40. Van Dillen (ed.), *Bronnen*, III, 63 nr. 133; cf. II, pp.774–75 nr. 1385
41. N.W. Posthumus, *De geschiedenis van de Leidsche lakenindustrie*, III (The Hague, 1939), 608–13; idem, 'Kinderarbeid in de zeventiende eeuw in Delft', *Economisch-Historisch Jaarboek*, 22 (1943): 49–67; J.C. Vleggeert, *Kinderarbeid in Nederland 1500–1874* (Assen, 1964), 9–11; Van der Vlis, *Leven in armoede*, 300–25; McCants, *Civic Charity*, 84–86; Van Eeghen, *De gilden*, 23; Spaans, *Armenzorg*, 330–34.
42. J.R. Bruijn, 'De personeelsbehoefte van de VOC overzee en aan boord, bezien in Aziatisch en Nederlands perspectief', *Bijdragen en Mededelingen betreffende de Geschiedenis der Nederlanden*, 91 (1976): 218–48, pp. 241–42, McCants, *Civic Charity*, 64–70; A. Zuurbier, *Het Burgerweeshuis te Haarlem 1765–1908* (unpubl. M.A. thesis, Leiden, 1990), 42–43.
43. McCants, *Civic Charity*, 70–82, 89, 200–202.
44. Van Eeghen, *De gilden*, 23–24, 107–108.
45. McCants, *Civic Charity*, 76.
46. J.L. van Daalen, *Geschiedenis van Dordrecht* (Dordrecht, 1931), 380: all trades where orphans were placed, except the brushmakers, were organized either in guilds or *confreries* (guild-like institutions). Cf. also the few data on other cities in the Dutch Republic in Groenveld et al. , *Wezen en boefjes*, 207–08, and Frijhoff, *Evert Willemsz*, 264–65.
47. Cf. also G.P.M. Pot, *Arm Leiden. Levensstandaard, bedeling en bedeelden, 1750–1854* (Hilversum, 1994), 65.
48. Van Eeghen, *De gilden*, 11.
49. GA Leiden, Archief Heilige Geest en Arme Wees- en Kinderhuis nr. 3863.
50. E.P. de Booy and J. Engel, *Van erfenis tot studiebeurs. De Fundatie van de vrijvrouwe van Renswoude te Delft* (Delft, 1985), 17–23, 51–57, 90–144, 161.
51. W. Frijhoff, 'Van onderwijs naar opvoedend onderwijs. Ontwikkelingslijnen van opvoeding en onderwijs in Noord-Nederland in de achttiende eeuw', in *Onderwijs en opvoeding in de achttiende eeuw. Verslag van het symposium, Doesburg 1982* (Amsterdam/Maarssen, 1983), 3–40, pp. 28–29.
52. Van Dillen (ed.), *Bronnen*, III, 353 nr. 680.
53. C. Wiskerke, 'De geschiedenis van het meekrapbedrijf in Nederland', *Economisch-Historisch Jaarboek*, 25 (1949–1951), 1–144, pp. 5–6.

54. Van Dillen (ed.), *Bronnen*, III, 437 nr. 840, 488 nr. 942, 508 nr. 977, 677 nr. 1440; the dyers in Rotterdam were not organized in a guild until 1717; H.C. Hazewinkel, *Geschiedenis van Rotterdam* (Zaltbommel 1974), III, 830.
55. For examples in Middelburg, Gouda and Leiden, see A. Dekker, 'Het ontstaan van de ordonnantie op de scholen van 1591 te Middelburg', *Archief Zeeuwsch Genootschap* (1941–1942), 21–24; Hulshof, 'De gilden', 139–44; and GA Leiden, Bibliotheek nr. 50840 *Ordonnantie van het schoolmeestersgilde binnen der stad Leiden* (Leiden, 1689); The database on guilds at the IISG (International Institute for Social History) also includes schoolmaster guilds in The Hague, Bois-le-Duc, Haarlem and Delfshaven (communciation by Jan Lucassen, Amsterdam, November 2000).
56. C.A. Davids, 'Ondernemers in kennis. Het zeevaartkundig onderwijs in de Republiek gedurende de zeventiende eeuw', *De zeventiende eeuw*, 7 (1991): 37–48 esp. 39, 41–44; C.A. Davids, J.A. van der Veen and E.A.. de Vries, 'Van Lastman tot Gietermaker. Claes Hendricksz. Gietermaker (1621–1667) en zijn leerboeken voor de stuurmanskunst', *Tijdschrift voor Zeegeschiedenis*, 8 (1989): 149–78.
57. C.A. Davids, 'Universiteiten, illustre scholen en de verspreiding van technische kenis in Nederland, eind 16[e] – begin 19[e] eeuw', *Batavia Academica*, VIII (1990), 3–34, esp. 5–6, 8, 12.
58. C.A. Davids, 'The Transfer of Windmill Technology From the Netherlands to North-eastern Europe From the 16th to the Early 19th Century', in J.P.S. Lemmink and J.S.A.M. van Koningsbrugge (eds), *Baltic Affairs: Relations Between the Netherlands and North-eastern Europe 1500–1800* (Nijmegen, 1990), 33–52, pp. 43–44; van Zyl, *Theatrum machinarum universale , of groot algemeen moolen-boek* (Amsterdam, 1734).
59. Goeree, 'Preface',in *d'Algemeene bouwkunst* (Amsterdam, 1681); van den Heuvel, `Willem Goeree (1635–1711) en de ontwikkeling van een algemene architectuurtheorie in de Nederlanden', *Bulletin KNOB*, 96 (1997): 154–76, esp. pp.167–69.
60. A. Lemmers, *Techniek op schaal. Modellen en het technologiebeleid van de Marine 1725–1885* (Amsterdam 1996), 15–42; P. de Clercq, `In de schaduw van 's Gravesande. Het Leids Physisch Kabinet in de tweede helft van de achttiende eeuw', *Tijdschrift voor de Geschiedenis der Geneeskunde, Natuurwetenschappen, Wiskunde en Techniek*, 10 (1987): 149–89; G. l'E. Turner, *Van Marum's Scientific Instruments in Teyler's Museum: Descriptive Catalogue* (Haarlem, n.d.), 173–86.
61. L. van Nierop, 'Gegevens over de nijverheid van Amsterdam bijeengelezen uit de advertenties in de Amsterdamsche Courant', *Jaarboek Amstelodamum*, 27 (1930): 271, 300 and 28 (1931), 119.
62. E.B.M. Lottman, 'De bijdrage van de Amsterdamse weeshuizen aan de bouwkundige opleiding in de achttiende eeuw', *Jaarboek Amstelodamum*, 69 (1977): 140–55; idem, `De bijdrage van de Rotterdamse en Schiedamse "tekenscholen" aan het bouwkundig onderwijs circa 1750–1850', *Rotterdams Jaarboekje* 9[de] reeks, 1 (1983): 243–72; C.A. van Swigchem, *Abraham van der Hart 1747–1820. Architect, stadsbouwmeester van Amsterdam* (Amsterdam, 1965), 323–27; N.B. Goudswaard, *Vijfenzestig jaren nijverheidsonderwijs* (Assen, 1981), 12–16; C.P. Krabbe, *Ambacht, kunst, wetenschap. De bevordering van de bouwkunst in Nederland (1775–1880)* (Amsterdam, 1997), 20–29, 37–41.
63. H.P. Meppelink, *Technisch vakonderwijs voor jongens in Nederland in de 19[e] eeuw* (Utrecht, 1961), 101–102, Goudswaard, *Vijfenzestig jaren*, 10–12; D. van Lente, *Techniek en ideologie. Opvattingen over de maatschappelijke betekenis van technische vernieuwingen in Nederland, 1850–1920* (Groningen, 1988), 82–83; H. Schippers, *Van tusschenlieden tot ingenieurs. De geschiedenis van het Hoger Technisch Onderwijs in Nederland* (Hilversum, 1989), 17; G.P.J. Verbong, 'Gescheiden paden', in H.W. Lintsen et al. (eds), *Techniek in Nederland*, vol. V, *Techniek, Beroep en bedrijf* (Zutphen, 1994), 51–84. p .61. For a recent, dissenting view, see Krabbe, *Ambacht*, 18–19.
64. C.A. Davids, 'From De la Court to Vreede: Regulation and Self-regulation in Dutch Economic discourse from c. 1660 to the Napoleonic Era', *The Journal of European Economic History*, 30 (2001): 345–289; Prak, *Republikeinse veelheid*, 279–84; C. Wiskerke, *De afschaffing der gilden in Nederland* (Amsterdam, 1938), pp. 96–118, 169–89; M.G. de Boer, 'De ondergang der Amsterdamsche gilden', *Tijdschrift voor Geschiedenis*, 47 (1932):

129–49, 225–45; H. Cohen-Koster, 'De afschaffing van de gilden in Haarlem', *Haerlem Jaarboek 1969* (Haarlem, 1970), 74–127, esp. pp. 89–93.

65. GA Leiden, Heilige Geest en Arme Wees- en Kinderhuis nr. 3862; the registers of apprenticed boys continue without interruption until 1870.
66. See the complaints discussed in Meppelink, *Technisch vakonderwijs*, 95–98.
67. Meppelink, *Technisch vakonderwijs*, 98.
68. P. Lourens and J. Lucassen, '"Zunftlandschaften" in den Niederlanden und im benachbarten Deutschland', in W. Reininghaus (ed.), *Zunftlandschaften in Deutschland und den Niederlanden im Vergleich* (Münster, 1999), 11–43.
69. Noordkerk (ed.), *Handvesten*, II, 456.

Chapter 5

Construction and Reproduction

The Training and Skills of Antwerp Cabinetmakers in the Sixteenth and Seventeenth Centuries

Bert De Munck

Apprenticeship in the Ancien Régime is included as a matter of course when studying the traditional trades, and rightly so: the apprenticeship system cannot be seen apart from the corporate organizational structures in which it existed.[1] As the study of traditional trades moves forward, re-evaluations in that area will have important consequences for studies of apprenticeship – and a great deal has changed since the introduction of the term *proto-industrialization*. The key terms used to describe craft guilds have long had pejorative connotations: exclusivity, conservatism and heredity.[2] Inevitably this has had a number of important consequences for the historical view of apprenticeship. Apprenticeship was approached primarily as an instrument in the hands of the masters, in the context of their control over the labour market and access to master status. Recently, however, other views of the trades have come to the fore:[3] the realization of complex market strategies such as investment in quality and innovation and the resulting opportunities created in certain sectors and professions.[4] On the European continent and in the Southern Netherlands in particular, remarkable cycles of product innovation and product differentiation have been observed.[5] In the final decades of the sixteenth and the first half of the seventeenth centuries import substitution, expansion of ranges and the use of artistic creativity enabled many urban sectors (addressing problems related to access to foreign markets) to recreate a flourishing export industry.[6]

Catharina Lis and Hugo Soly believe that such a development was only possible because of the way trades and production networks had been organized; they not only pointed to the role of major producers in this process, but stressed the importance of the innovative and progressive forces that were manifested within and because of the trades, rather than the reverse.[7] This sheds interesting light on the role of apprenticeship and learning processes. It is only logical that a need for innovation and creativity bring about a well organized, vital apprenticeship system that fulfils an essential role within the trades. Large-scale entrepreneurs, who often played leading roles in the trades,[8] would have everything to gain from allowing knowledge, creativity and skills to develop.[9] The complexity of this hypothesis should be borne in mind, however. Discussions on the transmission of methods and techniques in the context of migrations and '*Wander*' (travel) phenomena indicate that it has not yet been established precisely when and under what conditions knowledge and skills were transferred most effectively. While in some instances new impulses were especially welcome, in others '*les secrets de métier*' (trade secrets) were jealously delineated and guarded. For example, a Wander obligation – despite the widespread principle of *imitatio* (imitation/emulation)[10] – was not necessarily organised with a view to the passing on of skills.[11] The same question should be asked with regard to apprenticeship. Were apprenticeships in fact organized to allow knowledge and skills to be passed on and developed? And if not, when did other considerations become more important?

The case study presented here examines the situation among cabinetmakers in Antwerp. We will see that in the late sixteenth and early seventeenth century – especially after the blockade of the Scheldt – a fairly drastic realignment of the Antwerp (export) economy took place. Manufacturers and merchants began focusing increasingly on products in which the loss of sizeable market shares was offset by operating in higher price categories.[12] Classic examples are the diamond sector, the gold- and silversmiths, and silk production, but cabinetmakers, too, began targeting a wealthier buying public. Luxury articles increasingly found their way to foreign markets,[13] and the importance of the art sector for cabinetmakers, as well as quality, became more prominent.[14] In the well known *cantooren*, for example, ornamentation became excessive, structural elements more complex, and different types of wood were more frequently found in a single cabinet.[15] This shift towards luxury and semi-luxury products had consequences for the apprenticeship system.[16] One of these may be that higher quality was required of the apprenticeships regulated by that particular trade. The length of an apprenticeship term could, for example, be increased, and the requirements for the master-piece that had to be submitted for evaluation (theoretically) at the end of that period could be made more complex and difficult.

In the first section of this chapter it will become apparent that the situation was more complex among the Antwerp cabinetmakers. The apprenticeship system cannot simply be reduced to the generation and transfer of skills and knowledge, for the evaluation of craftsmen should be viewed in a wider perspective. It will be shown that the apprenticeship system (especially one of its major aspects, registration and income fees) was indeed important for regulating the labour market, albeit in a surprising way: it was diametrically opposed to corporate 'exclusivity'. The master-piece, moreover, was indeed important for evaluating apprentices or journeymen and for sanctioning certain skills, but it did not become correspondingly more complex and demanding. The evolution of the trial reflects evolutions in the product market as well as in the labour market. Changes in productive structures from the late sixteenth century on led to increased specialization, along with a lessening of overall skill levels. To preserve the image and prestige of the masters and their products, the importance of skills and quality gradually shifted to a representative level. Subsequently, this chapter will examine the 'construction' of skill and the preservation of the product quality in a broader sense. It is known that certain skills were (and are) not valued in direct proportion to their importance in the production chain, and that the perception of skills differs according to the status of the groups involved, distinguishing, for example, schooled journeymen from common labourers.[17] There is a similar issue for the employers. The appreciation of a particular (luxury) product depends at least partly on a belief in the skill of the artisan. Therefore, an important question is the extent to which apprenticeship and the master-piece, the central concepts in the corporate production system, played a role in the construction of artisan skills and of the quality of their products. This chapter will begin by questioning the construction of the cabinetmakers trade.

Construction of the Cabinetmaker

As has often been the case for trade disputes, many of the conflicts and legal proceedings among the cabinetmakers were centred on defining precisely which work they had the right to engage in, and to which work they had exclusive rights.[18] Initially, the disputes between cabinetmakers and carpenters appeared to be the most important, for there were many overlapping areas in the market segment targeted by the two groups. One crucial dispute led to a ruling in 1435 that would serve as a basis for centuries to come. The work of carpenters was strongly anchored in the construction sector, while the cabinetmakers concentrated primarily on the manufacture of furniture.[19] What is striking is that both groups were involved in the construction and furnishing of homes. In reality, therefore, the market was the same; it was only defined who could do what in that particular market, i.e. for the same (local) clients.[20] But from that time onwards, cabinetmakers were distinguished from carpenters according to skills. While carpenters worked with beams and large constructions, cabinetmakers worked with plane and chisel.[21] It is little wonder that further conflicts arose with sculptors and tableau carvers. In 1477 there was a dispute about which group should be allowed to make the substructures of altar tables and tableaux.[22] The problem was that cabinetmakers' journeymen had been making those substructures, so that the monopoly of the masters was circumvented. Yet for the cabinetmakers it was not simply a matter of jealously guarding their monopoly, for in the course of the conflict they stated that the sculptors were not capable of doing the job themselves.[23] It was precisely because of the overlap in market segments that dealt with an artistic craft that there arose particular sensitivity about the skills required. Cabinetmakers only made the substructures, while the more artistic carving work was reserved for the members of the Saint Luke's guild, but the cabinetmakers could not resist pointing out their own abilities as well.[24] The conflict marked the birth of a long territorial dispute that from the beginning was linked to having special skills and competence.

The positions became even more sharply defined in the course of the sixteenth century. In 1518 a discussion arose, again between carpenters and cabinetmakers, about the marketing of goods and the use of glue. The carpenters claimed that they were fully within their rights in manufacturing cabinetmaking products, to the extent that they were able to make these and as long as they did not transport the products to the market or use glue.[25] Nevertheless, the authorities found in favour of their opponents, with the result that all 'panel work' continued to be the preserve of cabinetmakers.[26] Panel work was defined as modern, attractive furniture built with a framework fitted with mortise and tenon joints, not rough boxes or heavy, coarse cupboards.[27] Cabinets were being built in a wide variety of sizes and shapes, and were becoming the core of the cabinetmakers' trade. Thus, in the process of defining the purview of each trade, distinctions were drawn between marketing of goods and contracting out of work, as well as regarding the 'art' of creating the product. In a new conflict in 1525, for example, the cabinetmakers commented that carpenters did not have to produce a masterpiece, and that anyone could begin practising the craft, including those who had no carpentry skill.[28] This time it was ruled that carpenters could make the same objects as cabinetmakers as long as they were fixtures, i.e. as long as they were immovable and could not be taken to the market. Thus was created a relationship between skill and the sole right to market and export furniture. Highly significant in this respect is that, in addition to the ban on building movable pieces and using glue, carpenters were not allowed to incorporate carving in their work.[29] The carving of corners and panels was already an important feature of more expensive furniture in the fifteenth century, but the emphasis on virtuosity associated with this skill only increased.[30] In short, cabinetmakers not only had to have the sole right to market such products, they also had to be recognized as the only ones able to make them. That all this was crucial especially for qualified masters (that is to say: guild members) is evident from legal battles with rag and bone merchants. The Antwerp cabinetmakers not only complained because these craftsmen – who were considered inferior – were imitating their pieces, but also because they were doing so with the help of free and unfree jouneymen.[31] We can assume that many of these rag and bone men or their journeymen were indeed incapable of doing this work themselves, but the issue is not whether cabinetmakers were or were not permitted to carry out their work. It is rather which cabinetmakers would be allowed to do so. In addition to the issue of skill, there was one of free and unfree labour. It did not matter whether or not the work was carried out on the instructions of rag and bone men. The point is that only masters were permitted to do (or supervise) such work. Significantly, and in contrast to free and unfree journeymen, only masters were required to produce a trial piece. A free cabinetmaker was therefore someone who was not only permitted to build certain pieces, but also someone with the skill to do so. The identity of the cabinetmaker was linked to the quality of the product and vice versa. The fact that the apprenticeship played a key role in this identity is self-evident.

Declining Importance of Apprenticeship?

To date, questions about the extent to which the different apprenticeships were tailored to the manufactured products have generally been limited to the length of those apprenticeships: was the length of the apprenticeship term related to the degree of difficulty of the trade to be learned?[32] If a discrepancy was observed between the complexity of the required skills and knowledge on the one hand and the length of the apprenticeship term on the other, the regulation of the labour market by the masters was deemed to be the force responsible. First, access to the trade was often closed to newcomers, which meant that the apprenticeship term tended to be longer than necessary to learn the requisite skills. Second, apprentices were often tied to their master for longer than strictly necessary so that they could be used as cheap labour. The efficient organization of apprenticeships was subordinate to the reproduction of a sufficiently large and flexible labour potential for a limited number of masters.[33] A relatively long apprenticeship term would be the consequence from both perspectives. Yet setting higher demands with regard to skills would also have given rise to longer apprenticeship terms. Seen from any perspective, therefore, a trend towards longer terms would have been expected. Nevertheless, this was not the case for the sixteenth and seventeenth-century Antwerp cabinetmakers.

In 1497 the apprenticeship term for cabinetmakers was increased from two to three years,[34] which in all likelihood is attributable to a real shift in the degree of difficulty of the craft. Not only did the increase in the training requirement occur in the context of distinguishing cabinetmakers from coopers (who engaged in a craft that was probably easier to learn than cabinet making)[35], there were major changes from the 'Roman' style of furniture to the Gothic during the fifteenth century.[36] Also important in this regard is the unusual addition that apprentices or masters could extend the period of apprenticeship even further as they saw fit.[37] While three years may have been sufficient for learning to build simpler furniture, the extended period may indicate the need for a longer training period to create products for more luxurious market segments. Therefore, the new privilege may have afforded the opportunity to respond flexibly to changing needs. At the same time, however, production remained largely linked to a set of standards, and a master who dared take on an apprentice for less than three years could expect a heavy fine. This suggests that the trade intended to apply quality norms and prescriptions.[38] The length of the prescribed apprenticeship definitely played a role in the guild's concern about product quality, albeit one that appears to have disappeared as the sixteenth century progressed. As early as 1515, the response to a complaint about neglecting the apprenticeship period was to prescribe a more difficult trial piece, rather than to require more stringent supervision for compliance with the apprenticeship terms.[39] Moreover, before the sixteenth century was half over, the apprenticeship term was again reduced to two years, precisely at a period in which cabinetmaking appears to have become more difficult.[40] Was the master-piece more important for the purpose of sanctioning skills than the length of the apprenticeship term? When the ebony workers were grouped with the cabinetmakers in 1621, following conflicts with the Saint Luke's Guild, the apprenticeship term for these craftsmen was also only two years.[41] Telling is the fact that the ebony workers acquired international fame in the seventeenth century by manufacturing and exporting luxury furniture. Their products were obviously finer, more complex work than the more stereotypical items of furniture of the fifteenth and early sixteenth centuries;[42] yet they were not required to have a longer apprenticeship term – quite the reverse. Despite frequent complaints about workmen who managed to enter the trade without the necessary skills, the short apprenticeship remained unchanged until the cabinetmakers merged with the carpenters in 1756.[43] In fact, the length of the apprenticeship was determined more by the free market than by the guilds. For the most part the terms agreed upon in indentures were longer than those prescribed, suggesting that the latter did not correspond to the difficulty of the trade.[44] It is true that in the negotiations between a master and the family of an apprentice, skills were not the only factor involved – the length of the term differed according to the price paid – but the inflexibility of the prescribed term underscores the difficulties the guilds faced as a consequence of specialization and product innovation.

Increasing Importance of the Master-piece?

Possible explanations for the short apprenticeship term are that only a few basic skills needed to be learned, or the specializations were specific and relatively simple. Do developments relating to creation of a master-piece support this hypothesis? That the trial piece was not simply an accidental survival from earlier periods can be demonstrated from the fact that they were only established somewhere between the end of the fifteenth and the beginning of the seventeenth centuries.[45] It is also not coincidental that at the end of the fifteenth century the cabinetmakers' trial piece entailed creating three items of furniture: two different cabinets and a table.[46] We can assume that this and other modifications of the trial piece occurred to some extent as a response to the change in the range of products manufactured.[47] Also important was the additional requirement that the items had to be of 'reasonable size',[48] which can be found several times. The ultimate piece of work had to meet a number of fixed dimensions and standards, which may indicate further standardization. Peter Stabel believes that apprenticeship (in medieval Flanders) was intended develop a system for adapting apprentices and journeymen to guild norms of standardized product quality.[49] But what precisely was tested in the trial piece, and how did this change during the sixteenth and seventeenth centuries?

As early as 1515 it became apparent that the requirements for creation of the master-piece were inadequate to control access to the labour market. The craft guild commented that some succeeded in producing the trial piece and becoming masters, yet knew very little of the craft. This was further exacerbated by the fact that the entrance fee was relatively low.[50] Yet the response by the trade was not to institute more stringent regulations, despite the fact that cabinetmaking really depended on skill, and cabinetmakers were better trained than, say, wood-breakers. They could well have responded to this situation by requiring a more difficult master-piece. But the plan that was put in place points in the opposite direction: the trial piece became simpler. Initially, the requirement was to build the three pieces according to a model, which as far as quality construction based on standards was concerned, was one step further than working according to precise dimensions.[51] In 1543, however, a new change occurred, caused by transformations in the market situation. Henceforth one piece would be sufficient. This single piece was to be in the form of a round or square (at the discretion of the deacons) *dressoir* (sideboard), which, it was added, had to be of better quality than had been required to date.[52] Officially, the justification was that this rationalization was introduced to relieve the burden on those wishing to enter the trade,[53] but the change also coincided with shifts in demand for the product. The ranks of well-to-do merchants and prosperous businessmen were growing, and the exporting of more expensive products was becoming more important.[54] To a certain extent this export market was concentrated in a specific type of cabinet, the 'art cabinet'. At the same time, an ever-increasing variation appeared within the boundaries of that range, and there are indications that in the same period and in certain circles the *dressoir* became a sort of status symbol.[55] The fact that only one cabinet now had to be built for the master-piece may have been the result of a strategy that adapted the transfer and sanctioning of skills to the product to be made, especially as freedom within the genre of cabinets had become greater. The strategy may have been to preserve sanctioning of the necessary skills, while also allowing a degree of flexibility.[56] For each apprentice or journeymen, the deacons could ad hoc decide precisely which dressoir had to be made. Consequently, they could not only adjust the pieces produced to changing tastes and norms, they could also tailor the evaluation of an apprentice to the specific training he had had.[57] After all, the production side played a role as well. Later this chapter will probe deeper into the relationship between small-scale masters, on the one hand, and large-scale merchants or entrepreneurs on the other, but for now it can be safely assumed that cabinetmakers often had their own individual specialities, which means that the subject matter of an apprenticeship was different in different workshops. Only by allowing a certain degree of flexibility in the master-piece could the craft continue to reproduce itself. This is particularly evident from the fact that when the ebony workers were incorporated with the cabinetmakers, the trial piece of the ebony workers was defined as the foot of a crucifix.[58] Anyone familiar with their magnificent work knows that this bore no relation to what they really did. At best, after abandoning the custom of requiring large, fixed models, only a few basic cabinetmaking skills were tested.

In the new cultural-economic context of baroque Antwerp, the inability of the guilds to require demonstration of skills in a meticulous master-piece as a condition for becoming a master did not necessarily imply a decline in the importance of the trial, but rather that such a trial may no longer have been a true test of the aspirant's ability to create the handmade products desired by the market. As with the apprenticeship term, the master piece and the work desired by the market were no longer the same. The trial even ceased to function as a tool for evaluating skills. The guild's accounts show no sign of masters having failed the test, casting doubt on whether the master-piece indeed functioned as a selective device. In 1543 it had been explicitly stated that any prospective master not able to make the required pieces properly had to study for an additional year, yet in subsequent ordinances the guild board no longer even considered the possibility of failure.[59] Moreover, while masters typically worked with journeymen on their premises, only masters were tested, implying that more than half the workforce was not. Unusually, in 1543 the carpenters did prescribe separate trials for journeymen and masters (one at the end of the apprenticeship term and the other upon becoming a master); later on only masters had to create such a test piece, leaving the majority of producers untested.[60] Indeed, it is puzzling why the requirement to produce a master-piece continued in force up to the end of the eighteenth century. In the following we will see that especially in the seventeenth and eighteenth centuries, the large *meubles d'apparat* (display cabinets) of the ebony workers and other cabinetmakers were rarely the work of the same artisan.[61] They were manufactured by a wide variety of specialized masters, probably working for large entrepreneurs, art dealers or rag and bone men. Did the latter use the guild's regulations to raise the quality of their renowned commodities, or did the majority of the (small) masters cling to the apprenticeship to defend their own standing?

The Creation of New Artisans and the Recruitment of Specialists

In all systems of education and training the goal is to create new expert practitioners. Thus it is legitimate to ask to what extent the social system among the Antwerp cabinetmakers was aimed at creating autonomous masters or craftsmen (i.e. producers who both designed the furniture and made it from start to finish). It is clear that at this time the degree of family continuity was relatively low, and that there were already a number of large, fairly integrated companies in the early sixteenth century. This is evidenced from the complaints that the large-scale masters often employed ten, twelve or even more 'piece workers' (*stuck werkers*) and made additional (illegal) profits on their work.[62] Despite the complaints, the average company size did not increase during the sixteenth and seventeenth centuries. In 1519 the craft chamber agreed to set the maximum number of employees at six,[63] and in spite of the low fines by seventeenth-century standards,[64] did not have to take up this issue again.[65] As late as 1755, in the merger with the carpenters, the maximum of six employees was felt to be perfectly acceptable.[66] Nevertheless, this does not mean that these were small-scale, autonomous companies led by one master operating independently. Gradually, the entire production became dominated by a handful of large-scale master-entrepreneurs. Their colleagues, often in their own studios, were only active in networks structured by a limited number of masters. In 1692, for instance, Hendrick Van Soest,[67] a merchant in ebony products, boasted that he was able to put more than fifty people to work.[68] Van Soest did not run an enterprise that was a single, large, integrated company, but coordinated a number of small studios and masters who worked for him. The concept was thus carried out by the entrepreneur, the product by other free masters at various locations.[69]

In this context was there any reason to close the ranks of the trade to new masters, or to limit the transfer of skills and knowledge to a small number of artisans within the confines of the trade? Was it not more logical for the large and powerful masters – who often dictated what happened within the trade[70] – to attract as many skilled people as possible, thus increasing their own ability to take on and contract out work and reducing the capabilities of competing groups? It has generally been believed that the role apprenticeship played in regulating the labour market was to make access to mastery of a craft more difficult. It would have primarily served as a means of limiting the number of masters – while at the same time swelling the pool of cheap labour. This was not the case for the Antwerp cabinetmakers or ebony workers – quite the reverse. The corporate structures were used precisely to attract and develop a maximum of technical knowledge and skill. As early as 1497 apprentices were more tightly bound to the trade. It was explicitly stated that those who had completed their apprenticeship in the cabinetmakers' craft were no longer permitted to engage in any other trade. The objective was that those who had completed training in cabinetmaking would spend the rest of their careers in that trade, or would be financially sanctioned.[71] When, in 1543, the craft membership fee was increased from 15 guilders to 23, the registration fee was also substantially increased.[72] The latter was raised from 18 to 30 pennies (*stuivers*), with the concession that apprentices were henceforth relieved of the requirement to pay candle money during their apprenticeship.[73] Rather than a deliberate closing of the ranks of the trade, these increases point to an adjustment for inflation.[74] The same can be said for the increase in 1595. From that time on, the entry fee was 24 guilders for masters' sons and 36 guilders for outsiders.[75] What is striking is that for the first time there was an explicit distinction between masters' sons and outsiders (although the distinction existed already). Nevertheless, it is not possible to conclude from this that an exclusivist policy was being pursued. Similarly, when, in 1621, the registration fee for ebony workers was defined, the amount set was not unusual. Entry for ebony workers was 30 guilders, and the registration fee was 20 pennies.[76] Even when the entry fee was raised by 13 guilders in 1647, it should not necessarily be interpreted as corporate exclusion. In this instance it was not a high rate of inflation that caused the increase, but trade debts.[77] Once again there was a simultaneous increase in the registration fee. The $1\frac{1}{2}$ guilders that had been customary was increased by 8 guilders for inhabitants of the town and 12 guilders for others (this meant a total of $9\frac{1}{2}$ guilders and $13\frac{1}{2}$ guilders, respectively).[78] That the purpose of these increases was not to close the ranks of existing masters is clear from the fact that it was also stipulated that journeymen could reduce their entrance fee (required to become a master) by a corresponding amount.[79] This had already been the case in 1497, implying that the guild had pursued an inclusive strategy all along.[80] Rather than making access to the trade more difficult, the idea was to bind potential labour and skills to the trade.[81]

The traditional rationale does not accord with the facts, and should be re-evaluated. The main concern of the Antwerp cabinetmakers was not to close the ranks, but rather to increase them, and to link to the craft particular knowledge and skills that might otherwise be used by competing groups.[82] This implies that apprenticeship could also be important for the inclusion of skills produced elsewhere. Yet, as far as can be ascertained, no compulsory system operated in the seventeenth-century Southern Netherlands comparable to the regulated Wander system that applied in Germany. Did migration play a role in this? Rainer Elkar believes that to answer this question it is important to ascertain whether there was any scope for innovations, before investigating the transfer of specializations and skills. In markets where quality was determined by product standards and product recognition, Elkar regards it as unlikely that major transfers of technical knowledge and skills took place. Crafts practised at the edges of artistic production – he refers to furriers, goldsmiths and tinsmiths – are more likely candidates, although specific conditions and regulations must be taken into account.[83] Knowledge that provided comparative advantage in a particular market segment was often protected, and schemes providing for the dissemination of that knowledge are likely to have been rare. Among the Antwerp cabinetmakers, however, there are indications that outside influences were important in the development of new product forms. In 1593 there was a conflict between the Saint Luke's Guild and the cabinetmakers, showing that a number of cabinetmakers were moving into new fields (e.g. 'inlaying' wood). Although they did not wish to join the Saint Luke's Guild, a number of masters developed strategies that could align seamlessly with the later ebony work.[84] At least one of these cabinetmakers had learned his craft in Augsburg, and he seems to have been most important in the acceleration of the ebony work in Antwerp.[85] Moreover, some eight years later a certain Hans Bernardus, who also played an important role in the development of the ebony industry, was admitted to the ranks of the cabinetmakers, and he was of German origin as well.[86] The fact that at least two German cabinetmakers were at the origins of the baroque ebony cabinet in Antwerp cannot be a coincidence, nor can their rapid incorporation into the cabinetmakers.[87] The use of the exotic ebony, which was initially the preserve of silversmiths, is said to have reached southern Germany from northern Italy at an early stage, and Augsburg is often referred to as the cradle of the southern German ebony cabinet.[88]

Thus, it was not an ingenious, powerful apprenticeship system that led to the development of innovative products, but rather an inventive organization of recruitment and production that did this. Product innovation and conquest of new market segments was not the result of the meticulous organization of efficient training, but of openness to new influences.[89] Significant in this respect is the comment made on the admission of Hans Bernardus to the trade. The German was forbidden to employ labourers or apprentices who had already learned cabinetmaking and were already incorporated in the trade.[90] Where we might expect that the local government or the leading masters would prefer to see the technical know-how brought by Bernardus spread among the Antwerp workers, the opposite was the case.[91] In practice, Hans Bernardus was required to employ foreigners.[92] Rather than training apprentices on Belgian soil, foreign craftsmen or masters had to be offered good working and learning conditions.[93]

The Construction of Quality

Nevertheless, as we suggested above, a certain 'de-skilling' occurred for each master apart. This decline in skill was not owing to the emergence of large integrated companies, but was rather associated with the continued existence of a large number of small craft studios led by an individual master. The apprenticeship system was to no avail here. Yet, there are reasons to believe that from the second half of the sixteenth century on, the cabinetmakers embedded the skill needed for their craft firmly in the trade itself – or rather, they continued to do so with a different strategy. The problem was that the product forms became increasingly complex and it became more difficult for customers to assess quality. Nonetheless, the cabinetmakers succeeded in turning their clients' uncertainty to their advantage, partly thanks to the apprenticeship system. The crux of the matter is that rather than being a means for achieving better product quality, the apprenticeship system should be seen as a representation and legitimization of that quality. The skills of the producers were defined rather than produced by the apprenticeship system, at least from the first decades of the seventeenth century onwards.

A few theoretical concepts will serve to clarify this. In recent economic theory – especially in the theories of 'convention' – the classical idea that there is a contractual coordination between actors making rational choices has been countered by the idea of coordinated practices embedded in 'tacit knowledge' and 'shared skills'.[94] The notion of an abstract confrontation between supply and demand mediated by the product price (agreed on by rational actors) ignores the various sets of conventions in which agreement between purchaser and vendor is necessarily embedded. While it is difficult to account for the structural lack of information the actors experience in orthodox or (neo)classical market theories,[95] the disagreeing theories assume that there were preceding (tacit) agreements or (implicit) mutual expectations about the value of certain characteristics of products and skills.[96] In other words, the confrontation between supply and demand that resulted in the price (valuation) of the product is always preceded by an objectification process that makes it possible to arrive at a common perception of the quality of that product.[97] One of the ways of achieving this objectification may have been the trademark, which assured or implied a certain level of quality.[98] The sculptors, for instance, had been obliged, at least since 1470, to burn the mark of the Saint Luke's Guild on every piece. This mark guaranteed that the piece had been inspected and therefore complied with certain norms and standards.[99] Placing such a mark on luxury and semi-luxury items provided a means of guaranteeing an otherwise unverifiable 'quality' and served to raise the price, in fact, a sort of *sur-prix* arose. In 1621 it was ruled that every piece sold as 'ebony work' made from Spanish wood had to be marked with the letter 'S'.[100] The reason for this ruling was that pieces made from the poorer quality timber were being sold as if they were ebony.[101] Apparently the difference was not always evident to lay people, and too many inferior pieces reached the market. This way the quality mark did not lead to a new form of standardization, but restored confidence in the (often very diverse) products.[102] In 1649 a complaint was lodged that brand new work was being sold at the Friday market, and by allowing this, clients were being cheated because of the poor quality of the pieces on offer. The cabinetmakers sought and were granted permission to distinguish this work for their customers via a trade mark, using the 'regular' mark of the craft.[103] From 5 March 1650 on, the cabinetmakers had permission to sell their work at the Friday market on the condition that they first took it to the deacons, made known the name of the rag and bone man who would be selling it, and burned on the trademark of the craft. In 1661 the ebony workers requested the same ruling for the same reason. They asked that no more Spanish wood or yellow wood be used, and if it was used that it had to be identifiable as such, and first inspected and signed by two elders.[104] That the intention was to maintain prices rather than to exclude alternative pieces and designs can be deduced from the fact that the deacons themselves bought the bad pieces to prevent them being sold at lower prices on the market. More important, the mark fitted in with increased scope for creativity and personal initiative in a market that was shifting towards the art sector. The point is that the mark had to be sanctioned, as is shown in the provisions resulting from a conflict with the panel makers of Saint Luke's. The products that had caused the conflict not only had to be marked, they had to be assured and approved by the deacons of the guild.[105] It was they who guaranteed the objective value of the quality mark. More generally, this was needed to guarantee the reliability of the quality of the producers, which could only be done by distinguishing it from the 'quality' of other producers. Above all, therefore, only masters could apply the trademark, that is to say: only artisans who had finished an official apprenticeship term and master piece. Hence the battle against unfree work fits entirely in this context, as does the apprenticeship. Apprenticeship legitimized the producer and, via the producer, the quality of the product.

Recently the conventions that may have operated in the valuation and construction of quality have been divided into three categories. The quality and saleability of a product would come about through standardization (*convention industrielle*), on the basis of personal factors (*convention domestique*), or by means of the market or price mechanism (*convention marchand*).[106] The hypotheses discussed in this chapter are related to the consequences these strategies could have had on the formal and substantive aspects of apprenticeship. An emphasis on one of the three factors would inevitably have had consequences for apprenticeships in the craft or occupational group where that particular strategy dominated. If, for example, the market mechanism dominated at any given moment, the production costs would have to be reduced as far as possible. An obvious step would be to simplify the production process, reduce labour and use apprentices as a form of cheap labour. The creative potential of apprentices or craftsmen would not really have been tested. By contrast, if at a given point among a particular occupational group, personal factors became important, it is not unlikely that relatives and contacts would become more important. Access to or membership in certain circles, origins, personal contacts and a good marriage would have been more significant than apprenticeship. For masters' sons, following in their father's footsteps would be more important than learning manual skills. Where standardization dominated, it would be reasonable to gear the training to the required standards. The content of the apprenticeship would then coincide closely with the expected result; the master-piece would be precisely defined and the curriculum would apply particularly for the occupational group in which the apprenticeship took place.[107] As we have seen from the cabinetmakers, who were concerned with export, they were likely to have had a system of product forms legitimized by standardization. (This was true up to the early sixteenth century.) Both apprenticeship and master-piece were indeed closely geared to the ultimate product, at least for furniture production. There are indications, however, that from the (final third of the) sixteenth century on, more and more cabinetmakers and ebony workers began manufacturing luxury and semi-luxury products, with the result that product standards gradually disappeared and product recognition was less a matter of course. This loss of confidence in the products had to be retrieved, particularly as there was now a different buying public. It is the way this new buying public judged and valued the product that should be studied.[108] By analogy with the *connoisseur*, who became famous in the sixteen and seventeenth-century art trade, conventional structures had to be built to restore confidence. The *convention marchand*, in which only the price mattered, was not the way to do this. Not only was there a continuous and inherent shortage of information, there was simply no objectified basis for assessing the product. What remained was the *convention domestique*, whose aim is to enter the product in a 'lineage of products, that are attached to a common origin, and by emphasizing special qualifications of persons and the importance of (regular) local networking'.[109] In other words, it is likely that among Antwerp furniture makers – particularly towards the end of the sixteenth and early seventeenth centuries, and despite the growing influence of art dealers and master-entrepreneurs – the network of regular masters (i.e. the guild) began to play a more prominent role. My argument would be that it was especially for these (small) masters that the apprenticeship system continued to be important – be it on a representative level.

The Construction of the Master

Harald Deceulaer and Marc Jacobs, who confronted the distinctions above with research on guilds in the Southern Netherlands, observe that in crafts where the *convention domestique* was important, access to the trade was the most expensive.[110] We have seen that the Antwerp cabinetmakers did not pursue an exclusive policy, but in practice heredity does seem to have played a more important role in certain periods.[111] In a document dating from the end of the sixteenth century, the same surname does not occur twice among the twenty-three cabinetmakers active at that time, indicating that heredity played a small role in becoming a master.[112] By contrast, of the thirty-five names found in an undated document from the mid-seventeenth century, a significant number of the same surnames occur more than once: Pauwels, Van Praet, Janssens, and possibly also Lits all appear twice, and Verbraecken appears three times.[113] Apparently these were mainly ebony workers, which suggests that the continuity was more common among the ebony workers. In 1678, however, no surname appears twice among those same ebony workers,[114] although the same surnames found a generation earlier do occur. Some of these names were to remain important until the end of the eighteenth century: Lits, Forchondt, Janssens, Claphouwers, Van Soest, Verbraecken and Peeters continued for at least two generations. Among the cabinetmakers, by contrast, the overall level of family continuity appears to have been relatively low and to have further declined in the eighteenth century.[115] With some caution, it can be concluded that continuity of names was most extensive among the ebony workers, especially in the first half of the seventeenth century, an era known for the pomp and splendour of the Baroque and the relatively strong demand for more expensive furniture. Yet, as we have seen, there are no indications that the financial threshold to the trade was raised significantly. The increase in entry fees was not so high among the ebony workers or the cabinetmakers that it made it prohibitive to become a master. Nor were creation of an apprentice's trial or the duration of the apprenticeship a high barrier. Becoming a master was not made progressively more difficult. Where Deceulaer and Jacobs claim that access to the trade tended to become more difficult as personal factors came to the fore, I would argue that some changes occurred in the family continuity quite apart from the entry threshold. Even more important may have been the fact that product-legitimizing strategies affected this. Was the strategy of the guild in line with family strategies or rather opposed to them?

In any case, differences within specific trades may have been greater than those between them.[116] It may be more fruitful to investigate which masters within a given trade were followed by their son than to concentrate on overall percentages. It may have been those masters that controlled the production chains who were followed by their sons, for it is the major names that recur most frequently: those who had more to transfer than manual skills and had more frequent contacts with clients. The Forchondts and the Van Soests, for example, were not primarily known for craftsmanship, but for their business skills. They did not make furniture; they designed furniture and set other masters to work. They were followed in this by their sons as a matter of course, probably not just because those sons had easier access to equipment, skills and techniques, but because they were continuing a name, a reputation. Designing was something they could learn equally well at home, from sketchbooks,[117] or the art academy,[118] and the knowledge they acquired about tastes and preferences from frequenting the milieux of their clients was more important than their ability to use a plane and chisel. As part of the notion of 'taste', skills cannot be distinguished from reputation or the perception of those skills. So for some masters, more important than completing an apprenticeship might have been an appreciation of the whole personality. As we have seen, the attractiveness of the product was linked to the manufacturer or vendor, which in fact was not the maker. Forchondt and Van Soest were, above all, merchants or deacons of Saint Luke's, and only secondarily were they masters in the craft of cabinetmaking.[119] The absence of a connoisseur in the world of luxury furniture in assessing the price and value of an investment may have implied increased reliance on name and reputation. Examples from painting, where the market value of the canvases of Peter Paul Rubens in the same period lost all relationship to the value of the raw materials or time invested in them, provide an idea of how successful the construction of a name or image could be. The price of a Rubens depended largely on the cultural and symbolic capital he had acquired throughout his career and on the willingness of purchasers to invest in that capital.[120] The same goes for other (luxury) products. It was not just the use of exotic timbers, silver, ivory, tortoiseshell, agate and similar materials that determined the value of a piece of furniture. The producer represented various forms of capital, derived from relationships and networks.[121]

It is not clear precisely when and how merchants and master-entrepreneurs were involved in the production process, but by the end of the seventeenth century, the production of luxury furniture was led and organized by a few large-scale entrepreneurs. Thus, to gain an idea of the significance of apprenticeship and skill, it is necessary to begin by assuming there was a clear difference between the large-scale (master-)entrepreneurs, on the one hand, and smaller-scale masters and craftsmen on the other. My hypothesis would be that it was not only the large-scale masters and entrepreneurs who profited from the legitimizing existence of a trade. Apprenticeships and master pieces continued to exist because both groups benefited from them, each in their own way.[122] The smaller-scale masters, whose status was subject to inflation, had little other option than to cling to the guild – i.e. to the apprenticeship system and the master piece making them 'qualified'. Despite their purely 'hands-on' activities, they stubbornly continued to identify themselves with their legitimized skills. It is perhaps in this context that the litigation against Guilliam Forchondt should be placed. He was the son of Melchior, who had been one of the greatest master-entrepreneurs in the sector. In the middle of the seventeenth century a number of smaller-scale masters complained that Forchondt no longer used any tools himself, and in fact was no longer capable of doing so.[123]. Forchondt was indeed someone who set other people to work rather than carrying out manual work himself. But why were those who worked in the craft so upset about whether or not he was still well versed in the skills? It may have been because the litigation was a response to the fact that art merchants began interfering in the production process and became masters in order to do so. Yet, the fact that it was precisely the smaller-scale masters (many of whom worked for Forchondt) who instigated this litigation does not necessarily mean that they were looking solely for advantage in the labour market. After all, sanctioning the skills of Guilliam Forchondt could objectively have had little impact on their own situation. The insistence that he, too, should be seriously tested by having to produce a trial piece points to the symbolic importance of the trial for the smaller masters. It was their way to uphold their status as craftsmen. The only way of compensating for the reduced value of their knowledge and skills was a symbolic confirmation of their own manual capacities through their continued identification with the hands-on making of the furniture concerned. This strategy was based upon the requirement to make a specific master-piece and the compulsory apprenticeship.[124] It was evidently important that, at least formally the corporate customs, including apprenticeship, should remain intact. In short, for these smaller-scale masters, too, apprenticeship had a primarily formal significance, which was separate from the actual reproduction of their skills.

Conclusion

This chapter has shown that Antwerp cabinetmakers began manufacturing luxury furniture – gradually in the sixteenth century and at an accelerated pace from the turn of the century – and that this shift had consequences for the apprenticeships organized within the trade. Paradoxically, the importance of apprenticeship waned at precisely the moment that the finished product started to become more luxurious and artistic. I have argued, therefore, that the emphasis shifted to learning basic skills and to recruiting as many specialists as possible.[125] However difficult the profession was, the apprenticeship term continued to be short (i.e. two years), and while the manufactured products became increasingly complex, the master-piece ended up simpler. It evolved from three precisely described (or models of) standardized pieces of furniture to one piece that tested only basic skills. Moreover, because the deacons of the guilds could ad hoc decide precisely which piece had to be made, it was possible to gear the evaluation of the apprentices to the product market, while allowing for a high degree of flexibility in the training. In a context of very different and sometimes highly specialized workshops it was necessary to adapt the trial to the specific training an apprentice or journeyman had undergone. In the meantime, registration and income fees were not applied for the purpose of preserving skills and technical knowledge for a group of insiders, but to maximize the available reservoir of skills and technical knowledge for the large-scale (master-)entrepreneurs. By financially rewarding those who stayed in the craft after finishing their apprenticeship and by attracting specialized craftsmen who had already studied elsewhere, the number of competent, available masters and free journeymen had to be increased.

An apprentice wishing to enjoy 'complete' training had little option but to 'shop' from studio to studio, and even then his later tasks would be primarily centred on carrying out manual work. The majority never reached the stage where they were themselves able to design products or shape the production process. Yet, if they wished to retain their former status, they had no option but to adhere to the corporate structures, and more specifically to the legitimizing and symbolic function of apprenticeship and master-piece.[126] In this they differed from the large-scale (master-)entrepreneurs, who often derived their symbolic capital from sources other than the trade. What they had in common was an awareness that the formal and symbolic properties of apprenticeship were more important than the actual development or transfer of skills and technical knowledge. Apprenticeships legitimized the producer and, via the producer, the quality of the manufactured product. By means of the common quality mark the trade played a substantial role in this process; after all, only a master who had completed an apprenticeship and had successfully finished the master trial was permitted to use the common mark.[127]

On the other hand, there was a shift towards '*les liens de proximité*' in the appreciation of products and producers.[128] In the end it was the large-scale master-entrepreneurs who conceived or invented art furniture; the majority of the masters only carried out manual work. Further research is called for into understanding the effects of the changing relations among large-scale merchants and entrepreneurs on the manufactured product and what that meant for the trademark and apprenticeship. Was a common mark important so long as the large (art) merchants were not themselves involved in the actual production process? Did personal marks arise as large-scale master-entrepreneurs began to engage in manufacturing luxury items? Maybe anchoring quality to a particular origin was increasingly achieved through handing on an occupation from father to son rather than through the trade itself? In any case the image of the designer or vendor was also important, as well as their 'knowledge' of taste. Their taste was the taste of their clients, and the quality or pricing of the product was embedded in convention structures relating to that taste.[129]

If a number of historians have focused their attention on the importance of the trade in the production of skill, the complexity of this notion has not been adequately understood. This case study shows that the existence, functioning and continuation of the early modern apprenticeship system among Antwerp cabinetmakers was more rooted in symbolic concerns than in actual skills and knowledge, which were often gained via alternative circuits.[130] The 'value' of skill cannot be determined objectively any more than can the quality of a given product. Prior to the basic interplay of supply and demand there have always been certain sets of collective, instituted and intentional conventions, both for employer and employee. Just as the leading master-entrepreneurs accorded a certain exclusivity to their products, small-scale masters and free craftsmen attempted to construe for their skills a quality that was (partially) isolated from the basic interplay of supply and demand. Up to a point skill was something artificial, and apprenticeship was more important for its formal, legitimizing, symbolic characteristics than for the learning processes that officially provided its content.

Notes

1. Many thanks to Catharina Lis and Hugo Soly for their critical comments on a first version of this article, as well as to the participants of the conference on apprenticeship in Alden Biesen (Belgium), 8 and 9 December 2000.
2. G. Crutzen, 'Principaux défauts du système corporatif dans les Pays-Bas autrichiens à la fin du XVIIIe siècle', *Revue de l'Instruction Publique*, 30 (1887): 277–302 and 361–78; ibid., 31 (1888): 1–24; H. Van Werveke, 'Ambachten en erfelijkheid', *Mededeelingen van de Koninklijke Vlaamse Academie voor Wetenschappen, Letteren en Schoone Kunsten van België*, 4, 1 (1942): 5–28. For Antwerp, see e.g. F. Prims, *Het herfsttij van het corporatisme te Antwerpen* (Antwerp, 1945).
3. Some important volumes: S. Kaplan and S. Koepp (eds), *Work in France: Representations, Meaning, Organization, and Practice* (London, 1986); M. Sonenscher, *Work and Wages: Natural Law, Politics and the Eighteenth-century French Trades* (Cambridge, 1989); C. Lis and H. Soly (eds), *Werken volgens de regels. Ambachten in Brabant en Vlaanderen, 1500–1800* (Brussels, 1994); idem, *Werelden van verschil. Ambachtsgilden in de lage landen* (Brussels, 1997); K. Schulz (ed.), *Handwerk in Europa vom Spätmittelalter bis zur Frühen Neuzeit* (Munich, 1999); W. Reininghaus (ed.), *Zunftlandschaften in Deutschland und den Niederlanden im Vergleich* (Wesfalen-Lippe, 2000).
4. B. Gustafsson, 'The Rise and Economic Behaviour of Medieval Craft Guilds', in B. Gustafsson (ed.), *Power and Economic Institutions. Reinterpretations in Economic History* (Aldershot, 1991), 69–106; S.R. Epstein, 'Craft Guilds, Apprenticeship, and Technological Change in Pre-industrial Europe', *The Journal of Economic History*, 58, 3, (1998), 684–713.
5. H. Van Der Wee, *The Growth of the Antwerp Market and the European Economy (Fourteenth–Sixteenth Centuries)*, 2 vols (The Hague, 1963); A.K.L. Thijs, 'Structural Changes in the Antwerp Industry From the Fifteenth to the Eighteenth Century', in H. Van Der Wee (ed.), *The Rise and Decline of Urban Industries in Italy and the Low Countries (Late Middle Ages – Early Modern Times)* (Louvain, 1988), 207–13; idem, 'Antwerp's Luxury Industries: The Pursuit of Profit and Artistic Sensitivity', in J. Van Der Stock (ed.), *Antwerp: Story of a Metropolis, Sixteenth–Seventeenth Century* (Antwerp, 1993), 105–13; C. Lis and H. Soly, 'Different Paths of Development: Capitalism in the Northern and Southern Netherlands During the Middle Ages and the Early Modern Period', *Review*, 20, 2 (1997): 211–42.
6. C. Lis and H. Soly, 'Exportgewerbe, Zünfte und kapitalistische Entwicklungen in den Nördlichen und Südlichen Niederlanden im späten Mittelalter und der Frühen Neuzeit', in Reininghaus (ed.), *Zunftlandschaften*, 45–70; Specifically for Antwerp: Thijs, 'Antwerp's Luxury Industries'.

7. C. Lis and H. Soly, 'Entrepreneurs, corporations et autorités publiques au Brabant et en Flandres à la Fin de l'Ancien Régime', *Revue du Nord*, 76 (1994): 725–44.
8. Lis and Soly, 'Exportgewerbe', 50 ff.
9. Compare Epstein, 'Craft Guilds, Apprenticeship, and Technological Change'.
10. K.W. Stratmann, *Die Krise der Berufserziehung im 18. Jahrhundert als Ursprungsveld pädagogischen Denkens* (Ratingen, 1967); P.L. Price, 'Learning Through Imitation: Some Examples', in *Children of Mercury: The Education of Artists in the Sixteenth and Seventeenth Centuries* (Minneanapolis, 1984): 49–58; P. Caspard, 'Pourquoi on a envie d'apprendre. L'autodidaxie ordinaire à Neuchâtel (XVIIIe siècle)', *Histoire de l'éducation* (1996, special issue on autodidaction ed. Willem Frijhoff), 86.
11. See e.g. R.S. Elkar, 'Lernen durch Wandern? Einige kritische Anmerkungen zum thema "Wissenstransfer durch Migration"', in Schulz (ed.), *Handwerk in Europa*, 213–33; see also W. Reininghaus, 'Wanderungen von Handwerkern zwischen Hohem Mittelalter und Industrialisierung. Ein Versuch zur Analyse der Einflußfaktoren', in G. Jaritz and A. Müller (eds), *Migration in der Feudalgesellschaft* (Frankfurt, 1988), 179–237; J. Ehmer, 'Gesellenmigration und handwerkliche Produktionsweise', in Jaritz and Müller (eds), *Migration*, 232–37; R. Reith, 'Arbeitsmigration und Technologietransfer in der Habsburgmonarchie in der zweiten Hälfte des 18. Jahrhunderts – Die Gesellenwanderung aus der Sicht der Kommerzienkonzesse', *Blätter für Technikgeschichte*, 56 (1994): 9–33.
12. A.K.L. Thijs, 'Nijverheid in de Zuidelijke Nederlanden', in *Algemene geschiedenis der Nederlanden*, vol. 7 (Harlem, 1980), 86–93; Thijs, 'Antwerp's Luxury Industries'; Lis and Soly, 'Different Paths of Development'.
13. C. Van Herck, *Antwerpse meubelkunst van de 16de tot de 18de eeuw* (Antwerp, 1952) (reprint from the *XXVIe Jaarboek van de Koninklijke Oudheidkundige Kring van Antwerpen*), 64.
14. Conflicts (concerning entitlements to certain work) with e.g. the timber-breakers and the carpenters gradually made way for conflicts with the Saint Luke's guild. In 1617, for example, there was a conflict with the tableau-makers about the making of frames, panels, altars, mirror-cabinets and the like, in which the cabinetmakers claimed that they had a historical right to perform these tasks (*'te maecken lysten, panneelen, aultaeren, sepulturen, spiegelcasten ende diergelycke')*, Antwerp city archive (Stadsarchief Antwerpen, SAA), Guilds and Crafts (Gilden en Ambachten, GA) 4334, f° 60v°–62v°; GA 4335, 11 December 1617 (copy). This claim goes further than the right to make substructures, which they were claiming in the fifteenth century.
15. R. Fabri, *Meubles d'apparat des Pays-Bas méridionaux, XVIe–XVIIIe siècle* (Brussels, 1989), 16 ff.; idem, *De 17de-eeuwse Antwerpse kunstkast. Typologische en historische aspecten*, (Verhandelingen van de Koninklijke Academie voor Wetenschappen, Letteren en Schone Kunsten van België, 53) (Brussels, 1991); idem, *De 17de-eeuwse Antwerpse kunstkast. Kunsthistorische aspecten* (Brussels, 1993).
16. It has been established, for example, that cabinetmakers from southern Germany, who also served as an example for the Low Countries, learned their trade in Italy, where they were not only said to have picked up manual skills, but also made acquaintance with the Greek pillars and the principles of proportionalism. Rainer Elkar cites the example of Peter Flötner, a Swiss cabinetmaker, who had learned his craft in Augsburg but who went to Italy to perfect his skills in decoration and proportion. R.S. Elkar, 'Schreinen in Franken. Handwerk zwischen Zunft, Kunst und Fabrik', in I. Bauer (ed.), *Möbel aus Franken. Oberflächen und Hintergründe* (Munich, 1991), 30.
17. At moments when demand for certain skills waned, or when alternative methods and techniques were more valued, certain groups would begin proclaiming their own skills as more important than they actually were. J. Rule, 'The Property of Skill in the Age of Manufacture', in P. Joyce (ed.), *The Historical Meanings of Work* (Cambridge, 1987), 99–118; P. Thompson, 'Playing at Being Skilled Men: Factory Culture and Pride in Work Skills Among Coventry Car Workers', *Social History*, 13, 1, (1988): 45–69.
18. A relative increase in the number of conflicts between different trades took place in Antwerp in the second half of the seventeenth century, at a time when the market was under pressure. H. Deceulaer, 'Conflicten en conflictregeling in de Antwerpse ambachtswereld,

1585–1796. Een verkenning van de juridische en sociaal-politieke aspecten op het lokale terrein', in Lis and Soly (eds), *Werken volgens de regels*, 152.

19. Cabinetmakers were forbidden from performing certain tasks, such as fitting doors and windows, floorboards etc. ('*doren, veijnsteren, steegers, alloyren, solders te leggenen oft plancken te leggene boven noch beneden inde huysen*'), while carpenters were forbidden from making certain items such as beds, tables etc., and from selling such items ('*trotsoenen, spennen, coetsen, bedtsteden, tafelen, schraegen, noch geenrehande gesend werck omme te vercoopen opde merckt ofte binnen hueren huysen*'). SAA, GA 4334, f°73–73v°; GA 4335, 15 March 1434 (1435) (copy).
20. The difference between heavy carpentry (carried out on buildings) and cabinetmaking or lighter woodworking emerged from the fifteenth century onwards. Cabinetmaking thus became a specific craft. R. Lemaire, *Beknopte geschiedenis van de meubelkunst* (Antwerp, 1949), 38. Some confusion naturally remained. In 1528, for example, on the basis of a ruling by the Council of Brabant on 25 March, it was decided that cabinetmakers could make windows, doors and roofs ('*vensteren ende deuren ende den dach vutten huyse sluyten*'). SAA, GA 4334, f° 20–21; GA 4335, 8 February 1528 (1529) (copy).
21. '*Der Schreiner setzt den Hobel an. Nicht Balken sondern Bretter, Leisten, Holzriemen fügen sich unter seinen Händen … Diese Eigenschaften ihrer Arbeit suchten die Schreiner hartnäckig gegen die Konkurrenz zu behaupten*', Elkar, 'Schreinen in Franken', 28.
22. '*De backen vande autaertafelen ende vanden tafereelen*', SAA, GA 4337, f° 5, (copy of 30 January 1477).
23. According to the cabinetmakers, it had been agreed that the sculptors would make certain elements ('*de backen vande autaertaeffelen ende taeffelreelen ende dat hueren ambachte aengaet … (totte beelden ende autaer dienende)*'), and if they were not capable they would have to call in cabinetmakers to do it for them, and not journeymen, apprentices or others ('*schrynmakers cnape oft die huer ambacht hanteren*'). SAA, GA 4334, f° 14–15; GA 4335, 17 December 1510 (copy).
24. Until the second half of the seventeenth century, conflicts regularly arose with 'nations' (factions) within the Saint Luke's Guild. E.g. SAA, GA 4575, *Sint Lucasgilde II: tafereel- en lijstmakers en beeldsnijders.*
25. SAA, GA 4334, f° 11; GA 4335, 24 November 1518 (copy).
26. '*Alle geschiecht werck daer panneelen inne staen tsy gesneden ofte ongesneden alleenelick*', SAA, GA 4334, f° 11; GA 4335, 24 November 1518 (copy).
27. '*Tresooren, spennen, coetsen, tafelen, geschiechte schutselen, schragens, andere gesneden oft gelymt werck*', SAA, GA 4334, 7v°–9v°; GA 4335, 6 August 1515 (copy). In the fourteenth and fifteenth centuries, partly because of the use of water sawmills, a separation occurred in the constructional parts and the closing fillings. A framework of stiles and cross-members was assembled using mortise, tenons and glue. The thin panels were slid into a groove. Lemaire, *Beknopte geschiedenis*, 34–43. According to Frans Defour 'the invention of the framed panel and the three-dimensional framework [was] the beginning of seven centuries art furniture', F. Defour, *Zeven eeuwen meubelkunst in België, XIIIe tot XXe eeuw, in Vlaanderen en Wallonië* (Antwerp, 1977), 24.
28. '*Oock die nyet tymmeren en connen*', SAA, 26 March 1525 (1526), f° 28–30v°, art. 4; GA 4335, 26 March 1525 (1526) (copy).
29. '*Dat is te wetene darcketten hoecken oft die kanten vanden panneelen uytsnuyden oft holen noch duerlichtige voyen oft panelen maken*', SAA, 26 March 1525 (1526), f° 28–30v°, art. 1–2; GA 4335, 26 March 1525 (1526) (copy).
30. Defour, *Zeven eeuwen meubelkunst*, 1–43.
31. SAA, GA 4334, f° 26–27; GA 4335, 13 December 1536 (copy).
32. A positive correlation was often found: A. Grießinger and R. Reith, 'Lehrlinghe im Deutschen Handwerk des ausgehenden 18. Jahrhundert. Arbeitsorganisation, Sozialbeziehungen und altägliche Konflikte', *Zeitschrift für Historische Forchung*, 13 (1986): 149–99, p. 152; I. Krausman Ben-Amos, *Adolescence and Youth in Early Modern England* (London/New Haven, 1994), 119–24. R. Reith, 'Zur beruflichen Sozialisation im Handwerk vom 18. Jahrhundert bis ins frühe 20. Jahrhundert. Umrisse einer Sozialgeschichte der deutschen Lehrlinge', *Vierteljahrschrift für Sozial- und*

Wirtschaftsgeschichte, 76 (1989), 1–27, p. 3, distinguishes according to period. In the late Middle Ages a tendency towards longer apprenticeship terms was found, probably because of specialization and rising quality standards. From the late sixteenth century on, it was the political and legal regulation of the labour market that caused longer apprenticeship terms.

33. K. Schultz, *Handwerksgesellen und Lohnarbeiter. Untersuchungen zur oberrheinischen und oberdeutschen Stadtgeschichte des 14. bis 17. Jahrhundert* (Sigmaringen, 1985); K. Wesoly, *Lehrlinge und Handwerksgesellen am Mittelrhein. Ihre soziale Lage und ihre Organisation vom 14. bis ins 17. Jahrhundert* (Frankfurt am Main, 1985); R. Endres, 'Handwerk-Berufsausbildung', *Handbuch der deutschen Bildungsgeschichte, Band I (15. bis 17. Jahrhundert: Von der Renaissance und der Reformation bis zum Ende der Glaubenskämpfe)* (Munich, 1987), 385; Sonensher, *Work and Wages,* 283. S.L. Kaplan, 'L'apprentissage au XVIIIe siècle. Le cas de Paris', *Revue d'histoire moderne et contemporaine*, 40, 3 (1993), 436–79, p. 450, found a positive correlation for Paris, but also important exceptions, owing to corporate exclusivity, the need for a moral education for the apprentices and the use of apprentices as cheap workers.
34. SAA, GA 4334, f° 1 ff.; GA 4335, f° 1, 14 June 1497 (copy).
35. In 1580 the apprenticeship for coopers was still only two years. B. Willems, 'Loon naar werken? Sociale mobiliteit in het Antwerpse kuipersambacht (1585–1793)', *Bijdragen tot de geschiedenis*, 82, 1–2 (1999): 31–62.
36. P. Eames, *Medieval Furniture in England, France and the Netherlands From the Twelfth To the Fifteenth Century* (London, 1977); Defour, *Zeven eeuwen meubelkunst.*
37. '*Ende niet min maer meer op dat men wilt'*, SAA, GA 4334, f° 1 ff.; GA 4335, f° 1, 14 June 1497 (copy).
38. SAA, GA 4334, f° 1 ff.; GA 4335, f° 3v°–4, 14 June 1497 (copy).
39. SAA, GA 4334, f° 7v°–9v°; GA 4335, 6 August 1515 (copy).
40. SAA, GA 4334, f° 31–33; GA 4335, 31 March 1543 (1544) (copy).
41. SAA, GA 4334, f° 65–66v°, art. 2; GA 4335, 28 April 1621 (copy).
42. F. Defour, *Belgische meubelkunst in Europa. Vlaams en Waals vakmanschap over de grenzen heen* (Roeselare, 1993).
43. It then became three years. SAA, GA 4345, 6 July 1756, f° 9r°, art. 1.
44. B. De Munck, 'Kiezen of delen? Sociale mobiliteit in ambachtsgilden (17de–18de eeuw)', in B. De Munck en D. Dendooven, *Al doende leert men. Leertijd en ambacht in het Ancien Régime* (Bruges, 2003), 25–39.
45. B. De Munck, 'Leren en werken in de praktijk. Beroepsopleidingen in het kader van ambachtsgilden: maatschappelijke en institutionele aspecten (13de–18de eeuw)', in De Munck and Dendooven, *Al doende leert men*, notes 18 and 19.
46. '*Een spenne, een tritsoer ende eenen rondeel disch oft viercante tafel*', SAA, GA 4334, f° 1 ff.; GA 4335, 14 June 1497, (copy). As regards the table, the guild council had the final say in whether it should be a round or square table, whereas the cabinets were strictly prescribed.
47. The trial changed 'because of certain significant reasons'. SAA, GA 4334, f° 1 ff.; GA 4335, 14 June 1497, (copy).
48. '*Ende elck stuck wercke op syne behoorlycke maete'*, SAA, GA 4334, f° 1 ff.; GA 4335, f° 1, 14 June 1497 (copy).
49. P. Stabel, 'Social Mobility and Apprenticeship in Medieval Flanders', in this volume.
50. Moreover, many workmen who were not cabinetmakers – wood-breakers who dabbled in gluing and the making of hard tables and other, similar '*schiechten wercke'* were explicitly referred to – were also engaged in making furniture and the like. SAA, GA 4334, f° 7v°–9v°; GA 4335, 6 August 1515, (copy).
51. SAA, GA 4334, f° 8–8v°; GA 4335, 6 August 1515 (copy).
52. SAA, GA 4334, f° 31–33; GA 4335, 31 March 1543 (1544) (copy).
53. SAA, 4334, f° 31–33; GA 4335, 31 March 1543 (1544) (copy).
54. H. Soly and A.K.L. Thijs, 'Nijverheid in de Zuidelijke Nederlanden', in *Algemene geschiedenis der Nederlanden*, vol. 6 (Harlem, 1980), 27–74.
55. Eames, *Medieval Furniture*, p. 59; cf. J. Van Damme, *Bijdrage tot de studie van de Antwerpse schrijnwerkers, hun ambacht en hun werk tijdens het coporatief stelsel* (Louvain, 1985, unpublished dissertation), 64.

56. The thesis that to some extent the making and evaluation of the master-piece matched (the quality of) the market commodity follows from the provision that anyone who did not do a good job of the master-piece (*'fraey, rustich ende neth'*) would have to train for another year (*'een jaere stil te staen ende beeter leeren eer hy wederomme beghinnen sal'*), SAA, 4334, f° 31–33; GA 4335, 31 March 1543 (1544) (copy); cf. GA 4334, f° 7v°; GA 4335, 6 August 1515 (copy).
57. M. Bimbenet-Privat, 'Goldsmiths' Apprenticeship During the First Half of the Seventeenth Century: The Situation in Paris', in D. Mitchell (ed.), *Goldsmiths, Silversmiths and Bankers: Innovation and the Transfer of Skill*, 1500–1800 (Stroud, 1995, Centre for Metropolitan History, Working Paper Series, nr. 2), 29, has argued that it was possible to tell an apprentice's specialization among the Parisian goldsmiths from the ad hoc master-piece.
58. SAA, GA 4334, f° 65–66v°; GA 4335, 28 April 1621 (copy).
59. SAA, GA 4335, Ordinance of 31 March 1543 (1544).
60. SAA, GA 4341, Ordinance of 31 March 1543, arts 6–7; GA 4345, Ordinance of 6 July 1756, arts 3–4.
61. See especially Fabri, *De 17de-eeuwse Antwerpse kunstkast.*
62. SAA, GA 4334, f° 22–22v°; GA 4335, 24 December 1519.
63. SAA, GA 4334, f° 22–22v°; GA 4335, 24 December 1519.
64. The file was three old shields. SAA, GA 4335, f° 26v°–27v°, 24 December 1519.
65. The ebony workers were subject to a similar rule in 1621: they could have five craftsmen, without the apprentices. SAA, GA 4334, f° 65–66v° and GA 4335, 28 April 1621, art. 54.
66. The cabinetmakers asked for a maximum of six labourers and an apprentice, instead of the twelve that was customary with the carpenters, who asked for an even higher maximum. SAA, GA 4345, *Contrarie redenen voor die dekens ...*, July 1756, f° 26–26v°; GA 4345, f° 10 ff.,16 July 1756.
67. The Musson and Forchondt families are well known to historians who have engaged in research on Antwerp. At the end of the seventeenth century the name Van Soest can be added. Cf. Fabri, *Meubles d'apparat*; idem, *De 17de-eeuwse Antwerpse kunstkast. Typologische en historische aspecten.*
68. SAA, Privilegekamer (PK) 780, f° 201–201v°; Fabri, *De 17de-eeuwse Antwerpse kunstkast*, 138.
69. There were ways to circumvent the legislation regarding the maximum number of employees in a workshop (accepting work in someone else's name, registering craftsmen and apprentices with other masters etc.) but the process described here was perfectly legal.
70. A man like Guilliam Forchondt was repeatedly elected as an elder in the ebony workers' craft. SAA, GA 4338, passim. If the largest-scale masters were not in the first instance the deacons of the ebony workers or cabinetmakers, but, like Hendrick Van Soest at the end of the seventeenth century, of Saint Luke's, this does not mean that their power in the cabinetmakers' craft was any less, since masters could be financially dependent on them. Moreover, any shortfalls in the accounts (in the eighteenth century) had to be made good by the departing deacons. Such a shortfall could amount to several hundred guilders, and the deacon by definition thus had to have a certain minimum capital.
71. SAA, GA 4334, f° 1 ff.; GA 4335, 14 June 1497 (copy).
72. From 1497, on the splitting of the coopers and the cabinetmakers, entry would amount to 2 pounds, 10 shillings Brabant groats. SAA, GA 4334, f° 1 ff.; GA 4335, 14 June 1497 (copy). In 1515 it was raised to 3 pound, 15 schilling (some 15 guilders). SAA, GA 4334, 7v°–9v°; GA 4335, 6 August 1515.
73. SAA, GA 4334, f° 31–33; GA 4335, 31 March 1543 (1544) (copy).
74. H. Van Der Wee, 'Geld-, krediet- en bankwezen in de Zuidelijke Nederlanden', in *Algemene Geschiedenis der Nederlanden*, 1979; vol. 6, 98–108; idem, *The Growth of the Antwerp Market and the European Economy.*
75. SAA, GA 4334, f° 50–51; GA 4335, 26 July 1595 (copy).
76. SAA, GA 4334, f° 64–66v°; GA 4335, 28 April 1621 (copy).
77. Virtually every craft that asked for a higher entry fee in the seventeenth century gave as the reason the (empirically verifiable) disruption of the balance between income and expenditure. Higher entry fees seemed to offer the only possible solution, especially since

the taxation of those who were already members of the craft (masters) seems to have been particularly difficult. E.g. SAA, GA 4334, f° 81v°–82v°; GA 4335, 19 April 1647 (copy).

78. SAA, GA 4004, f° 6–7, 29 April 1647; SAA, GA 4334, f° 81v°–82v°; GA 4335 (copy).
79. SAA, GA 4004, f° 6r°–7r°, 29 April 1647; GA 4334, f° 81v°–82v°; GA 4335 (copy).
80. SAA, GA 4334, f° 1 ff.; GA 4335, 14 June 1497 (copy).
81. In 1735 18 of the 21 guilders entrance fee was paid at the beginning of the apprenticeship, as a registration fee. SAA, GA 4335, f° 134v° ff.
82. Even regarding the financial problems of the trades, it may have been more rewarding to adopt an inclusive strategy than to raise the income from fees. Some trades indeed seem to have tried to raise the number of entrants instead of the sum each newcomer had to pay.
83. Elkar, 'Lernen durch Wandern?'.
84. The cabinetmakers were not permitted to carve figures or inlay wood (*'figueren belden ende anderssints te snyden ende in hout te leggen'*). Strikingly enough, it was the painters of Saint Luke's who instigated legal proceedings. The issue was, after all, the colours of the images, which was their preserve. The cabinetmakers defended themselves with the argument that they did not use paint for the inlaying of all manner of colours in wood (*'nyet en schilderen maer gebruyckten tot het inneleggen hout van alderhande coleuren'*). Moreover, their work involved the use of a plane, which was a cabinetmakers' tool, while inlayers used glue, which only cabinetmakers were allowed to do. SAA, GA 4334, f° 48–49v°; GA 4335, 24 December 1593 (copy).
85. Two cabinetmakers were in legal dispute with Saint Luke's, Joris Pistor and Hans Govaert. It was Pistor who trained in Augsburg. SAA, GA 4334, f° 48–49v°; GA 4335, 24 December 1593 (copy). Alfons Thijs has pointed to a document in which Joris Pistor boasted that he was 'the inventor of the inlaying of wood'. SAA, Notariaat 2876, 16 November 1593. A.K.L Thijs, 'De Nijverheid', in *Antwerpen in de XVIIe eeuw* (Antwerp, 1989), 131–51, p. 135.
86. SAA, GA 4334, f° 60; GA 4335, 26 September 1605 (copy). According to the cabinetmakers, the first ebony workers to set up in Antwerp were Melchior Forchondt and Franchois Van Stryp, in 1600. SAA, Proces D 4868, 1620. According to the accounts of the Saint Luke's Guild, however, they were Hans Bernardus 'the German' (*'den duyts'*) in 1600 and Melchior Forchondt in 1612. Other names among the ebony workers suggest a German origin: Peter Van Ceulen, Peter Wolffart, Coenraet Wolffs. Fabri, *De 17de-eeuwse Antwerpse kunstkast. Typologische en historische aspecten*, 25. Some simply registered with Saint Luke's as 'frame-makers', however, because that way they only had to pay half the fee.
87. When the emphasis shifted to French furniture at the end of the seventeenth century, we also see French names appearing in the account books: Gaillaird in 1693 among the ebony workers, Beauclair (1730), Grandjean (1730) and Ballieu (1734) among the cabinetmakers. SAA, GA 4336, Cabinetmakers' account book. None of them came directly from France, but the fact that they were major masters and not born in Antwerp may point to the same mechanisms. They were accepted into the craft without a murmur and developed into leading figures. SAA, Burgherbook, parts VI and V.
88. H. Kreisel, *Die Kunst des deutschen Möbels. Möbel und Vertäfelungen des deutschen Sprachraums von der Anfängen bis zum Jugendstil. Ester Band: Von den Anfängen bis zum Hochbarock* (Munich, 1968), 103–07.
89. As stated, a wooden or ebony piece of furniture was rarely if ever the work of one cabinetmaker alone. In addition to cabinetmakers and inlayers, silversmiths were also often involved, as well as embroiderers, carvers, painters, mirror-makers etc. The market advantage for Antwerp furniture makers was precisely that they were brought together in efficient networks through wealthy master-entrepreneurs. Names such as Forchondt and Musson acquired their international fame by rapidly deploying or attracting the available skills, not by ensuring a good transfer or development of those skills.
90. SAA, GA 4334, f° 60, GA 4335, 26 September 1605 (copy).
91. In eighteenth-century Austria, where a policy of population growth was being encouraged and where there was also a commitment to attracting as much technical skill and knowledge as possible, foreign masters who trained indigenous young people were actually rewarded. Reith, 'Arbeitsmigration', 14.

92. As early as 1602, for example, one Peeter Wolfhocker began training with 'Hans the German' ('*Hans den Duyts*'). P. Rombouts and T. Van Lerius, *De liggeren en andere historische archieven der Antwerpsche Sint Lucas Gilde* (Amsterdam, 1961), vol. I, 420. As has been stated elsewhere, foreigners were often more likely to be rejected by the brotherhoods than by the masters. Sonenscher, *Work and Wages*, 73–98.
93. For Josef Ehmer, 'Worlds of Mobility: Migration Patterns of Viennese Artisans in the Eighteenth Century', in G. Crossick (ed.), *The Artisan and the European Town, 1500–1900* (Aldershot/Brookfield, 1997), p. 172–200, the Wander system produced more flexible labour markets. Towns such as Antwerp often encouraged immigration by affording advantages to immigrants. Very probably the deacons – who were among the elite of the town – had the power to maximize the flexibility of the labour market in all kinds of ways. Soly and Thijs, 'Nijverheid in de Zuidelijke Nederlanden', 37. E.g. in most towns in the province of Brabant, training that had been completed in another free town – including outside Brabant – was regarded as valid. M. Jacobs, 'De ambachten in Brabant en Mechelen (12de eeuw-1795)' in *De gewestelijke en lokale overheidsinstellingen in Brabant en Mechelen tot 1795* (Brussels, 2000), vol. II, 591.
94. J.-P. Dupuy, F. Eymard-Duvernay, O. Favereau, A. Orléan, R. Salais and L. Thévenot, 'Introduction', *Revue Économique*, 40 (1989): 141–45 (special issue on *L'économie des conventions*); A. Orléan (ed.), *Analyse économique des conventions* (Paris, 1994 [2nd edition, 2004]); N. Baverez, B. Reynaud and R. Salais, *L'invention du chômage* (Paris, 1986); R. Salais and L. Thévenot (eds), *Le travail: marchés, règles, conventions* (Paris, 1986); T.R. Schatzki, K. Knorr Cetina and E. von Savigny (eds), *The Practice Turn in Contemporary Theory* (London/NewYork, 2001). Many of the 'convention theories', which align seamlessly with the practice theories, use concepts from L. Boltanski and L. Thévenot, *De la justification. Les économies de la grandeur* (Paris, 1991). See also M. Jacobs, 'Actornetwerk. Geschiedenis, sociale wetenschappen. De nieuwe Annales en het werk van Boltanski en Thévenot: een (re)view-artikel', *Tijdschrift voor sociale geschiedenis*, 22 (1996): 260–89.
95. P.-Y. Gomez, *Qualité et économie des conventions* (Paris, 1994). See also G.A. Akerlof, 'The Market for Lemons: Qualitative Uncertainty and the Market Mechanism', *Quarterly Journal of Economics*, 84 (1970): 488–500; and J. Stiglitz, 'The Causes and Consequences of the Dependence of Quality on Price', *Journal of Economic Literature*, 25 (1987): 1–48.
96. For the product market see F. Eymard-Duvernay, 'Conventions de qualité et formes de coordination', *Revue économique*, 40 (1989): 329–59; idem, 'Coordination des échanges par l'entreprise et qualité des biens', in Orléan (ed.), *Analyse économique*, 331–58. See also R. Salais and M. Storper, *Les mondes de production* (Paris, 1993).
97. See also H. Deceulaer and M. Jacobs, 'Qualities and Conventions: Guilds in 18th-century Brabant and Flanders: An Extended Economic Perspective', in S.R. Epstein, H.-G. Haupt, C. Poni and H. Soly (eds), *Guilds, Economy and Society* (Sevilla, 1998), 91–107.
98. '*L'identification des produits par une marque obéit fréquemment à une telle rationalité, qui s'écarte fortement de la rationalité marchande*'. Eymard-Duvernay, 'Conventions de qualité', 345.
99. J. Van Der Stock, 'Antwerps beeldhouwwerk: over de praktijk van het merkteken', in M. Smeyers and C. Van Vlierden, *Merken opmerken. Merk- en meestertekens op kunstwerken in de Zuidelijke Nederlanden en het Prinsbisdom Luik. Typologie en methode* (Louvain, 1990), 127–45; see also K. Van Vlierden, 'Het waarmerken van de beeldsnijproductie in de zuidnederlandse centra', in *Het laatgotische beeldsnijcentrum Leuven* (tentoonstellingscatalogus) (Louvain, 1979), 405–36; H. Nieuwdorp, 'De oorspronkelijke betekenis en interpretatie van de keurmerken op Brabantse retabels en beeldsnijwerk (15de–begin 16de eeuw)', *Archivum Artis Lovaniense. Bijdragen tot de geschiedenis van de Kunst der Nederlanden* (Louvain, 1981), 85–89.
100. SAA, GA 4334, f° 66; GA 4335, 28 April 1621 (copy).
101. From 1617 on, cabinetmakers were required to apply their mark on artists' panels they had made, which led to discussions with Saint Luke's. SAA, GA 4334, f° 60v°–62v°; GA 4335, 11 December 1617, art. 4. See also R. Fabri, 'Aan- en afwezigheid van merktekens op 17de-eeuwse Antwerpse kunstkasten', in Smeyers and Van Vlierden, *Merken opmerken*, 212.

102. This appears from the discussion with the tableau-carvers in 1617 on the making, painting and staining of frames, altars, mirror-cabinets, etc. SAA, GA 4334, f° 60v°–62v°; GA 4335, 11 December 1617 (copy).
103. SAA, GA 4337, f°27 ff., 26 July 1649.
104. SAA, GA 4337, f° 139–139v°, 30 May 1661.
105. SAA, GA 4334, f° 60v°–62v°; GA 4335, 11 December 1617 (copy).
106. Eymard-Duvernay, 'Conventions de qualité'; cf. Deceulaer and Jacobs, 'Qualities and Conventions'.
107. That is not to imply that there was an ideal situation in which apprenticeship operated 'as it should'. Here, too, for example, it is quite possible that the apprentice learned only 'hands-on' skills, not conceptual ones.
108. The transition to the various forms of Baroque was naturally linked to an orientation towards a potential buying public: '*(u)ne clientèle élégante pour des meubles précieux*', Fabri, *Meubles d'apparat*, p. 61; Fabri, *De 17de-eeuwse Antwerpse kunstkast*, 176–84.
109. Deceulaer and Jacobs, 'Qualities and conventions', 94.
110. Deceulaer and Jacobs, 'Qualities and conventions', 96–97; H. Deceulaer, 'Guildsmen, Entrepreneurs and Market Segments: The Case of the Garment Trades in Antwerp and Ghent (Sixteenth to Eighteenth Centuries)', *International Review of Social History*, 43 (1998): 1–29.
111. The fact that seventeenth-century Antwerp trade and export had a pronounced familial character has been observed several times. The firms were often comprised of family members, correspondence was conducted in Flemish, and trade relations were often limited to the circle of brothers, uncles and cousins. It may be that this also often applied to the production side. K. Van Der Stichelen, 'Productiviteit en samenwerking in het Antwerpse kunstenaarsmilieu, 1620–1640', *Driemaandelijks tijdschrift van het Gemeentekrediet*, 172 (1990): 5–15.
112. SAA, GA 4337, f° 72, 15 November 1594 (copy). We must of course take account of the fact that the given 'identical family name' is highly unreliable. S. Cerutti, 'Group Strategies and Trade Strategies: the Turin Tailors' Guild in the Late Seventeenth and Early Eighteenth Centuries', in S. Woolf (ed.), *Domestic Strategies: Work and Family in France and Italy, 1600–1800* (Cambridge, 1991), p. 117. For instance, there may be an important difference between trades and periods in which a number of masters had more than one son enter the same craft, and trades and periods in which it was customary that only one son followed his father, for example, where more capital was required.
113. SAA, GA 4337, f° 140.
114. SAA, GA 4338, *Opden 28 July 1678.*
115. SAA, GA 4336, Cabinetmakers' account book; GA 4344, Carpenters' account book.
116. A textbook example of comparing trades: L. Van Buyten, 'Arbeid en commercie op het einde van het Ancien Regiem: ondernemers, ambachtsmeesters en werklui te Leuven rond 1789', in *Leuven anno 1789* (Louvain, 1989), pp. 75–76.
117. The best known are perhaps those of Hans and Paul Vredeman De Vries. The former died in 1605 in Antwerp. The latter published important work in 1630.
118. Although in the Royal Art Academy of Antwerp the disciplines of architecture, perspective, and geometry only really began to be taught in the eighteenth century, the great interest in those disciplines in the wood and construction sectors indicates an existing demand for lessons that went further than imitations 'from life', in which mainly painters and sculptors seem to have acquired skill. Cf. Koninklijke Academie voor Schone Kunsten Antwerpen, Inventaris Rolland, 317 (30), *Naemlijsten van de ingeschreven voor de classen der grondregels van de geometrie, architecture en prospectieve in de Koninklijke Academie van Antwerpen* (according to the regulations of 22 April 1780), (1780–1801).
119. Rombouts and Van Lerius, *liggeren*, vols I and II.
120. Z. Zaremba Filipczak, *Picturing Art in Antwerp, 1550–1700* (Princeton, 1987), 73 ff.
121. Although the manual skills of someone like Guilliam Forchondt were under discussion, he was renowned among his contemporaries for his design drawings. It is no coincidence that his father was famous, and he enjoyed a strong reputation within Saint Luke's. Fabri, *De 17de-eeuwse Antwerpse kunstkast*. The 'grafting' of symbolic capital from other areas onto a

given product must moreover be understood almost literally. On the doors and panels of some cabinets (*cantoren* or *scribaenen*) it was not uncommon for familiar works, e.g. by Rubens, to be copied. Fabri, *De 17de-eeuwse Antwerpse kunstkast. Typologische en historische aspecten*, 117.

122. B. De Munck, 'La reproduction d'une crise. L'apprentissage des menuisiers et des charpentiers à Anvers (XVIe–XVIIIe siècle)', *Revue du Nord* (2003) (Nr. 17 hors série, éds. G. Bodé and Ph. Marchand, *Formation professionnelle et apprentissage (XVIIIe–XXe siècles)*, Actes du colloque international *L'histoire de la formation technique et professionnelle en Europe du XVIIIe siècle au milieu du XXe siècle*, Villeneuve-d'Ascq, 18–20 Janvier 2001), 31–51.

123. SAA, Proces A 868, 31 September 1648; Insolvente Boedelkamer 728/2, proces 1637. Fabri, *De 17de-eeuwse Antwerpse kunstkast. Typologische en historische aspecten*, 115.

124. The problem was precisely that Forchondt had never been registered as an apprentice. SAA, Proces A 868, *Repliecque voor* ..., art. 5.

125. It is not even clear for the frequently researched field of the art sector in the sixteenth century to what extent there was any specialization. There are indications that *'(l)e peintre se transforme en chef d'entreprise'* (the painter transforms into a manager). J.-P. Sosson, 'Une Approche des structures économiques d'un métier d'art: la corporation des peintres et selliers de Bruges (XVe–XVIe siècles), *Revue des Archéologues et Historiens d'Art de Louvain*, 3 (1970): 91–100. But especially the development in the seventeenth and eighteenth centuries is still fairly uncertain.

126. Whether they tried to create alternative forms of symbolic capital – e.g. training with a major master, seeking out other social groups in an academy, marrying into leading families, and so on – needs to be researched further, but the fact that the major master-entrepreneurs were more successful in this is generally accepted.

127. Personal marks were not discussed anywhere, although they definitely occurred at least from the seventeenth century onwards. One of the few personal marks to have been found is that of Michel Verbiest (M.V.), who was known for his great skill. Fabri, 'Aan- en afwezigheid', 201–15. But on the whole, collective marks seem to have been more important than personal marks up to the end of the *Ancien Régime*; this appears from research on the Antwerp gold- and silversmiths and pewterers. B. De Munck, *Leerpraktijken. Economische en sociaal-culturele aspecten van beroepsopleidingen in Antwerpse ambachtsgilden, 16de–18de eeuw* (Brussels, 2002, Unpublished doctoral thesis), 379–400.

128. Eymard-Duvernay, 'Conventions de qualité', 244.

129. Neither the marketed furniture pieces nor the working hours etc. were tied to fixed or prestructured prices. It seems that price negotiations dominated. Fabri, *De 17de-eeuwse Antwerpse kunstkast. Typologische en historische aspecten*, 25–71.

130. Data available for the eighteenth century in particular show that the routes followed by apprentices cut right across the formal structures. Cabinetmakers' apprentices, for example, turn up later as apprentice carpenters or also worked on an unfree basis at the same time. De Munck, 'La reproduction'.

CHAPTER 6

LEARNING BY BREWING
APPRENTICESHIP AND THE ENGLISH BREWING INDUSTRY IN THE LATE VICTORIAN AND EARLY EDWARDIAN PERIOD

Jonathan Reinarz

In the introduction to his wife's memoirs, Charles Flower, the Stratford-upon-Avon brewer and Shakespeare enthusiast, claimed that, when he first learned to brew in the middle of the nineteenth century, he literally began at the copper side. From there he 'went through the brewery under the direction of [his] father'.[1] At this time, the firm brewed approximately three times a week and, according to Charles, that left him with much time for office work, among other tasks. Not just confined to the brewery that his father, Edward, had built in 1831, Charles collected cash from customers, kept the firm's account books and even did some of the brewery's sales work, otherwise known as travelling.[2] Even more surprising, in October 1846, when Edward Flower left Stratford to visit relatives in America, the firm was left entirely in the hands of his sixteen-year-old son. Seemingly given little say in the matter, Charles claims the experience taught him 'the necessity of managing'.[3] A year later, with his father back in charge of business affairs in Stratford, he was sent for approximately a month to stay with the Fordhams, other relatives in Hertfordshire and owners of the Ashwell Brewery, in order to study their methods of brewing and malting.[4] While perhaps not having received the most systematic of educations, Charles Flower could proudly claim on the occasion of his retirement more than four decades later that he had 'worked in all areas of the brewery' and 'done a part of all the work'.[5]

The way in which Charles describes his introduction to brewing is almost presented as one would depict the practices of a bygone age. Those who gathered on the banks of the Avon in the summer of 1888, when he announced his retirement, and heard him speak of his training would certainly have been aware that apprenticeship had become a struggling institution in many trades and, if not in the process of transformation, was in danger of dying out all together, replaced by technical training in a new, more scientific age. Its future in the brewing industry could not have looked any better. Faced with the emergence of zymotechnology, the science of fermentation, in the last decades of the nineteenth century, brewing did not appear to be a subject that could be mastered should it have been pursued as casually as it was by Charles Flower. Rather than examine such macrohistorical developments, however, this chapter will continue to focus on events in a town not ordinarily associated with the brewing industry, and concentrate on the experiences of pupils who received their training at Flower & Sons, Stratford-upon-Avon's largest employer in the second half of the nineteenth century. Not only are Flower & Sons' records among the most complete of any English provincial brewery, but also the firm's training programme was extremely popular among those interested in pursuing a brewing career in late Victorian and early Edwardian England. As such, these findings are more representative of developments nationally than they might at first appear and are certainly more informative than those contained in other surviving brewing archives. Besides giving considerable insight into the daily routines of their young brewers in training, Flower & Sons' records suggest the institution of apprenticeship, though appearing archaic in an age of technical training, continued to be valued by English brewers, as well as their pupils, well into the twentieth century. Though informal in nature and broad in its content, the brewer's apprenticeship was judged appropriate to the class of individual it was intended to attract and, perhaps most importantly, allowed the industry's leaders to reproduce successive generations of brewery managers.

Apprenticeship: Historical Introductions

While apprenticeship was not the only means of acquiring skill in past centuries, it was, arguably, the single most important. Originating from the rules of the medieval craft guilds, the institution of apprenticeship was formalized in England by an act of government in 1563. In general, apprenticeship involved the drafting of a contract, or indenture, binding a young servant to a master and vice-versa. Usually in exchange of a fee and a designated term of service, generally lasting between four and seven years, a master agreed to teach an apprentice the secrets of a trade, and assumed responsibility for the pupil's moral welfare, as well as providing board and lodgings. Further acts in 1597 and 1601 were particularly concerned with the apprenticing of poor children, though pauper apprentices were guaranteed a written indenture only in 1691. For the next century, this statutory system of apprenticeship appears to have guaranteed employment and limited competition, and, in this manner, maintained workers' earnings, while also ensuring a certain level or standard of workmanship. By the late eighteenth century, however, this system had broken down in many industries, including textiles, as masters gradually withdrew from their workshops and economic and social change weakened the authority and organization of guilds. Furthermore, apprentices became ever more difficult to control, Defoe having bewailed their insubordination as early as 1726, many having absconded from their masters in the following decades.[6] Further weakened as a result of children, often very young, being sent to work in factories and sweated trades, apprenticeship was brought into great disrepute and is said to have been formally buried with the repeal of the 'poisonous' Elizabethan Statute of Artificers in 1814.[7] With the absence of any legislated safeguards, exploitative forms of industrial training increased, flourishing in the nineteenth century, but dying away gradually as parish officers, reflecting changed perceptions of childhood, began to invest in children's formal educations by sending them to schools, rather than to textile mills, among other demonized sites of manufacture, in 'cartloads'.[8] Although some small masters and unions may have, for a time, safeguarded the existence of apprenticeship, few effectively limited the numbers of new entrants to trades, leading boys and young men to seek out better-paid entry positions, free from the restrictions of indentures. No longer regarding apprenticeship as entirely inappropriate to the needs of modern industry, employers in many originally apprenticed occupations henceforward preferred theoretical and formal technical education in colleges and universities. As a result, by the start of the twentieth century, these trends had run their full course, for, if we follow the interpretation of apprenticeship as put forward by some influential contemporary observers, such as Olive Dunlop, the institution no longer existed.[9] Should it have reappeared on occasion, these cases were interpreted as anomalies, if not illusory, most employers having dispensed with any systematic method of instruction, not to mention written contracts. What will be argued here instead is that such views themselves were illusory and that apprenticeship as an institution was more flexible than its rich tradition suggests, allowing it in some circumstances to change, or even adapt, and, consequently, survive in certain industries, such as brewing, beyond the late nineteenth century.

A Portrait of the Brewer as a Young Man

As was the case in previous centuries and a diversity of trades, many brewers' first apprentices were their own sons or other male relatives, primarily nephews. Following in an uncle's or father's footsteps, however, was not always the most direct route into the brew house and few pupils received training that one might regard as appropriate to a career manufacturing alcoholic beverages. Although Charles Flower entered the family business in 1845, his education had begun some years earlier and certainly did not betray his career intentions. He attended several grammar schools in the Midlands, where he met other budding industrialists, some of whose businesses would even supply his firm with the raw materials for brewing when the contemporaries became adults. Charles Flower also lived for a year in the London home of a family friend, Philip Rathbone, who, in his own words, became 'the model of an English gentleman'.[10] As was usual at the time,

Flower learned little that modern observers would regard as directly related to business. As an active participant in Rathbone's social circle, Charles did, however, learn the importance of music and dance, skills that would allow him to move comfortably in respectable society thereafter. Interestingly, years later, the industrialist still used his spare time in the brewery to practise music.[11] Presumably, this was also when he familiarized himself with the works of William Shakespeare, whose collected works Flower republished in later life. Charles remained with the Rathbones until 1845, when he returned to Stratford and was actually taught how to brew.

Usually only after having received a preliminary liberal arts education did such young men acquire a practical knowledge of brewing. Like most ordinary brewery labourers, brewers' pupils picked up their skills by carrying out tasks in the brewery; they learned by doing, or, as the title of this chapter states, by brewing. This general introduction to business was characteristic not only of brewers, but was the accepted practice in numerous other vocations, whether carried out in Lancashire mills or Staffordshire potteries.[12] In fact, the importance of such practical instruction was growing in numerous fields in the nineteenth century, including professions such as medicine, where bedside learning would remain central to training long after the emergence of the laboratory.[13] Not surprisingly, few brewers questioned what appeared a common entrance to both professional and industrial careers.

Though it may come as a surprise to some, Charles Flower's earliest and perhaps most colourful, if not unusual, experiences were similar to those of other nineteenth-century brewers. Take, for example, the case of Alfred, son of John Izzard Pryor, the well-known Hertfordshire brewer, whose life has been documented in detail elsewhere.[14] Although Alfred Pryor entered the brewing trade a decade before Charles Flower began to brew in Stratford, they were, without a doubt, contemporaries, should one judge by their introductions to the trade. Although Pryor's education included lessons in mathematics, mensuration, accounting, surveying and the use of globes, his father also advised him to resume his interest in dancing soon after commencing his industrial training.[15] Furthermore, like Charles, Alfred Pryor spent a period of time at another firm in order to acquire some general rules of business administration practically. Instead of remaining in England, however, he travelled to Hamburg where he worked for two years with a close friend of the family; as many business skills were not trade specific, a number, like accounting, could often be learned while working in another industry. Eventually, after a somewhat informal start, Pryor returned to the family's Baldock brewery, not far from the Fordhams' Ashwell Brewery, where he acquired 'a knowledge of the Brewery Department by getting up to brew with Mr Tranter [the head brewer]'.[16] Perhaps never quite certain of his son's abilities, John Izzard Pryor, shortly afterwards, on one of his many visits to the brewery, was pleasantly surprised to see Alfred 'with his apron on looking like a brewer'.[17] Appearance would be equally important to brewers after fortunes had been made, occasions when former pupils as easily disposed of the brewer's gown and assumed the role of gentlemen. It is in these contexts, moreover, that their training in music and dance increased in value.

Although most nineteenth-century gentlemen entrepreneurs would not have received any formal scientific or technical education, few English brewers were promoted to positions of responsibility within their firms without having learned the practical side of their trade, or aspects of business administration in general. For example, it was recognized that to succeed in the industry one had to have, as claimed by Charles Flower, a knowledge of all a trade's branches. Consequently, the rudimentary training of many businessmen, such as Flower, despite its imperfect arrangement, had its benefits and did slowly evolve into a more systematic, though always flexible, form of instruction used to train successive generations of senior brewing staff. Although resembling an artefact of the past, the apprenticeship of brewers, albeit in a modified form, became standard in the trade for the remainder of the nineteenth century and beyond. If nothing else, its longevity alone should indicate that the institution performed certain valuable functions for manufacturers of drink. Determining exactly what these were, however, is not always clear to a contemporary audience.

By the last decades of the nineteenth century, Flower & Sons, among other provincial breweries, was well known throughout England for the training they offered young, prospective brewers. Successful applicants, and not just family and friends, were given the opportunity to learn all aspects of the brewing trade during a period of instruction lasting approximately two years. Since many brewers employed traditional craftsmen, such as coopers, maltsters and even carpenters and joiners, largely due to the great number of retail premises they controlled and maintained, breweries continued to instruct many tradesmen as well. However, through working alongside these artisans, brewers' apprentices acquired a broader, though perhaps diluted, knowledge of the industry's diverse trades and generally went on to occupy more responsible positions than did ordinary labourers. Spending very little time in each section of the brewery, apprentices were not expected to become specialists in any one field of production. Nevertheless, in time, many went on to become specialists in the management of these particular firms.

Despite the fact that brewing pupils were never expected to master a particular task during their period of instruction, and certainly none claimed to perfect any particular skills during the apprenticeship, they were a privileged elite. Most workers employed at breweries during this period, including at Flower & Sons, on the other hand, received very little training. The majority of ordinary brewery workers in Stratford comprised rural labourers who were recruited by the firm soon after they drifted into the town from nearby agricultural districts.[18] Once employed at the brewery and earning little more than the average agricultural labourer, these workers learned by 'picking up', namely, learning by doing; few received any systematic instruction and rarely moved between departments as they had done when brewing was seasonal only a few years earlier, before the introduction of refrigeration equipment. Training for draymen and maltsters was also seen to be unnecessary. Equally unnecessary were apprentices' indentures, or any form of printed contract, though brewers were not yet prepared to dispense with apprenticeship entirely. Although pupils' standard certificates are rarely found in brewing archives of this era, these having been far more common in the eighteenth century, the specific nature of apprenticeship as practised at Stratford, as at many other provincial breweries, is revealed in copies of letters written by the firm's owners and managers to the parents and guardians of brewing pupils. Not surprisingly, these also tend to shed far greater light on the details of a training programme than do standard indentures, on which names alone seem to vary. If this chapter has a primary goal, it is to use this rich evidence in order to build a comprehensive picture of pupils' experiences of the trade and shed greater light on what has been described as apprenticeship's wide world of unexplained events.

Institutionalising Instruction

As one might expect, not all breweries could contemplate the establishment of such an apprenticeship programme. Although members of the general public knew little about commercial brewing, many recognized that a firm's size had some bearing on an apprentice's education. While pupils at the smallest firms could expect to receive considerable attention from their masters, those in medium-sized firms usually had the additional advantage of modern machinery and more up-to-date methods.[19] The product brewed was also of some importance. By this time, Flower & Son 's brewery had begun to brew pale ale, which rapidly increased in popularity during the nineteenth century and ousted porter as the nation's drink of preference.[20] Not nearly the size of London's largest breweries, Flower & Sons also had certain technological advantages that ensured a steady flow of apprentices after Charles took over the firm from his father and rebuilt it in 1870. By this time, for a provincial brewery, located in a region not traditionally associated with brewing, its production facilities were very modern, and advertised as such.[21] For example, the brewery had already introduced refrigeration to production in the 1860s, years earlier than most breweries, whether in town or country.[22] By 1878, the firm had installed the latest pneumatic malting facilities and continued to invest in the reputation of both plant and product. As a result, pupils regularly came to the brewery to receive instruction in both malting and mashing. Finally, there was always the question of living environment, for many parents hesitated in sending their children to urban centres, such as London, despite the career advantages this might have entailed. The distractions, dangers and vices of the big city, which were said to appeal to and threaten the youth in particular, were often highlighted in literature of this period. The safety of a provincial environment, given the possibility of exercising greater supervision, for example, had long been used by the region's medical schools in order to attract students and it does not seem unlikely that this strategy would have been employed to equal effect by brewers and other industrialists.[23] To go to London, some warned, 'has often been like the blight that affects the opening bud'.[24] Besides being a small community, Stratford had the added advantage of being a centre for English literary culture, which increased its value as a place of education and learning.

This was only heightened following the construction of the first Shakespeare Memorial Theatre in 1879. Without a doubt, these characteristics were used to maximum effect by the Flowers, who had already established reputations as Victorian England's greatest Shakespeare promoters by the 1860s.[25] As a result of these combined factors, between 1870 and the outbreak of the first world war, in total, approximately three dozen brewing pupils were apprenticed in Stratford, though actual numbers may have been somewhat greater, as the company's letter books for the nineteenth century are more complete than those for the early twentieth century.

Flower & Sons' training scheme proved a successful one, judging by the assent it received from many distinguished brewing families, though, in subsequent years, this itself contributed to the firm's popularity. During the last years of the nineteenth century, the brewery hosted the sons of several prominent English brewers as pupils. In 1887, a year before Flower & Sons' incorporation, London brewer Robert Courage sent his son to Stratford as an apprentice.[26] Half a decade later, one of Flower & Sons' new directors, Stephen Moore, formerly employed as head brewer at the Notting Hill Brewery in London, wrote to another metropolitan brewer, Spencer Charrington, offering to train his son in the 'art' of brewing.[27] Finally, in the last brewing season of the nineteenth century, Charles Tetley of Leeds requested a place for his son due specifically to the Warwickshire firm's modern equipment and facilities.[28] Though connections usually aided access to apprenticeship during an earlier period, ties of familiarity had, by this time, lost some of their advantages. Although more personal than communications with the average apprentice's parents, the fees and conditions which governed agreements with acquaintances were no different from those made with absolute strangers. In Flower's own words, business arrangements between relatives were subject to equally strict regulation, 'for fear of misunderstanding'.[29] Some were even turned away if the firm already hosted two new learners. If anything, the approval received from other brewers may even have inflated the cost of training and discouraged the brewery's directors from lowering their apprenticeship premium until the closing years of the nineteenth century.

Compared with the educations of most tradesmen, a brewing apprenticeship was among the more prestigious forms of industrial training. Apprenticeship fees listed in a Register of the Brewers' Company from 1725 regularly surpass £200.[30] While some pupils paid £300, occasionally the training cost nearly double that sum, making a brewer's education among the most expensive of apprenticeships.[31] In the late eighteenth century it continued to rank alongside those of bankers, apothecaries, merchants and jewellers.[32] For much of the second half of the nineteenth century Flower & Sons demanded a premium of £400, half of which was to be paid when a pupil was invited to undertake instruction at the brewery, the remainder at the completion of training. In 1892, the firm made its first exception in response to complaints from Henry Burton and accepted a pupil for £300. By 1894, further critical comments reduced the fee to £200, a premium that endured less than ten years. On 17 February 1903, one young man even became a pupil for £100.[33] Improvements in technical education, competition in the trade and the brewery's need for instant capital, given a decline in its London trade in 1900, had reduced the cost of a brewer's training to a quarter of its original sum in just over a decade.[34] Nevertheless, until the firm was sold to Whitbreads in 1969, it would continue to accept apprentices, who rapidly assumed more responsible positions in the industry.[35]

This, however, did not stop people from criticizing the training's cost. In response to claims that fees were too high, Charles Flower informed Mr Cutler, whose son, Rupert, came to Stratford in 1886, that the firm had never taken less, even when pupils wished to stay for only a few months. He also reminded such demanding parents that the trade offered limited places to apprentices and that Flower & Sons certainly did not take on pupils indiscriminately. Few were accepted and parents were assured their sons would associate only with men of 'superior' quality, something that was more easily demonstrated the following year when Robert Courage's son joined the firm. Interestingly, Flower & Sons used similar methods to justify the higher price charged for their ales, which were generally marketed to appeal to middle-class, rather than working-class, drinkers.[36] Significantly, most barrels and bottles, as well as the firm's letterhead, were affixed with Shakespeare's portrait to further bolster their image of gentility.

Perhaps such claims to respectability, when applied to the cost of apprenticeship, only fostered a desire for social mobility and effectively justified or even blinded parents to an apprenticeship's actual financial costs. For example, many paid the first instalment of a premium only to realize they could not afford a second payment. Nevertheless, a family's financial condition could easily change over a two-year period, particularly during the years considered here. Regardless of cause, as such appeals became more frequent, the firm modified apprenticeship once more and made their method of payment more flexible. Some struggling or otherwise resourceful pupils were offered opportunities to work off what amounted to early student loans. When notified that Revd Brodie could not afford the second of his son's premiums, the brewery's managers immediately made alternative arrangements. As had been decided in the past, the directors permitted Wyndham Charles Brodie to work off his outstanding debt in a very practical manner that worked to the benefit of the firm: he was offered the positions of brewer or bookkeeper at a rate of £105 a year. Similar arrangements were made in 1876, when the firm offered Arthur Fagge, son of Aston Cantlow's vicar, a salary of £150 a year to help in the brewery offices. Of this salary, £100 was to be deducted in the first two years. Were he to prove satisfactory in this post, Fagge would be refunded £100 in his third year. While the firm's generosity appeared limitless, should debtors have refused such an offer, full payment was always demanded, but usually such drastic measures could be avoided. Furthermore, such pupils may have acquired more practical experience than other apprentices, but few of these struggling candidates went on to become brewery directors, most having spent their careers in far less prestigious posts.

As with insolvent guardians, the brewery did not tolerate apprentices' indiscretions. For example, in November 1878, the firm's proprietors were informed by C.L. Stephens that one of their pupils had suffered certain undisclosed 'misfortunes'.[37] Possibly having speculated unwisely or even gambled away his savings, a former student, unable to find employment, could not repay his debtors and requested the firm refund his premium. This, not surprisingly, the managers were unwilling to do. Instead, they advised Stephens to use his influence in order to help the pupil obtain a position at Allsopps, the Burton brewers. Alternatively, the firm was willing to lend him some money, but only if the pupil's creditors paid half his debt and he worked off the rest. The directors regarded the former solution to be the better, for, after such a poor display of initiative, the student needed to demonstrate that he could 'make himself a capable man of business'.[38] While this particular pupil obviously failed in this respect, others seem to have regularly achieved their primary goal. Of the dozen candidates who visited the firm during these years only four were ever dismissed or abandoned their apprenticeships before completion. Furthermore, one can only expect the flexible terms offered helped keep the number of failures lower than might otherwise have been the case.

The flexible nature of apprenticeship arrangements is equally reflected in the way in which young men were indentured. Traditionally, most apprenticeships involved pupils entering into written contracts with a master, or, in this case, a brewer; at Flower & Sons, as at other firms, such as Watneys of London, apprentices entered the brewery's service by way of an oral agreement.[39] Luckily for the historian, as mentioned earlier, all correspondence concerning these arrangements is recorded in Flower & Sons' letter books. Not surprisingly, given their informal nature, details could vary with each case. Nevertheless, even the most erratic system soon develops some regularity and such was the case at the Stratford firm. After an initial letter of introduction, the managers usually invited prospective pupils and their parents to the brewery to view the premises and introduced them to the production process, as well as any senior staff members who happened to be present. As one would imagine, only those issues which arose during this initial encounter were addressed by the firm. If parents were satisfied with what they saw and heard – and most undoubtedly were, breweries having been industrial showpieces of the Victorian period – and the brewery had room for an additional pupil, a young man would be taken on, and then only after an initial payment was made. Although a receipt was issued by the company secretary, no written contract outlining an apprentice's duties or the firm's obligations was drafted. When questioned on this matter in 1899 by Charles Tetley, whose son had recently begun an apprenticeship, the directors stated that never in the past had they issued any form of agreement.[40] While such inquiries led them to describe the duties of apprentices more thoroughly in their letters, and suggest indentures had been more common a generation previously, by not radically changing existing arrangements, or ever drafting a contract, the brewery maintained a very flexible system of instruction for many more years. Neither should it be forgotten that brewery workers remained unorganized until the interwar period. In this sense, brewers' apprenticeships generally contrasted with the great amount of regulation which otherwise characterized the trade in these years. Furthermore, by retaining an unwritten contract, brewers were also able to separate apprenticeship from the multitude of ordinary, if not coarse, aspects of the trade. More specifically, this form of indenture, in contrast to agreements made with many tradesmen and suppliers, was based largely on trust and, as such, distinctly resembled a gentlemen's agreement, thereby reflecting the status to which many brewers openly aspired.

The Anatomy of Apprenticeship

In her survey of English apprenticeship over three centuries, Joan Lane suggests apprentices have traditionally been dependent on their masters for food, shelter and clothing.[41] As such, masters have often assumed the role of the surrogate or foster parent. By the late nineteenth century, however, brewers' apprentices no longer fitted or even aspired to this model. While William Hawkes, one of the firm's first pupils, resided in the Flower family home, those apprentices who came to Stratford after 1870 lived in lodging houses located in the town.[42] The 1871 census, for example, lists Arthur Fagge as a lodger in the home of Hannah Osborne. In that same year, Francis Lawrence Talbot and a young bank clerk, Charles Hensmen, were recorded by an enumerator as living in the home of Thomas Kite, a local printer. A decade later, the living conditions of pupils appear unchanged. One of the firm's apprentices, Gilbert Thwaites, who also became one of its directors in 1896, lodged with Thomas Pearson, a railway passenger guard, for the duration of his tutelage. Perhaps, given the cost of apprenticeship, the firm's directors believed private accommodation was something most pupils' families would provide without hesitation. In any case, the cost of living in Stratford would have been considerably more reasonable than residing in London or many other large conurbations. Most brewers' apprentices, on the other hand, probably desired the independence their wealth afforded them.

Only if lodgings were not immediately available when they first arrived in Stratford did pupils live in the homes of the brewery's owners or managers, and then only for short periods of time. For example, Mr Aikenson's son spent only his first night in Stratford at the brewery house with Flower & Sons' head brewer and one-time pupil, Francis Talbot.[43] Three years later, in 1886, Charles Flower wrote to Mr Cutler to inform him that his son was welcome to stay with him at Avonbank, the brewer's Spanish-style villa, until more suitable accommodation could be found.[44] This, however, is the same Cutler who questioned the brewery about the size of its premium, and, in this respect, Flower's concessions may have been made to appease a particularly difficult parent. No other documents refer to apprentices living with staff or directors.

Despite not taking pupils into their homes, brewery owners and managers did take an interest in pupils' social lives, leading such arrangements to contrast markedly with more anonymous, business-oriented forms of instruction, which steadily proliferated in these years. To some extent, this heightened interest in a pupil's personal life might still have been considered an obligation despite the disappearance of other aspects of apprenticeship once regarded as traditional. In any case, this was at least practicable, if not always desirable, despite the fact that pupils lived outside of the brewery and managers' homes, largely given Stratford's size, not to mention the close and personal manner in which the Flower family continued to manage everyday events at the brewery. Not surprisingly, of particular concern to brewers were their apprentices' moral standards. In a letter written in 1876, Archibald Park, a brewery manager, informed the father of a pupil that his son had formed 'some very undesirable acquaintance'.[45] Interestingly, Park also reveals this to have been Charles Flower's observation. It is likely that Flower had always exercised influence over pupils' relationships and considered this an integral part of apprenticeship. Unlike other provincial brewers, who moved outside of the towns in which they first established their businesses, the Flowers always lived in Stratford. Consequently, letters contain references to other impassioned observations and advice. A decade later, for example, Charles Flower assured the father of a prospective apprentice that his son would not 'become intimate with anyone but gentlemen', a promise that was perhaps easier to keep in Stratford than in London.[46] On another occasion, in 1878, the firm wrote to Mr W. Nelson, the father of a pupil whose progress was anything but satisfactory. In particular, the directors were least impressed with the boy's lack of attention while at work in the brewery. Consequently, he was encouraged to 'buy and keep a horse and so get a certain amount of active healthy exercise instead of too much really idle time on his hands'.[47] Though not appearing to be the most useful of advice, such comments did indicate the brewery took their supervisory responsibilities extremely seriously throughout these years and reflect the degree to which solutions to any difficulties were often very class specific. Reference to a horse, for example, reinforced the gentlemanly qualities required of all pupils wishing to take on positions of leadership at breweries in these years. Furthermore, and along these lines, although the firm was rapidly becoming one of the larger, more successful provincial breweries, personal relations between master and apprentice suffered less than one would have expected; in fact, contact between the two was not reduced. What had reduced over the years, however, was the length of each pupil's period of instruction.

Although encompassing a wide range of activities, training at the brewery was relatively short compared to traditional apprenticeships, or even certain vocational courses for that matter.[48] By 1870, breweries had replaced apprenticeship time, the lengthy period during which boys were systematically introduced to tasks and given adequate time to practise and perfect their new skills, with learning time, which provided pupils merely with instructions essential to developing an understanding of the trade suitable for managerial purposes.[49] According to Charles More, whose study of workers' skills concentrated on a wide variety of trades, the average apprenticeship in 1870 lasted five years.[50] Most masters regarded twenty-one as the appropriate age for an apprentice to finish his education. Longer periods of instruction, however, had been common in breweries years earlier. In 1848, Edward Kelsey, one of

Edward Flower's first pupils, second only to Charles Flower himself, arrived to begin an apprenticeship that he completed in 1855.[51] By 1870, however, no pupils stayed for more than two years with the firm unless offered employment after their periods of instruction were successfully concluded. At other English breweries, apprenticeship also lasted only two years.[52]

After the training period was shortened, the average age of apprentices naturally increased. Rather than reduce the age at which apprentices completed their training, this merely delayed the age at which pupils were accepted. Once again, according to the 1871 census, Flower & Sons' pupils, Arthur Fagge and Francis Talbot, were seventeen and nineteen years of age respectively. Gilbert Thwaites, who began his training ten years later, was also nineteen when he was instructed in brewing. The ages of no other apprentices are recorded in either the censuses or Flower archives. Should these samples be representative of the entire group, however, it almost seems inaccurate to group brewers' apprentices among traditional boy labourers. Most enjoyed financial independence, their own accommodation and membership in a social circle comprising older, 'respectable' members of the brewing trade. Furthermore, unlike those pupils in trades that accepted numerous learners at one time, brewers' apprentices also managed to live up to employers' high expectations and were rarely described as rowdy or unruly, perhaps due largely to their relative isolation and social position.

This, however, did not imply that pupils were free of apprenticeship's numerous strict duties. For example, in a letter to Charles Doggett dated February 1883, Charles Flower claims he had 'enough of pupils who think they can just look on at their own time and convenience'.[53] Pupils had regular duties and hours, which, though rarely described in letters, were clearly laid out in writing when the firm accepted Wyndham Charles Brodie as a pupil. On this particular occasion, Charles Flower assured the young man's father that his son would be instructed in 'every branch of our business in all its details, including brewing, malting, cooperage, sales and bookkeeping'.[54] When the time came for a pupil to learn the business of malting, instruction would consist of 'following the maltster round, listening to him + pick up information'.[55] Another pupil accompanied a brewery manager when he purchased barley at the local corn exchange. On such outings, he was instructed on the most important features to 'look' for when buying a sample of barley. This task, among others, comprised a day that started at nine a.m. and ended at five p.m., clearly much shorter than that of the ordinary brewery labourer.[56] Pupils would spend several consecutive months in each main branch of production, including the maltings and actual brew house, and shorter terms with ancillary workers, such as coopers and carpenters, unless otherwise requested. Again, longer periods were spent in the firm's offices and with sales staff. Importantly, these were also usually undertaken in the last year of the apprenticeship.

While apprentices learned a wide array of subjects, the brewery never provided a great deal of scientific training, though trade journals endlessly proclaimed the importance of science to brewing in these years.[57] While the firm occasionally encouraged pupils to attend courses with consultant chemists, who advertised such courses in trade journals and taught the elementary principles of chemistry to all interested individuals for a modest fee, few did so. Many appear to have had no time for such classes, apparently, and perhaps rightly, convinced promotion depended on other factors. Nevertheless, while chemists had their critics, there were many supporters of scientific education within the brewing trade, and most brewers supported the creation of an English school for brewing, as had appeared earlier in the century on the continent. While the establishment of such an institution at Birmingham, located only twenty miles from Stratford, was perhaps the greatest challenge to the apprenticeship system during these years, older methods of training appeared far better at producing managers than did some months in a university laboratory. Moreover, technical education would never provide the connections that apprentices made during their years at a brewery, and scientific information and assessment, after all, could always be purchased from consultant chemists.[58] The fact that most institutions began to construct model breweries in order to instruct in the principles of brewing must only have convinced brewers that their practical teaching methods were equal if not superior to those offered at technical colleges and chemical firms.[59]

Should they have desired some technical training, however, nineteenth-century brewing pupils did not always have to leave the brewery in order to receive training relevant to the production of beer. Those pupils instructed at Flower & Sons for the decade between 1889 and 1899 may have received some scientific instruction from a resident chemist, but only rarely was a chemist included among a provincial brewery's regular staff. Generally, only the largest Burton brewers employed chemists throughout these years.[60] More often, pupils were recommended to acquire some scientific knowledge outside the firm. This was the case in May 1867 when Charles Flower wrote to Mr Brooke to inform him that his son had been accepted as a pupil at the brewery. After outlining the usual apprenticeship terms, Flower stressed the importance of a chemistry course to those wishing to learn the trade.[61] Arrangements were made for Brooke's son to attend classes with Dr John Attfield, head of the Pharmaceutical Society's own laboratory since 1862, to learn 'all that [was] necessary' in order to understand the science of brewing.[62] Similar arrangements had been made in 1870 for Revd Brodie's eldest son. Surprisingly, however, this was also the last occasion the brewery arranged for a pupil's scientific education. As this perhaps indicates, a classical education continued to have its supporters at a number of English breweries well into the twentieth century.[63]

Although unwilling to incorporate scientific training into their apprenticeship programme, managers at Flower & Sons appear to have understood the importance of periodically updating an education. Several other members of the trade also demonstrated the understanding that one's education never ends. According to Charles Flower, legislative changes, alterations in excise laws and technological improvements all encouraged brewers occasionally to learn their trade afresh. Widespread acceptance of this belief led many established, operative brewers to take advantage of Flower & Sons' training scheme. Consequently, not every pupil who came to the brewery did so to learn all aspects of the brewing trade. Many were improvers, the twentieth- century equivalent of journeymen, or tramping artisans. As the name implies, these individuals had already received some training, but, realized they required additional instruction in aspects of the trade, perhaps due to technological innovations, or the lack of particular facilities at the firms where they had completed their apprenticeships. Many came to the brewery for a few months, but did not undertake any office or sales work.[64] Although such people received less-extensive training, or stayed for shorter lengths of time, they paid the same fees as other apprentices and were subject to conditions resembling those of other pupils. In 1871, for example, the firm's letter books describe the case of an improver, who stayed at the brewery for only a fortnight after paying the usual fee. For this reason, however, it was also understood that the brewer could, in the future, regularly call on the brewery staff for assistance free of charge.[65] The fee charged also effectively provided access to a brewer's social network. In this case, though the cost of the premium might still have outweighed the value of the knowledge acquired, perhaps simply a recommendation from Flower & Sons when applying for a subsequent post would have further justified what might at first seem a considerable expense.

Given such arrangements, Flower & Sons also realized a successful apprenticeship programme could easily become a liability. Although hosting many pupils and improvers, the firm had traditionally attempted to keep their methods secret. If cases of industrial espionage in the late nineteenth century were indeed rare, frequent reports of patent infringements would have added to brewers' insecurities. Furthermore, not a day seemed to go by in the late nineteenth century without a report of some attempt to forge the labels of successful brewers, such as Bass and Guinness, or even those of the strongest regional brands. As a result, in 1867, when arrangements were made to accept Mr Brooke's son as a pupil, Charles Flower demanded he promise 'not to impart to any one what he may learn that is peculiar to our business or mode of brewing'.[66] Furthermore, after leaving the firm, he was not to become engaged in any Brewery within twenty-five miles of Stratford-on-Avon without their consent.[67] Whether these efforts were always successful is uncertain. Between the years 1870 and 1914, however, no correspondence suggests apprentices breached the conditions of their informal contracts, neither do trade journals contain references to such cases. Nor should we expect to find such evidence. According to certain senior members of the trade, fears of industrial espionage had largely died out by the early twentieth century.[68] Brewery visits were in fact becoming common and were even recognized by some leading firms for their advertising value. More commonly, brewers agreed that apprentices required wider experience than was offered by their host firms if they were to assume the managerial position for which they had been trained.

Although the usual term of apprenticeship at Flower & Sons, as at other English breweries, lasted only two years, the firm's directors admitted that pupils did not leave the programme sufficiently trained to manage the average middle-sized provincial brewery. On several occasions the board of directors advised guardians that pupils should not expect to obtain a supervisory position immediately after completing their training. In general, the brewery's managers believed an apprentice required two additional years of work experience before he was adequately prepared to take on such a post.[69] Brewers' apprentices were expected to spend much of their time improving their skills once they had obtained a permanent, subsidiary position with a firm. Interestingly, no one ever suggested the term of apprenticeship should be lengthened.

Although few immediately became managing brewers, most learners obtained employment soon after completing a two-year apprenticeship. In a letter to the parent of one potential pupil, Charles Flower claimed the firm accepted apprentices only if they had some definite prospect of entering into business after having received their training. While this might appear an exaggeration, this does not seem to have been an empty claim. Between 1870 and 1914, the firm never hosted more than two apprentices at one time and regularly turned down candidates when no vacancies were available. Often the firm hosted only one. Even in the first decade of the twentieth century, when the firm experienced its greatest financial difficulties, at no point did the directors accept more pupils in order to increase revenue. Moreover, not all brewers took apprentices. For this reason, unlike many other branches of the economy, the brewing trade was never flooded with apprentices. Neither should the social education of apprentices be forgotten, as this essentially prepared them for positions of responsibility in almost any industry.

In any case, Flower & Sons made considerable efforts obtaining employment for their pupils, if they could not offer successful candidates, such as Talbot and Thwaites, a place themselves; many of the brewery's best apprentices, after all, were offered employment in Stratford after their two-year introduction to the trade. One of the company secretary's many duties was to write letters of recommendation for past pupils. One such letter was written in April 1898 to Truman, Hanbury, Buxton & Company and, in his recommendation, Flower & Sons' secretary, although unfamiliar with the ex-pupil's business capacity, considered him 'thoroughly trustworthy', and found him 'very neat in what little book work he had to do'.[70] Arthur Hartcup, who applied for a position at Morgan's Brewery in Norwich, was also praised. Brewery manager and director, Stephen Moore, testified to Hartcup's knowledge of brewing and to his 'careful hand work in the brewery';[71] apparently the brewery had had other plans for Hartcup, for they were also 'sorry to lose his service'.[72] Though often very personal, such comments appear to have had less to do with the success of a candidate than did the recommendation itself. As a brewery that ran a popular apprenticeship programme, however, Flower & Sons could afford regularly to lose such members of staff and most, not surprisingly, were quickly replaced with other young and knowledgeable recruits. On the other hand, apprentices could not do without the recommendation of their masters, and most entering new posts were quickly reminded of perhaps the most tangible benefits such training offered: connections. And, this, equally worth reiterating, was something most consultant chemists or instructors at technical colleges could not offer their pupils.

Conclusion

In many ways, the subject of apprenticeship in England continues to be dominated by studies carried out over a century ago.[73] Inspired by the politics of late-Victorian and Edwardian society, these polemical works address a limited range of issues related to industrial training, but specific to their age. Besides describing apprenticeship's decline in a number of industries, these works were written with the intention of exposing its worst abuses.[74] Not surprisingly, despite their valuable and enduring insights, these studies have little to say about apprenticeship's success stories and the institution's elites, which undoubtedly included brewers' pupils. Working in an 'age sensitive to its social diseases', social reformers predominantly addressed the institutions' abuses, of which there were many.[75] Most described apprenticeship in pessimistic terms, if not likening it to a form of 'ritual servitude'.[76] This particular form of industrial slavery, however, was rarely found in breweries. Although many industrial apprentices were assigned unskilled and demeaning work, brewing apprentices learned a broad array of tasks, both in the brewery and its offices. While many would have learned the importance of cleaning brewing vats, this duty was always carried out by brewery labourers. The firm assured parents and guardians that a generous premium entitled a pupil to learn 'all the knowledge [the firm was] able to impart'.[77] Apprentices would learn 'everything except experience' and, in this way, were freed from the dull, monotonous tasks found and undertaken by an army of youths in numerous Victorian workshops.[78]

Nevertheless, before we begin to praise the nineteenth-century brewer too enthusiastically, it is perhaps worth remembering that ordinary brewery workers received no formal training at all. Most workers, even those who required a great deal of knowledge in order to perform their duties adequately, were left to pick up various tasks and trades by repeatedly carrying out the jobs associated with their posts. Most would have waited far longer to advance in the trade and generally carried out the repetitive duties that apprentices were spared. As non-unionized labourers, they also left fewer records, and their history, unlike that of the industry, both nationally and internationally, remains to be written. What is clearer is that, in the late nineteenth and early twentieth centuries, brewers' apprentices were the only workers receiving any systematic training in the industry. Given the practice's flexibility, brewery owners and managers were freed of the obligations which encouraged many other trades to dispense with traditional apprenticeships before the end of the nineteenth century. Although the establishment of a school for brewing and malting in Birmingham appeared to signal the end of apprenticeship in the trade, the institution proved to be secure at a number of breweries, including Flower & Sons, for many more years. Not wishing to minimize the contributions such innovative programmes, as well as consultant chemists, made to brewing, commentators rightly argued that chemists could not teach all that was required to run efficient breweries.[79] While often providing valuable scientific instruction, such courses were regarded only as supplementing a brewing pupil's learning. Managerial and administrative skills could still only be acquired practically, they were by Charles Flower fifty years earlier. Most who requested literature on the subject of brewers' training from trade journals were informed that such skills could still be learned only when one 'passed through the fire'.[80] As a result, while many operative brewers and their chemists may have taken advantage of new, specialist forms of technical training, those pupils more interested in management displayed little interest in these developments. Science, after all, accounted for only a fraction of the material that comprised the usual brewing apprenticeship. Furthermore, as was argued by some of the most competent men in the trade, few such courses could provide the contacts needed to excel in an industry dominated by gentlemen.[81] Consequently, as long as the new technical courses taught only science, the industry would continue to produce its own brewers. Ironically, while many had feared that placing apprenticeship in the hands of industry owners would lead to its inevitable demise, in the case of brewing, this autonomy seems to have been crucial to its survival. Perhaps as ironic, though brewers' pupils would continue to learn their trade by doing (in this case, brewing), they were often undertaking very little practical work at breweries during their apprenticeships. Nevertheless, as important as any practical training apprentices undertook was the social and moral instruction these young men acquired during their periods of indenture, both inside and outside the brewery, during and after working hours. Besides cultivating an influential social network, brewers' apprentices worked alongside their masters and, as such, daily witnessed the way in which one exercised the skills of leadership, whether in the brew house, office or, more famously, the many social events sponsored by English brewers such as the Flowers.

Finally, though Charles Flower's memoirs refer to the brewer having carried out a part of every branch of production, a fact that was announced, quite appropriately, at one of the firm's social gatherings, he could not, like his father, claim to have trained his son in the art of brewing. Unlike Edward, Charles did not pass the business to a son because he did not have one. Neither did he have any daughters. As a result, it was equally important for he and his wife, Sarah, to record their lives and experiences in a memoir, which has, without a doubt, greatly enriched this particular study. To say that Charles died childless, however, would be to ignore the significance of the apprenticeship tradition at the Stratford brewery, as well as its revival at a time when the institution appeared to be in decline elsewhere. While the exact influence of the couple's lack of children on the training programme is uncertain, it may very well have triggered its resurgence in these years. As a result, like many relatives before and after him, Charles was still able to surround himself with a very large family and, in this way, while perhaps serving as someone's model of an English gentleman, reproduce a long line of brewers and thereby ensure himself a lasting legacy in the industry to which he devoted his entire productive life.

Notes

1. S. Flower, *Great Aunt Sarah's Diary* (Stratford, 1964), p.4.
2. Ibid.
3. Ibid., 6.
4. Ibid. Despite the family connection, contact between the Fordham and Flower families was irregular after Charles's visit to the firm.
5. *Stratford Herald*, 20 July 1888.
6. D. Defoe, *The Complete English Tradesman* (1738), 16.
7. J. Lane, *Apprenticeship in England, 1600–1914* (London, 1996), 2.
8. Lane, *Apprenticeship in England*, 247.
9. O.J. Dunlop and R.D. Denman, *English Apprenticeship and Child Labour* (London, 1912), 19; C. More, *Skill and the English Working Class* (London, 1980), 46.
10. Flower, *Great Aunt Sarah's Diary*, 4.
11. Ibid., 5.
12. P. Joyce, *Work, Society and Politics* (London, 1982), p.24; S. Pollard, *The Genesis of Modern Management* (London, 1965), 109.
13. T.N. Bonner, *Becoming a Physician: Medical Education in Britain, France, Germany, and the United States, 1750–1945* (Baltimore, 2000), 15–16, 34–44, 48–52.
14. G. Curtis, *Chronicle of Small Beer* (Hereford, 1970).
15. Curtis, *Chronicle of Small Beer*, 25. A detailed account of Pryor's training is also given in T. Gourvish and R. Wilson, *The British Brewing Industry, 1830–1980* (Cambridge, 1994), 242–44.
16. Curtis, *Chronicle of Small Beer*, 31.
17. Ibid., 32.
18. J. Reinarz, 'An Easy Transition: Brewery Life and Labour in the Midlands, 1870–1914', *Midland History*, 28 (2003): 149–68.
19. N.B. Dearle, *Industrial Training: With Special Reference to the Conditions Prevailing in London* (London, 1914), 347–49.
20. R. Wilson, 'The Changing Taste for Beer in Victorian Britain', in T. Gourvish and R. Wilson (eds), *The Dynamics of the International Brewing Trade Since 1800* (London, 1998), 94.
21. *The Stratford Herald*, 28 January 1870.
22. Reinarz, 'An Easy Transition', 93–95.
23. Bonner, *Becoming a Physician*, 226–27; J.T.J. Morrison, *William Sands Cox and the Birmingham Medical School* (Birmingham, 1926), 20–21.
24. Bonner, *Becoming a Physician*, 227.
25. S. Beauman, *The Royal Shakespeare Company* (Oxford, 1982), 11.
26. Shakespeare Birthplace Trust Record Office (SBTRO hereafter), DR 227/110.
27. Ibid.
28. Ibid.
29. Ibid., DR 227/106.
30. P. Mathias, *The Brewing Industry in England, 1700–1830* (Cambridge, 1959), 23.
31. Ibid., 23–24.
32. Lane, *Apprenticeship in England*, 23.
33. SBTRO, DR 227/110. The last correspondence contained in the private letter book is dated 9 June 1904. Letters do not refer to pupils after Best's arrival. Consequently, arrangements governing brewing apprenticeships after this date are unknown.
34. For a lengthy discussion of the firm's financial crisis in the first decades of the twentieth century, see J. Reinarz, 'A Social History of a Midland Business: Flower & Sons, 1870–1914' (unpublished Ph.D. thesis, University of Warwick, 1998), especially pp. 47–57.
35. T. Gourvish, *Norfolk Beers from English Barley* (Norwich, 1987), 155–56.
36. SBTRO, DR 227/168.
37. Ibid., DR 227/106.
38. Ibid.

39. *Brewers' Journal*, 15 July 1898. Watneys, the London brewers, also charged pupils £200 for an apprenticeship lasting two years.
40. SBTRO, DR 227/110. Mitchells & Butlers, the Birmingham brewers, appear to be an exception to this rule. As opposed to Flower & Sons, (M&B) issued written indentures to their pupils, Courage Archives (hereafter CA) CA/C/217–23.
41. Lane, *Apprenticeship in England*, 2.
42. Flower, *Great Aunt Sarah's Diary*, 1.
43. SBTRO, DR 227/110.
44. Ibid.
45. Ibid., DR 227/106.
46. Ibid., DR 227/110.
47. Ibid., DR 227/106.
48. More, *Skill and the English Working Class*, 212.
49. Gourvish and Wilson, *The British Brewing Industry*, 244–45.
50. More, *Skill and the English Working Class*, 70–71.
51. SBTRO, DR 227/140.
52. H. Janes, *The Red Barrel* (London, 1963), 129. Again, M&B appear to be the exception to the rule. Their apprenticeship lasted three years during the last decades of the nineteenth century.
53. SBTRO, DR 227/110.
54. Ibid. Although Brodie learned about the cooper's work, he was not permitted to perform it himself. Coopering had been protected by legislation in England at an early date in the Act 23 HVIIIc.4.
55. SBTRO, DR 227/110. These details were described in a letter dated 30 May 1899 from Francis Lawrence Talbot to Charles Tetley.
56. SBTRO, DR 227/110. Fellows's progress was reported in an anonymous letter to his father dated 1 December 1902.
57. See, for example, *Brewers' Journal*, 15 August 1883.
58. J. Reinarz, 'Kendall & Son, Stratford-upon-Avon: The Business of a Brewers' Chemist in the Nineteenth and Twentieth Centuries', *Warwickshire History*, XI, 3 (2000): 108–19; R. Weir, *The History of the Distillers Company, 1877–1939* (Oxford, 1995), 86.
59. *Brewers' Journal*, 15 December 1884.
60. R. Bud and G.L.K. Roberts, *Science versus Practice: Chemistry in Victorian Britain* (Manchester, 1984), 59.
61. SBTRO, DR 227/106.
62. Ibid. See also, A. Morson, *Operative Chymist* (Amsterdam, 1997), 193.
63. See, for example, H. Brown, 'Reminiscences of Fifty Years' Experience of the Application of Scientific Method to Brewery Practice', *Journal of the Institute of Brewing*, 22 (1916): 345.
64. SBTRO, DR 227/110.
65. Ibid., DR 227/106.
66. Ibid.
67. Ibid.
68. S. Neville, *Seventy Rolling Years* (London, 1958), 44.
69. SBTRO, DR 227/106.
70. Ibid., DR 227/110.
71. Ibid.
72. Ibid.
73. G. Howell, 'Trade Unions and Apprenticeship', *Contemporary Review*, 3 (1877); R.A. Bray, 'The Apprenticeship Question', *The Economic Journal*, 19, 75 (1909); R.H. Tawney, 'The Economics of Boy Labour', *The Economic Journal*, 19, 76 (1909); R. Bray, *Boy Labour and Apprenticeship* (London, 1911); Dunlop and Denman, *English Apprenticeship;* Dearle, *Industrial Training*.
74. See, for example, Bray, *Boy Labour and Apprenticeship*.
75. Dunlop and Denman, *English Apprenticeship*, 309.

76. Howell, 'Trade Unions', 72; and More, *Skill and the English Working Class*, 47. In the printing trade, for example, apprenticeship was regarded as a way for masters to obtain cheap labour. For a complete description of this argument see T.A. Skingsley, 'Technical Training and Education in the English Printing Trade', *Journal of the Printing Historical Society*, 9 (1979): 24–26; and 10 (1980): 1–12.
77. SBTRO, DR 227/106.
78. Ibid.
79. See, for example, J.E. Bowley, 'The Consulting Brewer, his Dangers and his Uses, with some Practical Brewing Notes', *Journal of the Federated Institutes of Brewing* , Vol. II (1896)
80. *Brewers' Journal*, 15 June 1884.
81. Neville, *Seventy Rolling Years*, 24.

Part III

Social and Cultural Contexts

CHAPTER 7

SILK WEAVER AND PURSE MAKER APPRENTICES IN EIGHTEENTH- AND NINETEENTH-CENTURY VIENNA

Annemarie Steidl

Over the last few decades, the perseverance and flexibility of preindustrial institutions and mentalities, of cultural and institutional frameworks during the process of modernization in the eighteenth and nineteenth centuries have become central themes in historical research. The study of preindustrial artisans provides key insights for an investigation into mobility and stability. The starting point of this chapter is that artisan trades should not be interpreted as some kind of fossilized relic. Rather, they should be understood as a flexible and ultimately very efficient means of regulating social mobility and dynamism.[1]

This chapter deals with questions about duration and stability of an apprenticeship within Viennese artisan-workshops. Until now, these questions have not received much attention among historians. The regular training of artisans, which included their time as apprentices and as journeymen, was already institutionalized in the late Middle Ages and was in existence in nearly the same form until the twentieth century. The extreme importance of that training has been seen as one of the central characteristics of preindustrial artisan production. Contrary to the long-argued thesis of a continuous decline of a society and economy where the processes of production and reproduction were combined and apprentices as well as journeymen shared the households of their masters during the process of industrialization, this chapter will show that this system endured for a long time.

However, the great dependency of the apprentices on their artisan masters did not necessarily result in stability and a successful completion of the apprenticeship. Indeed, the cohabitation of the master and his family with their apprentices and journeymen can be seen as an efficient way of dealing with an unsteady labour market. In order to survey the transformation of a preindustrial society to the modern world, the long period of the eighteenth and nineteenth centuries has been chosen for consideration. What impact had reforms to the guild system and changes to the economic law which accompanied the accession to the throne of the Empress Mara Theresia in 1740?

During the eighteenth century, a type of 'state guild organization' was developed in the Habsburg Empire, in which guilds and the apprenticeship system were directed and also protected by the state. From the end of the eighteenth and, in particular, in the first half of the nineteenth centuries, the influence of the guilds slowly receded, though they were not completely abolished. The Commercial Law of 1859 formally dissolved the guild system but established compulsory 'trade associations', which preserved many tasks and organizational traditions of the guilds.[2] Changes to the economic law had different impacts on the apprentices in crafts and trades. While in some workshops the system of apprenticeship continued during the nineteenth century and was even expanded, in other artisan sectors the training of apprentices vanished and the cheap labour force of unskilled young men and women became more and more important.

Preindustrial small-scale production in cities like Vienna was characterized by a great variety of economic and social conditions. Different kinds of production and economic success came under the umbrella terms 'crafts' and 'trades'. The life-patterns of masters, journeymen and apprentices differed a lot within the general area of crafts and trades. Changes in the operating methods of small-scale production came with the advance of industrialization, thus affecting the apprenticeship system. In some sectors, such as the textile trades, this process had already started during the eighteenth century, while in other crafts the engagement of apprentices was astoundingly persistent until the middle of the nineteenth century. By analysing the Viennese purse makers and silk weavers, who carried out markedly different activities, a variety of employment conditions and practices will be shown and a homogenous picture of apprenticeship will be avoided.

What impact had the economic conditions and the social status of crafts and trades on the duration of an apprenticeship and did it change during the process of industrialization? Could the age of apprentices, their sex or their kinship and contacts have influenced the terms of training? How stable was the system of apprenticeship and how many young artisans did actually finish their training period? Were there chances for those who failed to complete their apprenticeships to earn their living in preindustrial societies? An analysis of these questions should elicit some new and differentiated insights into the stability and flexibility of the apprenticeship system in small-scale production in the eighteenth and nineteenth centuries.

The research results, presented here, are part of a more expansive project about mobility and stability in the Viennese craft guilds, 1740–1860.[3] Vienna is very well suited as a field for research into these questions. The prominent position of the city within central Europe and the specific characteristics of the Austrian guild system have to be taken into account in any study of Viennese artisans in the eighteenth and nineteenth century. In the late seventeenth century, Vienna became the permanent residence of the monarchy, and thus the capital of the Habsburg Empire. Following the end of Turkish attempts to capture the city, Vienna experienced rapid population growth along with a rapid rise in economic activity: in 1683, the city and its suburbs contained about 80,000 inhabitants; in 1710, about 113,000. At the end of the eighteenth century the population exceeded 232,000. Thus Vienna was by far the largest and the most rapidly growing urban centre in the German-speaking world and in all of central Europe.[4] It was only in the first half of the nineteenth century that Berlin's population surpassed that of Vienna. Therefore, Vienna can be considered on a par with other European capitals, such as Paris or London.[5]

Artisans formed an important part of the Viennese population. During this time approximately one-third of all inhabitants were engaged in crafts or trades, either as independent masters, journeymen or apprentices, or as their family members.[6] In 1820, for example, Vienna and its suburbs counted 159 trade corporations, of which 150 were civic guilds and 9 were privileged committees.[7] The number of master artisans rose from 23,000 in 1837 to 118,000 in 1910, an increase which more or less paralleled the general growth of population. Out of a total of 306,000 working people counted by the census of 1869, between 50 and 75 percent were apprentices and journeymen in crafts and trades.[8] Consequently, the official economic policy concentrated attention on the Viennese commerce.[9]

The strong position and endurance of the Viennese guild system means that extraordinarily rich source materials, such as apprentice enrolments, journeymen registers, listings of masters and workshops, minutes of guild meetings, ordinances, statutes etc. are still available. They are preserved in the Viennese Municipal Archive. Mainly, they consist of registers of persons, which have, until now, scarcely been exploited.[10] These documents, generated by the guilds by order of the state authorities, served as an instrument for controlling the guild members, their journeymen and apprentices. Guild records were a prerequisite for the creation of a relative homogeneous group of artisans.[11]

I have confined my research to apprenticeships. As a result, there are two kinds of records with which the present research deals: so-called apprentice enrolments (*Aufdingbücher*), and at the successful completion of the apprenticeship, *Freisprechbücher*.[12] The Viennese guild of silk weavers also kept special books of enrolment for female apprentices, the *Lehrmädchenprotokolle*. These are marvellous sources. By analysing these protocols, one can study gender differences in apprenticeship. On female artisans, there is only extremely scanty information, and no other Viennese artisan guild produced such rich source material. At the beginning of the nineteenth century, silk weavers with a special licence founded their own committee. This committee recorded their apprentices in nearly the same way as the guild masters. Based on these serial documents a comparison between apprentices who passed their training with a guild master and those engaged in workshops ran by artisans with a special licence, is possible.

The Viennese Purse Makers

Small and specialized crafts such as that of the Viennese purse makers could only be found in cities. Only urban centres could provide enough demand for purse makers' products; there was no real demand for bags and trunks in rural areas.[13] In other words, this was exactly the kind of traditional activity upon which the general historical picture of artisans has usually been based.[14] Purses have been produced in Vienna since the fourteenth century: the first master was mentioned in the year 1367.[15] A brief overview of the workshops in existence indicates that the purse-making sector was relatively stable in terms of numbers of independent masters and experienced few changes during the period under investigation. A public enquiry of 1736 quoted thirteen masters and two members of the municipal guard (*Stadtguardia*).[16] A statistical survey of the Habsburg Empire in 1834 counted sixteen workshops in the city of Vienna and four in the surrounding area of Lower Austria.[17]

Besides bags, trunks and knapsacks, the purse makers also manufactured furniture, such as leather armchairs.[18] The processing of the different materials, such as leather, timber, fabrics for the lining of the bags and metal for the fittings, made it necessary to acquire a number of different skills. Therefore there were highly attractive opportunities for purse makers to become engaged in other trades such as cabinet making or lock making or to work outside the guild-ruled sectors. In other words, in periods of low activity in their own sector journeymen, especially, were able to work elsewhere as unlicensed craftsmen. Unfortunately, however, the sources do not tell us anything about specialized workshops, for example, if there were masters who only produced saddle-bags or workshops the only products of which were chairs.

Managing a purse maker's workshop does not seem to have been particularly profitable, judging by the fact that this sector was always at the lower end of the tax-paying scale. In the middle of the eighteenth century, eleven Viennese masters paid an average of 7.30 florints, which was as high as the taxes paid by the tailors and cabinetmakers, but far less than the taxes of the tanners or the bakers, who paid, on average, between 25 and 35 florints.[19] A few statistics will give a brief overview of the size of the purse-making sector. The Viennese guild registers list the names of 58 independent purse makers in the period between 1781 and 1854, as well as those of 4 widows who managed the workshops of their deceased husbands. From 1724 to 1861, 495 journeymen were engaged in these Viennese workshops and 347 apprentices were newly enrolled in the apprentice books in the period between 1710 and 1854.[20]

At the end of the period under discussion, in the second half of the nineteenth century, the census of the Habsburg Empire in 1869 mentions 70 independent purse makers, 4 widows who managed their own workshops, 3 spouses who ran the purse makering business with their husbands, 192 male and 6 female labourers and 152 apprentices in the city of Vienna and its suburbs. In the villages surrounding the city there were 5 independent masters, 3 widows, 29 male and 5 female labourers, and 9 apprentices.[21] If one compares the numbers of purse makers in 1834 and 1869, the difference is quite incredible. The enormous increase in the number of workshops and labourers occurred mainly in the period 1860 to 1871, when a lot of new techniques were introduced and restrictions on the guilds were lifted (after the Commercial Law of 1859 had formally dissolved the guild system). As this was also a period of high economic growth for the city, the Viennese market grew rapidly. The number of purse makers increased by no less than 55 percent due to the establishment of a large number of small workshops; an increase which was accompanied by a simultaneous decline in the average tax payment from 15 to 11 florints.[22]

The Viennese Silk Weavers

Evidence of silk weaving in Vienna dates from the fourteenth century, but was of no economic relevance until the beginning of the eighteenth century. The silk weavers' guild, which received their first articles in 1710, was founded by a very small group of artisans. Six masters laid out the proposed guild articles, submitted them to the provincial authorities and finally received their confirmation by Emperor Joseph I.[23] The sector experienced enormous growth during the eighteenth century, supported by a carefully directed economic policy of the mercantile state. At the turn of the eighteenth century, the production of silk became Vienna's most important industrial activity in terms of the number of independent masters and labourers.

It was during the reign of Empress Maria Theresa that silk weaving experienced the highest economic upswing. Silk weavers were state-aided, either through legal measures or by direct financial subsidies. Vienna was the residence of the royal court, domicile of numerous aristocrats, government and municipal officers, as well as the home of entrepreneurs and rich merchants,[24] therefore a large part of the available assets was concentrated in the city. These circumstances guaranteed the function of the city as centre of demand. The presence of a special social stratum in a preindustrial capital made it possible that the numerous silk weavers still produced for a local market.[25] In the eighteenth century only a very small part of the Viennese silk fabrics were exported outside the territories of the Habsburg Empire.[26]

After 1780, there began a steep upward trend in silk production. The Viennese trade statistics in 1794 recorded 29 entrepreneurs, manufacturing silk on 3,000 looms. Until 1801 the number of looms inside the town had grown to 8,000.[27] Two hundred and thirty-five guild masters and 600 artisans with special licences had their domicile in Vienna in 1813, their workshops and manufactories gave work to more than 6,000 journeymen, 800 to 900 apprentices and 7,000 to 8,000 female labourers.[28]

In eighteenth and early nineteenth century Vienna, not only did different forms of silk production exist simultaneously with each other – master weavers, domestic industry, manufactories and, after 1803, even factories – but also all kinds of people were engaged in weaving. It was more or less a cooperation between artisans and protoindustrial production, dominated by the putting-out system, but with small centralized manufactories.[29] Hardly any difference can be found between entrepreneurs, guild masters and silk weavers with a special licence and it is nearly impossible to categorize them. Even in contemporary documents the titles 'entrepreneur' or 'guild master' were used arbitrarily, independent of the size of the workshop or manufactory, their economic success and their social status.

The increased activity of the Viennese silk industry lasted until the 1840s. Silk production supplied a luxury market, thus the economic situation was much more stable in comparison with other textile goods. During the revolutionary crisis in 1848 the economic decline of the Viennese masters was consolidated, making a recovery impossible. Only the wealthy producers or manufacturers could deal with the revolutionary crisis, which put the handloom weavers in an even weaker position. In 1850 the establishment of the Customs Union among the different countries in the Habsburg Empire dealt a final blow to the Viennese silk industry.[30] In the following thirty to fourty years, while the handloom weavers gave up their profession, the wealthy entrepreneurs moved their factories to far-away towns in the Habsburg provinces, in Bohemia, Moravia and Austrian Silesia. They continued to weave silk fabrics with much lower production costs, because of the cheap labour force in the provinces.[31] By 1875 only three thousand people were still engaged in the Viennese silk industry, while silk production had declined by one-fifth since 1850.[32] Today, there is only one factory still producing silk in Vienna, called *Flemich*.

The Enrolment of the Apprentices

Enrolment as an apprentice, confirmed by registering in the *Aufdingbuch*, was the usual way to start a career as an artisan. Additional to the acquisition of new skills, the apprenticeship served as a means of absorbing the customs of the guild system. For boys from rural areas the apprenticeship could be seen as a period of integration and acculturation.[33] A locksmith who came from Bohemia to Vienna for his apprenticeship in the nineteenth century tells us in his autobiography that it was usual for young boys from his village after finishing school to tramp to Vienna in order to learn a craft and improve their knowledge of German.[34] Therefore, the fact that an apprenticeship served not exclusively as training in artisan skills has to be taken into consideration. The training functioned as a way, more or less, of assimilation into the new environment of the city and the social and cultural vicinity of small-scale production. 'Young men whose horizons had been limited to their families and home towns were given the chance to enjoy broader contacts and experiences'.[35]

In the workshop of 75 Viennese masters, 347 apprentices started their training between 1710 and 1857. The decision to hire an apprentice depended on the economic situation of the masters. The number of enrolled apprentices varied considerably in the eighteenth and nineteenth centuries as can be seen in figure 7.1. In his research on the economic situation of

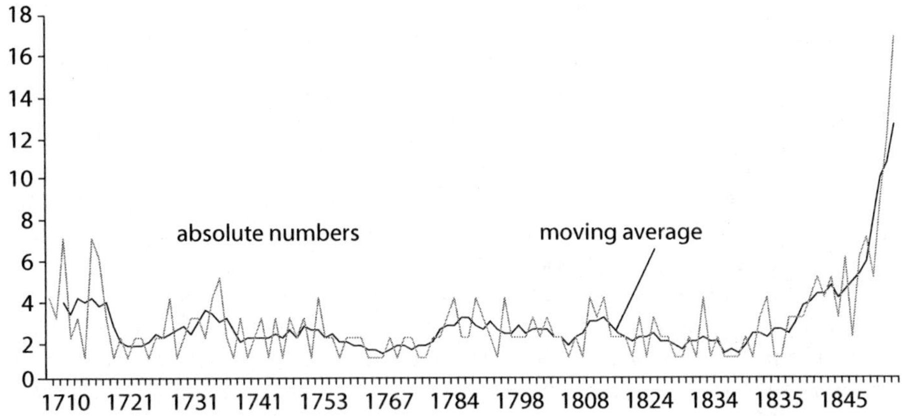

Figure 7.1 *Yearly Enrolment of New Apprentices in the Viennese Purse Makers' Guild (1710–1854)*

Sources: Viennese Municipal Archive, Guilds/Books, 54/1. Five years moving average.

Viennese crafts and trades, Alfred Klose clearly demonstrates a decline in the level of taxes paid by the purse makers between 1749 and 1756.[36] The number of enrolled apprentices decreased simultaneously with the poor economic situation, but the worst of the crisis had been overcome by 1780 and was then followed by a boom period during the Napoleonic wars.[37] Although it is difficult to prove direct causality between the effects of the continental blockade and the demand for the purse makers' products, the generally good state of the Viennese economy seems to have led the city's inhabitants to favour expenditure on consumer goods. After a pause between 1809 and 1840, the number of apprentices increased enormously up until the 1860s, although neither the changes in trade legislation nor the economic situation seem to have influenced the situation as much as technological improvements.

Only the enrolment registers for the period 1790 to 1903 were preserved for the silk weavers. 6,450 new apprentices were recorded during these years (see figure 7.2). In comparison with the purse makers this figure offers another perspective. Most obvious is the peak for new enrolments in the 1790s. The Napoleonic wars resulted in falling rates for enrolments in apprenticeships. The increase at the beginning of the 1840s and the 1850s can be explained by organizational changes. The guild masters and the artisans with a special licence were associated in 1848, therefore apprentices who had started their term of training in the workshop of an artisan with a special licence were newly enrolled in the guild.[38] The sharp decline in newly incorporated apprentices beginning in the middle of the 1850s was clearly affected by the abolition of the guilds in 1859. The new trade law changed the prerequisites for managing a silk-weaving workshop. The silk industry lost its status as a handicraft, therefore the weavers did not need to finish an apprenticeship for running their own workshops.[39] The period between the 1850s and the 1860s brought a decline in new enrolments of apprentices to almost one-tenth of what it had been in the first decades of the nineteenth century. By 1869 only one-third of all Viennese artisan workshops still engaged an apprentice.[40] From the middle of the 1870s hardly anyone started a career in a silk weaver's workshop.

From the end of the eighteenth century, silk weavers with a special licence were allowed to train their own apprentices, although these boys had to be recorded in the *Freisprechbuch* of the guild until 1811.[41] To start a career in the workshop of an artisan with a special licence could be an advantage for the boys, because despite lower fees, the training equipped them to run their own workshop and become a member of the guild, as apprentices enrolled by guild masters. The silk weavers' guild also kept special books of enrolment for female apprentices.

From 1790 to 1819, 887 apprentices were recorded as being in the association of silk weaver artisans with a special licence (see table 7.1). The enrolment of apprentices was much affected by economical up- and downswings: after a sharp decline at the end of the eighteenth and the beginning of the nineteenth centuries, the enrolments of apprentices reached a peak in the late 1800s. The abolition of the guilds had a deep impact on the apprenticeship system of young male and female silk weavers. Between 1859 and 1861 the number of Viennese silk-weavers' workshops and manufactories

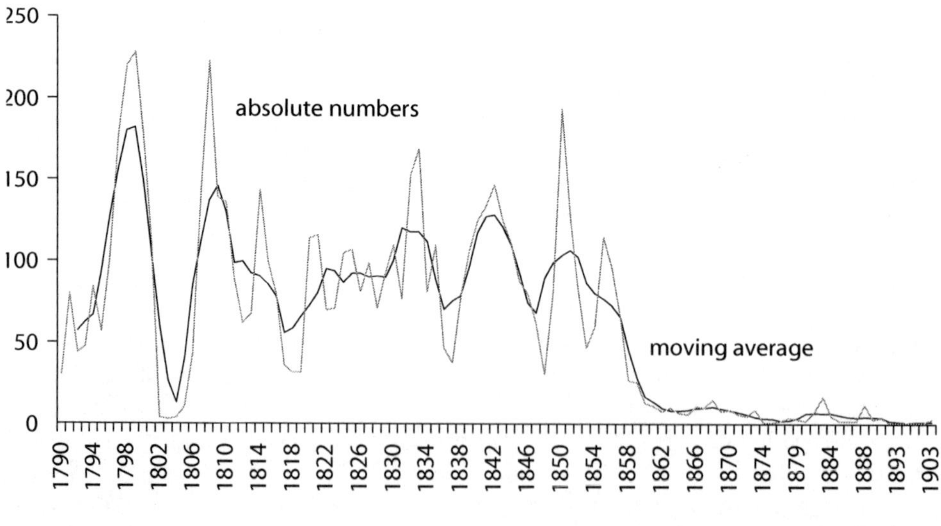

Figure 7.2 *Yearly Enrolment of New Male Apprentices in the Viennese Silk Weavers' Guild (1790–1903)*

Sources: Viennese Municipal Archive, Guilds/Books, 50/22, 23, 25. Five years moving average.

Table 7.1 *Numbers of Apprentices Newly Enrolled by Viennese Silk Weavers (1790–1903)*

Period	Female Apprentices*		Male Apprentices** (by the Guild)		Male Apprentices (Special Licence)		Total	
	n	%	n	%	n	%	n	%
1790–1799			1,011	79.0	269	21.0	1,280	100.0
1800–1809			834	58.7	586	41.3	1,420	100.0
1810–1819			767	96.0	32	4.0	799	100.0
1820–1829			900	100.0			900	100.0
1830–1839	730	43.5	947	56.5			1,677	100.0
1840–1849	251	20.5	971	79.5			1,222	100.0
1850–1859	516	38.6	821	61.4			1,337	100.0
1860–1869	152	61.0	97	39.0			249	100.0
1870–1879	56	60.2	37	39.8			93	100.0
1880–1889	27	33.8	53	66.2			80	100.0
1890–1899	12	57.1	9	42.9			21	100.0
1900–1903	1	25.0	3	75.0			4	100.0
Total	1,745		6,450		887		9,082	

Sources: Viennese Municipal Archive, Guilds/Books, 50/22, 23, 25, 30, 31, 57.
* Either engaged by a guild master or by an artisan with a special licence.
** After 1848 this column includes all male apprentices, either engaged by a guild master or by an artisan with a special licence.

Table 7.2 *Age of Male and Female Silk Weaver Apprentices at the Start of their Training (1830–1903)*

Period	Male Apprentices From 10 to 16 y.		Male Apprentices Over 17 y.		Female Apprentices From 10 to 16 y.		Female Apprentices Over 17 y.	
	n	%	n	%	n	%	n	%
1830 – 1839	41	93.2	3	6.8	249	90.9	25	9.1
1840 – 1849	459	83.8	89	16.2	88	96.7	3	3.3
1850 – 1859	605	72.7	227	27.3	370	96.4	14	3.6
1860 – 1869	77	79.4	20	20.6	139	91.4	13	8.6
1870 – 1879	20	51.3	19	48.7	55	98.2	1	1.8
1880 – 1889	12	22.6	41	77.4	24	88.9	3	11.1
1890 – 1903	2	18.2	9	81.8	9	75.0	3	25.0
Total	1,216	74.9	408	25.1	934	93.8	62	6.2

Sources: Viennese Municipal Archive, Guilds/Books, 50/25, 30, 31, 57.

declined by 9 percent; in the same period the number of newly enrolled female apprentices decreased from 222 in 1859 to 80 in 1861 (63 percent).

The registers of the guilds also give information about the age of the apprentices. An analysis of 91 apprentices of the purse makers in the period 1789 – 1857 showed that 76 percent were aged between thirteen and fifteen years.[42] Comparatively few decided on a career as a purse maker in later life.

None of the female or male apprentices who started their career as silk weaver artisans between 1830 and 1903 was under ten years of age. According to the analysis of the guild documents, there was no child labour in the Viennese crafts and trades in the eighteenth and nineteenth centuries. The usual age for starting a career as an artisan must have been between thirteen and fifteen years.[43] In the *Manufakturordnung für Seidenfabriken auf dem Land* (guild statutes for silk weavers in the countryside), which was enacted by Empress Maria Theresa in 1768, a lower age limit for the young male and female apprentices was fixed at thirteen years.[44] Table 7.2 shows a difference between young men and women. In the 1830s over 90 percent of the female and male apprentices started their term of training aged between ten and sixteen years. While the age of young female silk weavers did not change during the period under investigation, starting in the middle of the nineteenth century, more and more male apprentices were enrolled at a later stage of their life. In the 1870s nearly half of the young men, who were engaged in a Viennese silk weavers workshop or manufactory were older than seventeen years. For those 'older' apprentices the career as a silk weaver was not their first choice. A short notice in the book of enrolment gives information about their former profession. Four hundred-and- fourteen of the young men engaged in the silk-weaving workshops between 1790 and 1903 had already completed another apprenticeship; eleven of them were even guild masters in another craft.[45]

The Duration of an Apprenticeship

Existing historical research concerning the length of an apprenticeship in the eighteenth and nineteenth centuries has usually been based on the analysis of guild articles.[46] The length of an apprenticeship was one of the regulations fixed in such articles. Most Viennese guild articles prescribed an apprenticeship of between three and five years, and up to six or seven years in a few exceptional cases. For example, in the articles of the purse makers' guild of 1562 the duration of an apprenticeship was fixed at four years.[47] None of the following guild articles – one in 1715 and another in 1737 – prescribed any regulations concerning the duration of the apprenticeship.[48] The articles of the Viennese butchers of 1819 prescribed a three-year term, likewise the guild articles of cloth makers in the year 1752.[49] The guild of the chimney-sweeps demanded a longer period of training. According to the articles of 1673 the term was fixed at five years, although for the sons of masters the training was shorter – three years.[50] However, the articles of the silk weavers' guilds in 1740 demanded a six-year term and masters who paid for the clothing of their apprentices were allowed to engage them for seven years.[51]

A number of reasons can be given for the shortening or the lengthening of an apprenticeship. It can be assumed that young artisans were trained after a shorter period than the fixed one in the articles of the guilds, therefore it was beneficial for the master to lengthen the duration of the training period and to keep the apprentices as cheap labourers. On the other hand, apprentices were excused from paying for their apprenticeship if they were willing to pass some extra years of training and to work for below the normal wages. During the seventeenth century this practice of extra years became increasingly common.[52] On the other hand, the sons of masters were privileged: their apprenticeship tended to be shorter in duration. But there were other grounds for reducing or extending an apprenticeship. The Viennese guild of the cart wrights fixed the duration of the apprenticeship according to the height of the boys. Small and weak apprentices had to train for a longer period.[53] Likewise an apprenticeship in a workshop of a Viennese bookbinder depended on the age and height of the boys.[54] The chimney-sweeps preferred younger apprentices for their ability to climb up narrow chimneys.[55] On the contrary, prospective producers of leather clothes (*Gollermacher*) had to be sixteen or seventeen years old, because of the hard and laborious work.[56] As was the practice in the Viennese guilds, the Munich crafts had a special arrangement concerning the recruitment of apprentices: boys from the lower strata of society were trained without paying the fees, but had to pass an extra year. This special arrangement was supposed to protect the young artisans from being unemployed and becoming beggars.[57] An analysis of apprentices in German crafts in the eighteenth century concludes: 'The higher the money for the apprenticeship the shorter the period of training'.[58]

The index of artisans refered to earlier in this chapter conveys a better and more differentiated picture of the practice and duration of an apprenticeship than guild articles. By means of nominative record linkage – watching the information of identical persons in the *Aufding-* and *Freisprechbücher* by machine – one can calculate the period between the entry upon the apprenticeship and its completion. These calculated durations vary considerably from those fixed in the guild articles. According to the analysis of the guild articles of the purse makers, 200 apprentices, or 68 percent of all who were recorded in the period between 1710 and 1857, had to train for four years; only seven percent were allowed to complete their term of training in a shorter period; and the remaining 25 percent worked as apprentices for more than four years. According to the calculated training periods from the index, however, more than 20 percent finished their apprenticeship within a shorter period and a couple of sons of Viennese masters completed their term of training within one year.[59] In the case of the pearl embroiderers only 17 percent of the sons of Viennese masters and 13 percent of the other young artisans passed their apprenticeship in the fixed period – five years for the sons of masters and six years for all the other apprentices. All the others finished their term of training earlier.[60]

Figure 7.3 displays a comparison of the official duration of an apprenticeship fixed in the book of enrolment and the actual length of service in the Viennese workshops of the silk weavers between 1791 and 1903. An

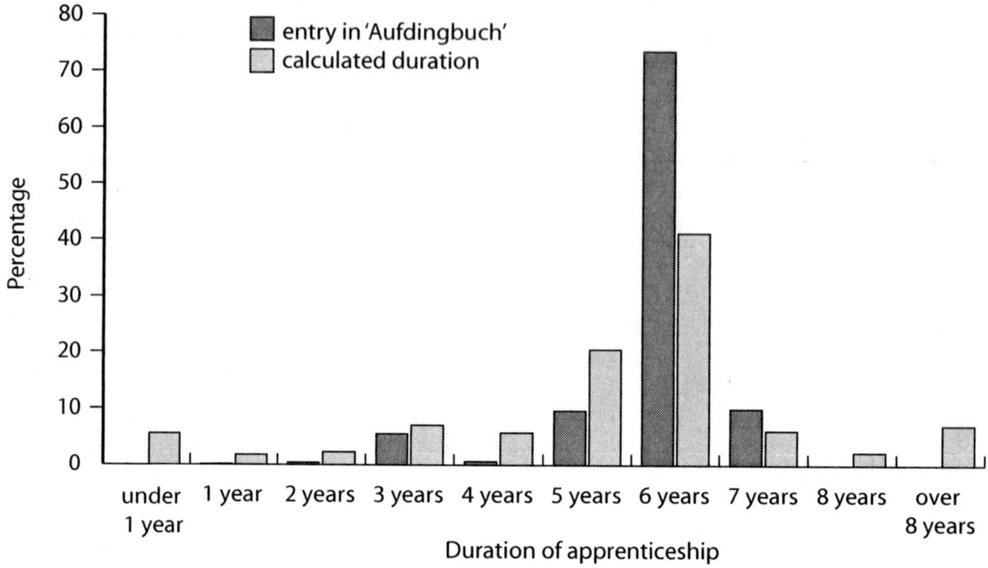

Figure 7.3 *Duration of Apprenticeship of Male Apprentices in Viennese Silk Weavers' Workshops (1791–1903)*
Source: Viennese Municipal Archive, Guilds/Books, 50/22, 23, 25, 57.

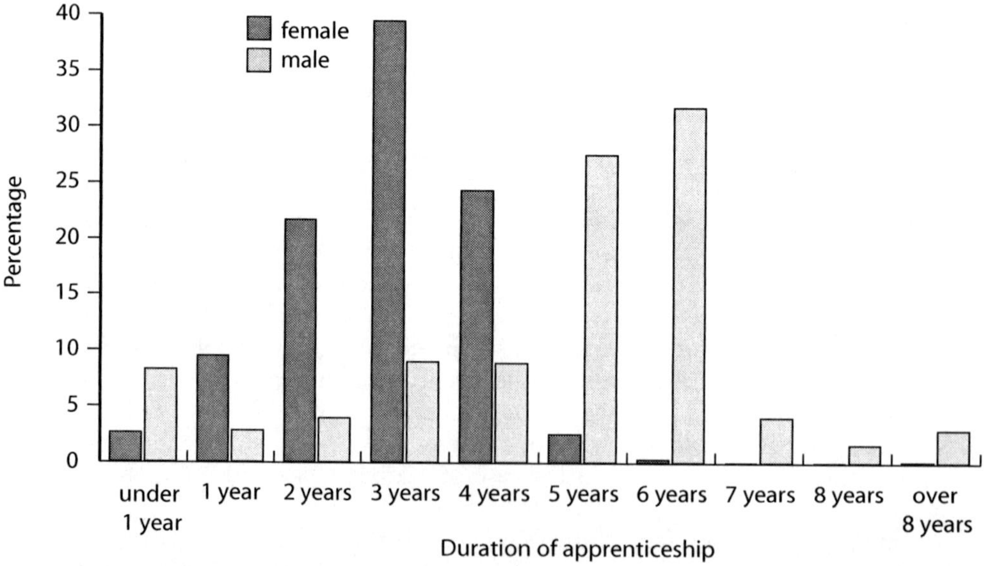

Figure 7.4 *Duration of Apprenticeship of Male and Female Apprentices in Viennese Silk Weavers' Workshops (1830–1903)*
Source: Viennese Municipal Archive, Guilds/Books, 50/22, 23, 25.

enormous discrepancy can be seen between the official and actual durations of training. A major percentage of the apprentices finished an ordinary training period of six years, but in addition we can see a broad variation in length of the apprenticeship between one and more than eight years. According to the calculated duration, only 41 percent of the silk weavers undertook an apprenticeship of six years; 43 percent finished their term of training in a markedly shorter period. Changing one's occupation was nothing unusual in the nineteenth century. Artisans with an apprenticeship in another sector did not have to complete the full term.[61] The sources do not give an explanation for the remaining 16 percent who had to work as an apprentice for more than six years. We only can assume that these were young men from the lower echelons of society, where the masters had to pay for their clothing.

Looking at figure 7.4, a comparison between the duration of an apprenticeship of male and female artisans, one can see major differences. While young women usually had to train for between two and four years, the apprenticeship of young men was markedly longer – between five and six years. The duration of an apprenticeship for male artisans was wide-ranging. These results lead to the conclusion that gender differences influenced the duration of apprenticeship. Female artisans were usually taught how to weave silk and velvet and after a relatively short period, from two to four years, as apprentices they were kept on as cheap labourers. It must be pointed out that trained female workers earned less money then journeymen. Since journeymen claimed much higher wages after the completion of the training period, masters were much more interested in lengthening the term of apprenticeship of the young men. Additionally the apprenticeship of male artisans which, after a period as journeymen, could lead to the position of a master, involved more than just weaving. Especially the sons of the leading masters – for example Beywinkler, Mestrozzi or Hebenstreit – were given additional training as pattern drawers. A special school for pattern drawing, the *Dessinateurschule,* was founded in Vienna in 1758.[62]

An apprenticeship could involve more than just the usual practice in artisan skills. In contrast to the terms of training of apprentices in the Viennese guild, in the German city of Krefeld an apprenticeship in silk-weaving skills lasted only three years.[63] To conclude, apprentices were cheap labourers and master artisans had the possibility to lengthen their training, which is exactly what they did.

The Stability of an Apprenticeship

Until recently the regular training period and the high stability of an apprenticeship were major assumptions of historical research.[64] The question of whether an apprentice successfully finished his or her training cannot be analysed on the basis of statues or articles. Therefore, historical research has not produced much evidence on the topic of stability.[65] A few results lead to the conclusion, that an apprenticeship was by no means a period of substantial stability. About 30 percent of French artisans in the eighteenth century did not finish their term, nearly the same as in Malmö (Sweden) in the first half of the nineteenth century. Steven Rappaport, who examined small scale production in London in the sixteenth century, concluded that only 41 percent completed their apprenticeships. In sixteenth and seventeenth-century Bristol only one third of all apprentices reached the status of a citizen.[66]

Indeed, not all apprentices finished their training in the same workshop where they had started and of course not all of them successfully completed their training. Data from several Viennese guilds in the eighteenth and nineteenth centuries offer some general information on this question (table 7.3). In the case of the bookbinders, only 20 percent terminated their apprenticeship in the second half of the eighteenth century. However, more than half of the locksmith apprentices gave up and never achieved the status of journeyman. Such high rates of capitulation can also be found in the case of the Viennese silk weavers. While more than 40 percent of the male silk weavers did not complete their apprenticeship between 1830 and 1903, only 14 percent of the young women stopped their training. Different reasons can be mentioned for this difference between the genders. The duration of a female apprenticeship was usually shorter than the male one, therefore it was easier to pass it. In addition, women did not have the same occupational opportunities as men. In the nineteenth century male workers had a wide

Table 7.3 *Stability of Apprenticeship in Different Viennese Crafts in the Eighteenth and Nineteenth Centuries*

Crafts	Period	Recorded Apprentices	Terminations	
			n	%
Bookbinder	1750–1804	385	77	20.0
Cooper	1861–1862	115	25	21.7
Haberdasher	1824–1857	1,831	477	26.1
Butcher	1844–1863	1,330	372	28.0
Chimney-sweep	1740–1867	716	203	28.4
Embroiderer of pearls	1665–1865	338	106	31.4
Cabinetmaker	1814–1840	121	43	35.5
Purse maker	1709–1854	347	137	39.5
Silk weaver	1810–1903	4,677	1,958	41.9
Locksmith	1785–1803	945	538	57.0

Sources: Bookbinder: Helga Skvarics, *Die Migrationsgeschichte der Wiener Buchbinder von 1750 bis 1800* (Wien, 1996, phil. Dipl.), 48; cooper: Viennese Municipal Archive, Guilds/Books, 68/10 (my own calculations); haberdasher: Viennese Municipal Archive, Guilds/Books, 41 (my own calculations); butcher: The Association of the Viennese Butchers, Aufding- und Freisprechbuch 1844–1862 (calculated by Heinrich Berger); chimney-sweep: Viennese Municipal Archive, Guilds/Books, 42/4, 5 (calculated by Heinrich Berger); embroiderer of pearls: Bauer, *Gold- und Perlsticker*, 10; cabinetmaker: Zatschek, *550 Jahre*, 107–08; purse maker: Viennese Municipal Archive, Guilds/Books, 54/9 (my own calculations); silk weaver: Viennese Municipal Archive, Guilds/Books, 50/22, 23, 25, 57 (my own calculations); locksmith: Friedrich Schembor, *Geschichte des Wiener Schlosserhandwerks von 1683 bis 1830* (Wien, unpublished manuscript).

range of different potential ways in which to earn their money, while women were mostly limited to textile work.[67] Therefore it was much harder for female labourers to change their employment.

The Master–Apprentice Relationship

The topic of apprentices absconding from their masters' households has often been mentioned in historical research.[68] Although this was one of the main reasons for the termination of an apprenticeship, running away need not directly end a career as an artisan. The apprenticeship was embedded in the master–servant relationship. An artisan household was based on a hierarchical structure, and apprentices were the lowest members of that hierarchy. Opportunities for apprentices to stand up to the power of the masters, their wives and the journeymen were marginal,[69] although the young men's parents, with whom they were often still in contact,[70] sometimes made use of their supervisory authority and their right to object to any violation on the part of the master.[71] However, the Viennese case also shows that parents used their powers to persuade young men to stay with their masters.

The tradition of moving into the master's household during the apprenticeship displays an astounding continuity in nineteenth century Vienna in comparison with German cities.[72] According to an analysis of samples of the Viennese census of 1857 and of 1869, three-quarters of all apprentices lived in their masters' households and only a few resided as subtenants or had their lodgings with their parents or other relatives.[73] As most of the Viennese apprentices in the nineteenth century were migrants from Bohemia or Moravia without their parents or relatives, they had to take their lodging in the masters' households. For young people without money or urban experience, living in the household of the employer was beneficial.

Sharing the household can be seen as a relationship between the family of the master and his subordinates. It has to be emphasized that it was not a relationship without conflicts and both partners did not have the same possibilities for shaping their daily life. On the one hand, apprentices could be engaged in daily domestic work – carrying water or looking after the children, and masters often ill-treated their young subordinates. Life could be hell in an artisan household, where bad food and inadequate lodging caused daily conflicts. On the other hand, the masters placed confidence in unfamiliar apprentices while incorporating them into their households, where they had the opportunity to deceive or rob the master's family. Daily conflicts between apprentices and their masters were not unusual in preindustrial societies, as can be seen in special paragraphs concerning these problems in the guild records[74] and complaints to the public authorities.[75] While journeymen had their special organizations and therefore a powerful tool to protest against the masters and the public authorities,[76] apprentices were not organized and their protests were individual and limited. 'Dropping out' of an apprenticeship was often the only way to defend against the arbitrariness of the masters.

Apart from individual acts of absconding, possibilities for protection were limited. Officially, apprentices could issue a public complaint against their masters. The most important reason for complaints was physical punishment.[77] However, public authorities admonished the guilds not to maltreat their subordinates. In 1775 the mayor and the council of Vienna sent a letter to all crafts and trades' organizations in which they complained about the ill-treatment of apprentices by their masters.[78] Another public admonition in 1845 argued again against masters who maltreated their subordinates.[79] Although it does not seem to have been common that artisan masters were judged for their malpractice in public, some of the apprentices did choose the legal route. In 1790 the father of the silk weaver apprentice Franz Hilbert wrote a letter to the Viennese town council in which he complained about the guild master Jakob Bernklau treating his son 'in a nearly inhuman way'. He asked the council if it would be possible for his son to complete his apprenticeship in another workshop.[80] And in 1849 two silk weaver apprentices wrote a letter of complaint about their master Adam Kostner. They also asked for permission to finish their apprenticeship in another workshop.[81] Complaint about the silk weaver Alois Zettin in the year 1844 led to the guild barring him from training further apprentices.[82]

Not all of the apprentices had to abscond; there were other means of protection, and sometimes even the lowest members of the hierarchy could gain their rights. One way was to move to another workshop and finish the apprenticeship under the care of another master. 13 percent (888) of all silk weaver apprentices in the period between 1791 and 1903 moved into another workshop during their training period and more than 22 percent (413) of all the young haberdashers who started their apprenticeships between 1824 and 1857 finished their term with another master.[83] Although only scanty information is available, it can be assumed that the reasons for the movement were manifold. For example, apprentices also had to find new workshops because of the deaths of their masters. Only in the Viennese silk weavers guild, widows who carried on the workshop of their deceased husband had the permission to engage apprentices, although they had to finish the last months of their apprenticeship in the workshop of a guild master.[84]

Besides running away, which either interrupted or ended the apprenticeship, there were other reasons which ended a career as an artisan. Masters could dismiss their apprentices, like the purse maker Erhard Hölzl who parted with his apprentice Franz Joseph Gnauß in 1716 because of the latter's 'dishonest behaviour' ('*in ganzsen unehrlichen verhalten*') or the apprentice Leonhard Gittner who was discharged by the silk weaver Josef Jakobi in 1853 because of his 'incompetence' ('*Unfähigkeit*').[85] Diseases and physical disability could also lead to cancellation of an apprenticeship contract. The purse maker Joseph Lezanzky, apprenticed in the workshop of Eduard Schlösser, ended his training in 1835 with the assent of the master because of physical disability.[86] Likewise the silk weaver Achatz Zettel had to give up his artisan career in 1816 because of problems with his eyes.[87]

Extremely scanty information is available concerning the future careers of apprentices who terminated their training period. The *Gewerbeenquete* (craft inquiry) from 1868 mentions that a lot of young artisans were able to use their skills after a very short period of training,[88] in other words, they could earn their living in crafts and trades without finishing their apprenticeships. Even in the first half of the eighteenth century, only a minority of the independent craftsmen in Vienna were incorporated into the guild system.[89] According to the commercial census of 1736 only 32 percent of the masters were guild members.[90] To supply the demand of the citizens a high number of craftsmen outside the guilds were needed. Therefore, in a big city like Vienna there always existed options to operate in crafts and trades without legal permission. The majority of the Viennese artisan recruits in the eighteenth and nineteenth centuries were migrants from central Europe. A lot of them remigrated to their point of origin after the ending of the apprenticeship, either as a journeyman or as a craftsman outside the guild system. In the countryside and in small villages the possibility to work as a 'freelancer' was also high – in Austria, they were called *Störer*.[91]

In preindustrial crafts and trades interrupting an apprenticeship did not necessarily mean an end to a career as an artisan. A lot of young artisans who absconded from their masters had the chance to continue their training in another workshop.[92] Most of the Viennese guilds consisted of a broad variety of workshops, in terms of social status. The economic development and the progress of industrialization in the nineteenth century intensified the social differentiation. Young artisans moved between the different workshops to finish their term of training with a master of higher social status. In the case of the Viennese silk weavers two types of licensed entitlement for running an artisan workshop existed simultaneously. The minority of the independent artisans were members of the guild, but the majority of the silk weavers carried on their activities with a special public licence. Apprentices who started their training with an artisan with a special licence often changed workshop to finish the apprenticeship with a guild master. The different levels of social status were reflected by the difference in fees that had to be paid for a successful completion. To finish an apprenticeship in the workshop of a guild master one had to pay 6 florins and 30 kreutzer. In the workshop of an artisan with a special licence the fees were much lower, only 2 florins.[93]

Another opportunity for runaways was to change their occupation. In the period under investigation more than 60 silk weaver apprentices restarted their careers in another craft. Because of the comparability of the skills, most of the drop-outs chose another textile trade, such as linen weaving, or weaving ribbons or veils, for the completion of their apprenticeships. If they restarted their career in a similar craft they did not usually have to go through the whole period of training. But there were also young artisans who changed their trade totally and decided on apprenticeships as carpenters, locksmiths, bakers or gold-beaters. Especially in times of war, when states raised the conscription, service in the army could also be an alternative for earning one's living. The young silk weaver Georg Franz Kriegs, born in Bamberg/ Germany, quit his apprenticeship in the workshop of the Viennese master Johann Kostner in 1815 and joined the army,[94] likewise the purse maker Joseph Kupfer, who ran away from his master in 1768.[95] In the second half of the eighteenth century the public authorities of the Habsburg Empire who were interested in young soldiers sent an order to the guilds: apprentices who wanted to shorten their period of training and join the army should be allowed to do so and they should be discharged from paying the full fees.[96] Between 1811 and 1861, 5 percent (242) of the enrolled silk weaver apprentices chose the trade of war instead of a career as an artisan. They only had to pass a curtate period of training and paid a reduced fee of 1 florin and 30 kreutzer.[97] But the social positions of the runaways should not be overestimated. Not all the young men who did not finish their apprenticeships had the chance to work in crafts and trades. Former apprentices could just as easily end up as beggars, as can be seen in an analysis of Viennese beggars at the end of the seventeenth century.[98]

In the nineteenth century, the social position of apprentices changed: in a lot of different crafts they became cheap labourers. This process started primarily in the so-called 'mass artisan sectors' with a high demand for workforce, such as the textile trades. 'In any case, from one end of the century to the other, it is clear that the status of the apprentice became assimilated to that of the industrial working class in general'.[99] Until the late eighteenth century, wages for apprentices were only known in the building and textile trades, sporadically in metalwork. These payments were mostly limited to the last year of apprenticeship.[100] During the nineteenth century, the payment of half of the journeymen's wages became typical after a short period of training in almost every craft and trade. Those sectors who suffered from a high degree of competition from the newly risen, factory-based production were the first who started to pay wages to the apprentices. Industrial workers were paid after a short period of training, therefore the masters had to give wages to their own subordinates, because otherwise they would lose their cheap labourers. The wages for apprentices could differ according to the workshop, hence the movement of the young artisans between these workshops was nothing unusual.

Although in the nineteenth century most of the Viennese artisans' sectors still produced on a small scale, other branches – such as building and construction – had already begun to organize themselves as larger enterprises in the course of the early modern period. During the eighteenth century, the silk-product sector likewise shifted towards protoindustrial activity based on a combination of centralized manufactories and the putting-out system. In the manufactories of the Viennese silk weavers it became usual to engage more than twenty apprentices at different periods of training at the same time. Some of these bigger workshops could afford to register more than ten new apprentices at once. These new types of enterprises were accompanied by the break-up of preindustrial relationships between masters and their apprentices. The modified status of the young artisans in the working process also affected the rules of the guilds. For example, masters in a lot of Viennese crafts and trades hired Jews and illegitimate boys and girls, even before the dissolution of the guild system in the middle of the nineteenth century.

Conclusion

Preindustrial crafts and trades were not some kind of fossilized relic. By analysing guild registers on Viennese apprentices I have tried to show that small-scale production should be understood as a flexible and ultimately very efficient means of regulating social mobility and dynamism. The chapters focused on the matter of stability and fluctuation of apprenticeships, as well as on the stability of the social position as an apprentice. By choosing the eighteenth and nineteenth centuries, changes in mobility and dynamism during the process of industrialization could also be taken into consideration.

The traditional picture of immobile artisans and an adjusted apprenticeship in preindustrial periods is based on the analysis of normative source materials, such as guild records. By studying the registers for apprentices one can get a better and more varied view of the practice and duration of an artisan training period. Viennese artisan masters had a variety of ways of shaping the duration of an apprenticeship. But it was not only the masters who benefited from the variability of the term of training: young men from the lower echelons of society saved their money by taking on an extra year, while the terms of training for the sons of Viennese artisan masters were shorter, likewise for journeymen who had already passed an apprenticeship in another craft or trade.

Based on the Viennese sources, gender differences in apprenticeships can also be seen. Although young women had the chance to start a career as a silk weaver, the course of an apprenticeship differed from that of the male artisans. During the progress of industrialization, the status of young apprentices shifted towards cheap labour force. Crafts and trades with a high demand for low-cost workers, such as textile industries, tended to engage more and more apprentices and to lengthen their training.

The question of whether an apprentice successfully finished or dropped out of his or her training period is one of the aspects of duration and stability which cannot be examined on the basis of guild articles. By analysing registers of the Viennese artisan guilds in the eighteenth and nineteenth centuries, a variety of options to deal with the institution of apprenticeship for masters and apprentices can be demonstrated. In some crafts nearly half of all young artisans did not finish their apprenticeship. Apprentices who stopped their training had the possibility to move to another workshop or they could start a new career in a different craft. Some of the young artisans joined the army or ended up as freelancers. Although scanty information is available on the future professional history of those young artisans who left the city, it can be assumed that a lot of them went back to their home towns and villages to work in crafts and trades outside the guild system. Vienna, as the capital of the Habsburg Empire, offered a broad variety of ways to earn one's living. Therefore the high degree of instability of apprenticeship must be seen as a phenomenon rooted in the big city, where social control is much weaker than in small towns and villages. To compare the situation of apprentices in Viennese guilds with other crafts in small towns and rural artisans, further research has to be done.

Notes

1. In the late nineteenth century the German historical school of economics generated a picture of rigid and back warded guilds, which were resistant to innovation. This stable picture has been challenged by social historians during the last thirty years but without any conclusion about the role of the guild system in the eighteenth and nineteenth centuries. See Wilfried Reininghaus, *Gewerbe in der Frühen Neuzeit* (Enzyklopädie deutscher Geschichte, vol. 3) (München, 1990); Josef Ehmer, 'Traditionelles Denken und neue Fragestellungen zur Geschichte von Handwerk und Zunft', in Friedrich Lenger (ed.), *Handwerk, Hausindustrie und die historische Schule der deutschen Nationalökonomie* (Bielefeld, 1998), 19–77; and Reinhold Reith, 'Lohn und Leistung aus der Perspektive der Historischen Schule der Nationalökonomie. Zum Problem der Wirtschaftsmentalität', in Lenger (ed.), *Handwerk*, 78–104.
2. Josef Ehmer, 'Tramping Artisans in Nineteenth-Century Vienna', in David Siddle (ed.), *Migration, Mobility, and Modernisation* (Liverpool, 2000), 158–78, p. 166.
3. Studies in the Viennese guild archives were funded by the Austrian Science Fund (P10807–Soz.). For their help and comments, I would like to thank the head of the project, Josef Ehmer, and the members of the team Sigrid Wadauer and Heinrich Berger. On published results see Josef Ehmer, 'Worlds of Mobility: Migration Patterns of Viennese Artisans in the Eighteenth Century', in Geoffrey Crossick (ed.), *The Artisan and the European Town, 1500–1900* (Aldershot, 1997), 172–99; Ehmer, 'Tramping Artisans', 164–85; Annemarie Steidl, *Auf nach Wien! Die Mobilität des mitteleuropäischen Handwerks am Beispiel der Haupt- und Residenzstadt* (Sozial- und wirtschaftshistorische Studien, vol. 30), (Wien/München, 2003); and Sigrid Wadauer, *Die Tour der gesellen. Mobilitat und Biographic im Kondwerk room 18. bis zum 20. Jahrhundert (Frankfurt, 2005).* (Wien, 2001, Ph.D. Thesis).
4. See Ehmer, 'Worlds of Mobility', 175.
5. Jürgen Bergmann, *Das Berliner Handwerk in der Frühphase der Industrialisierung* (Berlin, 1973); Helga Schultz, *Berlin 1650-1800. Sozialgeschichte einer Residenz (*Berlin/DDR, 1987); Michael Sonenscher, *Work and Wages: Natural Law, Politics and the Eighteenth Century French Trades* (Cambridge, 1989); Steven L. Kaplan, *Provisioning Paris: Merchants and Millers in the Grain and Flour Trade During the 18th Century* (Ithaka NY, 1984); and Steven Rappaport, *Worlds Within Worlds: Structures of Life in 16th Century London* (Cambridge, 1989).
6. Josef Ehmer, 'Ökonomischer und sozialer Strukturwandel im Wiener Handwerk – von der industriellen Revolution bis zur Hochindustrialisierung', in Ulrich Engelhardt (ed.), *Handwerker in der Industrialisierung. Lage, Kultur und Politik im späten 18. bis ins frühe 20. Jahrhundert* (Stuttgart, 1984), 78–105.
7. Andreas Baryli, 'Gewerbepolitik und gewerberechtliche Verhältnisse im vormärzlichen Wien', in Renate Banik-Schweitzer et al. (eds), *Wien im Vormärz* (Wien, 1980), 17–21.
8. Ehmer, 'Tramping Artisans', 166.
9. See Karl Pribram, *Geschichte der österreichischen Gewerbepolitik 1740–1860*, vol. 1 (Wien, 1907) and Andreas Baryli, 'Kontinuitäten der österreichischen Gewerbepolitik vom Vormärz bis zum Jahr 1883', *Christliche Demokratie*, 4 (1984): 345–51.
10. For more information about the sources in the Viennese Municipal Archive see Heinrich Kretschmar, *Archivinventar 'Innungen'* (Veröffentlichungen des Wiener Stadt- und Landesarchives, Reihe A, Heft 2) (Wien, 1987).
11. Sigrid Wadauer, 'Der Gebrauch der Fremde. Wanderschaft in der Autobiographik von Handwerkern', *Österreichische Zeitschrift für Geschichtswissenschaft* (*ÖZG*), 2 (1998): 159–87, p. 162.
12. At the beginning of an artisan training every boy was registered in the apprentice enrolments, listed under the name of the master who engaged the apprentice. The evidence varies according to the guild. Normally, the register contained the first and last name of the apprentice, the name of the master (or his widow, who had carried on the workshop of her deceased husband), the date of enrolment, the duration of the apprenticeship, the entry fee, and information as to whether or not the new apprentice was the son of a Viennese master.

The place of birth, the age of the boy at the enrolment or his date of birth, and dates of persons who acted as guarantors for the apprentice as well as the masters and journeymen who witnessed the enrolment were not recorded in every document. Records concerning the breaking-off of an apprenticeship and information about the intended new career of the apprentice can only scarcely be found. After the successful completion of the apprenticeship, the young men's names were again recorded in a special book, called *Freisprechbuch*. Most of the Viennese guilds had their own records for the completion of an apprenticeship, but some of them only made an entry in the book of enrolment. The *Freisprechbuch* is much less informative than the *Aufdingbuch*. Normally it contains the name of the apprentice, the date of completion of the apprenticeship, the name of the master with whom the boy finished his training, and the fees for the successful completion.

13. In a letter to the government of Lower Austria the Vienna purse-makers' guild lamented 'daß auf dem Lande die Taschnerprofession ganz entbehrlich und bloß ein Bedarf ... ist, wo viele Reisearbeiten zusammen kommen' [Purse-makers are unnecessary in rural areas and there is only a demand for their products if a lot of people are travelling]. Vienna Municipal Archives, Guild Books, 54/38.
14. Reinhold Reith, 'Arbeitsmigration und Gruppenkultur deutscher Handwerksgesellen im 18. und frühen 19. Jahrhundert', in *Scripta Mercaturge*, 23 (1989): 1–35, p. 17. For more information about the Viennese purse makers see Heinz Zatschek, *Aus der Vergangenheit des Taschner-Handwerks in Wien* (Wien 1954, unpublished manuscript).
15. See Erwin Bandion, *Wiener Gewerbe und Industrie 1804–1850* (Wien, 1949, PhD. thesis, 11).
16. Viktor Thiel, 'Gewerbe und Industrie', in Alterthumsverein zu Wien (ed.), *Geschichte der Stadt Wien* (Wien, 1911), 411–523, p. 479.
17. *Statistische Tafeln der Österreichischen Monarchie* (Wien, 1834).
18. Viennese Municipal Archive, Hauptausschußakten, 17/1688.
19. Alfred Klose, *Die wirtschaftliche Lage der bürgerlichen Gewerbe in Wien von 1749 bis 1775* (Wien, 1957, PhD. Thesis), 121.
20. Viennese Municipal Archive, Guilds/Books, 54/1, 2, 5, 6.
21. Gustav Schimmer, *Die Bevölkerung von Wien und seiner Umgebung nach dem Beruf und der Beschäftigung. Auf Grundlage der jüngsten Volkszählung* (Wien, 1874), 93. This high number of workers seems to be even higher when we take into consideration that the census was conducted in winter (31 December 1869), because at this time of year the number of journeymen was lowest.
22. Christian Salmeyer, *Das gewerbliche Kleinbürgertum in Wien. Zu seiner wirtschaftlichen und politischen Entwicklung in der zweiten Hälfte des 19. Jahrhundert* (Wien, 1980, PhD. Thesis), 42.
23. Helene Deutsch, *Die Entwicklung der Seidenindustrie in Österreich 1660–1840* (Studien zur Sozial-Wirtschafts- und Verwaltungsgeschichte, vol. 3) (Wien, 1909), 53–54 and Sylvia Lausecker, *Vor- und frühindustrielle Produktionsformen am Beispiel der Wiener Seiden- und Baumwollindustrie 1740–1848* (Wien, 1975, PhD. Thesis).
24. See Günther Chaloupek, 'Wirtschaftsentwicklung, merkantilistische Wirtschaftspolitik und die Wiener Wirtschaft bis Joseph II (1790)', in *Wiener Geschichtsblätter*, 31 (1976): 13–31.
25. In 1765, after the death of the emperor Franz Stephan, his widow, Maria Theresia, ordered a year- long mourning of the royal court. In consequence, the silk industry declined because only black silk was demanded. Moritz Dreger, 'Beginn und Blüte der Wiener Seidenweberei', *Kunst und Kunsthandwerk*, 18, 1/2 (1915): 325–400, p. 337.
26. Herbert Hassinger, 'Der Außenhandel der Habsburgermonarchie in der zweiten Hälfte des 18. Jahrhunderts', in Friedrich Lütge (ed.), *Die wirtschaftliche Situation in Deutschland und Österreich um die Wende vom 18. zum 19. Jahrhundert* (Stuttgart, 1964), 61–98, p. 82.
27. See Stephan Ritter von Keess, *Darstellung des Fabriks- und Gewerbewesens im österreichischen Kaiserstaate*, vol. 1 (Wien, 1819–1824), 300.
28. Franz Bujatti, *Geschichte der Seiden-Industrie Österreichs, deren Ursprung und Entwicklung bis in die neueste Zeit* (Wien, 1893), 69.
29. Markus Cerman, 'Proto-Industrialization in an Urban Environment: Vienna, 1750–1857', *Continuity and Change*, 8 (1993): 281–320, p. 286.

30. See Cerman, 'Proto-Industrialization', 292.
31. Deutsch, *Die Entwicklung*, 206.
32. Günther Chaloupek, 'Der unvollendete Boom. Die Entwicklung der Wiener Wirtschaft in der Ära des Liberalismus', in *Wien in der liberalen Ära* (Wien, 1978), 34–36.
33. Rappaport, *Worlds Within Worlds*, 294.
34. Pavla Vošhlíková (ed.), *Auf der Walz. Erinnerungen böhmischer Handwerksgesellen* (Wien/Köln/Weimar, 1994), 273.
35. Steven R. Smith, 'The London Apprentices as Seventeenth-Century Adolescents', *Past and Present*, 61 (1973): 149–61, p. 160.
36. Klose, *Die wirtschaftliche Lage*, 121.
37. Günter Chaloupek, 'Kleingewerbe und Handwerk im 18. Jahrhundert', in *Geschichte der Stadt Wien*, vol 4. (Wien,1991), 118.
38. Viennese Municipal Archive, Guilds/Documents, 50/24.
39. See *Die Gewerbeordnung vom 20.12.1859* (Brünn, 1907).
40. Salmeyer, *Das Gewerbliche Kleinbürgertum*, 21.
41. Boys who were recorded in the guild registers had to pay their fees to the guild. Viennese Municipal Archive, Hofkammerdekret vom 24. Dezember 1811, Guilds/Documents, 50/25.
42. Viennese Municipal Archive, Guilds/Books, 54/1.
43. Most of the Viennese carpet maker apprentices were over fourteen years at the start of their carreer. Heinz Zatschek, *550 Jahre jung. Die Geschichte eines Handwerks* (Wien, 1958), 132; the average age of apprentices in Viennese chimney-sweeps' workshops was between thirteen and fourteen years. Else Reketzki, *Das Rauchfangkehrergewerbe in Wien. Seine Entwicklung vom Ende des 16. Jahrhunderts bis ins 19. Jahrhundert* (Wien, 1952, PhD. Thesis), 76.
44. 'Sammet- Taffet und andere glatten Seidenzeuge-Manufacturs-Ordnung vom 24. März 1768', *Codex Austriacus*, Suppl. 4, (1704): 1072–84.
45. The 414 'older' apprentices had already been trained as: 347 weavers, 11 master weavers, 11 soldiers, 9 commercial servants, 9 tailors, 6 gauze makers, 4 shoemakers, 3 haberdashers, 3 ribbon weavers, 2 clothiers, 2 gold smiths, 1 stocking weaver, 1 dyer, 1 calico printer, 1 locksmith, 1 tinsmith, 1 steel worker and 1 gem cutter.
46. See, for example, Reinhold Reith, *Arbeits- und Lebensweise im städtischen Handwerk. Zur Sozialgeschichte Augsburger Handwerksgesellen im 18. Jahrhundert (1700–1806)* (Göttinger Beiträge zur Wirtschafts- und Sozialgeschichte) (Göttingen, 1988).
47. Viennese Municipal Archive, Guilds/Books, 54/8; see also Zatschek, *Aus der Vergangenheit*, 116.
48. Viennese Municipal Archive, Kaiserliche Privilegien der bürgerlichen Taschner von 1715. H.A. Akten, 5/1715 und Satz und Ordnung deren gesambten Taschner-Gesöllen und Jünger von 1737. H.A. Akten, 2/1737.
49. See Karl Fajkmajer, *Festschrift der Wiener Fleischhauergenossenschaft* (Wien, 1912), 67, and Ritter von Keess, *Darstellung des Fabriks- und Gewerbewesens*, vol. 2, 261. According to the records of the butchers' guild in the Viennese suburbs, their apprenticeship was fixed at three years.
50. Viennese Municipal Archive, Handwerksartikel, AR 6/1664, F. 62 and Privileg Kaiser Leopolds, AR 7/1673, F. 78.
51. Viennese Municipal Archive, Handwerksartikeln für die Seiden-, Schleier- und Dünntüchelmacher, gegeben vom Bürgermeister und Rat der Stadt Wien, 12. Februar 1740. Guilds/Documents, 50/23, nr. 1.
52. Zatschek, *550 Jahre jung sein*, 43. Regulations for the lengthening of an apprenticeship can also be found in other German-speaking countries. See, for example, Helmut Bräuer, *Handwerk im alten Chemnitz. Studien zur Sozial- und Wirtschaftsgeschichte des Chemnitzer Handwerks von den Anfängen bis zum Beginn der industriellen Revolution* (Chemnitz, 1992), 69.
53. Heinz Zatschek, *Handwerk und Gewerbe in Wien. Von den Anfängen bis zur Erteilung der Gewerbefreiheit im Jahre 1859* (Wien, 1949), 162.
54. Maria Menzel, *Wiener Buchbinder der Barockzeit* (Wien/Graz/Köln, 1972), 58.

55. Heinz-Peter Mielke, 'Schornsteinfeger', in Reinhold Reith (ed.), *Lexikon des alten Handwerks. Vom späten Mittelalter bis ins 20. Jahrhundert* (München, 1990), 215–16.
56. Thiel, 'Gewerbe und Industrie', 101.
57. Uwe Puschner, *Handwerk zwischen Tradition und Wandel. Das Münchner Handwerk an der Wende vom 18. zum 19. Jahrhundert* (Göttinger Beiträge zur Wirtschafts- und Sozialgeschichte, vol. 13) (Göttingen, 1988), 242–43.
58. Andreas Grießinger and Reinhold Reith, 'Lehrlinge im deutschen Handwerk des ausgehenden 18. Jahrhunderts', *Zeitschrift für Historische Forschung*, 13 (1986): 149–99, p. 153. In sixteenth-century London paying off years of apprenticeship was also common. See Rappaport, *Worlds Within Worlds*, 321.
59. Viennese Municipal Archive, Guilds/Books, 54/9.
60. Franz Bauer, *Die Zunft der Gold- und Perlsticker in Wien* (Wien, unpublished manuscript, 11).
61. Viennese Municipal Archive, Verordnung Nr. 97, 1. Februar 1785, Guilds/Documents, 50/24.
62. For the history of the *Dessinateurschule* see Maria Braun-Rohnsdorf, 'Dessinateurschulen und Mustersammlungen', *Ciba-Rundschau*, 114 (1954): 4206–11.
63. Peter Kriedte, *Die Stadt am seidenen Faden. Haushalt, Hausindustrie und soziale Bewegung in Krefeld in der Mitte des 19. Jahrhunderts* (Göttingen, 1992), 111.
64. See, for example, Helmut Prösler, *Das gesamtdeutsche Handwerk im Spiegel der Reichsgesetzgebung 1530 bis 1806* (Berlin, 1954); Michael Stürmer (ed.), *Herbst des Alten Handwerks. Zur Sozialgeschichte des 18. Jahrhunderts* (München, 1979), and Kurt Wesoly, *Lehrlinge und Handwerksgesellen am Mittelrhein. Ihre soziale Lage und Organisation vom 14. bis 17. Jahrhundert* (Frankfurt/Main, 1985).
65. See Reinhold Reith, 'Zur beruflichen Sozialisation im Handwerk vom 18. bis ins frühe 20. Jahrhundert. Umrisse einer Sozialgeschichte der deutschen Lehrlinge', *Vierteljahrschrift für Sozial- und Wirtschaftsgeschichte* (*VSWG)*, 76 (1989): 1–27; and Elke Schlenkrich 'Der Alltag der Lehrlinge im sächsischen Zunfthandwerk des 15. bis 18. Jahrhunderts', *Medium Aevum Quotidianum*, 4 (1995).
66. Sonenscher, *Work and Wages*, 109–110; Lars Edgren, 'Crafts in Transformation? Master, Journeymen and Apprentices in a Swedish Town, 1800 – 1850', *Continuity and Change*, 1 (1986): 363–83, p. 369. In the case of the London brewers between 1540 and 1580, 40 percent finished their apprenticeship, 15 percent died, 1 percent of the young men quited their term because of marriage and 44 percent left their masters. Between 1540 and 1590, only 55 percent of London carpenters' apprentices completed their training. Rappaport, *Worlds Within Worlds*, 77 and Ilana Krausmann Ben-Amos, Adolescence and Youth in Early Modern England (Yale, 1994).
67. See Annemarie Steidl, 'Trost für die Zukunft der Zurückgelassenen.' Die Funktion der Witwenpensionskassen im Wiener Handwerk im 18. und 19. Jahrhundert', in Josef Ehmer and Peter Gutschner (eds), *Das Alter im Spiel der Generationen. Historische und sozialwissenschaftliche Beiträge* (Wien/Köln/Weimar, 2000), 320–47.
68. See, for example, Schlenkrich, 'Der Alltag', 102–11; Petra Eggers, 'Hamburger Handwerkslehrlinge der Schuhmacher und Schiffszimmerer Zunft im 18. und 19. Jahrhundert', *III. Internationales Handwerksgeschichtliches Symposium,* vol. 1 (Veszprém, 1987), 143–52; Kathrin Keller, *Zu materiellen Lebensverhältnissen kleiner gewerblicher Warenproduzenten am Beginn der Übergangsperiode vom Feudalismus zum Kapitalismus (Ende des 15. bis Anfang des 17. Jahrhunderts) – dargestellt am Beispiel von Leder- und Textilgewerbe in Leipzig* (Leipzig, 1987, PhD. Thesis); and Friedrich Lenger, *Sozialgeschichte der deutschen Handwerker seit 1800* (Frankfurt/Main, 1988), 30–31.
69. Grießinger and Reith, 'Lehrlinge', 151 and Andreas Grießinger, *Das symbolische Kapital der Ehre. Streikbewegungen und kollektives Bewußtsein deutscher Handwerksgesellen im 18. Jahrhundert* (Frankfurt/Berlin/Wien, 1981), 59.
70. Some of the apprentices returned to their fathers' houses before they started to travel around as journeymen. This finding leads to the conclusion that they did not lose contact with their parents during their apprenticeship. See Sigrid Wadauer, 'Diese Frage kommt mir

oft wie ein Gespenst vor. Alter und Generationsbeziehungen in der Autobiographik von Handwerkern', in Ehmer and Gutschner (eds), *Das Alter*, 348–82.

71. In his autobiography a carpenter remembered the admonition of his father: 'aber wir müßten bei dem, was wir uns gewählt hatten bleiben, und wehe, wir würden aus der Lehre davonlaufen, an den Ohren würde er uns dorthin zurückführen' [We had to stay with whatever artisan we chose and if we would abscond from our masters' house he would take us back even if he had to force us]. Karel Šacek, 'Erinnerungen eines Tischlers', in Vošhlíková (ed.), *Auf der Walz*, 104–05.
72. See Reith, 'Zur beruflichen Sozialisation', 10.
73. Josef Ehmer, *Soziale Traditionen in Zeiten des Wandels. Arbeiter und Handwerker im 19. Jahrhundert* (Frankfurt/New York, 1994), 81.
74. For example, in 1819, the guild statutes of the Viennese butchers defined that it was forbidden for artisan master to use their apprentices as shepherds for more than a year. The statutes also fixed special fines for masters who offended against that rule. See Fajkmajer, *Festschrift*, 67.
75. In 1835, a public statement complained that new apprentices were exposed to the arbitrariness and cruelty of their masters and that the parents most often had to pay for a better treatment of their sons. See Lausecker, *Vor- und frühindustrielle Produktionsformen*, 211.
76. For more information about journeymen's protests see Grießinger, *Das symbolische Kapital.*
77. See Eggers, 'Hamburger Handwerkslehrlinge', 143–52 and Josef Ehmer, *Heiratsverhalten, Sozialstruktur, ökonomischer Wandel. England und Mitteleuropa in der Formationsperiode des Kapitalismus* (Göttingen, 1991), 178.
78. See Vienna Municipal Archives, Brief vom Magistrate der k.k. Haupt- und Residenzstadt Wien an sämtliche Wiener Zünfte, 3. März 1845. Guild Documents, 50/24, nr. 6.
79. 'Die k.k. Polizei=Oberdirektion hat aus den an dieselbe gelangten Berichten der k.k. Polizei=Bezirks=Direktion die Wahrnehmung gemacht, daß viele Professionisten am hiesigen Platze das ihnen beziehungsweise auf ihre Lehrjungen zustehende Recht der häuslichen Züchtigung in einem solchen Grade mißbrauchen, daß von den Letzteren mehrfache Klagen gegen ihre Lehrherrn geführt werden, bei deren Untersuchung in Folge der beigebrachten wundärztlichen Befunde sich zeigte, daß die Kläger und rücksichtlich die Lehrjungen, statt einer häuslichen Züchtigung, Mißhandlungen erlitten hatten, welche an den Mißhandelten nicht nur Merkmale zurückgelassen, sondern dieselben auch auf gewisse Zeiträume zur Arbeit unfähig gemacht haben. In Folge eines von der hohen Polizei=Hofstelle erlassenen hohen Auftrages ist auf das Benehmen der Gewerbesleute in besagter Beziehung ein besonderes Augenmerk zu richten, und jene, welche sich solcher tirannischer Behandlungen schuldig machen, die Befugniß zur Lehrjunge=Aufdingung zu entziehen.' Viennese Municipal Archive, Brief vom Magistrate der k.k. Haupt- und Residenzstadt Wien an sämtliche Wiener Zünfte, 3. März 1845. Guilds/Documents, 50/24, nr. 6.
80. Viennese Municipal Archive, Brief von Johann Hilbert an den Wien Magistrat, 16. April 1790. Guilds/Documents, 50/24, nr. 6.
81. Viennese Municipal Archive, Ratschläge und verschieden Akten 1849–1863, Guilds/Documents, 50/17, nr. 11.
82. Viennese Municipal Archive, Brief des Magistrats der k.k. Haupt- und Residenzstadt Wien an die bürgerliche Seidenzeugmacherzunft, 23. Mai 1844. Guilds/Documents, 50/25, nr. 8.
83. Viennese Municipal Archive, Guilds/Books, 50/22, 23, 25, 57 and 41. My own calculations.
84. See Steidl, '... Trost für die Zukunft der Zurückgelassenen', 320–47.
85. Viennese Municipal Archive, Guilds/Books, 54/9 and 50/25.
86. A short note in the book of enrolment says: 'wurde auf sein ersuchen mit Einverständnis des Lehrherrn mit Taufschein und Schulzeugnis entlassen' [This apprentice wished to be dismissed. His master agreed and he got his certificate of baptism and his school certificate]. Vienna Municipal Archives, Guild Books, 54/9.
87. Viennese Municipal Archive, Guilds/Books, 50/23.

88. 'Enquete der Niederösterreichischen Handels- und Gewerbekammer über die Wünsche des Handels-, Gewerbe- und Arbeiterstandes im Kammerbezirk bezüglich der Revision des Gewerbegesetzes vom 20. Dezember 1859' (Wien, 1868), 50.
89. Steidl, *Auf nach Wien*, 78–85.
90. Thiel, *Gewerbe und Industrie*, 435.
91. See Schlenkrich, 'Der Alltag', 112–13.
92. See also Albrecht Bruns, *Die Arbeitsverhältnisse der Lehrlinge und Gesellen im städtischen Handwerk in Westdeutschland bis 1800* (Köln, 1938, PhD. Thesis), 50–51.
93. Viennese Municipal Archive, Guilds/Books, 50/22, 23, 25, 57.
94. Viennese Municipal Archive, Guilds/Books, 50/23.
95. Viennese Municipal Archive, Guilds/Books, 54/9.
96. Ilse Holzhey, *Die Zünfte im Kampf mit den Landesfürsten 1527–1832* (Graz, 1965), 51.
97. Viennese Municipal Archive, Guilds/Books, 50/23, 25.
98. See Helmut Bräuer, *'... und hat seithero gebetlet' Bettler und Bettelwesen in Wien und Niederösterreich zur Zeit Kaiser Leopolds I.* (Wien/Köln/Weimar, 1996), 130.
99. Yves Lequin, 'Apprenticeship in Nineteenth-Century France: A Continuing Tradition or a Break With the Past?', in Steven L. Kaplan and Cynthia J. Koepp (eds), *Work in France. Representation, Meaning, Organisation, and Practice* (Ithaca/London, 1986), 459.
100. For more information about wages for apprentices see Reinhold Reith, 'Zur sozialen Lage der Handwerksgesellen und Lehrlinge vom späten 18. bis ins frühe 20. Jahrhundert. Sparfähigkeit, Sparmöglichkeiten und Sparmotivationen', *Zeitschrift für bayerische Sparkassengeschichte*, 6 (1992): 57–82.

CHAPTER 8

SOCIAL MOBILITY AND APPRENTICESHIP IN LATE MEDIEVAL FLANDERS

Peter Stabel

Introduction

The last few decades have seen a dramatic increase in historical literature on apprenticeship and guilds in early modern Europe, but not for the late medieval period in Europe.[1] Historians may have been daunted by the apparent lack of sources or the seemingly one-sided information in the normative sources.[2] While these critics may be correct in their assessments of the economic and social realities of entrepreneurship, the guild statutes that have come down to us (although vague) can also provide indications of ideologies, cultural modes and social customs. A comparison of existing regulation with contemporary litigation in urban courts, surviving apprenticeship contracts, or scarce quantitative data about guild membership, moreover, sheds useful light on indicators of change as well as on some continuities.[3]

Apprenticeship was one of the cornerstones of social and economic organization in the preindustrial city. It was characterized by hierarchical and paternalistic views of society, but also by ideals of guild fraternity and solidarity.[4] It was used to transfer knowledge, but even more important, to transfer status. Apprenticeship was considered a threshold to social mobility, as well as an effective barrier against undesirable intruders. The system became a rite of passage for the young and a way of preserving political power, social prestige and economic capital in the hands of influential masters. It was the ultimate tool for establishing qualification, maintaining authority and defending social boundaries.

But how effective was this threshold? The little quantitative data we have about late medieval migration suggests that society in that period was highly mobile. People moved back and forth among countryside and towns, or among various urban settlements, looking for opportunities. Migration could be temporary and seasonal: domestic and unskilled labour moving from countryside to towns or the other way around. But migrational flows of skilled labour were important, and because most skilled labour was organized in the corporate economy, these flows included many guildsmen. Masters sought better entrepreneurial opportunities, journeymen better employment, and apprentices better training conditions. Furthermore, skilled labour often followed a pattern of step migration, moving from smaller towns to larger centres.[5] Hence social mobility of skilled artisans within guild structures also had a geographic dimension. As will be demonstrated, apprentices moved up the ladder of the guild hierarchy to become masters, but not necessarily in the same town. Journeymen, as well as masters, often moved to other cities to settle as skilled wage earners or entrepreneurs.

Guild authorities could not always control the mechanisms of social mobility completely, even if they wanted to. Geographic mobility added to the difficult situation. Mechanisms to recognize and acknowledge training in other towns, and even in other guilds, as well as to adopt skills acquired elsewhere, were widely accepted because reciprocal relations between towns and guilds were inevitable. But this openness contained a paradox. Apprenticeship became an issue in the political and economic competition among cities. This was not only because it was important to preserve a monopoly on economic expertise and skill, but also because of the status aspects of guild organization in a system of *monopolistic competition*.[6] The good fortune of the urban industries, especially the cloth industries, which had an international clientele, depended on standard quality that allowed clear identification of the textiles of a particular city on the export market and differentiated these from similar textiles manufactured in other cities and production regions. Distinguishing wares from those of competitors and establishing standardized quality were therefore crucial for the survival of the urban industries. Guarding and defending that quality was paramount in the strategies of guilds. No wonder training and product control became so crucial in the organization of craft guilds. It was essential that newcomers, apprentices, journeymen and masters quickly adapted to the economic standards set by the guild.

Start of a Career? Becoming an Apprentice

In 1422 the Ghent tapestry weaver Jan Vroetaert went before the highest guild institution in the city, the *opperdeken* (senior dean), to declare that he had taken Pieterkin Beelaert as an apprentice for a period of five years.[7] This seemingly ordinary event – in Ghent there must have been dozens of such contracts daily – reveals important facts about the position of apprentices in a guild-regulated economy. Peter's father gave young Peter into the custody of another man for a period of five years. In exchange for training and board, young Peter had to work for his new master and obey him as he would have obeyed his father. The agreement must have been to the benefit of both parties. The tapestry master was even prepared, if necessary, to take over Peter's entrance fee of 4 Flemish pounds (about 96 days' worth of wages for a skilled craftsman), if his father were not able to pay himself.

Guild statutes reveal very little about the relations between masters and apprentices. Often they only mention the fact that apprentices were not allowed to abandon their posts and that masters were not supposed to lure away another master's apprentices. This indicates that abiding by the contract must have been a burning issue. Contracts preserved in the registers of the Flemish aldermen reveal further details about the aims and ambitions of individuals.[8] Although there has not yet been a systematic study of apprenticeship in this period, some mechanisms about orphan-apprentices in the largest city in Medieval Flanders, the cloth city of Ghent, can be identified.[9] Young orphans were placed in the custody of a craftsman, and had similar conditions and restrictions to those of other apprentices. Theoretically, they had to serve their master, obey him, and work at his premises in exchange for training, socialization and board. Marianne Danneel believed that at the end of this training they would be able to assimilate more easily in the 'rigid' guild system of Ghent.[10]

An analysis of written apprenticeship contracts (even though many were concluded orally) reveals a diverse social reality. The presence or absence of specific conditions in the contracts depended on the balance of power between the contracting partners. The political situation, the general economic cycle, and especially the condition of the labour market determined which party enjoyed a stronger position. Before each contract was signed there were negotiations about the conditions of apprenticeship (*besprec*). The length of the apprenticeship was a particular subject of negotiation. Although it could vary from one guild to another, the guild statutes only set the norm. Individual negotiations did not necessarily follow the prescribed length. The apprentice's career after his training was finished was also an important issue: would the apprentice continue to work for the same master and for what wage? Attention was paid to the quality of accommodation and board and to the actual training to be received (technical skills as well as instruction in reading and writing).[11] In return, the apprentice's guardians paid the master a fee, which could vary from a yearly sum (often decreasing as the apprentice became more skilled and performed more efficiently) to a loan to be refunded partly or (sometimes) completely at the end of the training. In the latter case access to capital and cheap credit, drawn from *weezengeld* (the inherited capital of orphans, usually invested in annuities), provided a strong impetus. Other stipulations in such contracts dealt with what the responsibilities were in the event of early termination because of death, disease or contractual violation. Ghent orphans started relatively late as apprentices and as journeymen: they were often between 19 and 29 years old.[12]

Unlike guild training in central Europe,[13] even a superficial analysis of the names of apprentices shows that in Flanders they were often apprenticed to close relatives (sometimes their own parents). This allowed for continuity of family businesses and a more cost-efficient integration of labour from the household to the workshop.[14] So apprentices learned their trade in the same social *milieu*, if not in the same occupational group or guild as the one they came from.[15] The master himself did the actual training in his own workshop. Occasionally, however, apprentices were also trained by journeymen or even by other masters. In 1463 a conflict arose between a master sawyer in Ghent and his apprentice's family because the boy had been trained by other masters and went from one workshop to another. The family argued that this would inevitably harm the quality of his training. They wanted their money back and threatened to withdraw the apprentice from his master's custody. But the practice must have been quite common. The aldermen decided in favour of the master.[16]

At the start of a career an apprentice was required to pay an entrance fee to the guild, which could vary, but until the fifteenth century these fees generally remained relatively low. Guild statutes from Bruges in the early 1440s show that most guilds required an entrance fee of 266 groats (a skilled mason earned 8 groats per day in this period).[17] A few guilds had lower entrance fees, and at least eight guilds did not specify the amount (nor was there any specific requirement that the apprentice had to be a *burger* or citizen of the city).[18] In smaller towns, such as Oudenaarde, entrance fees for an apprentice or master were even lower, but there were important differences among the various guilds.[19]

Masters' children always had an advantage. They usually had to pay only a fraction of the other apprentices' fees. In Oudenaarde a tailor's children only paid 5 groats to the guild in the late fourteenth and fifteenth centuries, while others paid 20 to 40 groats (depending on whether or not they were citizens). The tanners' guild demanded an entrance fee of 140 groats, but citizens only paid 5 groats (only a small fraction of the regular fee levied on outsiders). In 1404 children of mercers and fine leather workers paid 10 groats, while burgers had to pay 105 groats and foreigners 185 groats. In 1418 the belt makers required 160 groats as an entrance fee, 380 groats for foreigners, but only 10 groats for master's children. The inflation of entrance fees was particularly marked for children of foreigners (that means non-burgers) and burgers, and was much less for masters' children. In 1418 the entrance fees for tailors' apprentices in Oudenaarde was raised from 30 to 40 groats for foreign apprentices, while the fees for masters' children remained the same. The mercers raised the entrance fee from 100 to 180 groats in 1478 for citizens, and to 360 groats for foreigners, but the entrance fee for masters' children remained unchanged (10 groats).

The period of training varied as well. Some guilds did not enforce a particular training period at all. This was usually the case for hereditary guilds, such as the butchers and fishmongers. In Oudenaarde aspiring butchers could follow in the footsteps of their fathers without any formal training period simply by paying a modest 10 groats as an entrance fee. But most guilds in Oudenaarde required at least a period of one (shopkeepers) to two years (bakers, belt makers, tanners and shoemakers). Other guilds required much longer periods. Sometimes the length of training depended on the status of the apprentice. The candle makers' and fruit sellers' guilds in Oudenaarde required a training period of one year for all apprentices, except for children of guild members, who only had to pay an entrance fee of 15 groats without requiring any training period (1364). But normally the training period was the same for foreign apprentices and masters' children.

In Bruges most guilds required a training period from three to four years. Some of the higher-status guilds, however, required six years (tanners, manufacturers of rosaries, goldsmiths), while others required only two years of training (sellers of old clothes, ropers, as well as highly specialized occupations such as glove- and purse makers and fine leather workers). In the larger guilds, such as the shoemakers, shippers, furriers, tailors, bakers or fruit sellers, the statutes did not require any formal training at all. Among fishmongers and butchers, two guilds where membership in the guild became a hereditary matter, apprenticeship was not regulated. There was no inverse correlation between the technical skills and the average length of apprenticeship contracts, as was the case in late medieval Burgundy.[20]

Although apprenticeship paved the way for many individuals to enter the formal economy, some sought guild membership for other reasons. Membership enabled people to enjoy the social networks and the political opportunities that guilds offered. Guilds were not always opposed to such strategies, but membership under false pretences could pose serious problems for the guild's economic activities. Therefore, guilds resisted unfair entry by intruders. For example, marrying a master's widow to gain entry to a guild was looked on with great suspicion, but even cases where apprenticeship itself was used to force entry to the guild were a major concern. In 1557 the Bruges candle makers opposed one of their masters who wanted to accept Thomas Lommelin, descendant of a rich Genoese family, as his apprentice. It was argued that Thomas was too old ('at thirty-six one is too old to learn anyway'), and that he would not be able to remain four years in his master's custody. But the real problem was that this reversed traditional role patterns. Master Joris Andries was a poor artisan who rented a room in Lommelin's house. The apprentice was a wealthy citizen who probably only wanted to enter the guild to enjoy its social contacts and political opportunities.[21]

Conditions of Apprenticeship

An early end to apprenticeship was always difficult for both parties. Accident or disease could prevent an apprentice from performing his duties in the master's household, or it could interfere with the quality of his training. The untimely death of a master could threaten an apprentice's career prospects. Often provisions were made so that a master's widow could continue the contract or another master had to be found. In Ghent masters often sued the guardians of their apprentices for any additional costs incurred to treat an apprentice who became ill. Sometimes the masters had success in their lawsuit. At other times, however, the master was supposed to care for his or her apprentice 'in sickness and in health'.[22] It is striking that none of the guild statutes deal with these eventualities. Without exception, these were dealt with through individual negotiations.

The only major concern for the guild authorities was the apprentice's loyalty. Both the guild statutes and the apprenticeship contracts almost always include a provision for breach of contract. Runaway apprentices must have been a substantial problem. Young people were difficult to discipline, and the hierarchical relationship to a master, the responsibilities of work and training, and the length of apprentice training must have made the situation even more difficult. Masters wanted to protect themselves against financial loss, so the guilds placed heavy fines on runaway apprentices. Contracts include clauses in which the training fee had to be paid in any case, or the master was allowed to keep the loan he had received earlier from the apprentice's parents or his guardians.[23] The only way a youngster could reintegrate into the guild community was by returning to his master and reimbursing him for the damage.[24] Only 'just cause' could be invoked to terminate the contract.[25] Apprentices' families often actively intervened to protect their child's interests. An apprentice was not abandoned to 'the kindness of strangers'.[26]

To protect the social and economic status quo, guild control was paramount. Hence, formal approval for an apprenticeship by the guild was strictly enforced. In 1397 the Ghent brewer Paul Van Innendale complained that his son Hendrik was not allowed to enter the brewers' guild, despite the fact that he had completed his apprenticeship and everything else 'a good apprentice should do for his master'. The guild refused because 'neither the dean nor his assistants were ever informed of his apprenticeship.' The council of the *opperdeken*, the highest guild court in the city, confirmed the decision, and Hendrik had to start his training period all over again.[27]

Formal approval was not only important for controlling access to the guild, it was also necessary to avoid unfair competition. In 1560 the Bruges authorities decided against a hat maker in a conflict with his guild. The guild had refused to register his stepson because he had not fulfilled all the administrative requirements for becoming 'free' in the guild. The guild claimed it had no way of knowing how long an apprentice had served his master. The hat maker argued that his apprentice was the son of a hat maker's widow, and it was the custom that sons of masters were not registered. The guild agreed that this was indeed the case, but that it was not applicable because membership could not be inherited via the mother in a second marriage. Hence all fees had to be paid that were required for any stranger seeking to enter the guild. This was especially true because in this case the boy had already been apprenticed in another guild of the city, the bakers.[28]

Apprentices' credentials were carefully investigated when they asked for recognition of their apprenticeship. Thus, in 1401, when Claes de Decker asked the tanners' guild of Ghent to recognize that the requirements of his apprenticeship had been fulfilled, the guild's officers looked into the matter. They asked the master where Claes had performed his apprenticeship and decided that he had only fulfilled five of the required six years. Claes was required to serve another master for one more year.[29]

Reciprocity was important for maintaining standards of guild quality and status. In 1535 Hendrik Andries was refused entrance to the Bruges candle makers' guild because he had been trained in the small neighbouring town of Damme. Although Damme apprentices were usually accepted in the Bruges guilds, the Bruges candle makers argued that in this case Hendrik could not be accepted because he was a citizen of Bruges and should not have received his training outside the city. Moreover, they added that Hendrik had previously worked in Bruges as a cooper, thus casting doubt on the craftsman's statement that he was skilled in candle making. Because he had gone to Damme to avoid the fees and the longer training period in Bruges, the final guild argument was a plea for the survival of the economic system of Bruges: what would happen to the guilds and the urban economy if everyone were allowed to do such a thing? Furthermore, the plaintiffs argued, he had been trained by a widow. The aldermen dismissed these arguments, requiring that the guild accept Hendrik as a new member upon payment of the customary dues.[30]

Women, as independent entrepreneurs, were usually allowed to have apprentices. Yet such a situation was always looked upon with great suspicion. Apprentices (and journeymen) could take advantage of this by trying to use marriage to an unmarried or widowed mistress to gain entrance to the guild. In 1360 the senior dean of Ghent decided an issue raised by the grocers' guild, that the newlywed husband of one of their members, the daughter of a grocer, had to serve a regular apprenticeship for a period of four years before he could enjoy the status of guild member.[31] Pieter Tavernier, who had married a barber's daughter, Mergriete Musch, experienced the same fate when he applied for entry to the guild. In order to be accepted as a barber, he had undergone the standard period of training. The guild encouraged him to do so, probably because they were even less enthusiastic about having women barbers in their midst.[32] The fear of unwanted new guild members was very prevalent. Hence the widow of a Bruges candle maker was forbidden in 1520 to accept a new apprentice because this apprentice was old enough to marry her. The widow argued that she was allowed to take him because guild solidarity guaranteed her the same opportunities as other masters. The guild, however, refused to believe that the apprentice would live for four years under the protection of the widow. But the main reason for their refusal was undoubtedly their fear that the apprentice would try to enter the guild by marrying the widow. The city authorities were not convinced by these arguments, however, and the widow was allowed to take on the apprentice.[33]

Various Outcomes of Apprenticeship

Not much quantitative data exist about the realities of apprenticeship in medieval Flanders. Thus, little information is available to show how many were able to obtain promotion within the guild, how long it took for apprentices to become masters, or whether they would make this move directly or first join the ranks of journeymen on the labour market. A limited analysis of the registers of guild matriculation and entrance fees can reveal some of the mechanisms on this path. The registers of matriculation in the tanners' and shoemakers' guilds in the small town of Oudenaarde demonstrate that becoming a master was a formidable threshold for young apprentices.[34] Of the 410 apprentices recorded between 1459 and 1506, only 29 were registered as becoming masters, a scant 7 percent of the total number. Undoubtedly this can be partially attributed to incomplete registration: only the masters who employed apprentices themselves are known, and in the case of Bruges, as will be demonstrated, not all masters had trained apprentices. Masters' sons and daughters were probably not registered if their parents had trained them. The data shows, nonetheless, the enormous difficulties involved in becoming a master: only a tiny minority of apprentices were able to take this step.

The register also allows an assessment of the period between the start of a craftsman's career and the date on which he began to train apprentices himself (table 8.1). The average period between these two milestones was 10.6 years (median = 9 years), but there were important differences. Some masters took apprentices shortly after they became masters: nine masters employed apprentices within four years after their own apprenticeship began (the standard period of apprenticeship was only four years). Many had to wait one, two or even three decades before they had their own apprentices. Other data for medieval Flanders reveal similar statistics. In Ghent the guild of coverlet weavers registered 231 masters and 89 apprentices between 1370 and 1396. Only three became masters after four, seven and nine years from the start of their apprenticeship. Most new masters seem to have been either masters' sons (and as such they were not registered) or newcomers in the city, having been apprenticed elsewhere.[35]

The sources in Bruges are more reliable. The bowyers (craftsmen who made bows for shooting), who practised one of the smaller crafts (in 1425 there were 38 masters), are typical for the many Bruges guilds involved in highly specialized industries. The statutes contain the usual descriptions regarding loyalty, length of training (four years) and entrance fees (26 groats). Apprentices did not have to be citizens of the city, but once they had been trained, local citizenship was a necessary condition for them to acquire the 'freedom' of the guild. To enter the guild, trained apprentices had to pay 480 groats (the equivalent of 60 days of work), while a master's son only had to

Table 8.1 *The Leather Guild in Oudenaarde (1459–1506): From Apprentice to Master*

Number of Years*	2	3	4	5	7	8	9	10	11	14	15	16	18	22	26	29
Number of Apprentices	4	3	2	1	2	2	1	3	1	1	1	2	2	2	1	1
Total	29															

*Period between the start of apprenticeship and the date when apprentices reappear as masters who accept apprentices of their own.

pay 26 groats (3.5 days of work).[36] Between 1385 and 1550, the guild clerks registered 358 apprentices, 349 journeymen and 267 masters.[37] Only 79 of the apprentices listed became masters (and only 23 of the journeymen who were registered did so). These figures show that the overwhelming majority of apprentices, for one reason or another, never became masters. If we consider only those apprentices registered before 1540 (allowing a period of about ten years to become a master), less than one-quarter (22.5 percent, or 79 of the 351 apprentices) eventually achieved the status of independent entrepreneur. The success rate of new journeymen (craftsmen who entered the guild after having had training in other 'free' cities) was even lower. (Bruges apprentices were not required to register to become journeymen following their training period.) Only about 6.8 percent (23 of the 341 journeymen who had registered before 1540) became masters in the guild. Those who had not previously been registered in the records as apprentices or journeymen comprised more than half the masters registered (131 of the 233). We must assume that these members had either been immigrant masters with enough capital to become masters in Bruges immediately, or that they had been masters' sons.

The cycle of new guild members, masters, apprentices and journeymen in the bowyers' guild is a good indicator for the cycle of the urban economy of Bruges during the late Middle Ages. As with many other very specialized crafts in the city, the bowyers and their dependent branches worked for markets beyond the local economy. In the late fourteenth and early fifteenth centuries, the number of new bowyers increased substantially, from an average of six in the 1390s to more than twelve in 1420. Beginning in the late 1430s their numbers showed a sharp decline, and there was a total stagnation of new bowyers in the 1440s, 1450s and 1460s: only some six or seven members are recorded. The late 1470s saw an end to the period of relative prosperity, and the number of new bowyers dropped sharply to four in the late fifteenth and early sixteenth centuries. Afterwards the bowyers nearly disappeared from the economic stage of the city.[38] This cycle not only reflects the decline of the very specific economic activity of bowmaking, it also coincides with the general cycle of the Bruges economy. But do periods of decline and growth have an impact on the open or closed character of such specialized craft guilds?

In general, periods that show many new apprentices seem to alternate with periods having many journeymen. Only in the 1420s and again from the 1450s to the 1460s are the numbers of new apprentices and new journeymen similar. The system of employing journeymen and apprentices, therefore, seems to have been very flexible. Each entrepreneur was able to adapt the employment structure of his workshop to his needs and requirements. It must be stressed that the fluctuating number of journeymen in the guild is unknown, because the lists only include those journeymen who came from outside Bruges. The analysis of the bowyers' registers is hampered by one important missing variable: the number of apprenticed sons of masters. It is probable that in periods with high numbers of new masters and low numbers of apprentices, more new masters came from within the guild.

Table 8.2 *New Bowyers in Bruges, 1380–1550 (Yearly Average)*

	Totals	New Masters	New Apprentices	New Journemen	New Apprentices/ New Masters	New Journemen/ New Masters
1380–1390	7.0	2.2	3.2	1.7	1.46	0.77
1390–1400	5.8	1.8	1.5	2.5	0.83	1.39
1400–1410	8.7	2.2	2.4	4.1	1.09	1.86
1410–1420	7.5	1.5	4.3	1.3	2.87	0.87
1420–1430	12.6	3.3	4.7	4.3	1.42	1.30
1430–1440	7.7	2.1	3.0	2.3	1.43	1.10
1440–1450	6	1.9	2.3	1.5	1.21	0.79
1450–1460	6.6	0.9	2.5	2.5	2.78	2.78
1460–1470	6.6	1.6	2.5	2.5	1.56	1.56
1470–1480	7.7	2.0	2.7	3.0	1.35	1.50
1480–1490	5.9	1.5	1.6	2.8	1.07	1.87
1490–1500	3.1	1.3	0.9	0.9	0.69	0.69
1500–1510	3.4	0.9	1.4	1.1	1.56	1.22
1510–1520	4.3	1.3	1.2	1.8	0.92	1.38
1520–1530	3.5	1.6	1.2	0.7	0.75	0.44
1530–1540	3.5	1.2	0.6	1.7	0.50	1.42

Apprentices had more opportunities to become masters in the late fourteenth and early fifteenth centuries (access was relatively easy, especially in the 1420s, and again in the 1460s). In the second half of the fifteenth century and in the early sixteenth century opportunities for social promotion in the guild of the bowyers were limited. More became masters in the early fifteenth century (in the 1420s up to 43 percent of all apprentices were able to become a master), and the average length of time between apprenticeship and becoming a master was substantially shorter (four to six years). As declining outlets caused the craft to become less prosperous, there were fewer opportunities to become a master. This was also true for the first period of economic difficulty in Bruges in the middle of the fifteenth century, when the average number of apprentices becoming masters fell from 1.2 to 0.3 per year (see table 8.2). In the 1460s, when the craft started recovering and the number of new masters rose again, opportunities for new apprentices also improved. Yet the average time between apprenticeship and becoming a master was longer than ever.

The opportunities for new journeymen in the Bruges bowyers' guild to become masters varied greatly. While opportunities for social mobility within the guild were good in the early fifteenth century, they decreased throughout the fifteenth and sixteenth centuries. Unlike the situation for apprentices, however, the changing economic cycle in the middle of the fifteenth century had not altered journeymen's opportunities in the least; instead of improving in the 1460s, promotions became even rarer. By the late fifteenth and in the sixteenth centuries it was almost impossible for new journeymen to become masters.

Similar data exist for the coopers' and the painters' guilds in Bruges (see tables 8.3 and 8.4).[39] In this commercial metropolis coopers provided an essential packing service, so their economic success was dependent on the general trade cycle. But they also performed a vital function for the local economy. Hence the cycle of matriculation was less variable. Between 1375 and 1500, 966 apprentices and 685 masters were registered. Only 164 of all registered apprentices in the city were able to become masters in this period, a scant 17 percent. As with the other Bruges guilds, masters' sons did not need to be registered. The opportunities to become a master were best in the early fifteenth century (especially in the 1400s, 1410s and 1420s, which were periods of relative wealth in Bruges), but opportunities declined in the 1430s (when Bruges experienced political turmoil) and towards the last quarter of the fifteenth century (when Bruges' international trade had completely declined). Data for the painters (guild of Saint Luke) reveal similar statistics, though they show a slightly better success rate for Bruges apprentices: between 1456 and 1550 almost 22 percent became masters there. But success rates could vary greatly. In the 1470s, as well as from 1510 to 1530 (when Flemish art had ostensibly passed its most illustrious period), apprentices found it relatively easy to become masters. In the 1460s, 1490s and 1500s, however, it had again become very difficult. There were clear differences between the various sectors of the painters' guild. The greatest opportunities for apprentices to become masters were as easel painters, glaziers or mirror makers, but it was more difficult for those who were canvas painters or saddlers. For the painters' guild there was no direct link to the cycle of the urban economy. Painting still flourished even after Bruges no longer played an important role on the international stage.[40]

Table 8.3 *Painters' Guild in Bruges: Success Rate of Apprentices*

Year	Painters' Apprentices	Apprentices becoming Masters (%)
1460–1480	221	21.7
1480–1500	99	18.2
1500–1520	99	21.2
1460–1520	419	20.8

Table 8.4 *Coopers' Guild in Bruges: Success Rate of Apprentices*

Year	Coopers' Apprentices	Apprentices becoming Masters (%)
1375–1400	193	14
1400–1425	236	26.7
1425–1450	194	16.5
1450–1475	158	14.6
1475–1500	185	10.3
1375–1500	966	17

The high percentage of apprentices who did not become masters requires further explanation: tables 8.3 and 8.4 compare two snapshots in time, becoming an apprentice and becoming a master. It is certainly possible that many things may have happened in the course of the period between the start of apprenticeship and eligibility for the apprentice to become a master. There are various reasons why an apprentice may not have finished his training. For one, death rates among adolescents in this period of recurrent plague were high. Crude annual death rates in fifteenth-century Flemish towns can be assessed at about 34 to 40 per thousand (figures for Hulst and Kortrijk).[41] Using the 34 per thousand figure means that within the twelve years (four years of training and eight years as a journeyman) 32 percent would have died.[42] Moreover, people often decided to change occupation. Still another factor was that in many cases an apprentice would leave his master before the end of the contract; further, many journeyman were not able or did not want to become a master, but preferred to remain in service (again, there could be several reasons for this, among which was especially the lack of start-up capital). Another rarely mentioned aspect of late medieval and early modern economies was the high geographical mobility of craftsmen. Social and economic success could also be sought in a different town or region. Although Bruges was at the top of the urban hierarchy in Flanders, the city had passed its economic peak by the 1450s, and young skilled workers may have preferred to seek opportunities elsewhere.

Those apprentices who were not masters' sons and had received their training in Bruges found it difficult to become masters. This is confirmed by an analysis of new masters in the coopers' guild (table 8.5): only 164 masters (24 percent) had been previously registered as apprentices in Bruges, 23 percent were masters' sons, but more than 53 percent were newcomers. Most masters, therefore, were immigrants who had received their training in a town other than Bruges. Some, however, could enter the guild without prior training: they were granted special permission, or they had received training in another guild.[43] Bruges apprentices had the best chances of becoming masters in the first half of the fifteenth century; later on promotion became the exception rather than the rule. Masters' sons, on the other hand, were well represented among masters throughout the period, and they were particularly numerous in the third quarter of the fifteenth century. Paradoxically, the decline of the Bruges market did not prevent newcomers from entering the coopers' guild on a massive scale in the 1470s, 1480s and 1490s, when both masters' sons and Bruges apprentices became very rare. The local citizens probably had a more accurate understanding of Bruges' declining need for the services they provided.

Similar processes can be seen in the painters' case (see table 8.6). Except for the final quarter of the fifteenth century, the data are less reliable and contain a greater number of unidentified masters. In the third quarter of the fifteenth century (when painters such as Petrus Christus and Hans Memling were active), most painters were recruited in Bruges itself (one quarter were masters' sons, and half of the masters were trained as apprentices in Bruges). The most renowned painters, who had almost all been immigrants to the city,

Table 8.5 *New Masters in the Coopers' Guild: Bruges, 1375–1500*

Years	Number of Masters Entering the Guild	Masters Previously Registered as Apprentices (%)	Masters' Children (%)	Masters Not Registered as Apprentices or Masters' children
1375–1400	99	9.1	31.3	59.6
1400–1425	114	44.7	26.3	28.9
1425–1450	137	38.0	19.7	42.3
1450–1475	159	13.8	31.4	54.7
1475–1500	176	17.0	10.8	72.2
1375–1500	685	23.9	22.9	53.1

Table 8.6 *New Masters in the Painters' Guild: Bruges, 1456–1550*

Years	Number of Masters Entering the Guild	Masters' Sons (%)	Apprenticed in Bruges (%)	Apprenticed Elsewhere (%)	Apprenticeship Unknown (%)
1456–1460	11	0.0	0.0	0.0	100.0
1461–1470	59	13.6	13.6	16.9	55.9
1471–1480	54	25.9	42.6	25.9	5.6
1481–1490	82	17.1	45.1	26.8	11.0
1491–1500	14	28.6	7.1	57.1	7.1
1501–1510	67	25.4	32.8	22.4	19.4
1511–1520	65	13.8	7.7	29.2	49.2
1521–1530	48	2.1	25.0	25.0	47.9
1531–1540	34	5.9	8.8	2.9	82.4
1541–1550	35	25.7	8.6	25.7	40.0
1456–1550	469	16.6	24.3	23.5	35.6

were exceptions in this guild. Less prestigious guilds recruited more widely among immigrants than did this highly specialized luxury industry. The impact of both masters' sons and newcomers, however, became more pronounced in the first half of the sixteenth century, while that of apprentices trained in Bruges declined. The painters' guild starts to resemble the other guilds in this period. Masters' sons were probably still able to conquer new markets, even when the art market itself was shifting to Antwerp.

Assuming every apprentice underwent the standard training period of four years, it took an average of more than seven years following the end of his apprenticeship before a bowyer could become a master (table 8.7). Only one apprentice became master immediately after his training period was over, but several succeeded after only one or two years; the longest period was thirty-two years, but most apprentices needed between five and seven years. The few immigrant journeymen who achieved the status of master did so somewhat sooner (an average of 6.7 years). The more successful journeymen, however, became masters after only one year as a journeyman, which suggests that they probably had some capital when they arrived in Bruges.

Table 8.7 *Apprentices Becoming Masters in the Bowyers' Guild (Bruges, Fourteenth to Sixteenth Centuries)*

	Totals	Yearly Average	Average Number of Years between Apprenticeship and Mastership	Min	Max	% of Apprentices becoming Master
1380–1400	6	0.6	3.5	0	6	19.4
1400–1420	13	0.7	4.3	1	8	35.1
1420–1440	23	1.2	6.2	0	16	43.4
1440–1460	5	0.3	9.2	4	11	17.2
1460–1480	18	0.9	11.2	1	32	52.9
1480–1500	6	0.3	6.3	2	15	20.0
1500–1520	5	0.3	8	3	13	23.8
1520–1540	3	0.2	8.3	1	16	10

The pattern for coopers and painters (table 8.8) is similar to that of the bowyers. On average a cooper needed almost ten years (9.8 years; the median was nine years) to become a master after his apprenticeship. The average time it took most coopers (40 percent of 164 apprentices) to achieve this was between nine and eleven years, although a significant minority (30 percent) achieved it in less than six years. In fact, 13 apprentices even worked for twenty years or more, perhaps as journeymen in the guild, before they eventually were able to join the ranks of the masters in the guild in the autumn of their careers. For painters the intervening period averaged 9.2 years: most took four or five years, which was longer than the bowyers but much shorter than the coopers.[43] There is no doubt that some must have pursued other occupations in the intervening period. Examples of townspeople trained within several guilds are numerous. In other instances – this was especially true for painters – craftsmen were active as journeymen in Bruges as well as in workshops elsewhere.

Table 8.8 *Years between End of the Prescribed Period of Apprenticeship and becoming a Master: Coopers' and Painters' Guilds in Bruges, 1375–1500)*

Years	Coopers	Painters
		4
1	1	1
2	7	2
3	4	2
4	14	6
5	9	11
6	16	4
7	11	10
8	7	8
9	15	12
10	24	9
11	11	5
12	6	2
13	5	5
14	5	6
15	3	3
16	6	4
17	3	1
18	3	1
19	1	
20	3	
21	2	
22	3	
23	3	2
24	0	1
25	2	
More		1
Totals	164	100

Labour Cost, Entrepreneurship and Apprenticeship

As training approached its end, apprentices became increasingly valuable assets to a master's workshop. Apprentices who stayed on after the end of their contract received real wages (sometimes these had been stipulated in the apprenticeship contract). Moreover, apprenticeship contracts always stated that the apprentices had to spend their time usefully (that is, useful for the master). They had to participate in the economic effort of the master's household and perform all necessary tasks for him. In fact, they became a form of (very) cheap labour.

Records from 1462 for the Bruges bowyers indicate not only the date when an apprentice was registered, but also the name of the master who employed him. Again it must be stressed that masters' sons were not registered. Masters who trained at least one apprentice in their career (more than half never had any apprentices at all) averaged no more than two apprentices in their professional lives, but most masters had only one. The figures reveal a sharp tendency towards concentration. More than half of all masters who did take on apprentices had only one apprentice in their whole carreer, while thirteen had only two (see table 8.9). If apprentices stayed with their masters for the compulsory period of four years, this means that most masters were involved in training for only very short periods in their careers. But there is also an important group of masters who were continually involved in training and employing other people's sons: Perchevael De Langhe had six apprentices in 26 years, Matheeus Crommelin had five apprentices in his long career of 46 years, and Martin De Rijcke had five apprentices in 32 years. Although a more thorough analysis may reveal many more interesting facts, it is clear that a substantial number of these apprentices were also trained by members of the extended family: very often apprentices had the same surname as their master.

The same holds true for the coopers' and painters' guild in Bruges. In the period between 1375 and 500 422 coopers were registered as having trained at least one apprentice (only 57 percent of all registered masters in the coopers' guild). On average each master who did take on apprentices employed 2.2 apprentices (median=2), and most Bruges coopers employed only one apprentice (see table 8.9); moreover, a significant minority continually had apprentices: between 1439 and 1476 Wouter Meyngheer trained eleven apprentices. Usually the training period of four years was respected, and coopers were not allowed to have more than one apprentice at

Table 8.9 *Masters Employing Apprentices in Oudenaarde and Bruges, Fifteenth to Sixteenth Centuries*

	Oudenaarde Tanners (1473–1506)		Bruges Coopers (1375–1500)		Bruges Bowyers (1462–1550)	
Apprentices Per Master	Masters	Total Apprentices	Masters	Total Apprentices	Masters	Total Apprentices
1	63	63	206	206	30	30
2	23	46	80	160	13	26
3	27	81	55	165	7	21
4	15	60	38	152	5	20
5	7	35	21	105	2	10
6	6	36	10	60	1	6
7	4	28	7	49		
8	2	16	3	24		
9	1	9	1	9		
10	1	10				
11	1	1	11			
13	1	13				
14	1	14				
Totals	151	411	422	941	58	113

the same time. But if an apprentice died or left his employer, coopers could take on a new one. A notable figure like Meyngheer had to do this on three successive occasions between 1457 and 1463.

The same pattern for employing apprentices can be seen in the painters' guild (see table 8.9). On average a master had only one apprentice in his career: half never had any apprentices, one quarter had only one, 20 percent had two to four apprentices, and a very small minority (a few individuals) continually had apprentices. The great masters, Hans Memling, Petrus Christus and Gerard David, only occasionally trained an apprentice. They probably relied on journeymen to enhance the scope of their workshop. A correlation with the economic cycle is clear: before 1490 painters averaged 1.5 apprentices, after 1500 only 0.5; before 1490 only 42 percent did not have apprentices, after 1500 no less than 67 percent of the masters no longer trained apprentices. In the heyday of Bruges painting, training was much more common than after demand for these paintings had declined.

In the small town of Oudenaarde, a large majority of tanners and shoemakers employed only one or two apprentices in their careers, while a slight minority was able to maintain apprentices continuously, and often several at the same time (see table 8.9). Joos De Dondere had 14 apprentices from 1478 until 1497; in 1489 he even employed three new apprentices. It was only in 1525 that the number of apprentices was limited to one for each master. At this time the length of apprenticeship was fixed at two years. The ordinance mentions the many abuses that had taken place in the city.[45] It is clear that the regulation was inspired by the practices shown in the registrations between 1458 and 1506: some masters had employed apprentices as cheap labour, undermining fair competition amongst guild members.

Furthermore, it is striking that those entrepreneurs who had many apprentices did not necessarily belong to the same group as the masters who employed immigrant journeymen.[46] From 1520 to 1546 the bowyer Jan Bourlee employed twelve new journeymen, but he is mentioned only twice as a master who trained an apprentice. Masters with many apprentices were only marginally involved in employing new journeymen. Perchevael De Langhe (with six apprentices and seven journeymen) is an exception. It is clear that there were two paths that did not necessarily interconnect.

Conclusions

Several conclusions can be drawn from these statistics. First, apprenticeship was a formidable threshold to becoming a master, but it was by no means the only one, and perhaps not even the most important one. Most new masters who were not masters' sons were immigrants. Members of the latter group were trained outside the city where they were eventually registered as master.[47] The second important conclusion is that migration must have been a crucial element in social mobility within the guild system. This was certainly true at the top of the urban hierarchy, where the process of step-migration culminated. Immigrants entered the city and became citizens and then guild members. As we have seen from the records of the Bruges bowyers, the immigrants to this guild usually avoided becoming journeymen, primarily because this path was usually a dead end. As a rule, once registered as a journeyman, it was very difficult to become a master. Incoming skilled artisans, therefore, often entered the guild as masters.

Apprenticeship was only a necessary step in a career. Many apprentices never became masters (excluding masters' sons, more than 75 percent). Only masters' sons had more secure future prospects. After completing their apprenticeships they were usually able to become masters quite easily. Starting capital could be advanced from within the household. Other apprentices could remain in the city, start off as journeymen, and eventually (after a shorter or a longer period, depending on their social background and their ambitions) save enough money for their entrance fees and starting capital. Only after they had fulfilled these conditions could they could become masters. For most accomplished apprentices, however, such an issue was not an option: they were forced to remain journeymen or to switch their occupation.

The world of skilled artisans and guild-regulated labour in the late medieval city was structured as a very complex social system. Various systems of social mobility, social exclusiveness and labour organization existed at the same time in a single locality. The conditions of apprenticeship were only marginally influenced by fixed guild regulations. Regulation was scarce and unspecific; guilds preferred to use social custom and negotiation as more decisive elements in establishing occupational relations. Hence a diversified system became possible. The social mobility enjoyed by masters' children was completely different from that of foreign apprentices or journeymen. The children of masters formed a stable group, and were the core of guild organization and political life within the guild. Once trained and independent, masters' sons were quickly able to establish their own workshops, avoiding the bottleneck of becoming journeymen. Many from this group were also able to enter the political organization of guilds (as guild officers or administrators; some could even aspire to a political mandate in the guild-dominated political system of Flemish cities). Those who were apprenticed outside their immediate social networks probably had much fewer opportunities to become masters. The majority remained journeymen after their initial training, or they changed jobs or moved away to take advantage of better opportunities in other places. The influx of newcomers, apprentices, journeymen and masters, followed the same patterns. Incoming apprentices and journeymen stood little, if any, chance of becoming masters. The only successful newcomers were those who had already experienced training elsewhere and who had gathered enough capital to become masters and start their own workshop. These new masters, foreigners in the city, could develop their own networks within the guild system, much as masters' sons did, although many of them probably lacked the advantages of already established networks.

Notes

1. On apprentices in early modern Europe see: James R. Farr, *Artisans in Europe 1300–1914*, Cambridge, 2000, 33ff. For medieval Europe, recent works of synthesis only rarely contain information about apprenticeship (for the Low Countries, see Pascale Lambrechts and Jean-Pierre Sosson (eds), *Les métiers au moyen âge. Aspects économiques et sociaux*, Louvain-la-Neuve, 1994). The survey by Steven A. Epstein, *Wage Labor and Guilds in Medieval Europe*, Chapel Hill (N.C.), 1991 focuses on Italian cities. Compare also Michael Mitterauer, 'Servants and Youth', *Continuity and Change*, 5, 1990, 11–38, and idem, 'Familie und Arbeitsorganisation in städtischen Gesellschaften des späten Mittelalters und der frühen Neuzeit', in Alfred Haverkamp (ed.), *Haus und Familie in der spätmittelalterlichen Stadt*, Cologne/Vienna, 1984 (Städteforschung, Darstellungen 18), 1–36.
2. Jean-Pierre Sosson, 'Les métiers, Normes et réalité. L'exemple des anciens Pays-Bas méridionaux aux XIVe et XVe siècles', in Jacqueline Hamesse and Colette Muraille-Samaran (eds), *Le travail au moyen âge. Une approche interdisciplaire*, Louvain-la-Neuve, 1990, 339–48.
3. Marc Boone, 'Les gens de métier à l'époque corporative à Gand et les litiges professionels (1350–1450)', in Marc Boone and Maarten Prak (eds), *Statuts individuels, statuts corporatifs et statuts judiciaires dans les villes européennes (moyen âge et temps modernes)*, Leuven, 1996, 23–48; Harald Deceulaer, 'Guilds and Litigation: Conflict Settlement in Antwerp (1585–1796)', in *ibid.*, 171–208.
4. Martha Howell, *Women, Production, and Patriarchy in Late Medieval Cities*, Chicago, 1986; Farr, *Artisans*, 33–37. On the function of apprenticeship in early modern economies see also Stephan R. Epstein, 'Craft Guilds, Apprenticeship, and Technological Change in Preindustrial Europe', *The Journal of Economic History*, 58, 1998, 684–713 and Bert De Munck and Dominiek Dendooven, *Al doende leert men. Leertijd en ambacht in het ancien régime (1500–1800)*, Bruges, 2003.
5. Peter Stabel, *Dwarfs Among Giants: The Flemish Urban Network in the Late Middle Ages*, Leuven, Garant, 1997, and various contributions in Simonetta Cavaciocchi (ed.), *Le migrazioni in Europa secc. XIII–XVIII. Atti della Venticinquesima settimana di studi, 3–8 maggio 1993*, Prato, 1994 (Istituto internazionale di storia economica F. Datini 25), in particular, Erik Thoen, 'Immigration to Bruges During the Late Middle Ages', 453–91.
6. John H. Munro, 'Industrial Transformations in North-west European Textile Trades, c. 1290–c. 1340: Economic Progress or Economic Crisis, Monopolistic Competition', in Bruce M.S. Campbell (ed.), *Before the Black Death: Studies in the 'Crisis' of the Early Fourteenth Century*, Manchester, 1991.
7. SAG (city archives of Ghent), series 156, no. 1, fol. 71r (register of the upperdean).
8. Guillaume Des Marez, *L'organisation du travail à Bruxelles au XVe siècle*, Brussels, 1904 and Léon Verriest, *Les luttes sociales et le contrat d'apprentissage à Tournai jusqu'en 1424*, Brussels, 1912. The most in depth study on contracts is Philippe Didier, 'L'apprentissage médiéval en France: formation professionnelle, entretien ou emploi de la main-d'oevre juvenile?', *Zeitschrift der Savigny-Stiftung für Rechtsgeschichte. Germanistische Abteilung*, 101, 1984, 200–55.
9. Marianne Danneel, *Weduwen en wezen in het laat-middeleeuwse Gent*, Leuven, 1996 and David Nicholas, *The Metamorphosis of a Medieval City: Ghent in the Age of the Arteveldes, 1302–1390*, Lincoln (Nebr.), 1987.
10. Danneel, *Weduwen*, 80–97.
11. Female apprentices could be identified in the guilds of the embroiderers, stocking makers, mercers (shopkeepers) and manufacturers of fine leather goods (Danneel, *Weduwen*, 83).
12. Danneel, *Weduwen*, 81.They can easily be compared with Peter Laslett's *Life-cycle Servants* (*The World We Have Lost*, London, 1971). See also on the relationships between age, apprenticeship and criminal behaviour: Guy Dupont, 'Patronen van jongerencriminaliteit in een laatmiddeleeuwse grootstad (Brugge, 1385–1550)', in Catharina Lis and Hugo Soly (eds.), *Tussen Dader en Slachtoffer. Jongeren en criminaliteit in historisch perspectief*, Brussels, 2001, 49–82.

13. Ad Knotter, 'Problems of the "Family Economy": Peasant Economy, Domestic Production and Labour Markets in Pre-industrial Europe', in Maarten Prak (ed.), *Early Modern Capitalism: Economic and Social Change in Europe 1400–1800*, London/New York, 2001, 135–60.
14. The same phenomenon can be recognized in late medieval Paris: Diane Frappier-Bigras, 'La famille dans l'artisinat du XIIIe siècle', *Le Moyen Age*, 95, 1989, 62–66.
15. Danneel, *Weduwen*, 90–91.
16. Danneel, *Weduwen*, 95.
17. The Bruges statutes are in the process of being published (Jan Dumolyn and Peter Stabel, *De Statuten van de Brugse Ambachten in de 15de Eeuw*, Brussels, Commission Royale d'Histoire).
18. RAB (State Archives Bruges), fonds Brugse Ambachten, No. 1, passim.
19. SAO (town archives of Oudenaarde), Ambachten, passim. See also Peter Stabel, *De kleine stad in Vlaanderen : bevolkingsdynamiek en economische functies van de kleine en secundaire stedelijke centra in het Gentse kwartier (14de–16de eeuw),* Brussels, 1995, 222–26; Marceline De Jaegher, *Sociaal-ekonomische strukturen te Oudenaarde in de XIVe en XVE eeuw*, unpublished thesis University of Ghent, 1973, 185–212.
20. Philippe Didier, 'Le contrat d'apprentissage en Bourgogne aux XIVe et XVe siècles', *Revue historique de droit français et étranger*, 54, 1, 1976, 35–57. See also Alessandro Stella, 'Travail, famille et maison: formes et raisons du placement dans les sociétés traditionnelles', *Médiévales*, 30, 1996, 35–44.
21. RAB, Charters with blue numbers, No. 8402; 25 September 1557.
22. Danneel, *Weduwen*, 87–89.
23. Danneel, *Weduwen*, 91.
24. Such a clause is present in most Bruges guild statutes: RAB, Ambachten, 1, passim.
25. A religious calling, another choice of occupation (after approval by the guild authorities), the fact that an apprentice could not physically or mentally perform his tasks, and unreasonably harsh treatment by the master were reasons invoked (Danneel, *Weduwen*, 92–93).
26. John Boswell, *The Kindness of Strangers: The Abandonment of Children in Western Europe From Late Antiquity to the Renaissance,* Chicago, 1988, 326ff., and the critical remarks in recent studies on Medieval Flanders: Danneel, *Weduwen*, 94–95 and Myriam Carlier, *Kinderen van de minne? Bastaarden in het vijftiende-eeuwse Vlaanderen*, Brussels, 2001.
27. SAG, series 156, No. 1, 40^1, 20 July 1397. A similar case ended with the same decision (SAG, series 156, No. 1, No. 41^2).
28. RAB, Charters with blue numbers, No. 9018 (6 July 1560).
29. SAG, series 156, No. 1, 44^1 (22 January 1401).
30. RAB, Charters with blue numbers, No. 8937 (21 April 1535).
31. SAG, series 156, No. 1, f 20r (20 June 1360).
32. SAG, series 156, No. 1, 47 and 47^1. The guild authorities refused to agree with the husband's argument that whoever married a barber's daughter would be as free in the guild as the other barbers, but they agreed that the wife, as the daughter of a barber, was permitted to carry out the trade.
33. RAB, Charters with blue numbers, No. 8296, 19 October 1520. The guild probably saw the reasonableness of this case afterwards, because only one year later they approved the widow's remarriage to the apprentice and the latter's entry into the guild after a period of apprenticeship (No. 8295).
34. SAO, Sint Amandsgilde, 1.
35. Nicholas, *The Metamorphosis*, 172–73.
36. RAB, Brugse ambachten, No. 1, f. 133r–138v.
37. RAB, Brugse ambachten, No. 42.
38. Raymond Van Uytven, 'Stages of Economic Decline: Late Medieval Bruges', in Jean Marie Duvosquel and Erik Thoen (eds), *Peasants and Townsmen in Medieval Europe: Studia in Honorem Adriaan Verhulst*, Ghent, 1995, 259–70.
39. SAB (City Archives of Bruges), series 336 (guild register). The number of entries in the coopers' guild has already been analysed in Jean-Pierre Sosson, 'La structure sociale de la

corporation médiévale. L'exemple des tonneliers de Bruges de 1350 à 1500', *Revue belge de Philologie et d'Histoire*, 44, 1966, 457–78. For the painters' guild, see Peter Stabel, 'Organisation corporative et production d'œuvres d'art à Bruges à la fin du Moyen Age et au début des Temps Modernes', *Le Moyen Âge*, 113, 2007, 91–134.

40. Stabel, 'Organisation corporative', 109–113.
41. Stabel, *De kleine stad*, 54–62; Erik Thoen, *Landbouwekonomie en bevolking in Vlaanderen gedurende de late middeleeuwen en het begin van de moderne tijden. Testregio: de kasselrijen van Oudenaarde en Aalst (eind 13de-eerste helft 16de eeuw)*, Ghent, 1988, 64–93; David Herlihy and Christiane Klapisch, *Les Toscans et leurs familles. Une étude du catasto florentin de 1427*, Paris, 1978, 454–55; and M.-Th. Lorcin, *Vivre et mourir en Lyonnais à la fin du moyen âge*, Paris, 1981.
42. See Stabel, 'Organisation corporative', 120–27.
43. This is confirmed by samples taken from the registers of new burgers (A. Jamees, *Brugse poorters*, Handzame, 1974, 1980 and 1990; R.A. Parmentier, *Indices op de Brugsche poorterboeken*, Geschiedkundige Publicatiën der Stad Brugge, 2, Bruges, 1938).
44. Stabel, 'Organisation corporative'.
45. RAB, Brugse ambachten, No. 42.
46. Stadsarchief Oudenaarde, Fonds Ambachten, 843/1, No. 2.
47. Peter Stabel, 'Stappen in een carrière: meesters, gezellen en leerlingen in de luxenijverheden van het laatmiddeleeuwse Brugge', in preparation.
48. On the Ghent coverlet weavers see: Nicholas, *The Metamorphosis*, 172.

Chapter 9

Apprentices in the German and Austrian Crafts in Early Modern Times

Apprentices as Wage Earners?

Reinhold Reith

Older studies of handicrafts history have generally focused on Guild ordinances containing articles of apprenticeship. These can indeed provide some important clues about social practices, but they tended to be merely normative overviews so they remain inadequate guides to actual practices.[1]

Educational sciences developed an early interest in the history of occupational education. They viewed guild training in the early modern period as integrated into an order of estates and governments, a static order where the requirements of tradition made any deviation from strictly observed norms impossible.[2] According to Stratmann training was based on a fixed catalogue of behaviours set by custom, habit, law and religion and the *imitatio* process (learning through imitation) permitted no weakening of custom. In this view traditionalism led to a crisis in artisanal education in the late seventeenth century. Then, Enlightenment pedagogy (viewed from this humanistic perspective as the real source of occupational education in industrial society) brought occupational training into the light.[3]

The earlier integration of apprentices into family and guild appeared to allow them so little manoeuvering room that apprentices were not considered significant subjects for research, so apprentices have remained among those groups that have received little historical attention until very recently. One recent study of the history of youth since the sixteenth century devotes only a few partial sentences to apprentices under the reading 'Feudal Society and Absolutism',[4] and 'seemingly voiceless' apprentices were' nt even given their own entry in a major anthology devoted to eighteenth century servants that was published in 1995.[5]

The new social history, with its interest in everyday life, has greatly altered the scientific picture of early modern times. Family history research, for example, has cast doubt on assumptions about the inheritability of handicraft trades and their presumed family-business structure, emphasizing instead the diverse combinations of family and nonfamily labour forces participating in artisanal production.[6] Recent studies in the social and economic history of handicrafts have studied not only the mobility of apprentices but also their living conditions and the conflicts associated with them.[7]

While apprenticeship contracts have often been used as source materials for French research (making the contractual nature of apprenticeship explicit),[8] apprenticeship contracts have been given little attention as potential sources in German-language research – except for that of Hektor Amman and Hellmut Gutzwiller.[9] There has been only one overview of the distribution and availability of such sources to date, and that just for Switzerland.[10] Even in the most recent German-language research, apprenticeship has been treated less as a contractual condition than as one of subordination – with apprentices integrated into the household (the *ganze Haus*) of the master under his doubled paternalist authority as both master and head of household. In this chapter I would like to explore this point by considering two representative studies from this genre.

The first is a 1937 dissertation by Bruns on the working conditions of apprentices and journeymen in Western Germany.[11] According to Bruns, there was a need for more detailed investigation of this topic 'since the failure of the labour laws of the liberal epoch just past [i.e. the Weimar Republic] provides an ideal occasion to look back at medieval ways of life that were integrated with a particular *Weltanschauung*, in order to possibly discover models and guidelines among them'. In Bruns' chronology – which had been developed from historical economics – the 'early days' of the crafts and trades extended up to the mid-fourteenth century, and the 'golden age' into the mid-fifteenth when the 'age of decline' set in. Wages for apprentices were said to have still been rare during the golden age and Bruns saw them as a sign of decay.

In 1962, Haberleitner published a study of the crafts and trades in Styria. He characterized the handicrafts of previous centuries as 'familism', where journeymen and apprentices were said to have been members of the master's family, where 'they stood under the master's protection and were subject to his discipline'.[12] Haberleitner focused on a concept of the household, '*das ganze Haus*', which has been surrounded by controversy in recent years.[13] A number of phenomena have been cited by those opposed to equating 'pre-modern' social forms with the household. These include: the early spread of wage labour; the importance of gainful self-employment by women; and limits to the authority of the male head of the household, as well as the high degree of mobility of journeymen.[14] Recent research – and especially historical, family research – has called attention to fault lines and contradictions in these communal living conditions, and warned scholars to avoid an exaggeratedly harmonious or idyllic interpretation of this household model.[15] For the purpose of analysis of the social forms of the crafts and trades, the term 'under the same roof-tree' seems more workable, since it proposes no *a priori* evaluation of social relationships.[16] Otto Brunner, however, was trying to describe 'concrete orders' with the term he coined, in this case the position of head of household. For him, the essence of household and the leadership of it was to be found in 'loyalty and honor, protection and nurture, counsel and aid', which he introduced as 'presumable source concepts' into the 'play with ambiguity'.[17] Algazi pointed out that the assumption of these terms does not derive from what is found in the source material, but 'rather, it results from preconceptions about what constitutes the 'essence' of authority.' Thus, the strong response elicited by phrases like 'protection and nurture' was attributable to, among other things, their political resonance at the time.[18]

Older research used the concept of the household to postulate a social form that was purportedly characterized by the 'authority of the head of household' and a 'relationship of protection and loyalty'. This characterization was claimed for apprenticeship, and the patriarchal conception did indeed seem to apply here. But this context makes it difficult to analyse apprenticeship as a contractual relationship or as an exchange relationship or transaction.[19] The concept of 'protection and nurture' made it difficult to integrate these very same wage-like services, since they could only be interpreted as paternalistic gestures or as welfare services – or, as we have seen, as a sign of decay!

The aim of this chapter is to take these wage payments as a starting point. I will take up the suggestion of S.R. Epstein to regard the workshop as a governance structure, the chief objective of which was to get the greatest possible benefits from familial and nonfamilial labour.[20] The apprenticeship contract and the guild are thus regarded as interdependent solutions to the problem of the conflicting interests of the parties to the contract – the master and the apprentice's legal guardian. This concept offers 'skills training' as a simple explanation for apprenticeship itself and for the origin of the guilds and their survival over many centuries.

Apprenticeship contracts mediate two key and interrelated requirements. The master had to be assured of recouping his investment (e.g. assurance that the apprentice would not run off), since at some point the apprentice could get a higher wage from another master who had not incurred any training costs. Without such assurances, no master would take on an apprentice. On the other hand, the apprentices had to be assured protection against improper behaviour by masters, such as mistreatment, exploitation or inadequate training. Completing an apprenticeship had to guarantee acquisition of sufficient skills to offer a chance to succeed in the labour market. Compatible skills guaranteed that masters would be able to find correspondingly well-qualified workers (journeymen), and they guaranteed that the apprentices would be able to find work anywhere in their chosen field – all in all, a reduction of the uncertainties of the labour market.

I would now like to turn the tables and, in contrast to older concepts, consider the teaching relationship as a labour relationship (though certainly keeping in mind that we are still dealing with the education of adolescents). With teaching relationships in which apprentices received a money wage or wage in kind as my point of departure, I wish to raise a few questions. Did such labour relationships exist? Since when and in which occupations did they exist? Which wage forms were typical? What was their distribution over time? Can the payment of a wage really be interpreted as a sign of decay? Why were they typical in some crafts and not in others? Which economic, social and technical factors can be identified?

Apprenticeship Contracts

Beginning in the fourteenth century there was an increasing differentiation in Central Europe between apprentices and journeymen in the crafts. Male apprentices were characterized as lerjunge, ler(n)knabe, ler(n)knecht or lerlinger,[21i] while female apprentices – particularly among weavers and tailors – were characterized as leretöchter or lermädgen, as well as lerdirne and maidlin[22] – almost all of which focused on the learning relationship.

Hektor Amman documented and published a whole series of apprenticeship contracts from the notary registers of the city of Freiburg in Switzerland.[23] These fourteenth and fifteenth century contracts were drawn up in concise language and are distinguished by their wide-ranging variety since there was as yet no unified regulation of apprenticeship. Nevertheless, some basic provisions recur in all of them.[24]

To begin with, all the parties to the contracts are named by surname, forename, occupation and place of residence, as are witnesses and guarantors. The contents deal with length of service, sanctions for not fulfilling their provisions, and the possibility of annulling them. Then, the duties of the master were enumerated – including board (and in some cases, a wine ration or a fixed cash allowance) and clothing for the apprentice, as well as the apprentice's wage. The amount of the apprenticeship premium varied widely. The apprenticeship premium and other payments or services due to the master were mostly made in instalments; the *Lichtgeld* was a fee that went to the guild. Occasionally, some of a wide range of supplementary provisions were added.

The extant contracts provide for terms of six months to twelve years. A one-year term of service was prevalent (at least in cloth weaving, the craft from which we have the largest number of such contracts), while contracts of two years were far less common, numbering only half as many as those with one-year terms. Third most prevalent are both contracts of less than a year and those of three or four years' duration. Service contracts of five to thirteen years do exist but are rather rare. 'The one-year or two-year apprenticeship thus constituted the norm'. These contracts did not clearly differentiate between apprentices and journeymen, and there are corresponding indications from other central European cities as well.[25]

First of all, we are confronted with what is still a complex set of rules that are difficult to sort out. From the fifteenth century at the very latest, an apprenticeship of two to three years was probably obligatory in most cases for many Austrian crafts,[26] while Göttmann documents this for the Middle Rhine area.[27] Wesoly refers to numerous articles of the Frankfurt guild bylaws of 1355 and 1377 that call for money, wax or wine to be paid at the commencement of the apprenticeship.[28] The training period generally lasted two to three years in the Upper Rhine area as well. Schulz detects a trend toward extending this term during the fifteenth and sixteenth centuries as in many cases, occupations were becoming more complicated as well as increasingly specialized.[29] In Saxony, too, the duration differed among the various crafts and grew longer during the second half of the sixteenth century. Terms ranged from two to five years, though the Leipzig goldsmiths required up to eight years. The three-year apprenticeship was the most common, with a trend toward longer terms from the sixteenth to the eighteenth centuries. By the seventeenth and eighteenth centuries, one-year apprenticeships were hardly to be found, and two-year terms were disappearing.[30] However, even in the late eighteenth century, the brewers in Regensburg went through apprenticeships lasting only two winters![31]

At all times and places, though, differences specific to particular crafts can be found. In the eighteenth century, apprenticeship terms ranged from two to eight years; three to four years was most common. Payment of a high apprenticeship premium ('purchasing the apprenticeship') could, among other benefits, shorten the term of service. If no apprenticeship premium was paid, then this might mean that the term would be extended – the apprentice learned 'a year for a year (free learning)'. On the other hand, for example, among the bakers of Augsburg, 'a big, strong man was often taken on without having to pay any apprenticeship premium, whereas a small, weak man would have to pay somewhat more'.[32] Of 682 apprentices in Regensburg between 1780 and 1800, 315 trained without paying an apprenticeship premium while 228 had to pay. Payment of the premium sometimes increased the chances of receiving good training.[33] The Augsburg goldsmiths noted that some children of poor parents were forced to train under a master who did inferior work because they lacked the money to be apprenticed to a consummate artist.[34]

Differences between individual cities and regions tended to diminish as a result of the migration of journeymen. There was, in any case, a tendency for equivalent conditions to prevail everywhere, although a shorter apprenticeship predominated in rural areas and rural crafts tended to follow the general trend after a time lag. There were, however, also clear differences specific to particular occupations. These could be observed in many different regions and were associated with differences in how work was done in individual crafts.

Even the fourteenth and fifteenth century contracts documented by Hektor Ammann contained rules having to do with wages and wage-like compensation. Among these – if compensation is considered in the broadest possible sense – were rules concerning time off and vacation. One contract dated 1421 obliged a master to give his *Knecht* every Saturday morning off. A weavers' contract provided for a month-long vacation every year.[35] Among late fifteenth-century Straßburg tanners apprentices were allowed to take off fourteen days off in the autumn each year (probably to help with the grape harvest). In return, the apprentice had to give the master 40 *Pfennigs* during the first two apprenticeship years and, in the third, 60 *Pfennigs* and a 'harvest goose'.[36]

The edited contracts mostly contain two wage forms: first, a share-wage, which established the fixed percentages of the total receipts that would go to, respectively, the master and the *Knecht*,[37] and second, the fixed annual wage or a wage for a specified contractual period. There were also individual contracts that called for a weekly or daily wage and, on rare occasions, a piece-rate wage. A considerable number of contracts included no provisions in this regard.

The following sections will explore more fully the issue of wage payments for apprentices in three areas: textile production, metalworking and the construction industry.

Wage Payments in Textile Production

In textile production,[38] and particularly in the weaving industry, wage payments to apprentices have been documented in numerous regions. The Nuremberg fustian weavers established wage scales for apprentices in 1535, 1582, 1593 and 1611. Sakuma therefore assumes that they were 'taken on as labourers in mass-scale production'.[39] In contrast to those of the journeymen, however, the apprentices' wages were set up in various categories depending on how many days an apprentice needed for a particular piece of work. Table 9.1 shows the wage rates for apprentice weavers (in denar = *Pfennig*) for the years 1535 and 1582 according to type of work (vertical) and time required (horizontal).

The apprentices' wage was indeed a piece-rate wage, but rather on a 'time scale' than a 'money scale'. This is perhaps the earliest evidence for the existence of a time-scale wage. These two types differ only in a formal sense – namely, in how the wage was calculated. 'In the case of a money scale, the actual number of pieces produced was the basis of the calculation, whereas, in the case of a time scale, the wage was figured according to the time required to produce a given number of pieces. In both forms, however, actual output was determined and used as the basis for the wage calculation'.[40]

First it must be pointed out that the apprentices' wages were far lower than those of journeymen. The shortest time segment would well have been that for the typical output of a journeyman, since, according to the regulations of 1582, the best-qualified apprentice could finish a *Schetter* (piece of linen) in six days, which corresponded to the output of a journeyman.[41] If we convert the wage scales into daily earnings, then it was possible to earn from 1 denar to 14 denar per day in 1535, depending on type of work and qualifications; by 1582, the range had risen to 1.4 denar to 25 denar after a transition to a more detailed and multifaceted output policy. What was the objective of this time scale? Most probably, the aim was to get apprentices – who were still unaccustomed to continual work at the loom – used to piece-rate production, since journeymen also received a piece-rate wage.[42] However, the 'time scale' was by no means unique to Nuremberg.

Table 9.1 *Wage Scales for Apprentices of the Nuremberg Fustian-Weavers 1535 and 1582*

1535 *days*	Schetter	Gugler	Ziech Einsiegler	Ziech Zweisiegler	Zwilch Barchent	Zwilch Mittler	Walenstück Einsiegler	Walenstück Zweisiegler	18er
6						10 (1.7)	10 (1.7)	6 (1.0)	
5	15 (3.0)					20 (4.0)	15 (3.0)	15 (3.0)	8 (1.6)
4	20 (5.0)	7 (1.8)	15 (3.8)		12 (3.0)	30 (7.5)	24 (6.0)	20 (5.0)	16 (4.0)
3	28 (9.3)	15 (5.0)	24 (8.0)	10 (3.3)	16 (5,3)		28 (9.3)	25 (8.3)	24 (8.0)
2		20 (10.0)	28 (14.0)	15 (7.5)	24 (12.0)				
1582 *days*	Zwilch Dreisiegler	Schetter Dreisiegler	Schetter Zweisiegler	18er Walenstück	Ziech dicke	Ziech schmale	Ziech gewürfelte*	Ziech gewürfelte**	
17	45 (2.6)								
16	50 (3.1)								
15	56 (3.7)								
14	63 (4.5)								
13	72 (5.5)								
12	90 (7.5)	64 (5.3)							
11	100 (9.1)	75 (6.8)	40 (3.6)	15 (1.4)					
10	112 (11.2)	90 (9.0)	48 (4.8)	20 (2.0)					
9	126 (14.0)	100 (11.1)	56 (6.2)	25 (2.8)					
8	144 (18.0)	112 (14.0)	66 (8.3)	32 (4.0)					
7		126 (18.0)	72 (10.3)	45 (6.4)					
6		150 (25.0)	84 (14.0)	56 (9.3)					
5				75 (15.0)	22 (4.4)				
4				90 (22.5)	28 (7.0)	15 (3.8)	18 (4.5)	12 (3.0)	
3					36 (12.0)	24 (8.0)	24 (8.0)	18 (6.0)	
2						36 (18.0)	28 (14.0)	24 (12.0)	

Wages in d (Denar = Pfennig). In parantheses: daily income (in d). * = 1600 threads (warp) ** = 1300 threads (warp)
Sources: Hironobu Sakuma, *Die Nürnberger Tuchmacher, Weber, Färber und Bereiter vom 14. bis 17. Jh.*, Nuremberg 1993, S. 216.

The Augsburg weavers (1549) did indeed demand a modest premium for a one-year apprenticeship, but the apprentice also received compensation – as soon as he could finish a piece of cloth in two days, the master was to pay him three *Pfennigs*; if he took three days, he got two *Pfennigs*; if he took longer, the master owed him nothing.[43] From 1569 to 1574, a two-year apprenticeship was required, but this regulation remained in force.[44] Thus, if an apprentice could complete a piece of cloth in two days, that corresponded to the minimum output that was to be expected of a journeyman. Whoever was unable to weave three pieces of material a week was not considered a journeyman (*Knappe*), but rather was merely a *Hautzinger*.[45] The fustian weavers in Carinthian Villach had a rule that was practically identical in 1557,[46] perhaps weavers who had migrated from Augsburg introduced it there.[47] The rules of the linen weavers in Linz (1572) also set a rather low wage for a piece of *Rupfen* or fine linen according to the number of years they had been learning their craft.[48]

Such wage payments have not only been documented for larger commercial centres. The rules of the Kefermarkt linen weavers in 1598 provided that the master give his apprentice two pairs of shoes, a smock and work shirts each year; but if the apprentice preferred money to the smock, the master was to give him a sum in cash.[49] Among the Görlitz cloth makers in 1603, apprentices were likewise to receive a little *Groschen* (penny) in addition to clothing.[50] In textile production in Bremen, an apprenticeship premium was not generally required, and apprentices (except those of the cloth-makers) received a wage from the very start. Among the linen weavers wages were paid by the length of cloth, in other trades by the piece. Otherwise, the apprentice had to take on ancillary tasks that journeymen working according to an output scale did not do.[51]

In Augsburg, apprentices' (*Lernknechte*) wages were revised or raised in 1610, and in 1625 the apprenticeship period was further increased to three years. There were evidently more wage increases before the mid eighteenth century, since a reduction that went into effect in 1739 returned the rates for certain sorts of work back to the level of 1610. In 1739, the council approved a reduction because demand had dropped and the available workforce was considerable after a large number of apprentices had been trained in the 1690s and 1730s. They continued to pay according to a 'time scale', the premium line of which was set disproportionately high to thus offer a strong incentive. From these wage scales, it can be assumed that the apprentices worked at the loom.

In any case, by the late eighteenth century wage scales were reduced again. The Nuremberg fustian weavers even abolished wages, and provided only a modest monthly allowance. The *loden* weavers in Nördlingen also paid very low wages. On the other hand, the demand for the products turned out by the Viennese silk weavers had increased so much that female apprentices were being accepted; furthermore, it was ruled that once apprentices had 'spent [a certain amount of time] on the loom, and begun to grasp the work', they would be assigned a daily quota and whatever they produced beyond that level would be compensated according to the journeymen's wage scale.

Among the silk ribbon weavers (*Bortenmacher* and *Posamentierer*), rather low wages were also traditionally paid. In Nuremberg (1601–1695), apprentices were to receive a wage of at least 12 *Kreuzer* during the fifth year of their apprenticeship. And the Ulm regulations of 1606 provided that apprentices who put in overtime to make 'Arras braiding' which was then very much in fashion would receive a piece-rate wage of 3 *Kreuzer*.

Wages Payments in the Metal Working Industry

There are also many examples of the compensation of apprentices in the metalworking industry.[59] In the sixteenth century knives became increasingly established as part of the standard table setting and knife production expanded.[60] Nuremberg, Steyr and Waidhofen were among the main centres. Annual production in Nuremberg is estimated at up to 4.5 million knives in 1557.[61] Knife smiths in Nuremberg and Wendelstein paid their apprentices a weekly wage in which over quota production was compensated by the hundred, as with journeymen. Apprentices in Waidhofen (1567) also received a wage; in the knife industry they were integrated into the production process first by being assigned individual job steps and then by working on the shoddy, 'mass-produced' goods.

Apprenticeship was divided into three phases in Nuremberg: two years of forging, a year-and-a-half working as a smith, and finally a year of finishing (*Praiten*).[62] In the first phase, the apprentice's weekly quota was either 600 normal blades or 150 small ones.[63] The weekly wage during the first half-year was 14 *Pfennigs*, in the second half 21 *Pfennigs* and in the second year 28 *Pfennigs*. If an apprentice forged more blades than the required quota, he was paid for the overage at the same rate as journeymen – 3 *Kreuzer* per hundred.[64] After two years at the forge the apprentice could either begin working as a journeyman forger, or he could continue learning the craft of the smith. During the next two years as a smith, he had to work and harden six hundred blades a week, for which his weekly wage was 72 *Pfennigs*. For the final finishing work, which he did for a year, he received 2 *Kreuzer* per hundred blades.[65] In Nuremberg and Steyr, more and more apprentices were taken on and this led to a growth of the craft as well as – in the wake of sales slumps beginning on the mid-sixteenth century – to signs of crisis in the sector.[66]

At Kirchdorf-Micheldorf, the most important centre of Austrian scythe production, the rules of 1595 and 1604 established wages for the apprentices according to the number of years they had been learning their craft. Learners received a weekly wage in exchange for a fixed production quota and received 12 *Pfennigs* for what they produced above and beyond that.[67] In Waidhofen during the second half of the eighteenth century, the wage was 5 *Kreuzer* a week during the first year, 7 *Kreuzer* in the second and 9 *Kreuzer* in the third. Occasionally the smiths tried to attract more apprentices through higher wage offers.[68] At both locations, the number of so-called boys (*Pueben*) was increased around the year 1700. However, those were not apprentices, but rather unskilled workers. The masters emphasized that the finished goods had to be processed better, so 'more lads were necessary as helpers' since every *Knecht* needed a boy as his assistant. These youngsters received a weekly wage.[69]

Innerberg's hammer smiths in 1575 had a tough job attracting labour to do their physically very demanding work. They were so hard put to find workers that they had to take woodsmen and other *Knechte* who either had a difficult time proving legitimate birth or had 'some other deficiencies', which is why these requirements were eliminated. The wage paid was 8 *Pfennigs* per hundredweight (*centner*) of forged iron.[70]

Among the nail smiths (*Zweckenschmiede*) of Steyr in 1580 apprentices received a bonus for higher output in addition to their fixed wage. Each first-year apprentice was to be given three yards of woollen cloth, as well as three shirts and three pairs of shoes. During the remaining three years of the apprenticeship, he had to file and stamp at least 300 nails a day, or to forge 600; whenever he made more than his weekly quota, he was due a 6-*Pfennig* bonus for each 300 filed and stamped nails or each 600 forged nails.[71] A similar scale featuring a number of different brackets was in effect for the Steyr awl smiths in 1580. The quota ('specified daily output') was 450 pieces in the second year, 500 in the third, and 600 in the fourth; in return, the master was to pay 3 *Kreuzer* a week in the second year, 4 *Kreuzer* a week in the third year, and 5 *Kreuzer* a week in the fourth year.[72]

It is known that the goldbeaters also paid wages, since this craft entailed an unusually long apprenticeship due to the demanding nature of the work. In 1556 the goldbeaters of Cologne required an apprenticeship of at least five years, while those of Nuremberg required seven years in 1554, as did those of Augsburg in 1676. The average age upon completion of an apprenticeship from 1750 to 1800 was 21 (with the majority between 19 and 23). During the final years of their apprenticeships apprentices could be assigned the job of beating gold. In 1627 they thus received a weekly wage of six *Kreuzer* during their last year, as well as either 20 *Gulden* or a 'journeyman's outfit' upon completion of the apprenticeship. This body of rules was surely also meant to keep the apprentices from running off – conflicts had to have developed during the long apprenticeships, and fatigue or inattentiveness could lead, for example, to the destruction of precious parchment forms. From 1690 to 1800, the goldbeaters registry noted that 26 of 404 apprentices ran away – 'took off', 'lit out' or 'resigned'.[73] In Nuremberg the fixed wages were virtually identical while the metal beaters in Fürth received 4 *Kreuzer* for an output of thirty forms a week.[74]

Wage Payments in the Construction Industry

The largest number of records available concerning wage payments are from the construction industry, where wages for apprentice carpenters, roofers, stonemasons and bricklayers had already become obligatory in the Late Middle Ages.[75] Most typically apprentices moved up to a higher pay bracket with each completed year of apprenticeship. The Regensburg rules of 1366 provided for first-year apprentice stonemasons, carpenters and roofing-tile layers to receive the same wage as day labourers, and 4 *Pfennigs* a day in the second year.[76] The carpenters of Straßburg (1478) mandated that each master provide his apprentices with sturdy shoes and white hose according to need, as well as four yards of coarse material for a jacket and four yards of *Zwilch* cloth for a smock. Furthermore, upon completion of the apprenticeships, the master was to give the apprentice the tools of his trade – in exchange for which apprentices were either to pay 4 Pounds or serve a fifth year. Moreover, apprentices had a claim to a 2-*Pfennigs*-a-week 'drinking allowance' until the master received full wages for him from the building contractor. Thereafter, the master had to pay 4 *Pfennigs*. The duration of apprenticeships soon had to be reduced to three years since it was getting difficult to attract apprentices. As for wages, masters were advised to work out agreements with each lad 'based on his physical build'. Wages were thus negotiable. Schulz does not regard this as a feature unique to Straßburg, since Basel contracts contained similar provisions after 1590.[77] In 1646, the Basel City Council commissioned a study of apprenticeship premiums and duration in a number of crafts and trades. Apprenticeship premiums were not customary in the construction industry where, as the bricklayers explained, young men were paid an appropriate weekly wage depending on how strong they were.[78]

Construction apprentices in Nuremberg were probably compensated by the fifteenth century. Up to the end of the eighteenth century, all these apprentices were entitled to a journeyman's wage in the third year of apprenticeship and they were already regarded as fully qualified workers by the second year.[79] Such wage payments were the rule in many different regions, and there is evidence that here, too, this was not only the case in large cities. The same rule applied to the carpenters in Kremsmünster, Austria in 1600 and the bricklayers in Waldhausen in 1629, where apprentices were to 'have the full wage to which they were entitled, but provide for their own room and board'; nevertheless, a portion of the daily wage went to compensate the master 'for his teaching and efforts'.[80]

There is a great deal of evidence of older apprentices due to the physical requirements. Among the Zürich stonemasons there were even married apprentices during the sixteenth century. In 1560, the masters found themselves unable to enforce a ban on marriages.[81] But the 1690/91 and 1715 rules in Nuremberg provided that only single people could be taken on as apprentices, and no one was permitted to marry during the apprenticeship.[82] In 1706, such a provision was added to the rules for carpenters in Augsburg, and during the second half of the eighteenth century there were only very rare cases of married apprentices.[83]

By the seventeenth and eighteenth centuries the wage tables for apprentices no longer called for a full daily wage. In Augsburg, the daily wage for apprentices came to 80–85 percent of the journeyman's wage; in Nuremberg it was 81 percent of the journeyman's wage from 1645 to 1797.[84] Nor were the wages cited in the tables paid out in full.[85] As a result, the masters were more than happy to take on more apprentices, while the journeymen sought to limit their number on each job (relative to the number of journeymen).[86]

Since construction work was hard physical labour, the apprentices were mostly older than those in other occupations. Where age data are available they suggest that in the eighteenth century construction industry males had to turn eighteen or nineteen before beginning an apprenticeship.[87] Before then most worked as so-called boys, who in Augsburg were on the same pay scale as the unskilled labourers (53–67 percent of the journeyman's wage in Augsburg and 71 percent in Nuremberg).[88] In Hildesheim, only those who had already worked as limestone mixers or helpers were accepted as apprentice roofers.[89] The fact that apprentice bricklayers in Wittgenstein (1725) received 83 percent of the journeyman's wage and the helpers got only 62.5–83 percent of that figure indicates that the former group was considered physically more productive.[90] In Augsburg, in any case, it was customary to work as a boy before becoming an apprentice. Thus even at the commencement of the apprenticeship the apprentices had a certain amount of on-the-job experience!

The Teaching Relation as a Labour Relation

The cursory consideration of three sectors presented here shows that apprenticeship conditions connected with the payment of wages were certainly not exceptional. Even though there are also indications of compensation in other occupations, it was by no means the rule, but it must be pointed out that the crafts discussed above comprised a major proportion of the entire workforce.[91] The payment of wages to apprentices was already common practice in the late Middle Ages.[92] It can be observed throughout the entire construction industry, and this was also true of textile production, metalworking and, later, book printing.[93] Moreover, there are a great many indicators that are still difficult to assess.

Besides clothing and tools being provided, there were cash payments in the form of money for drinks, allowances and bathing stipends. The time-based wage, with raises after each apprenticeship year completed, could be paid for a day, a week or a longer period of time, and there was also the bonus for completing the apprenticeship designed to assure that the apprentice did not 'run away'. Piece-rate wages played a role in textile production, though mixed forms were more common. On the basis of a fixed quota, excess output was paid for by the piece. The time-scale wage was said to constitute an incentive and these forms of compensation were to be found especially in production for export.

What about the distribution over time? Can the payment of wages really be regarded as a sign of decay when focusing on the early modern period gives the impression that there is a tremendous amount of evidence for the compensation of apprentices, particularly for the sixteenth century? In the eighteenth century, it seems to have been used more restrictively, so Bruns' explanation that the guilds had to pay wages because the economic situation had deteriorated and parents were said to have preferred to place their sons in manufactories is most certainly wrong.[94]

Evidence of compensation increases again in the second half of the nineteenth century. In 1853 in Berlin, for example, apprentices in numerous crafts and trades received a wage. In the construction industry, half of the journeyman's wage was typical. When the apprentice was not provided with room and board, the master paid a stipend for that purpose.[95] As small retail trades came under stronger competitive pressure as they did in the second half of the nineteenth century, wage payments (20–40 percent of the journeyman's wage) were typical.[96]

As far as distribution over time is concerned, it must be kept in mind that bodies of regulations have come down to us first and foremost from the so-called 'golden age' and there has been less interest in the so-called 'period of decline' (seventeenth and eighteenth centuries). Furthermore, these rules usually just established a framework; everything was stipulated in detail in the contracts, which is why more attention should be focused on them.[97]

Apprenticeship terms were generally longer at the end of the early modern period than at the beginning. Population growth during the sixteenth and eighteenth centuries exerted a certain amount of pressure on the labour market, but we must not lose sight of another factor – rising qualifications. A look at the 'world of goods', where there was considerable change going on even before the eighteenth century, reveals that there were numerous product innovations and variations.[98] This led to an increasing demand for higher qualifications, and a one-year or two-year apprenticeship hardly sufficed any longer. In late sixteenth-century Augsburg there was an attempt to extend the apprenticeship period as the council complained that there were too many 'technically inept and inexperienced' masters. Journeymen weavers were allowed to become masters 'so easily and prematurely' that many were reportedly unable to turn out anything better than thin fustian.[99]

This also brings up a problem in training in the occupations in which the journeymen received payment by result. For one thing, apprentices could be assigned ancillary tasks or certain preproduction and postproduction activities; on the other hand, they could be allowed to independently fabricate individual pieces – usually of lesser quality.[100] Particularly (but not only) in the larger workshops, training tended to be the job of the journeymen. Among book printers the apprentice was assigned to a journeyman who was supposed to teach him in return for an 'instructional fee'. According to the Leipzig regulations dated 1606, the 'instructors' often bore considerable blame for the fact that there were so many bad typesetters. The apprentices could even work on the press after only half a year, but in typesetting (except for removing old type) it took a while to gradually integrate him into the work.[101]

Now we finally come to the question of why compensation (a wage) was customary in some occupations and not in others. Here we can offer only a few suppositions. Our sample includes, above all, crafts engaged in export production or in a construction industry that mostly consisted of large firms. In nearly all these occupations, the age of the apprentices was relatively high, and in a few of them the apprentices worked as helpers prior to the apprenticeship: 'boys' among the scythe smiths, 'blackers' among the book printers, 'lads' or 'helpers' in the construction industry, and 'half-apprentices' or 'rinsers' in the case of the weavers. Even before beginning their apprenticeships they had gathered a certain amount of experience that enabled them to make a rapid transition into 'productive' activities. In the construction industry it was surely the physical preconditions and a familiarity with how things were done on the construction site that made possible the use of apprentices (some of whom were the sons of married journeymen).

What about skills in the export-oriented crafts and trades? They produced mostly standardized articles, including mass-produced goods – shoddy wares in the case of knife makers, thin fabrics or ribbons with a simple texture among the weavers, and so on. Sometimes the production steps could be clearly divided from one another and this could raise problems for the apprentices because if they were only able to work on certain products or had mastered only certain processes, their later chances on the labour market were quite limited. Such training objectives could be precisely regulated. Two Freiburg contracts dated 1409 and 1411 obliged the master to train his *Knecht* to weave broadcloth and special types of material were also named.[102]

In the export crafts and trades apprentices could therefore be rapidly integrated into the production process when demand was high enough. In order to assess the flexibility and the supply elasticity of urban export crafts and trades, therefore, the labour of apprentices must be taken into consideration to a greater extent than is commonly the case. In occupations in which an apprenticeship premium was demanded, it was obviously not a case of directly product-specific qualifications, but rather had to do with a set of skills. Thus, in the bodies of rules and contracts in such cases, there were also rather general demands – the master was to teach the craft 'without keeping anything secret'.[103] Or, as in the 1356 case of the needle makers in Lübeck, that he would teach the boy so much as to enable him 'to be able to earn his own bread'. Or – as the Lüneburg hat makers put it in 1574 – to be able to make a proper hat.[104]

The reciprocal duties between masters and apprentices were often enforceable even when there was no notarized agreement as authorities beyond the guilds had a strong interest in the quality of training and disputes were handled by the business courts in the large manufacturing towns. These conflicts are especially enlightening because before the courts reached a decision they heard the testimony of parties and witnesses, and trade representatives submitted a statement.

Complaints against individual masters had many sources. The most frequently repeated complaints were over the abuse of apprentices; the provision of bad and insufficient food; and finally the employment of apprentices for noncraft work and the failure to provide training in the appropriate skills for the trade.[105]

The Augsburg craft tribunal, for example, heard charges that the apprentice 'could certainly learn more if he were used for more than just taking care of the children', that he 'had not learned anything', that the master 'does not teach the essentials' to his apprentice and treats him badly, or that the master 'never shows him anything from the trade', 'never gives him new tasks to complete', or 'never let him near a chair or showed him how to set one up'.[106] A cabinetmaker's apprentice in Würzburg complained that 'instead of training in the trade he had to carry earth, and in addition there was nothing but quarrels and strife in the house'.[107] These complaints were closely examined by the justices as the apprentices sought to change masters through them. Sometimes the master on trial sought to prevent the 'escape' of an apprentice into the service of another master by arguing that the apprentice was just lazy, careless or unwilling to work.[108] Not all charges were grounded and the statement of the trade representative carried a lot of weight. In one case where the trade representative certified that the master was an 'honorable and good worker' he was entrusted by the judge to determine what the youth had learned so far.[109]

When charges were upheld the masters were warned or the fee was set aside to be paid only at the end of the apprenticeship. If the judge considered the master's incompetence proven, the master had to refund part of the apprenticeship fee ('*a proportione*') and the apprentice was allowed to change masters; occasionally a master was even forbidden to take on further apprentices.[110] When, for example, an Augsburg lace maker's apprentice charged in 1722 that he had not learned anything from his master, who had only taken him along to the market, the master was required to teach the apprentice and to take on a journeyman, or face losing the apprentice.[111] This was painful for the master for several reasons: he would have lost not only part of the apprenticeship fee but also the labour of the apprentice. An Augsburg cabinetmaker, who had 'very hardly used' his apprentice, apologized, saying that after he had had a beer he had drunkenly thrown a plane at the boy's head when he was very 'sluggish at work'. At the same time, he asked that the apprentice not be taken away from him as 'he had already taught and fed the youth for an entire year and now that he was finally useful it would be very hard to do without him'.[112] The father of an apprentice sued a master purse maker in the Regensburg court (Hansgrafenamt) for beating his son black and blue, hitting him with a plank until it broke. The master apologized, saying he could not deny that he had sometimes beaten the apprentice for his laziness, but he said it was not as bad as claimed. It would be very hard for him if the father now had the apprentice given to another master 'as only now was he useful', so he offered to give the youth a year of apprenticeship without fee. The justice warned him that he should 'refrain from harsh treatment and improper blows going beyond ordinary punishments', otherwise he would lose the second half of the agreed upon apprenticeship fee along with the apprentice.[113] But these complaints and court hearings by no means indicate a crisis in vocational training in the eighteenth century.

Finally, the importance of acquiring social skills is in no way undervalued here, and the master's household remained the main social space where apprentices acquired them – at least until the practice of apprentices living and boarding in their masters' households faded in importance (in Central Europe that began only in the second half of the nineteenth century, but in England the numbers of 'outdoor apprentices' had already begun to grow in the eighteenth century.[114]

Nonetheless, this review shows that apprenticeship functioned as a relationship of reciprocal claims and associated conflicts–at the same time as it was a paternalistic power relationship. These reciprocal claims seen in the contested cases that appeared in court, in addition to wage payments for apprentices, demonstrate that the analysis of apprenticeship only in terms of power relationships is too superficial. All of these arrangements lend themselves to a reading as labour contracts governing working conditions. Apprentices (with the exception of masters' sons) were therefore also non family workers whose labour conditions depended on many circumstances that took different forms in textile production, metalworking and construction (as well as book printing). The demand for labour power for export production played a central role along with the age (and the work experience) of the apprentice. And explicit employment agreements were most likely to be made where handicrafts competed with other economic sectors for young workers.

Notes

1. See for example Arno von Dirke, *Die Rechtsverhältnisse der Handwerkslehrlinge und Gesellen nach den deutschen Stadtrechten und Zunftstatuten des Mittelalters* (Berlin-Steglitz, 1914).
2. Karlwilhelm Stratmann, *Die Krise der Berufserziehung im 18. Jahrhundert als Ursprungsfeld pädagogischen Denkens* (Ratingen, 1967), 21.
3. Walter Georg and Andreas Kunze, *Sozialgeschichte der Berufserziehung. Eine Einführung* (Munich, 1981).
4. Winfried Speitkamp, *Jugend in der Neuzeit. Deutschland vom 16. bis zum 20. Jahrhundert* (Göttingen, 1998), 21, 24.
5. Gotthardt Frühsorgle, Rainer Gruenter and Beatrix Freifrau Wolff Metternich (eds), *Gesinde im 18. Jahrhundert* (Hamburg, 1995). Franz Eder (*Gesindedienst und geschlechterspezifische Arbeitsorganisation in Salzburger Haushalten des 17. und 18. Jahrhunderts*, 41–68, 41), characterized servants as a "seemingly voiceless and overly diverse group" that included both journeymen and apprentices.
6. Michael Mitterauer, 'Zur familienbetrieblichen Struktur im zünftischen Handwerk', in Herbert Knittler (ed.), *Wirtschafts- und sozialhistorische Beiträge* (Munich, 1979), 190–219; ibid., 'Gesindedienst und Jugendphase im europäischen Vergleich', *Geschichte und Gesellschaft*, 11 (1985): 177–204.
7. On apprentices see: Kurt Wesoly, *Lehrlinge und Handwerksgesellen am Mittelrhein. Ihre soziale Lage und ihre Organisation vom 14. bis ins 17. Jahrhundert* (Frankfurt, 1985); Andreas Grießinger and Reinhold Reith, 'Lehrlinge im deutschen Handwerk des ausgehenden 18. Jahrhunderts. Arbeitsorganisation, Sozialbeziehungen und alltägliche Konflikte', *Zeitschrift für Historische Forschung*, 13 (1986): 149–99; Reinhold Reith, 'Zur beruflichen Sozialisation im Handwerk vom 18. bis ins frühe 20. Jahrhundert. Umrisse einer Sozialgeschichte der deutschen Lehrlinge', *Vierteljahrschrift für Sozial- und Wirtschaftsgeschichte*, 76 (1989): 1–27; Elke Schlenkrich, *Der Alltag der Lehrlinge im sächsischen Zunfthandwerk des 15. bis 18. Jahrhunderts* (Krems, 1995); Knut Schulz, 'Handwerk im spätmittelalterlichen Europa. Zur Wanderung und Ausbildung von Lehrlingen in der Fremde', *Jahrbuch des Historischen Kollegs* (Munich), 1996: 69–97; and Annemarie Steidl, *Auf nach Wien! Die Mobilität des mitteleuropäischen Handwerks im 18. und 19. Jahrhundert am Beispiel der Haupt- und Residenzstadt* (Wien, 2003).
8. Philippe Didier, 'Le contrat d'apprentissage en Bourgogne aux XIVe et XVe siècles', *Revue historique de droit francais et étranger* , 54 (1976): 35–57. Natalie Zemon Davis, 'Women

in the Crafts in Sixteenth-century Lyon', *Feminst Studies,* 8 (1982): 47–80. Kathryn L. Reyerson, 'The Adolescent Apprentice/Worker in Medieval Montpellier', *Journal of Family History* , 17 (1992): 353–70. Anne-Marie Cocula, Contrats d'apprentissage du XVIIIe siècle: quelques enseignements d'une moisson aquitaine, *Revue d'histoire moderne et contemporaine,* 40 (1993): 423–35.

9. Hektor Amman, *Mittelalterliche Wirtschaft im Alltag. Quellen zur Geschichte von Gewerbe, Industrie und Handel des 14. und 15. Jahrhunderts aus den Notariatsregistern von Freiburg i. Uee., 1.–3. Lieferung* (Aarau, 1942–1952). He is basically supported by Hellmut Gutzwiller, 'Das Handwerks-Lehrlingswesen in Freiburg i. Ue. im Ausgang des 14. und zu Beginn des 15. Jahrhunderts', *Freiburger Geschichtsblätter,* 47 (1955/56), 14–34.
10. See the overview of western Swizerland in: Karljörg Landolt, *Das Recht der Handwerkslehrlinge vor 1798 im Gebiet der heutigen Schweiz* (Ph.D. Thesis University of Freiburg, Näfels, 1977), 65 ff.
11. Albrecht Bruns, *Die Arbeitsverhältnisse der Lehrlinge und Gesellen im städtischen Handwerk in Westdeutschland bis 1800* (Ph.D. Thesis University of Cologne, 1938), 1, 14 and 33.
12. Odilo Haberleitner, *Handwerk in Steiermark und Kärnten vom Mittelalter bis 1850* (Graz, 1962), 7.
13. Otto Brunner, 'Das "Ganze Haus" und die alteuropäische "Ökonomik"', in ibid., *Neue Wege der Verfassungs- und Sozialgeschichte,* 2nd edn, (Göttingen, 1968), 103–27; Hans Derks, 'Über die Faszination des "Ganzen Hauses"', *Geschichte und Gesellschaft,* 22 (1996): 221–42.
14. Valentin Groebner, 'Außer Haus. Otto Brunner und die "alteuropäische Ökonomik"', *Geschichte in Wissenschaft und Unterricht,* 46 (1995): 69–80.
15. Josef Ehmer, 'Wohnen ohne eigene Wohnung. Formen des Zusammenlebens in städtischen Unterschichten des 18. und 19. Jahrhunderts', in ibid., *Soziale Traditionen in Zeiten des Wandels. Arbeiter und Handwerker im 19. Jahrhundert* (Frankfurt, New York, 1994), 52–100.
16. Under the title 'Under the Same Roof-Tree' Edward P. Thompson criticized (Times Literary Supplement, 4 may 1973, 485–87) the work of Peter Laslett, *Household and Family in Past Time* (Cambridge, 1972).
17. Gadi Algazi, 'Otto Brunner, Konkrete Ordnung und Sprache der Zeit', in Peter Schöttler (ed.), *Geschichtsschreibung als Legitimationswissenschaft 1918–1945* (Frankfurt, 1997), 166–203, 174 ff.
18. Ibid., 178 f.
19. Wage in kind was also seen as payment for work – but not as paternalistic care. Groebner, 'Außer Haus', 73 f; ibid., *Ökonomie ohne Haus. Zum Wirtschaften armer Leute in Nürnberg am Ende des 15. Jahrhunderts* (Göttingen, 1993). See also Reinhold Reith, *Lohn und Leistung. Lohnformen im Gewerbe 1450–1900* (Stuttgart, 1999), 18 f., passim.
20. S.R. Epstein, 'Craft Guilds, Apprenticeship, and Technological Change in Preindustrial Europe', *The Journal of Economic History,* 58 (1998): 684–713.
21. Pauline Hollnsteiner, *Das Lehrlings- und Gesellenwesen Österreichs im 15. Jahrhundert* (Ph.D. Thesis, University of Vienna, 1937), 3.
22. Dirke, Die Rechtsverhältnisse der Handwerkslehrlinge und Gesellen, p. 5; Rudolf Wissell, *Des alten Handwerks Recht und Gewohnheit, vol. I,* (Berlin, 1929), 393 ff. In the thirteenth and fourteenth centuries, many guilds in the towns of the Holy Roman Empire admitted girls to apprenticeship, but in the late fifteenth and sixteenth centuries some guild ordinances and statutes specifically prohibited the practice, while others simply masculinized the language. See James R. Farr, *Artisans in Europe 1300–1914* (Cambridge, 2000), 39; and Merry Wiesner-Hanks, A Learned Task and Given to Men Alone: The Gendering of Tasks in Early Modern German Cities, *Journal of Medieval and Renaissance Studies,* 25 (1995): 89–106.
23. Amman, *Mittelalterliche Wirtschaft im Alltag.*
24. See Gutzwiller, 'Handwerks-Lehrlingswesen'.
25. Gutzwiller, 'Handwerks-Lehrlingswesen', 16.
26. See Hollnsteiner, *Das Lehrlings- und Gesellenwesen,* 20 ff.

27. Frank Göttmann, *Handwerk und Bündnispolitik. Die Handwerkerbünde am Mittelrhein vom 14. bis zum 17. Jahrhundert* (Wiesbaden, 1977), 69.
28. Wesoly, *Lehrlinge und Handwerksgesellen am Mittelrhein*, 50 ff.
29. Knut Schulz, *Handwerksgesellen und Lohnarbeiter. Untersuchungen zur oberrheinischen und oberdeutschen Stadtgeschichte des 14. bis 17. Jahrhunderts* (Sigmaringen, 1985), 248.
30. Helmut Bräuer, *Gesellen im sächsischen Zunfthandwerk des 15. und 16. Jahrhunderts* (Weimar, 1989), pp. 19 f; Schlenkrich, *Der Alltag der Lehrlinge im sächsischen Zunfthandwerk*, p. 49.
31. Grießinger and Reith, 'Lehrlinge', 152.
32. Reinhold Reith, *Arbeits- und Lebensweise im städtischen Handwerk. Zur Sozialgeschichte Augsburger Handwerksgesellen im 18. Jahrhundert*, 1700–1806 (Göttingen, 1988), 105.
33. Grießinger and Reith, 'Lehrlinge', 154.
34. Sylvia Rathke-Köhl, *Geschichte des Augsburger Goldschmiedegewerbes vom Ende des 17. bis zum Ende des 18. Jahrhunderts* (Augsburg, 1964), 14.
35. Gutzwiller, 'Handwerks-Lehrlingswesen', 31.
36. Schulz, *Handwerksgesellen und Lohnarbeiter*, 257 f.
37. The share-wage was widespread in the exporttrades, especially in textile production (weavers, shearers, fullers and dyers). Weavers' employees were customarilly paid one-third of the profits. Gutzwiller, 'Handwerks-Lehrlingswesen', 21. For more on wage forms, see Reith, **Lohn und Leistung**, 122 ff.
38. An overview of textile production can be found in: Rudolf Holbach, *Frühformen von Verlag und Großbetrieb in der gewerblichen Produktion, 13.–16. Jahrhundert* (Stuttgart, 1994), 47–208. For wage forms in textile production see: Reith, *Lohn und Leistung*, 121–55.
39. Hironobu Sakuma, *Die Nürnberger Tuchmacher, Weber, Färber und Bereiter vom 14. bis 17. Jahrhundert* (Nuremberg, 1993), 215.
40. Rudi Schmiede and Edwin Schudlich, *Die Entwicklung der Leistungsentlohnung in Deutschland. Eine historisch-theoretische Untersuchung zum Verhältnis von Lohn u. Leistung unter kapitalistischen Produktionsbedingungen* 3rd edn, Frankfurt, New York, 1978), 500.
41. Sakuma, *Die Nürnberger Tuchmacher*, 218. The warp of a Schetter had a minimum of 1,600 threads.
42. Up to 1589 the linen and fustian weavers in Nuremberg first claimed a two-year apprenticeship, later a three-year term. Sakuma, *Die Nürnberger Tuchmacher*, 295.Ibid., 295 f.
43. The Augsburg weavers also employed half apprentices (halbe Lehrknechte), – probably spoolers. Claus-Peter Clasen, *Die Augsburger Weber. Leistungen und Krisen des Textilgewerbes um 1600* (Augsburg, 1981), 90.
44. Clasen, *Augsburger Weber*, 95.
45. Clasen, *Augsburger Weber*, 93. In 1555 the local authorities restricted admissions to handweaving so that 'not so many clumsy, inexperienced young people would become masters'. In the view of the council, the number of poor weavers was so great because the 'Knappen' were 'so promiscously and too soon allowed to become masters', despite the fact that they still could not weave more than a narrow fustian. The ordinance required that apprentices be first certified at the age og eighteen and that the apprenticeship period should be extended to two years. In 1574 new rules were established and a two-year term was claimed.
46. Karl Dinklage, *Geschichte der Kärntner Arbeiterschaft*, vol. I, (Klagenfurt, 1976), 44. 'Ninth: when an apprentice can work a cloth in three days the master shall give him two Pfennigs, when he works it in two days the master should give him one Kreuzer, but if he takes longer than three days working on one cloth the master is not liable'. Haus-, Hof- und Staatsarchiv Wien, Allgemeine Urkundenreihe; Österr. Akten: Kärnten Fasz. 21/22; Handschrift Blau 339.
47. Josef Kallbrunner, 'Zur Geschichte der Barchentweberei in Österreich im 15. und 16. Jahrhundert', *Vierteljahrschrift für Sozial- und Wirtschaftsgeschichte*, 23 (1930): 76–93, 88 ff.
48. Alfred Marks, Das Handwerk der Linzer Leinenweber im 16. Jahrhundert und seine Stellung im Landesverband, *Historisches Jahrbuch der Stadt Linz*, 1949: 179–97, 183 f.

49. Josef Schwarzlmüller, *Die Berufslaufbahn Lehrling – Geselle – Meister in den Handwerkszünften Oberösterreichs* (Vienna,1979), 55.
50. Schlenkrich, *Der Altag der Lehrlinge im sächsischen Zunfthandwerk*, 87.
51. Elisabeth Höfinghoff, *Die bremischen Textilgewerbe vom 16. bis zur Mitte des 19. Jahrhunderts* (Bremen, 1933), 23 f.
52. Clasen, *Augsburger Weber*, 102. In the period between 1603 and 1605 (within three years) there were registered 727 full-and 37 half-apprentices (p. 106).
53. The masters hired 303 new apprentices in just the years between 1730 and 1739; thus the 90 apprentices who were admitted to the trade inthis period (not including masters' sons) can be identified. See Claus-Peter Clasen, *Textilherstellung in Augsburg in der frühen Neuzeit, vol. I: Weberei* (Augsburg, 1995), 75.
54. Stadtarchiv Augsburg, Handwerkerakten Weber, Fasz. XVIII, 30. V. 1739 and 25. VIII. 1739. The masters claimed that high wages corrupted the apprentices, that they would drink and gamble away on Sundays and holidays what they had earned during the week; thereby becoming accustomed to a dissolute life even during the apprenticeship.
55. Pius Dirr, 'Augsburger Textilindustrie im 18. Jahrhundert', *Zeitschrift des Historischen Vereins für Schwaben*, 37 (1911): 1–106, 17.
56. Walter Riedl, *Die rechtliche Stellung der Lehrjungen und Gesellen des Nürnberger Handwerks in der Zeit vom Ende des Dreissigjährigen Krieges bis zur Einverleibung der freien Reichsstadt in das Königreich Bayern im Jahre 1806* (Diss. jur., Erlangen, 1948), 33; W.H.K. Ebert, *Die Lodweberei in der Reichsstadt Nördlingen* (Nördlingen, 1919), 52.
57. Helene Deutsch, *Die Entwicklung der Seidenindustrie in Österreich*, 1660–1840 (Vienna, 1909), 88 f. 'Therefore the master shall in any event provide the necessary clothing and underwear or this sum shall be returned at the end of the apprenticeship. Fully trained apprenticeses may work on their own for producers'.
58. August Jegel, *Alt-Nürnberger Handwerksrecht und seine Beziehungen zu anderen* (Neustadt/Aisch, 1965), 412. Eugen Nübling, *Ulm's Kaufhaus im Mittelalter. Ein Beitrag zur deutschen Städte- und Wirtschaftsgeschichte* (Ulm, 1900), 226 f.
59. See the references concerning the fifteenth century, in Hollnsteiner, *Der Lehrlings- und Gesellenwesen*, 30 ff.
60. See the overview of knife production from the thirteenth to the sixteenth centuries in Holbach, *Frühformen von Verlag und Großbetrieb*, 243–77.
61. Kurt Keller, *Das messer- und schwertherstellende Gewerbe in Nürnberg von den Anfängen bis zum Ende der reichsstädtischen Zeit* (Nuremberg, 1981), 24 ff.
62. Keller, *Das messer- und schwertherstellende Gewerbe*, 213. The apprenticeship period was set at four-and-a-half years in 1575.
63. Keller, *Das messer-und schwertherstellende Gewerbe,* 213.
64. Ibid.
65. Ibid., 215.
66. Ibid, 242; Irmgard Hack, *Eisenhandel und Messererhandwerk der Stadt Steyr bis zum Ende des 17. Jahrhunderts* (Ph.D. Thesis, University of Graz, 1949), aftermath.
67. Franz Fischer, *Blaue Sensen. Sozial- und Wirtschaftsgeschichte der Sensenschmiedezunft zu Kirchdorf-Micheldorf bis zur Mitte des 18. Jahrhunderts* (Graz/Cologne, 1966), 71. Work clothes were provided in addition to the basic wage.
68. Kurt Semellechner, *Sensenerzeugung und Sensenhandel in Waidhofen an der Ybbs von der Gegenreformation bis zu den Josephinischen Reformen* (Ph.D. Thesis, University of Vienna, 1972), 53. The scythe-smiths of Rottenmann provided clothing after the first year of apprenticeship; see Haberleitner, *Handwerk in Steiermark und Kärnten*, 27.
69. Fischer, *Blaue Sensen*, 56 f. *Semellechner, Sensenerzeugung und Sensenhandel*, 64 ff.
70. Haberleitner, *Handwerk in Steiermark und Kärnten*, 16 and 26.
71. Schwarzlmüller, *Berufslaufbahn*, 55.
72. Ibid.
73. Reith, *Arbeits- und Lebensweise*, 186 ff.
74. Hans Voit, *Die Nürnberger Gold- und Silberschlägerei* (Nuremberg, 1912), 16; Friedrich Morgenstern, *Die Fürther Metallschlägerei. Eine mittelfränkische Hausindustrie und ihre Arbeiter* (Tübingen, 1890), 24.

75. For wage systems in construction see the overview in: Reith, *Lohn und Leistung*, 90–121.
76. Dirke, *Die Rechtsverhältnisse der Handwerks-Lehrlinge und Gesellen*, 31.
77. Schulz, *Handwerksgesellen und Lohnarbeiter*, 260 f.
78. Ibid., 262.
79. Peter Fleischmann, *Das Bauhandwerk in Nürnberg vom 14. bis zum 18. Jahrhundert* (Nuremberg, 1985), 252). For a list of references concerning the Swiss regions (Bern, Luzern, Winterthur) see: Landolt, *Das Recht der Handwerkslehrlinge*, 112 ff.
80. Schwarzlmüller, *Berufslaufbahn*, 57.
81. Klaus Strolz, *Das Bauhandwerk im Alten Zürich unter besonderer Berücksichtigung seiner Löhne* (Aarau, 1970), 34. The council declared that the masters could verbally discourage apprentices from marrying, but that they could not punish them for it.
82. Fleischmann, *Das Bauhandwerk in Nürnberg*, 260.
83. Reith, *Arbeits- und Lebensweise*, 201; Klaus Schwarz, *Die Lage der Handwerksgesellen in Bremen während des 18. Jahrhunderts* (Bremen, 1975), 185. Heinz Moser, *Die Steinmetz- und Maurerzunft in Innsbruck von der Mitte des 15. bis zur Mitte des 18. Jahrhunderts* (Innsbruck, 1973), 88 f.
84. Reith, *Arbeits- und Lebensweise*, 220 f. Rainer Gömmel, *Vorindustrielle Bauwirtschaft in der Reichsstadt Nürnberg und ihrem Umland, 16.–18. Jahrhundert* (Stuttgart, 1985), 210.
85. Hans-Jürgen Gerhard, 'Quantitative und qualitative Aspekte von Handwerkereinkommen in nordwestdeutschen Städten von der Mitte des 18. bis zur Mitte des 19. Jahrhunderts', in Ulrich Engelhardt (ed.), *Handwerker in der Industrialisierung* (Stuttgart, 1984): 51–77, p. 59. Gerhard supposed that only a part of the wages was payed out and that the apprentices had a lower net income than journeymen. In the Braunschweig construction industry of 1798 the masters did not pay the full wage in the first year. See Grießinger and Reith, 'Lehrlinge', 188.
86. In 1711 the Dresden journeymen carpenters charged that some masters 'took two to three, possibly even four apprentices' and that there were some construction sites with three apprentices and one or two journeymen, thereby damaging the customers' interests. Stadtarchiv Dresden, Innungsakten Z 16 a Zimmerleute: Acta die sämtlichen Zimmergesellen wider ihre Meister betr. 13. 1. 1711 and 17. 1. 1711. For competiton in the construction-industry labour market in the 1790s see Grießinger and Reith, 'Lehrlinge', 187 ff.
87. William Gerber, *Die Bauzünfte im alten Hamburg. Entwicklung und Wesen des vaterstädtischen Maurer- und Zimmerergewerbes während der Zunftzeit* (Hamburg, 1933), 40. Schwarz, *Die Lage der Handwerksgesellen in Bremen*, 185.
88. Reith, *Arbeits- und Lebensweise*, 221. Gömmel, *Vorindustrielle Bauwirtschaft*, 210.
89. Karl Heinrich Kaufhold, *Das Handwerk der Stadt Hildesheim im 18. Jahrhundert. Eine wirtschaftsgeschichtliche Studie* (2nd edn Göttingen, 1980), 112.
90. Joachim Naumann, *Arbeitswelt und Lebensformen des Bauhandwerks im wittgensteinischen Territorialstaat der Neuzeit,1550–1850*, (Ph.D. Thesis, University of Marburg, Augsburg, 1972), 167.
91. Farr also underestimated the importance of wage payments to apprentices: 'These hand-picked and potential future masters received food, clothing, lodging, and training in return'. Farr, *Artisans in Europe*, 33 f.
92. See also Hollnsteiner, *Lehrlings- und Gesellenwesen*, 30 f.
93. Rudolf Wackernagel, *Rechnungsbuch der Froben und Episcopius, Buchdrucker und Buchhändler zu Basel 1557 bis 1564* (Basel, 1881),74.
94. Bruns, *Arbeitsverhältnisse*, 37.
95. E.H. Müller and C.F. Schneider (eds), *Jahresbericht des statistischen Amtes im Königlichen Polizei-Präsidio zu Berlin für das Jahr 1853* (Berlin, 1854), 65–100.
96. Reith, 'Zur beruflichen Sozialisation', 24 f; Karl Thiess, *Die Lohnverhältnisse in Berlin seit 1882* (Ph.D. Thesis, University of Heidelberg, Berlin, 1894), 19 ff. Johann Pollitzer, *Die Lage der Lehrlinge im Kleingewerbe in Wien* (Tübingen and Leipzig, 1900), 51–58.
97. Schulz, *Handwerksgesellen und Lohnarbeiter*, 258.
98. John Brewer and Roy Porter (eds), *Consumption and the World of Goods* (London, 1993); Reinhold Reith, 'Technische Innovationen im Handwerk der frühen Neuzeit? Traditionen,

Probleme und Perspektiven der Forschung', Karl Heinrich Kaufhold and Wilfried Reininghaus (eds), *Stadt und Handwerk in Mittelalter und früher Neuzeit* (Cologne, Vienna, 2000), 21–60.

99. Clasen, *Augsburger Weber*, 93.
100. In Augsburg, a centre of ribbon manufacturing, similar charges were brought by apprentices (or their parents) against masters before the trade court over the course of the eighteenth century: so, for example, in 1724 a fringe maker's apprentice asked for reassignment to another master because he had already served more than four years and still could not weave more than one sort of fringe. Another apprentice wanted to change masters 'because he had not learned anything from him' and had so far 'produced only one sort of work'. Stadtarchiv Augsburg, Protokolle des Kunst-, Gewerbs- und Handwerksgerichts (KGH) 9. II. 1724, p. 80; and 21. V. 1792, p. 289.
101. Stadtarchiv Leipzig, Titelakten XLVI 495, pp. 33a–34b. See Albrecht Kirchhoff, 'Material, Arbeit und wirtschaftliche Resultate in den Leipziger Buchdruckereien bis 1650', in: *Zeitschrift für Deutschlands Buchdrucker 1* (1889), 107 and 134. The Frankfurt ordinances of 1598 allowed no more than two apprentices per press, but in cases of journeymen shortages 'or similarly considerable factors' it permitted these 'restrictions to be set aside'. Benno Schmidt (ed.), *Frankfurter Zunfturkunden bis zum Jahre 1612*, vol. I (Frankfurt, 1914), 171. For the designation of apprentices see: Sven Steffens, 'Le nom de l'apprenti : une analyse du vocabulaire socio-professionel', *Revue Belge de Philologie et d'Histoire,* 79 (2001): 591–617. See also Reinhold Reith (ed.), *Lexikon des alten Handwerks. Vom späten Mittelalter bis ins 20. Jahrhundert* (Munich, 1991).
102. Gutzwiller, 'Handwerks-Lehrlingswesen', 16.
103. This was generally expressed in formulaic terms: *et sibi nihil celare in dicta eorum arte, prout bonus et fidelis ac probus magister docere tenere famulum suum.* Gutzwiller, 'Handwerks-Lehrlingswesen', 16.
104. Dirke, *Die Rechtsverhältnisse der Handwerks-Lehrlinge und Gesellen*, 29. Eduard Bodemann, *Die älteren Zunfturkunden der Stadt Lüneburg* (Hannover, 1883), 115 (*'eme de meister einen kloppenden hot schall maken lehren'*).
105. See Grießinger and Reith, 'Lehrlinge', 164–82; Petra Eggers, 'Hamburger Handwerkslehrlinge der Schuhmacher- und Schiffszimmerer-Zunft im 18. und 19. Jahrhundert', in *III. Internationales Handwerksgeschichtliches Symposum, Veszprém 1986*, vol. I (Veszprém, 1987), 143–52, 145 f. and 147 ff.
106. Stadtarchiv Augsburg, KGH 7. I. 1726, p. 11 f.; 22. VI. 1729, p. 192; 22. VI. 1740, p. 320 f. ; 25. II. 1771, p. 34; 17. V. 1773, p. 129 f.; 21. II. 1774, p. 40 f.; 7. II. 1791, p. 71 ff.; 14. III. 1791, p. 149 ff.; and 21. V. 1792, p. 289.
107. Stadtarchiv Würzburg, Protokolle des Oberrates 14. III. 1783.
108. For runaway apprentices see: Grießinger and Reith, 'Lehrlinge', 177 ff.; Reith, 'Zur beruflichen Sozialisation', 22 ff.; Schlenkrich, *Der Alltag der Lehrlinge im sächsischen Zunfthandwerk*, 112 ff. and; Steidl, *Auf nach Wien*, 252–61.
109. Stadtarchiv Augsburg, KGH 14. II. 1791, p. 150 f. and 23. III. 1791, p. 160 f.
110. For instalment payments of the apprenticeship fees see Gutzwiller, 'Handwerks-Lehrlingswesen', 36. Grießinger and Reith, 'Lehrlinge', 179 and Hermann Lenzen, *Lehrlinge und Gesellen in der Reichsstadt Köln. Ein Beitrag zur Wirtschafts- und Sozialgeschichte des deutschen Volkes* (Ph.D. Thesis, University of Cologne, 1920), 128.
111. Stadtarchiv Augsburg, KGH 2. IX. and 16. IX. 1722, p. 63, p. 68.
112. Stadtarchiv Augsburg, KGH 26. V. 1723, p. 173 f.
113. Stadtarchiv Regensburg, Protokolle des Hansgrafenamts 8. II. 1790, p. 28.
114. Josef Ehmer, *Heiratsverhalten, Sozialstruktur, ökonomischer Wandel. England und Mitteleuropa in der Formationsperiode des Kapitalismus* (Göttingen, 1991), 173 ff.; and Reith, 'Zur beruflichen Sozialisation', 10–14.

Conclusion

Chapter 10

Reconsidering Apprenticeship
Afterthoughts

Steven L. Kaplan

After a long period of gestation, a colloquium lives two lives, one hot, the other cold; the first fleeting albeit often powerfully memorable, the second protracted, albeit sometimes prematurely forgotten. The first is collective, the actual meeting of the participants, a time of great intensity, excitement, even incandescence, if the current passes and the fruitful play between give and take, confrontation and solidarity, dialogue and debate is sustained. The second life is emotionally anticlimactic and intellectually rather fragmented and solitary. It is a transition from a phase of poetry to one of prose: from stimulating exchange to more or less demanding revision, a process framed by poles of torment and insouciance. The voyage towards publication is for some a road movie, for others a *chemin de Damas*, for still others a pedestrian express ride. I had the good fortune to be part of the trip at the outset, where I served as critic and (let's say) heuristic synthesizer, and at the end, where I have been asked to exercise similar functions. I propose these 'afterthoughts' not as a canonical conclusion – the elegant introduction does that job, as it were, pre-emptively – but as a critical and provocative homage to the excellent scholarship of this book. I question a number of approaches, challenge certain assumptions, (re)problematize some issues, seek elucidation of various points, venture connections and disconnections, and indicate areas where further research would be welcome: prolegomenon for a return ticket to the heat.

In one way or another, with allowance for national differences in architecture and decor, much of the recent 'revisionist' historiography concerning guilds and the broader world of work derives from a repudiation of the *'ganze Haus'* paradigm. Logically, the predicate to Reinhold Reith's study is a rejection of the idea of handicrafts as 'familism', of the tendentious and/or idealized conflation of premodern social forms with the household. Pointing to myriad phenomena that impugn such an interpretation (e.g., the precocious proliferation of wage labour, the striking mobility of journeymen, the widespread engagement of women in self-employed work, and the limited authority of the male head of household), Reith shows how the view of apprenticeship as an expression of patriarchal organization has obscured its critical role as a contractual or exchange relationship. This organicist-nurturant model troubles Reith particularly because it diminishes the wage nexus either to a mere gesture of paternalism or to a marker of decay. Manifestly seduced by an argument according primacy to the wage factor, Reith reverts prudently at the end of his essay to a more balanced appreciation: apprenticeship 'functioned as a relationship of reciprocal claims and associated conflicts – at the same time as it was a paternalistic power relationship'. Quite rightly, however, he admonishes that 'the analysis of apprenticeship only in terms of power relationships is too superficial'.

The problem with Reith's formulation, from my perspective, is that if he genuinely acknowledges that the 'paternalistic-power' dimension bears significant weight, as I think it does, then he cannot be satisfied with the version passively inherited from an historiography that he considers globally deficient. The ganze Haus paradigm is discredited: thus he needs to reread entirely the paternalistic power relations, both in terms of representation (the doctrine proclaimed by the actors themselves as profession of faith and/or propaganda) and as practice (the various inflections of domination/ subordination). The very robustness of Reith's own research obliges him, it seems to me, to redefine paternalism and power and to rethink the ways in which they operated in light of his (and others') rich findings. I am not convinced that we can make sense of apprenticeship without reference to the (demystified and deconstructed) *'haus'*. We need a new conception of the 'haus', rebuilt with a balanced blend of revisionist Feng Shui.

The demolition of the old 'haus' – demystification-cum-deconstruction – requires a close re-examination of the notion/myth of a golden age to which Reith adverts. What are its origins and how do they vary from nation to nation, culture to culture? What are its diverse functions (lyrical master narrative, nostalgic anchor, conventional baseline, etc.)? How does it fare over time? (Eclipse as a result of Enlightenment/Revolution? Flowering in the wake of the counter-revolutionary culture wars and the messianic corporatism of the 1930s?) More broadly, we need a better understanding of the historiography of apprenticeship inside and outside the corporate orbit: its political, cultural and epistemological conditions of production. Benighted or not, this historiography merits disaggregation and analysis rather than sweeping stigmatization and dismissal.

Equally impatient with 'traditional views' that associate apprenticeship with 'maintaining the status quo and reproducing the established social order', Bert De Munck and Hugo Soly forswear the perspective in which training became inseparable from upbringing. Yet it does not seem necessary (or useful) to me to forsake the notion of upbringing in order to construe corporate institutions as compatible with the development of capitalism, market play, technological innovation, etc. We need to reproblematize 'upbringing' as a crucial aspect of apprenticeship because it covers the whole range of learning *off* the shop floor. It would be a radically excessive allergic reaction to the *gemeinschaft* conservatism of the ganze Haus genre to narrow the spectrum of apprenticeship to 'learning on the shop floor', to borrow De Munck and Soly's phrase. Far too much of the apprentice experience would be left out, in my view – much of what we call, doubtless too nebulously, socialization.

For example: what does it mean for a youth (age and gender differentials are crucial here) to leave his/her family, to install him/herself in another family? What are the psychosomatic dimensions of this experience (reaching puberty; exploring sexuality; developing emotional autonomy or heteronomy)? What sorts of interactions occur with other actors? What are the protocols of commensality where social relations congeal into structures? Does the youth bond with his foster parents? Does the master's wife play a special, pedagogical role as in the Japanese case? Is the stereotype of journeymen lording it over and hazing apprentices a sufficient characterization of their relations? Does religion play any role in this 'upbringing'? How porous are the separations between life and work in the apprentice's world? However idiosyncratic or harsh, it is surely insufficient to treat upbringing as a subcategory of the abuse of apprentices.

In the same spirit, even if De Munck and Soly understandably deplore the boosterist emphasis of the traditional(ist) historiography on the vocation of apprenticeship to mould 'a new member of the community', it is well to remember that this was the objective of numerous guilds and many (albeit by no means all) masters. The fabrication of the 'good worker' was both a normative and instinctive objective. Sundry apprentices comfortably settled into this mould (which ones? relatives or relations of the master? young ones? the timid or weak? those with clear ambitions to ascend?). These were the apprentices, presumably, who did not follow the journeymen to the whorehouse when they were old enough (what was the canonical sociobiological age?), who went to mass, who spied on the journeymen and denounced their tricks to the master, who curried favour or sullenly complied with all demands, etc. Other apprentices resisted, subverted or rebelled in multiple ways. Do they present a different profile, follow a different trajectory, begin (rudimentarily) and end with a different habitus?

A baker apprenticed in Normandy at fourteen years of age, desperate to escape the cold and hunger of his rural home in the late 1920s, assiduously toiled to please his master. The latter expressed surprise one day when he noticed his disciple signing the raw bread-form [*pâton*] – deploying a razor-like instrument to cut incisions into the surface – with his left hand. Queried as to his method, the unnerved youth blurted apologetically 'I always do as you do'. 'Yes', acknowledged his master, 'but I am left-handed and you are right-handed!' This is hyperbolic *imitatio*, the style of learning that appears to have dominated in the shops studied herein.

In fact, we know very little about the techniques of teaching/learning that characterized apprenticeship. Surely nothing was more consequent for most apprentices, as the degree and timing of their emancipation/autonomization depended intimately on how much/how well/how fast they learned, and virtually all the contracts heralded the master's obligation to teach, in some cases even to pledge to withhold no secrets. Yet in some ateliers the apprentices and their parents or tutors denounced the failure of the master – by design, negligence or technical ineptitude – to impart the promised skills; in others the apprentices paid crippling homage to the division of labour (like Reith's weaver who knew how to do only one type of fringe after more than four years' labour); in still other situations the master farmed out the task of teaching to journeymen of extremely variable pedagogical disposition. Surely in certain crafts acute observation on the apprentice's part did not on its own suffice to acquire competence, especially if s/he did not have the opportunity to practise under some sort of critical monitoring. One wonders about the epistemic foundations of shop floor work: did masters have a conscious sense of the threshold level at which the lack of imparted and practised knowledge penalized commercial outcomes? Or in some less concrete way compromised the social order? Extreme diversity, here and elsewhere, hampers our ability to generalize. In late medieval Flanders, in old-regime Paris, and surely in many other sites, certain families negotiated for the children to learn to read and write, a task regularly assumed by the 'master's' wife in late twentieth century Japanese apprenticeship, whose finality was management rather than production per se. If apprentices did not acquire esoteric knowledge likely to power their (linear) ascension, we know that many became competent generalists, versatile enough as journeymen to move across (and thus blur) corporate boundaries in search of employment.

In light of his research on Antwerp cabinetmakers, Bert De Munck displaces and recasts the function of skill and skill reproduction, even as he chafes against the classical view, endorsed by several of his coauthors, construing apprenticeship centrally as a labour market regulator, modulating access to mastership and swelling the pool of cheap labour. Rather than rendering access to the trade more difficult, the idea in Antwerp was to attract a maximum of technical knowledge and to bind it to the trade. Rather than a means of assuring product quality, to which it seems to contribute little directly, apprenticeship 'legitimizes' the producer 'and, via the producer, the quality of the product'. On one level, this view seems close to the orthodox one, for apprenticeship never claimed to guarantee the product, merely to distinguish its maker. De Munck seems to go a step further, suggesting that (local, institutional) apprenticeship itself contributed very little to the shifting fund of knowledge, mobilized most effectively by larger entrepreneurs, that resulted in reliable and innovative products. Symbolically and psychologically, the legitimation compensated, in particular, the mass of small producers for the reduced real value of their apprenticeship-traceable skills. Apprenticeship may have launched the brilliant careers of the foreigners whose arrival energized and transformed the trade – unfortunately, De Munck says nothing about their training – but it seems to have implicitly deskilled the native practitioners, while at the same time serving as a durable anxiolytic for those who succeeded in performing/producing the masterpiece and attaining corporate consecration. In any case, his contention that product markets decisively, albeit often elliptically, shape the behaviour of labour markets will bear heavily on future research. While De Munck's guilds are no longer the custodians of quality, a task appropriated by the marketplace, they have the intelligence to find other reasons to render themselves indispensable. Allowing for differences in product nature – say, substituting textiles for fancy cabinets – this system may have certain points in common with the surprisingly open world of 'monopolistic competition' evoked by Peter Stabel.

On different grounds, Reith joins De Munck in questioning the primacy accorded to education in the apprenticeship process. Their work stands in paradoxical counterpoint to the dominant theme of this book, for it tends to the conclusion that while apprentices were enormously important, (prescriptive) apprenticeship was not. Reith does not wholly ignore adolescent education, but in his revisionist perspective earning matters more than learning. Inverting the classical paradigm, he construes the teaching relation as primordially a labour relation. Redressing the historiographical (im)balance, he imputes to the actors a maximizing logic in which the workshop functions as a governing structure whose chief objective is to extract the greatest possible benefits from family and non family labour.

Although Reith brings to bear an impressive array of evidence in favour of his thesis, certain critics will tax him for the (once congenially venial, now irremissibly mortal) sin of economism. There is an implacable linearity in the trajectory of his apprentices that seems not to pay sufficient attention to variability of lived experience, of life's accidents, asperities and allures. 'Boys' do on-the-job-training in order to qualify as apprentices, the apprentices rush to learn as fast as they can to get to the loom, and then they hasten to attain the productive threshold that will entitle them to the status of journeymen and thus to a revised wage. Echoing Larry Epstein's vigorous suggestion that the guild system is quintessentially about reducing uncertainties in the labour market and that apprenticeship is principally a mechanism for resolving the conflicting interests of masters and young workers, Reith is tempted to evacuate a whole range of social, cultural and psychological variables (e.g., the fashioning of the submissive subject, the age-and gender-specific needs of children, intrashop conflict of various sorts, the anxieties and aspirations of parents, etc.), in favour of a more easily measurable dynamic.

Somewhat defensively, at the end of his robust demonstration, he claims that 'the importance of acquiring social skills is in no way undervalued here'. But why is it not *valued*? Could one not incorporate, conceptually if not statistically, as part of an exchange relationship if not precisely in a wage package, certain forms of psychic income such as kindness or certain kinds of social currency such as docility? Polemically and tactically, Reith's emphasis on the wage strikes me as right on the mark. Strategically, however, it may prove counterproductive to throw out the baby with the bathwater. Here, too, a closer critical reading of the historiography he rejects might have proved fruitful. The ganze Hause exegetes wistfully espoused the contemporary lament that the wage portended decay. It is perhaps worth asking why (many of) the actors viewed the wage relation in these more-or-less apocalyptic terms and how they accounted for it. What kinds of interests were they venturing to defend? Representations can be used here, not to dispense with, but to illuminate the complexity of the reality that Reith is attempting to restitute.

Peter Stabel and Annemarie Steidl, among others, join Reith in underlining the ways in which apprentices (if not apprenticeship) contribute, not to the rigidity, but to the flexibility of the system of production and distribution as well as to the labour market itself. Reviled in our age of Davos and globalization as a diabolical tool of manipulation, flexibility (flexploitation?) seemed to be more-or-less fully integrated as a value and a method – and as a negotiating card – in much of the corporate world and in the broader universe of relations between employers and apprentices.

The guild's role is relativized in many of the papers. To the extent that the guild is the site of apprenticeship, it is not always clear to what extent the apprentice is genuinely integrated into corporate life. In fifteenth century Bruges, Stabel refers squarely to a fee that the apprentice pays in order to enter the guild. Several centuries later, in Paris, the apprentice, like the journeymen, is confined to the distant periphery: only masters enjoy *droit de cité*. Yet we suspect that at one time apprentices and 'valets' or journeymen were embraced in many French guilds (and their confraternities) as fellow, albeit junior, members. When and why were they expelled, and was this expulsion, either in terms of a subtle and slow evolution or a brusque defenestration, a widespread European phenomenon? Steidl reminds us that the status of the apprentice often depends upon the size and structure of the shop in which he functions. Morphology aside, scale in itself, as historians have recently begun to show in many other domains, carries telling consequences. Everyone seems to concur implicitly that some form or other of necessity induced or drove children or youth to become apprentices. But we need a more searching reflection on motivation, that takes into account the multiplicity of possible incentives and constraints, including ostensibly diffuse cultural appetites that may also be tinged with economic rationality (Steidl's Bohemian village boys who tramped to Vienna to improve their knowledge of German even as they acquired a trade).

Virtually all apprenticeships issue from a contract. Their study generates perspectives that would not have found purchase a number of years ago. The first, reinforced by other angles of analysis, casts in relief the extraordinarily mobile nature of the world of work and of the society *tout court*, not so long ago celebrated for its lethargic sedentarity. The second accentuates the frequently negotiated, fluid nature of the contracts, once portrayed as procrustean frameworks. Karel Davids notes that it was commonly an oral arrangement in the northern part of the early modern Low Countries, as does Stabel for a slightly earlier period in Flanders, where he insists on their precocious responsiveness to market forces and the political environment. Based on trust and geared to facilitate flexibility, it was a similarly oral 'gentlemen's agreement' for Jonathan Reinarz's nineteenth-century brewers.

I think that the written contracts merit more careful attention than they habitually receive. Historians of my generation assailed our predecessors who rashly and/or complacently extrapolated lived reality from prescriptive or normative texts – especially corporate statutes, but also putatively standardized contracts. Social historians today are often reproached, not always justly, for failing to 'read' texts with sufficient 'closeness' and cunning, with a sharp enough sensitivity to the play of language, to the ambiguity or equivocality of certain formulations, to the very meaning of words. To do so quite self-consciously is not to acknowledge the primacy or autonomy of the discursive, but rather to understand better the conditions of production of the discourse and its possible significations on the one hand and the relation between norms and behaviour on the other.

Concerning the statutes, Reith, Steidl and, more volubly, Davids warn of their perfidies and blindspots; Stabel contends quite rightly that they can be 'very useful' without exactly showing how and with what methods. With a fresh and empathetically sceptical gaze, we need to ask again: what are the statutes? What are their purposes and aporias? Are they always the same, and how are we to interpret sameness and difference? I believe that we need to reproblematize systematically the formal statutes, scrutinize their genesis, decode if not deconstruct the texts themselves, interrogate them with fresh questions and rethink their pertinence, as referential or prescriptive sources, or as indicators in other ways. We need to envisage a sociology of reception: how did the actors read the texts that supposedly governed their comportment? What did it mean for a master to transgress a statute? What were the relations between the statutes and other forms of regulation, unwritten or partially written: conventions, usages, etc.? We need to do the same with the contracts, especially the simultaneously transparent and opaque stereotypical clauses rather than the individualized stipulations, the latter already inviting us to *croiser* and corroborate these specific arrangements with other sources that help us to measure the passage from engagement to action, from discourse to practice.

The duration of the time of apprenticeship is one of the most interesting pieces of information that the contract supplies, often in contradiction with the norm prescribed in the statutes when guilds are involved. Great variability is the rule, even within the same craft or guild. Sons of masters, if they were required to undergo a mandatory training period, enjoyed a shorter indenture. In almost every case studied, the family constitutes a sort of extraterritorial space in which a most favoured son/daughter policy is systematically applied, concretely translated into lower fees and less exigent masterpieces as well as shorter service periods. In Vienna Steidl found a socially stratified system, the poorer apprentices paying less for the training but staying longer. Masters commonly accorded time rebates in exchange for money, despite guild prohibitions. (In Augsburg, big, strong baker boys did not obtain reduced service periods, but rebates on cost – not the sole instance in which anthropometric criteria came into play.)

In France, there is often a logical relation between the time of service and the difficulty of the craft, clockmakers plausibly serving twice or three times the length of shoemakers or tailors. Elsewhere, the relation between skill requirements and duration is problematic. De Munck links the variation in duration, ranging from one to three or more years, to shifts on the demand side of product markets, emphasizing once again the capacity of the system to adapt rapidly to changed circumstances. One-year apprenticeships were not uncommon in fifteenth century Switzerland or seventeenth century Antwerp. These training periods seem derisory compared to the epic, ten-year odyssey in confectionery undertaken by Mary Louise Nagata's "M" in contemporary Japan, where school education apparently has still not superseded apprenticeship. For the moment we are impotent to map out any patterns over the long term and across cultures. Clearly we still require a massive quantitative investigation – exquisitely contingent on the highly uneven carrying capacity of the sources – in order to obtain baselines for comparison and generalization of not only duration of apprenticeship, but also age of entry (and of completion where traceable), cost of engagement (fees to master, to guild, to municipality, to other sponsors or patrons), penalties for absence or abandonment, and other kindred data.

Another significant question that warrants attention concerns the proportion of apprentices living with/within the master's family, and the nature of that experience. Again, this theme should not be passed over because it suffered the stigma of the ganze Haus grand narrative. The stakes are considerable on multiple levels. Is this a context for a certain nurturing and foster-parenting? Is it an opportunity to harvest insights on family/household dynamics in general? Is the apprentice a commensal, sharing the same food at a common table, or is s/he relegated to a symbolically inferior and pragmatically 'other' station? Is living under the master's roof a site for conflict and alienation issuing in the sort of malicious vengeance wonderfully epitomized by Robert Darnton's account of the 'great cat massacre' in which an overbearing master's wife paid a heavy price for her relentless officiousness? Are the lines between domestic and 'professional' labour blurred or sharply etched? Is the apprentice incorporated in non work-associated activities such as praying or church-going or collective leisure activity? Does s/he live in a certain promiscuity or enjoy a minimum of privacy, factors critical to her or his emotional development and general wellbeing? Vis-à-vis sons and daughters, is there a bonding process or friction and jealousy? Are journeymen present, and do they subject the apprentice to the classic gamut of hazing, or is there some sort of reciprocity in which the apprentice obtains some compensation in the form of protection, assistance or instruction? Beyond the evident tension between learning and labour evoked by De Munck and Soly, is the household/family experience the crucible for the crystallization of a contentious spirit (germination of a consciousness of rights, drawn from nature or convention, quickened by a sense of distinction of the genre: 'we [apprentices or journeymen, owners of skills] are not lackeys') or the itinerary of the kind of sustained ideological tutelage exercised by a more or less sympathetic master over a more or less needy/compliant apprentice adumbrated by the Marxist historian Albert Soboul (a useful reminder that ganze Haus idyllicism is not the appanage of the political right).

Living in or just working in, the apprentice is often discontent even when s/he is openly docile. His/her doleful lament denouncing abuse and diverse *misère* resonates through many of our stories. The sources of recurrent complaint are physical abuse by the master directly (beatings whose varying degrees of brutality express varying thresholds of rationality), psychological abuse (harassment, breaking the spirit, *domptage*, more or less ritualized humiliation), systematic assignment to effect domestic chores/deficit of real learning (beyond mistreatment and mortification lurks the sense of betrayal and contractual violation and a blow to self-interest as well as self-esteem), and bad and/or inadequate food, by no means a trivial matter (where the claims of dignity vie with those of appetite and taste). Even as she records these grievances, Steidl remarks that the master, too, takes a risk in admitting strangers into the intimacy of his household. In Paris, masters deplore a litany of horrors allegedly committed by vengeful or merely wicked journeymen and less frequently by apprentices, including theft, sabotage of work and assault, especially against the wife. Resolutely sceptical of a focus that places too much emphasis on 'the power-paternalistic relationship', Reith notes that while much friction occurred, 'these complaints and court hearings by no means indicate a crisis in vocational training in the eighteenth century'. One is inclined, then, to ask: what did they indicate?

Given their very nature and their extremely irregular inscription in the record, these data are obviously radically less susceptible than, say, wage evidence, to serial treatment. It might nevertheless be worthwhile attempt to to quantify and periodize complaints. We need a more exhaustive geography of grievance mechanisms for apprentices, institutional and informal or customary. Where can they go to complain, and what are their chances of obtaining justice and/or satisfaction? Stabel invokes the Bruges municipality as a possible site of recourse, but was it composed of persons whose interests were imbricated in corporate life? Karel Davids' apprentices in seventeenth-century Amsterdam enjoyed a privileged form of redress as a result of their right to report on their treatment by their masters, not to the guild hierarchy, but directly to the regents of the municipal board of orphans. Steidl relates that the city council of Vienna in the second half of the eighteenth century took a direct interest in protecting ill-treated apprentices, thus showing that it construed the public interest/public order in terms that transcended simply facilitating business. What was the composition and vocation of the trade courts that Reith cites? Where else does one encounter characteristically more specialized jurisdictions such as this to adjudicate labour strife? How commonly do parents or other sponsors become involved in defending their children and wards? Logically, the apprentices would turn to them first when they were not too far away.

Many contracts explicitly anticipate the ultimate recourse of frustrated or tormented apprentices: flight. Stabel suggests grounds for the embedding of loyalty (the best-case/normative scenario), but intimates that runaways were quite frequent, a finding with which Steidl seems to concur. For the apprentice, panicked or lucid, this step constituted an extreme measure, for the consequences could be enormously deleterious for his (more rarely her) future and the financial penalties onerous for their families. We need to distinguish between the capricious or temporary *fugue* and the act of veritable, probably irreversible desperation. For certain masters, flight merely confirmed the anthropology of youth widely shared at the time: young people as inherently unruly, naturally mutinous, potentially dangerous.

Symmetrically, it would be fruitful to pay more systematic attention to the recriminations of masters against workers, apprentices included. We need to try to move beyond seductive impressionism (the convergent observations of percipient eighteenth-century commentators such as Restif de la Bretonne and L.-S. Mercier that the burgeoning insolence of workers is linked to their growing capacity to read and thus learn dangerously subversive ideas) and equally beguiling teleology (the temptation to view the highly disparate but ostensibly thickening signs of workplace/labour-market insubordination in post-1750 France as the logical portent of a more or less inexorable revolutionary explosion). Are there signs here and elsewhere of a trickling down of the Enlightenment from the salon to the shopfloor, from the opera to the marketplace? In a series of muscled measures targeted to impose much tighter controls on the movement and behaviour of workers, the French state seemed to acknowledge an acceleration of insubordination, the vector of which was often illicit (thus clandestine) association. Are there signs of a parallel anxiety and tightening of monitoring and repression in other states, territories or cities?

It goes without saying that all apprentices were not fugitives, rebels, malcontents or simple drop-outs. For measuring 'success' however, we lack both clearcut criteria and data. Stabel reports that 75 percent of apprentices, sons of masters excluded, never reached mastership and over a third did not complete their apprenticeship, a bleak assessment echoed by Steidl. Impressionistic French evidence eddies in the same direction, but it is clear that we need longitudinal studies throughout Europe in order to reconstitute a compelling picture. Besides masters' sons, do 'outsiders' who complete their training share common characteristics that distinguish them? Is there even a more distinctive sociology for those who do go on to produce a master-piece and ascend to mastership? Other questions that surge to mind will be even more difficult to answer. At what point and why does an aspiring apprentice abandon the trajectory? Are institutional factors (putative guild exclusivism or sclerosis), financial barriers (lack of capital for admission and commercial establishment) or product-market factors (a highly unfavourable business cycle, chronic over-supply or under-demand) the decisive influences? Yet we must be careful not to equate 'success' with canonical completion tales. Recent research emphasizes the alternative paths available that may yield success in different terms: switching professions, moving on (geographical mobility), finding remunerative and/or steady employment outside the corporate structure or setting up illicitly, for instance.

The accounting of various apprenticeship outcomes will be facilitated by a better mapping of boundaries, real and imagined, porous and impermeable: the spaces of free and unfree work, of incorporated and privileged space, of licensed and tolerated work, of defiantly renegade, 'false', or illegal work, etc. In addition to cataloguing opportunities for operating as unlicensed craftsmen or 'freelancers' in the country and probably also in the city and for obtaining 'special licenses' whose prerogatives included the right to take guild-bound apprentices, Steidl suggests that the phenomenon of unsanctioned work was widespread: 'in a big city like Vienna there always existed options to operate in crafts and trades without legal permission'. Often styled *'chambrelans'* (because they set up shop discreetly/clandestinely in dismal rooms in residential quarters), more pejoratively 'false' workers (in part because they instinctively sought refuge in the *fauxbourgs*), and more generically 'ouvriers sans qualité', these artisans and merchants pullulated in eighteenth-century Paris, and most likely in many other cities as well, in the interstices of the urban core as well as in the suburban periphery. Until we take the full measure of their presence, unveil the myriad ways in which they connected with legal/corporate work through subcontracting and other arrangements, fathom their pragmatic (and not merely their formal) relations with public authorities (police, municipality) etc.) and take stock of their role in the labour market, we will have a seriously incomplete and necessarily flawed notion of the processes of production as well as reproduction in the world of work. We need a comprehensive inventory of the cohabitation (and conflict) of different structures and systems: corporate and nonguild, open and underground, small and large, artisanal, proto-industrial and quasi-industrial (small centralized manufactories), entrepreneurial/innovative and routinized/customary, export-oriented and locally focused, putting out of all genres, etc.

The flowering of parallel/complementary/competitive systems invites us to reflect on noncorporate alternatives to or vectors for apprenticeship. If, in the end, Davids acknowledges the guilds as 'very valuable institutions' for economic and social regulation and for nourishing the general welfare, the whole thrust of his chapter argues for their superfluity in the governance of apprenticeship in the Dutch Republic. Numerous guilds, notably in the distribution sector, did not even have a dedicated category for apprenticeship in their by-laws. (Once again it seems imperative to differentiate by the production of specific goods and services, whose organization and markets elicit different styles of behaviour: thus, for example, the case of the distribution-oriented Parisian master *épiciers* [grocers], many of whom viewed their journeymen as quasi-equal 'disciples' rather than utterly subordinate quasi-servants.) Apprenticeship thrived outside the guilds, whose agency proved unnecessary for enforcing contracts that depended on trust and kin-vetting or for supervising training that local magistrates or special organizations (*neringen*) monitored. Major suppliers of apprentices such as orphanages (and presumably even more tellingly the charitable organizations called *Fundaties*) exercised institutional leverage over guilds, obtaining most-favoured-son advantages for their wards. Davids makes clear the advantages that the apprentices and their sponsors (and, more nebulously, the 'urban elites', to whom Davids somewhat wishfully imputes collective 'long-term strategy') procured from this corporate cannibalization, but he does not deal with the putative benefits that the guilds derived from a system that neutered them.

Even as the guilds entered their so-called 'consolidation' phase during the long eighteenth century, craft training shifted increasingly from the workshop to the classroom. Logically, then, the trauma of guild abolition, at least as far as it concerned apprenticeship, was very much mitigated in the northern Netherlands. Marat's unexpectedly passionate defence of the guilds in 1791 as the indispensable stewards of apprenticeship could not have applied here.

We need to know globally just how common Davids' scenario was in early modern Europe and more specifically what were the nature of the relations – political, ideological, economic, social – between 'urban elites' and guilds. The school model seems to have been far more compelling in the Dutch Republic than in the somewhat ethereal worlds of nineteenth-century brewers or twentieth-century Japanese enterprises of various sorts.

In opposition to Reith and De Munck, Clare Crowston accords primacy to education in the apprentice process. Yet, in a more limited and equivocal way, she comforts their contention that prescriptive apprenticeship is not coterminous with the apprenticeship story. Like Davids, Crowston explores parallel trajectories of training. If she will allow me a paronomastic moment, when she writes that the general tendency has been to construe apprenticeship through the *prism* of the guild system, I think she really means the long-term mental *prison* of historiography. In sympathy with Davids, Crowston thoughtfully frees us from this thraldom. But she does so in a self-consciously ambiguous narrative, for most of the 'education' that she discusses remains embedded in the corporate nexus in contrast to the examples of Amsterdam iconoclasm. Unlike Reith's 'boys' who do their pre-apprenticeship in hands-on fashion at work, Crowston's children are prepared in a very different manner, primarily in schools shaped by a Christian and conservative critique of the deficiencies of corporate socialization, considered to be insensitive to the different stages of childhood and adolescence, and to the ever-dynamic connection between moral and professional development.

Ideologically, however, the parish school and the guild shared the conviction, punctuated by slightly different emphases, that salvation depended both on a religious engagement and on the sustained practice of a trade. The alternative amounted to spiritual and social disorder: idleness and/as sinfulness. For the partisans of the parish school, the master intervenes too late to assure the formation of the 'good' worker: tractable, passably pious, decidedly productive. The right habits had to be inculcated earlier, starting at the age of seven or eight. With this foundation, the master-in-guild could then make apprenticeship work for the benefit of his ward, his shop, his corporation and the society at large. (Bachelier's drawing- school model offers a much more radical alternative to institutional apprenticeship, while the intransigent corporate-scepticism of the St-Eustache Company and its refusal to subsidize guild apprenticeship are more surprising and merit closer examination.)

In this perspective, the labour market is less critical than the larger social organization of which it is an emanation and an instrument. Whereas for Reith, the social follows the economic, for Crowston the former precedes and shapes the latter. Reith intimates that the wage (as invisible hand?) will educate/socialize the apprentice through and into a rational world view and a propensity to behave more or less consistent with this logic. For Crowston's local elite, only a very visible and active hand can establish the basis for a durable equilibrium. She focuses squarely on 'perceptions' rather than practices. Yet even had she taken the wage more seriously – her dismissal of its impact on master-apprentice relations in the Parisian/French context is too peremptory – it seems doubtful to me that this factor would have modified the interpretive framework. Crowston's apprenticeship is more hybrid and less linear than commonly portrayed, and her guild world is less monolithic and more supple and variegated, in the spirit of revisionist historiography.

We should also look for possible variants of the contract called *allouage* in France. As a rule closely modelled on the apprenticeship transaction, though applicable in one-room shops, in privileged spaces and in quasi-factories such as Oberkampf's *manufacture des toiles peintes,* allouage promised training, sometimes with more individualized attention than apprenticeship characteristically proffered, and the usual gamut of (asymmetrical) reciprocities. It took place, however, outside the corporate sphere even when the contract was signed by a guild master, for it specifically could not qualify the youth for the making of the master-piece and eventual entry into the guild as a master. It was not necessarily shorter than apprenticeship and not always less expensive, even as it limited the range of opportunities available after completion of the time. Thus we need to understand the allure that it manifestly had for many families who entered into this arrangement. (For instance, it clearly facilitated the training of girls and it enlarged the choice of masters available to parents of children of both sexes.) It enabled nonmasters to perform master-like training and it probably permitted masters to increase their stock of cheap labour by avoiding, in this circuitous manner, the limit imposed on the number of apprentices that one could take at one time.

These interrogations point inexorably to a seminal question that is not the subject of this book, yet infiltrates it at many points: given the (ostensibly) growing irrelevance of guilds in many domains, including apprenticeship, why do so many artisans and merchants remain in them or continue resolutely to seek entry? If the trajectory towards admission looms as relatively unproblematic, say, in the fifteenth and sixteenth centuries, it becomes increasingly less so subsequently. One explanation that finds favour in some of the chapters here is a variant of a sort of rational-action theory: a cost-benefit calculation in the end seals decisions. Conceived as a naturally/narrowly economic choice by some, this formulation worries others, who seek to resist its reductionist momentum by reckoning cost-benefit in more catholic fashion: in addition to the hard, material interests at play, they take into account the softer power of social, cultural and political capital. The staggering diversity of corporate experience renders cross-'national' comparison difficult. Internal organization and governance, recruitment practices, masterly status and the place of the guilds in the larger social and political structures vary significantly over space and time, in all likelihood more so than the play of market forces, though the latter by no means escape cultural conditioning. Jean-Pierre Hirsch has shown us just how delicate it is to construe 'economic' motivation: rationality in this regard is not always what it seems to be, especially as capitalism penetrates more and more deeply into commercial and corporate relations. Other scholars have underlined the weight of a noneconomic rationality in shaping both individual (masterly) and collective (corporate) decisions. To understand the character and influence of apprenticeship both inside and outside corporate orbit, we need to clarify our sense of the vitality and viability of the guilds. A less Manichean sense of corporate 'interests' will help us appreciate why guilds could simultaneously evince fierce resistance (Stabel) to interlopers on the one hand, and welcome them, quite profitably, on the other. A more differentiated view of corporate and masterly stakes would help make sense of the disparity of interests within a guild. An entrepreneurial core of (relative) leviathans may operate in a different economic universe from the legion of lilliputians, but both types of master may be heavily invested in the guild for other (concordant or divergent) reasons. I remain fascinated by the Parisian master draper – in fact, a sort of international banker/broker – who still takes his turn as a guild beadle, donning a black gown and scrupulously patrolling to uncover usurpers. Accommodation of difference may prove to be a marker not of incoherence but of strength. For a long time there was a temptation to conflate the trade with the guild, and to allow the (institutional) latter to eclipse the (economic) former. These days the danger may be rather in overlooking the guild, dismissed as preternaturally *ringard* or cast in superficial and stereotypical terms, sometimes derived from its formal self-representation.

Obviously the relationship between corporations and apprenticeship is similarly complex. Certain guilds are active parties to the contract, which becomes a tripartite affair. The regulatory interests of the guild as a collectivity often clash with the entrepreneurial interests of a master as individual. (Limits on numbers of apprentices per shop, prohibitions against 'debauching' the apprentice of a colleague, surveillance of treatment, etc.) In the labour market, from the corporate viewpoint, the rebelliousness of masters is no less ominous than the allegedly congenital mutinousness of journeymen and apprentices. Nor is the interest of the master in apprenticeship reducible to simple explanation, e.g., cheap or regulated labour flows. Surely De Munck and Soly are right in asserting that 'the economic means of individual masters may have determined whether they could take on apprentices.' One can, however, imagine a master without such means straining to take on an apprentice precisely to assert his status as a master, in some sense to affirm his very existence. The essentialist inclination of many French masters, well into the nineteenth century, was to associate their rank with the prerogative of binding apprentices. Certainly this was one of the reasons why the free-riding *agrégés,* who had opted initially to remain outside the new corporate world inaugurated after Turgot's abortive attempt at abolition in 1776, began gradually to return to the fold: re-entry was the only way they could recover their right to conduct apprenticeship, as much to enhance their status as to enable them to command cheap labour, to which they had access through other channels. On the other hand, Stabel reports that over half the masters in his purview trained only a single apprentice lifelong. French journeymen complained that many masters did not possess basic craft skills. Collectively masters were reluctant to share trade secrets, yet they wanted to be the only ones with the right to dispense them, if one is to judge by their antagonism to efforts to offer technical training through schools, a sometimes deeply resented expropriation of popular culture.

For those agrégés to whom I just referred and many other corporate actors, mastership was also defined as a kind of insurance policy: the right to transmit certain corporate/professional prerogatives to a wife upon her husband's demise. Habitually, the widow could carry on the trade, but could not take apprentices. We need a closer look at the relation between prescription and practice in this arena. Steidl points to an exception, hedged by a tension between the virtues of continuity and the resurgence of mistrust: the wives of deceased masters in the Viennese silk weavers' guild had permission to engage apprentices, but the latter had to finish the 'last months' of service in the workshop of a guild master, presumably to obtain ritual cachet. Ubiquitous in the world of work, yet in some basic, taxonomic sense often socially anomalous and worrisome, widows beg for the historian's attention, as do the women's guilds, cast in the image of the men's, but often quite different in practice and even in discourse, and the mixed communities which were unevenly and frequently uneasily integrated. The more we learn about women (married or celibate) and widowed masters/mistresses, the more sharply we will apprehend the experience of female apprentices, whose itinerary does not mechanically produce that of the boys.

Like gender, religion is often a pretext for and marker of exclusion, though not much is said about it in these papers. In France, Roman Catholicism was officially a sine qua non for ascension to mastership, and the confraternity is consubstantial to the corporation. In the Dutch Republic, Davids tells us, guilds showed neutrality on the religious question, 'except towards Jews'. Gendered female in terms of certain of their social and moral defects, Jews embodied both threatening and useful properties that made them at once pariahs and coveted partners. In the latter situation, as mediators of all sorts, they enjoyed officious affiliation and more rarely formal admission to certain guilds. In the former capacity, they served as scapegoats for all seasons. Many corporations and many trades had their Jews of one sort or another, all the more exasperating because invariably present even when systematically excluded. We need a closer look at visible and invisible minorities: how and where they operated, how they reproduced via apprenticeship and other processes, and to what extent they penetrated the majoritarian/dominant world.

Apprenticeship has emerged as a major question of social, economic and cultural history. Indicated above are numerous vectors of 'intensification' of research in order to deepen our understanding of how apprenticeship worked, what it did, how it fit into larger patterns, and so on. The agenda is rich and it solicits historians of virtually all methodological confessions, for we need quantitative investigations, discursive analyses, ethnographic monographs, historical and economic sociology, etc. We can also imagine a sphere of 'extensification', inserting the study of apprenticeship not only into the realm of the history of work, but also the history of childhood, adolescence and the family, and the history of institutions, power, social movements, etc. Opened to the larger society beyond the world of work, apprenticeship issues in the quasi-universal practice of mentoring. Not only Rousseau's Emile fits into this framework, but, each in his or her own way, so do the Princesse de Clèves and Monsieur Jourdain, Candide and Gil Blas, the

Chevalier des Grieux and Manon Lescaut, Marianne and the Marquise de Merteuil, the Comte Almaviva and Figaro, Julien Sorel and Fabrice del Dongo, Eugène de Rastignanc and Lucien de Rubempré, Emma Bovary and Frédéric Moreau. Learning how: this is a process common to the dance floor and the opera, the battlefield and the boudoir, the hunt and the bank, the dinner table and the classroom. In one way or another, learning how crosses class, gender, race, ethnicity, religion and most other barriers. Research on mentoring requires, even more urgently than apprenticeship, life-cycle studies and the reconstitution of individual trajectories. Apprenticeship in the world of work certainly is not reducible to mentorship; yet mentoring implies some sort of apprenticeship. It might prove fruitful to map out some of the conceptual and social connections between the two itineraries.

As we have seen, these essays raise some significant methodological issues, explicitly in pragmatic terms, and tacitly in more theoretical ways. One sensitive area in this regard is social history. In the U.S.A., it has been under assault and on the defensive. Driven in part (but only in part) by the 'linguistic turn', by the withering of Marxism and by a postmodernism that in some versions reduces the authority of the fact to merely another expression of oppression, this onslaught has relegated the social to a kind of historiographical purgatory. The situation in France is somewhat less gloomy, perhaps because many practitioners of social history, comfortably ensconced in the archives (when they are open), simply move ahead, carton by carton, *le nez dans le guidon*. Social history there, however, enjoys nothing of the prestige, not to speak of the hegemony, of yore. Polemically, it is cast as an object of archaic nostalgia if not of frank shame. A considerable number of the more self-conscious players are manifestly demoralized.

Beyond the infernal couple U.S.A-France (certain old-timers in France even blame the importation of 'American theory' for the ruin of their profession, by which they mean Derrida, Foucault and Lacan, *inter alia*), other distinguished European centres of research seem far more unruffled. I am struck by the serenity with which our Dutch- and German speaking colleagues pursue their brands of social history. Part of their resilience probably derives from their refusal to be drawn into contentious disputations that result in pigeon-holing and caricaturing certain ways of doing. The vocation of social history, as Braudel ambitiously forged it, was to 'federate' the branches of history and indeed all the social sciences. Even as it offers a wide berth to theoretical engagements of all types, social history must take into account agency as well as structures, the *doing* as well as the *saying*, the conditions of production as well as the products, objects as well as subjects, the short term as well as the long run, the fast as well as the slow, etc. It is well, moreover, to keep in mind Bill Sewell's prudent admonition that it is never wise to code the social as purely material: it should be marked at once as material and symbolic, as economic and cultural, as practice and discourse. The rest, as they say in France, 'c'est du cinéma', the vernacular in scholarly circles for epistemological regression.

Notes on Contributors

Clare Crowston is Associate Professor of History at the University of Illinois at Urbana-Champaign, United States of America. She teaches and researches early modern France, with interests in the history of work, women and gender, fashion, and material culture. She is the author of *Fabricating Women: The Seamstresses of Old Regime France, 1675–1791* (Durham, 2001). She is currently working on two projects: a study of credit, fashion and sex in eighteenth-century France, and a coauthored study of apprenticeship in France from the seventeenth to the nineteenth century, with Steven L. Kaplan and Gilles Postel-Vinay.

Karel Davids holds the Chair of Economic and Social History at the *Vrije Universiteit Amsterdam*, Free University of Amsterdam, The Netherlands. He has just finished a book on *The Rise and Decline of Dutch Technological Leadership: Technology, Economy and Culture in the Netherlands, c.1350–1800*, and is now working on a global comparative history of the relations between technology and culture between c.500 and 1800. A Dutch translation of a collective volume edited jointly with Jan Lucassen, *A Miracle Mirrored. The Dutch Republic in European Perspective,* has just been published.

Bert De Munck studied history at the *Vrije Universiteit Brussel*, Free University of Brussels, Belgium, where he wrote a Ph.D. thesis on 'Apprenticeship in the Antwerp Guilds (1500–1800)'. Since 2004 he has been a Lecturer in the Department of History at the University of Antwerp, Belgium, teaching social and economic history of the early modern period, history and social theory, European ethnology and heritage, and the history of the guilds. He is also a member of the Centre for Cultural and Urban History at the same university. He has published many articles on the history of guilds, labour and (vocational) education.

Steven L. Kaplan is Goldwin Smith Professor of European History at Cornell University, United States of America, and *Professeur invité* at the Université de Versailles-Saint-Quentin, France. A specialist in the history of subsistence and work in early modern and revolutionary France, he has written extensively on guilds, and on bakers and bread, both historically and in the present day. His most recent works are *La fin des corporations* (Paris, 2001) and *Le Retour du bon pain: Une histoire contemporaine du pain, de ses techniques, et de ses hommes* (Paris, 2002). He is completing a major project – inspired by a devastating collective food-poisoning in the town of Pont-Saint-Esprit and entitled *Le Pain maudit* – dealing with the provisioning system in the context of the taut relationship between State and society in France, 1948–1958.

Mary Louise Nagata is a *membre associé* with the Ecole des Hautes Etudes en Sciences Sociales, Centre de Recherches Historiques, in Paris, France. Her most recent publication is *Labor Contracts and Labor Relations in Early Modern Central Japan, 1672–1873* (Routledge-Curzon Press, 2005). New research concerns primarily the family and demographic practice of Kyoto residents in the nineteenth century, focusing on 1843–1868, the twenty-five years leading up to the Meiji Restoration. This will be the theme of her next book with the provisional title 'Family, Firm and Community in Early Modern Kyoto'.

Jonathan Reinarz is a Wellcome Lecturer at the Centre for the History of Medicine in the University of Birmingham Medical School, United Kingdom. He is currently writing a history of the Birmingham teaching hospitals and has recently commenced a Wellcome-funded projected examining the history of medical education in provincial England between 1800 and 1939. He has published on various aspects of economic, social and medical history, including technological change, apprenticeship and the brewing industry.

Reinhold Reith is Professor of Economic and Social History at the Department of History at the University of Salzburg, Austria. He studied History and Political Science at the University of Constance and taught at the Universities of Constance, Berlin and Vienna. His major interest and empirical research concern artisans, wages, labour, food, environment and technology. His publications include *Lohn und Leistung: Lohnformen im Gewerbe 1450–1900* (Stuttgart 1999); he edited *Lexikon des alten Handwerks: Vom späten Mittelalter bis ins 20. Jahrhundert* (Munich, 1990/91).

Hugo Soly is Professor of Early Modern History and Director of the Centre for the Study of Pre-Industrial Production Processes and Labour Relations at the *Vrije Universiteit Brussel*, Free University of Brussels, Belgium. His research interests span the period 1300 to 1850, and he writes in five major areas – urban development and urbanism, poverty and poor relief, 'deviant' behaviour, industrialization, and craft guilds. He is currently working on perceptions of work in pre-industrial Europe. His publications include *Disordered Lives: Eighteenth-Century Families and Their Unruly Members* (Cambridge, 1996), with Catharina Lis. He has edited *Charles V and His Time, 1500–1558* (Antwerp, 1999), and with Catharina Lis, Jan Lucassen and Maarten Prak *Craft Guilds in the Early Modern Low Countries: Work, Power, and Representation* (Aldershot, 2005).

Peter Stabel is Senior Lecturer in the Department of History at the University of Antwerp, Belgium. His research has focused primarily on urban networks, urban textile industries and marketing systems in late Medieval Flanders. Recent publications include 'Guilds in Late Medieval Flanders: Myths and Realities of Guild Life in an Export Oriented Environment', *Journal of Medieval History*, 30 (2004), and 'Italian Merchants and the Fairs in the Low Countries, 12th–16th Century', in *La Pratica dello Scambio* (Venice, 2003).

Annemarie Steidl is a post-doctoral associate at the Department of Economic and Social History of the University of Vienna, Austria. Her research has focused primarily on the history of artisans, migration in the eighteenth and nineteenth centuries, and gender history. She is currently working on a major project dealing with transnational migration in Central Europe from 1860 to 1914. Recent publications include *Auf nach Wien! Die Mobilität des mitteleuropäischen Handwerks im 18. und 19. Jahrhundert am Beispiel der Haupt- und Residenzstadt* (Vienna, 2003), and with Engelbert Stockhammer and Hermann Zeitlhofer, 'Relations among Internet, Continental and Transatlantic Migration in Late Imperial Austria', *Social Science History*, 31, 1 (2007): 61–92.

Index